Brassey's
ALMANAC
THE
PENINSULAR
WAR

Brassey's
ALMANAC
THE
PENINSULAR
WAR

PHILIP J. HAYTHORNTHWAITE

BRASSEY'S

First published in Great Britain in 2004 by Brassey's

An imprint of **Chrysalis** Books Group plc

The Chrysalis Building
Bramley Road
London W10 6SP
www.chrysalisbooks.co.uk

Distributed in North America by:
Casemate Publishing, 2114 Darby Road,
Havertown, PA 19083, USA

British Library Cataloguing-in-Publication Data
A record of this title is available on request from the British Library.

ISBN 1-85753-329-1

Library of Congress Cataloging in Publication Data available

Printed in Great Britain

CONTENTS

INTRODUCTION

William Napier began the preface of his great history by remarking that 'For six years the Peninsula was devastated by the war of independence. The blood of France, Germany, England, Portugal, and Spain, was shed in the contest . . .'; yet the war of 1807-14 in the Iberian peninsula is sometimes regarded as not being among the most significant of Napoleonic campaigns. There might appear some justification for this, in that Napoleon himself spent only a matter of weeks campaigning in Spain (a period involving some of the most dynamic operations undertaken by the French in the region); but such a perspective might be to under-rate the significance of the Peninsular War.

The most profound consequences of the war were experienced by the nations of the Iberian peninsula itself, notably in Spain, where the war is generally known as 'la Guerra de Independencia'. Military action in the Peninsula was not unknown during the previous century - notably during the War of the Spanish Succession (1701-14), between Portugal and her allies against Spain towards the end of the SevenYears' War (1761-62), and against France at the beginning of the French Revolutionary Wars - but none of these approached the cataclysmic consequences of Napoleon's war.

Apart from the death, misery and economic collapse occasioned by the war itself, its longer-term effects on Spain were equally or even more profound, notably in the burgeoning conflict between what might be termed most succinctly as progressive liberalism and reactionary absolutism, the resolution of which took many years and much bloodshed. The monarchy, having been removed by Napoleon with barely any dissent from its head, even though restored in the person of Ferdinand VII, lost much of its influence; and neither the nobility nor church, so influential in Spain before the Peninsular War, ever recovered their former power, even after Ferdinand's reversion to absolutism. Neither did Spain's place in international affairs ever recover; already in decline, the usurpation of its throne completed its collapse as one of the major European powers. Economically and financially, the country was ravaged by the war, which was one direct cause of the collapse of Spain's empire in the New World, as colonies threw off control from Madrid, not only securing their own independence but depriving Spain of the colonial revenue that had been so important to national finances. The 'war of independence' against French occupation and usurpation of the throne introduced into Spain, notably with the 1812 constitution, the beginning of the conflict between liberalism and less progressive ways which was to give rise to subsequent conflicts, including the revolt of 1820 and the French invasion of 1823, the Carlist War of 1834-39, the civil war of Espartero's revolt of 1840-43 which briefly dispossessed the reigning monarch, a near revolution in 1854, a proper revolution in 1868, and a renewed Carlist War of 1873-76. The consequences of the Peninsular War even resonated into the Spanish Civil War of 1936-39.

Although Portugal's monarchy was not actually disposessed, it was absent in Brazil for the whole of the Peninsular War; and if there were no attempt at political reform during the war to match the Spanish 1812 constitution, and no colonial revolt, the failure of the monarchy to return from Brazil at the end of the war caused great resentment. The Regent (from 1816 King John VI) only returned home in 1821, after the 1820 revolution which established a constitutional monarchy; an attempt to reintroduce the previous absolutism led to the civil war of 1823-24, followed by the dynastic 'Miguelite Wars' of 1826-34, involving (1827-28) a renewed British expedition to Portugal. Unrest and insurrection continued until 1851, and the stability of the country was again under threat later in the century, involving even the assassination of King Carlos I and the crown prince in 1908. Portugal also lost the jewel of its colonial territory, Brazil, which having been the seat of the monarchy throughout the Peninsular war became almost the head of its own mother country; in 1822 Brazil's independence was declared, with John VI's son being proclaimed as constitutional emperor Pedro I, independence being recognised by Portugal in 1825.

For Britain, intervention in the Iberian Peninsula gave the British government a degree of authority in negotiations with its allies which might not have been so marked had the British war effort been restricted largely to maritime and financial considerations. Arguably one of the most profound aspects of British involvement was in the development of the British Army. Prior to the Duke of Wellington's command, the British army's successes had been limited and the overall campaign record very patchy; but the consequences of sustained success in the Peninsula, leading to enhanced morale and confidence, are still evident in regimental tradition and consequent esprit de corps. This is manifested in such diverse commemorations as the use by the King's Own Royal Border Regiment of French drums captured by the 34th Foot at Arroyo dos Molinos, or the use by the King's Royal Hussars of Joseph Bonaparte's silver chamber-pot as a punchbowl.

The wider consequences of the Peninsular War, or its influence as one of the determining factors of the Napoleonic Wars in general, are less certain. On more than one occasion, while absolving himself of any criticism for initiating the war, Napoleon emphasized its dire consequences. 'That unlucky war ruined me; it divided my forces, obliged me to multiply my efforts, and caused my principles to be assailed; and yet it was impossible to leave the Peninsula a prey to the machinations of the English, the intrigues, the hopes, and the pretensions of the Bourbons . . . All the circumstances of my disasters are connected with that fatal knot: it destroyed my moral power in Europe, rendered my embarassments more complicated, and opened a school for the English soldiers. It was I who trained the English army in the Peninsula. Events have proved that I committed a great fault in the choice of my means; for the fault lies in the means much more than in the principles . . . that unfortunate war in Spain was a real affliction, and the first cause of the calamities of France . . .'[1].

Nevertheless, it is debatable how great an effect the Peninsular War actually had in its widest context. The difficulties of attempting to sustain the demands of a war on two fronts, most notably from 1812 onwards, are obvious, and while lack of numbers was not a primary cause of Napoleon's defeat in Russia in 1812, the experienced troops that remained committed to the war in Spain would have proved extremely useful, at the least, in the campaigns of 1813-14. Napoleon's intransigence to accept a negotiated peace may have been the vital factor which led to his downfall, but the drain on resources occasioned by the Peninsular War was still a constant factor, its unpopularity with the army damaging morale, and the burden it placed upon the system of conscription helped to erode domestic support. 'That unlucky war' may not have been the prime cause of Napoleon's ruination, as his statement above might suggest; but it certainly exerted a notable influence.

Spellings

The rendition of proper names relating to the Iberian peninsula has been a cause of some difficulty from the period of the war itself. Within the Peninsula, with more than one principal language, the spelling of place-names has varied (for example Badajoz and Badajos), and some have altered since the early nineteenth century. A number of locations have not only their indigenous spelling, but variations accepted

1 Las Cases, E.A.D.M.J., *Memoirs of the Life, Exile and Conversations of the Emperor Napoleon*, London 1834, Vol. II, pp. 134-5, 296.

as universal in other principal languages in which histories of the war have been written; for example Lisboa (English Lisbon, French Lisbonne), La Coruña (Corunna, La Corogne), Zaragoza (Saragossa, Saragosse), Cataluña, (Catalonia, Catalogne). Where accepted English spellings exist, they are generally used in this work (e.g. Tagus instead of Tajo, or French Tage).

Variations in the spellings of indigenous names without a 'foreign' spelling are also common; what was often termed Baylen, for example, is now Bailén. This factor is demonstrated by the spellings of the British Army's battle honours, notably those carried on the clasps of the Military General Service Medal. If none of the Peninsular honours are as opaque as that for the clasp for 'Port Spergui' on the Naval General Service Medal (which concerned an action in 1796 on the coast of Brittany at Erqui), the spellings are often different from those which are now common. Vimeiro and Albuera, for example, appear as the battle-honours 'Vimiera' and 'Albuhera'; English histories and the battle-honour usually refer to Vittoria, Spanish and more modern works to Vitoria. Fuentes de Oñoro is now common, while the battle-honour is 'Fuentes d'Onor'; in British dispatches it appears both as 'Fuentes de Honor' and 'Fuentes Onova'[2], and may be found in French works with the alternative name of Pozo Bello, from the nearby location from which the British 85th and 2nd Cacadores were driven on 5 May. The first major British action of the war was at 'Roleia' according to the battle honour, the spelling of which was only amended to 'Rolica' more than a century after the events (by an Army Order of 1911). Both Napier and Belmas refer to the action as Roriça, Londonderry to both 'Roliça' and (in the chapter-heading) to 'Loriça'; Gurwood's published edition of Wellington's dispatches uses the spelling 'Roliça', but when the same dispatch was originally printed in the *London Gazette* (3 September 1808) it appeared as 'Roleia'. (Such an alteration between two early published versions is not unique; in the same document, for example, 'OEbidos' (with diphthong) was changed to 'Obidos', and the spelling of Miles Nightingall's name was corrected). Foz do Arouce (or Foz de Arouce) appears in some sources as 'Foz de Aronce', a consequence, it has been speculated[3] of a printer's error in Napier's history[4], while French sources, at the time and subsequently, use the equally incorrect spelling 'Arunce' or similar. Spellings of place-names in southern France are equally vulnerable to confusion: Arriverayte, an important crossing-point of the River Saison, for example, was spelled 'Arriverete' by

2 *London Gazette*, 26 May 1811.
3 Oman, Sir Charles, *History of the Peninsular War*, Oxford 1902-30, Vol. IV p. 155.
4 Napier, W.P.F., *History of the War in the Peninsula and South of France*, 1831 edn., Vol. III, pp. xi & 470.

Wellington and 'Riveyrete' by Soult, while the Spanish decoration for the 'Batalla de Tolosa' refers to Toulouse, rather than to the Spanish town of Tolosa, some 20 km. south of San Sebastian, where an action occurred in June 1813.

Potentially even more confusing are cases in which an action was given quite different names; for example, the British Barossa and Salamanca are generally known as Chiclana and Les Arapiles respectively by the French. The celebrated action now known as Garcia Hernandez appears in Wellington's despatch as La Serna[5]; similar examples are not uncommon.

Variations may also be found in the spellings of personal names. This is, perhaps, unsurprising in the case of names foreign to the writer; for example, the unfortunate French general Francois-Xavier Schwarz, captured at La Bispal, appears as 'General Swarty' in British despatches[6] (in which Bagur appears as 'Beger', La Bispal as 'Besbal'); the distinguished Major Ernst von Burgwedel, who led the 3rd Hussars of the King's German Legion at Benavente, appears as 'Bagwell' in some British accounts. Not only foreign names may be found mis-spelled, especially in early sources: Wellington used the correct spelling of Robert Craufurd's surname, for example, but Londonderry called him 'Crawford' and Napier used both correct and incorrect versions (the latter being corrected in later editions). Nightingall's name, frequently rendered as 'Nightingale', initially appeared incorrectly in the *Army List*, and as late as 1815 that publication still used two versions of the spelling. Even in relatively modern sources, variations in the spellings of both personal and place-names may be encountered.

5 *London Gazette* 16 August 1812.
6 *Ibid*. 24 November 1810.

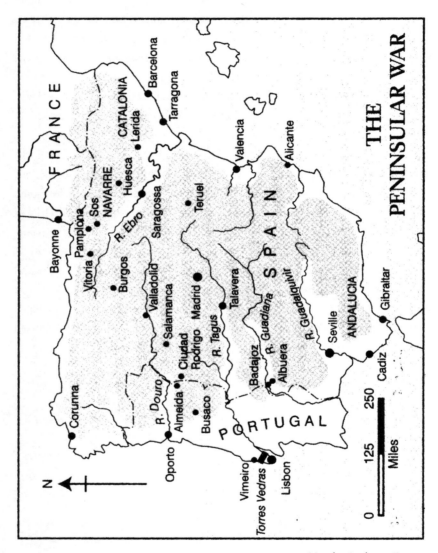

THE PENINSULAR WAR

Map by Anthony Evans

CHRONOLOGY

This chronology of the Peninsular War covers many of its most significant events, but does not include all of the many minor skirmishes. It should be noted that the dates of some events are recorded variously; for example, the date of Arthur Wellesley's ennoblement as Viscount Wellington is often quoted as 4 September 1809, whereas the announcement was actually made on 26 August. (With commendable circumspection he noted that he refused to use his new title until he had seen it confirmed in the Gazette, which must have been on 16 September, when he added to a letter a note that 'This is the first time I have signed my new name'[1]).

The full names of individuals are given in the following only upon the occasion of their first mention, and for similar reasons of brevity the various ranks of general officer are not usually distinguished in the Chronology; for example, the holders of such ranks as *Général de Brigade, Général de Division, Mariscal de Campo,* etc., are all just identified as 'General'.

The fact that events were occurring simultaneously throughout the Peninsula and beyond can complicate the chronology of any particular operation; thus, in many cases, where an occurrence does not relate directly to the events listed immediately before or after it, dates are given in parentheses to indicate where details of the relevant preceding or subsequent events may be located within the chronology.

1806

21 November: Napoleon issued the 'Berlin Decrees', intended to exclude British trade from continental Europe, declaring that Britain was under blockade and that no vessel from Britain or a British possession would be allowed access to any port under his control. It was the start of the 'Continental System', later reinforced by the Milan Decrees. (7 July, 23 November 1807).

1807

24 March: Duke of Portland became British Prime Minister, whose administration sanctioned involvement in the Peninsula. (26 September 1809).

7 July: by the Treaty of Tilsit between Napoleon and Tsar Alexander I, Sweden and Portugal were to be forced to comply to the Continental System. (21 November 1806, 12 August 1807).

---

[1] The sources of the direct quotations are listed at the end of the chronology. The above is taken from *Dispatches of Field-Marshal the Duke of Wellington*, ed. J. Gurwood, London 1834-38, Vol. V p. 158.

2 August: General Jean-Andoche Junot appointed to command the 'Corps of Observation of the Gironde'. (18 October).

12 August: to compel Portugal to accept the Continental System, French and Spanish ambassadors threatened a break in diplomatic relations with the Prince Regent, John (Joao) of Portugal. (7 July, 20 October).

30 September: Portuguese reaction to Napoleon's demands being deemed insufficient, the French and Spanish diplomats quit Lisbon.

11 October: Ferdinand, Prince of the Asturias, requested Napoleon's help against his father, King Charles IV of Spain. (27 October).

18 October: Junot's Corps of Observation of the Gironde crossed the Bidassoa into Spain, en route for the occupation of Portugal. (2 August, 23 November).

20 October: Prince John of Portugal reluctantly declared war on Britain, in an attempt to pacify Napoleon, making sure that Britain knew he was acting under duress. (12 August).

22 October: a secret convention between Britain and Portugal sought to preserve relations in the face of French pressure, arranged British assistance should the Portuguese royal family be forced to flee, and pledged British support for their rights. (29 November).

27 October: Treaty of Fontainebleau signed between France and Spain, arranging for the occupation and dismemberment of Portugal. Manuel Godoy, Charles IV's minister, having discovered Ferdinand's correspondence with Napoleon (sometimes styled the Escor-ial conspiracy), the king arrested Ferdinand on a charge of treason. Subsequently he was released, but it exemplifies the hostility existing within the Spanish court. (11 October).

8 November: Prince John ordered the detention of the remaining British subjects in Portugal; the British ambassador, Lord Strangford, remonstrated and requested his passports. (20 October).

17 November: Strangford joined the fleet of Admiral Sir Sidney Smith (flagship HMS *Hibernia*) off the Portuguese coast, and a blockade of the Tagus was begun. (27 November).

22 November: Following Junot, the Second Corps of Observation of the Gironde, under General Pierre Dupont, crossed into Spain. (18 October; 8 January & 10 April 1808).

23 November: Napoleon issued the first of his Milan Decrees to reinforce the Continental System, authorising the confiscation of any ship that had called at a British port, and of all goods not certified as having originated outside British territories. (23 November 1806, 17 December 1807). The leading elements of Junot's corps reached Abrantes by forced march. (12, 30 November).

27 November: Strangford returned to Lisbon to demand that either the Portuguese fleet be surrendered, or be used to transport the royal family to Brazil. (17 November).

29 November: with a British naval escort, the Portuguese royal family departed for Brazil in the fleet of Vice-Admiral Manuel d'Acunha Sottomayor (flagship, *Principe Real*). (6 December, 19 January 1808).

30 November: Junot marched into Lisbon with about 1,500 men of his army. (23 November, 1 February 1808).

6 **December**: having detached part of his fleet to accompany the Portuguese to Brazil, Sir Sidney Smith returned to the Tagus where the Russian fleet of Vice-Admiral Seniavin had anchored, en route home from the Mediterranean, and since Tilsit officially hostile to Britain. (29 November, 3 September 1808).

7 **December**: a British expedition bound for the Portuguese territory of Madeira, under Maj.Gen. William Beresford, left Cork, escorted by the fleet of Admiral Sir Samuel Hood (flagship, HMS *Centaur*). (24 December).

11 **December**: exemplifying the continuing state of war between Britain and Spain, the British 18-gun brig-sloop HMS *Grasshopper* (Capt. Thomas Searle) captured the Spanish 12-gun brig *San Josef* (Capt. Antonio de Torres) at Cape Negrete, near Cartagena.

17 **December**: Napoleon issued his second Milan Decree, that any neutral vessel that had submitted to British naval authority would be regarded as an enemy and be liable for confiscation. (23 November).

24 **December**: Hood's fleet with Beresford's expedition arrived at Madeira. (7 December)

26 **December**: the Portuguese authorities surrendered Madeira without resistance, thus denying its use to the French. Two battalions were left there as garrison.

1808

8 **January**: Napoleon's third military force, the Corps of Observation of the Ocean Coast, under Marshal Bon-Adrien-Jeannot de Moncey, entered Spain. (22 November 1807, 21 June).

19 **January**: the Prince Regent of Portugal and the court landed at Bahia in Brazil. (29 November 1807).

1 **February**: Junot was appointed governor-general of Portugal. (30 November 1807).

13 **February**: reconnoitering the mouth of the Tagus, boats from the 20-gun HMS *Confiance* (Capt. James Yeo), under Master's-Mate Robert Trist, captured the anchored French gun-vessel *No. 1* (Enseigne de Vaisseau Gaudolphe).

15 **February**: the British 10-gun brig HMS *Raposa* (Capt. James Violett) was destroyed to prevent capture after running aground near Cartagena.

16 **February**: French troops seized Pamplona from the Spanish, without resistance.

20 **February**: Marshal Joachim Murat was appointed 'lieutenant of the Emperor' and commander of all French forces in Spain. (10 March).

29 **February**: French troops seized Barcelona from the Spanish, without resistance.

5 **March**: San Sebastian surrendered by the Spanish under threat of French assault.

10 **March**: Murat crossed the Bidassoa, taking command of all French troops in Spain (20 February, 24 March).

13 **March**: at Valladolid one of Dupont's divisional commanders, General Jean-Pierre-Firmin Malher, was killed when shot

through the head by a ramrod fired accidentally by one of his own men during an exercise. At Vivero (a port north of Corunna) a landing-party from the British frigate HMS *Emerald* (Capt. Frederick Maitland) captured the port's two forts, which enabled them to burn the French 8-gun schooner *Apropos* in the harbour.

17 March: mob violence in Aranjuez led Godoy to hide from a populace which believed he intended harm to the king and queen. The unrest was quelled next day when Ferdinand, Prince of the Asturias, addressed the crowd.

18 March: prompted by the rising, Charles IV announced that Godoy was relieved of his duties and banished. Figueras was seized by the French, without resistance.

19 March: Godoy was arrested; Charles IV abdicated in favour of his son, Ferdinand VII. Marshal Jean-Baptiste Bessières was appointed commander of the Corps of Observation of the Western Pyrenees. (14 July).

24 March: Murat entered Madrid. (10 March, 2 May).

10 April: Dupont occupied Aranjuez. (22 November 1807, 23 April).

20 April: Ferdinand arrived at Bayonne, lured by Napoleon into captivity. (19 March, 20 April).

23 April: serious riot at Toledo, suppressed by the arrival of elements of Dupont's force. (10 April). In the Tagus, a British attempt was made to capture the Portuguese 20-gun brig-corvette *Garrota*, which had been taken over by the French. Boats from the frigate HMS *Nymphe* (Capt. Conway Shipley) and 18-gun sloop HMS *Blossom* (Capt. George Pinot) were driven

off after Shipley was killed while boarding. **30 April**: King Charles IV and Queen Maria Luisa joined Ferdinand at Bayonne. (20 April, 6 May).

2 May: the 'Dos Mayo' in Madrid, a popular rising against the French and in support of the royal family, suppressed by Murat. (24 March).

6 May: Ferdinand having been forced to relinquish the throne, Charles IV was prevailed upon by Napoleon to abdicate in his favour. (30 April, 10 May).

7 May: off Cape Trafalgar, a Spanish mistico was captured and four gunboats destroyed by HMS *Redwing* (Capt. Thomas Ussher), the last Spanish naval losses before the cessation of Anglo-Spanish hostilities.

10 May: Ferdinand formally abdicated his rights to his father's throne. (6, 24 May).

18 May: British 10-gun brig HMS *Rapid* (Capt. Henry Baugh) destroyed by batteries in the Tagus while attempting to cut out two merchantmen.

24 May: Napoleon nominated a representative body from Spain to convene at Bayonne to appoint a new king (10 May, 6 June). First insurrection against the French at Saragossa. (31 May).

25 May: government of the Asturias officially declared war on Napoleon, the first Spanish province to do so. (30 May).

29 May: insurrectionary junta formed at Lerida in Catalonia (the province's chief city, Barcelona, being occupied by the French general Philibert-Guillaume Duhesme).

30 May: an Asturian delegation (the Vizconde de Matarosa (Toreno) and Don Andrés de la Vega) embarked at Gijon in a Jersey privateer, to seek assistance from Britain (25 May, 4 June). Galicia rose against the French.

31 May: in Saragossa, José Palafox y Melzi declared resistance to the French in the name of the rightful dynasty of Spain. (24 May, 8 June).

4 June: Asturian delegation arrived in London, with news of the Spanish insurrection and a plea for British assistance (30 May, 15 June). The Junta of Seville, claiming the title of Supreme Junta of Spain and the Indies, declared war on France in the name of Ferdinand VII. In Catalonia, French general François-Xavier Schwarz, marching against insurrectionists at Manresa, was turned back by Spanish local forces at Bruch, the first organised skirmish of the war. (15 June).

6 June: a junta of insurrection (against French occupation) proclaimed at Oporto; the commander of the Spanish force there, General Belesta, took prisoner the French governor (General François-Jean-Baptiste Quesnel du Torpt) and marched to Galicia to help its new junta (18 June). Joseph Bonaparte was named as new king of Spain (24 May, 15 June). General Jean-Antoine Verdier (from Bessières's corps) dispersed insurgents at Logroño. Bessières's cavalry commander, General Antoine-Charles-Louis Lasalle, defeated a Spanish force at Torquemada (12 June).

6-7 June: mob rising in Valencia exterminated the French mercantile community; the instigator, Canon Baltasar Calvo, was subsequently executed by the Junta of Valencia for this barbarity.

7 June: first real action of the war occurred when Col. Pedro de Echavarri, commander of the Cordova district, attempted to defend the crossing of the Guadalquivir against Dupont; the Spanish were dispersed and Dupont sacked Cordova, prompting much retaliation (2-3 July). Segovia was captured by General Bernard-Georges-François Frère of Dupont's corps.

8 June: Spanish force of the Marquis of Lazan, marching from Saragossa, was defeated by General Charles Lefebvre-Desnouettes' French force at Tudela (31 May, 14 June).

9 June: Spanish ships and shore-batteries began to fire on the French ships of Vice-Admiral François-Etienne Rosily-Mesros at Cadiz; on the following day he began negotiations (14 June).

10 June: Duhesme won a small action at Llobregat in Catalonia.

12 June: French generals Pierre-Hugues-Victoire Merle and Lasalle defeated Spanish general Gregorio Garcia de la Cuesta's Army of Castile at Cabezon; Valladolid was captured without resistance. Advancing on Saragossa, Lefebvre-Desnouettes defeated a Spanish force rallied by Lazan at Mallen (8 June).

14 June: Palafox's army from Saragossa was defeated by Lefebvre-Desnouettes at Alagon. Andalusian forces captured the French warships at Cadiz, mainly survivors from Trafalgar: Rosily-Mesros's flagship *Héros*, ships of the line *Algésiras*, *Argonaute*, *Neptune* and *Pluton*, and 40-gunner *Cornélie* (9 June). French 74-gunner *Atlas* taken by Spanish forces at Vigo.

15 June: British foreign secretary George Canning declared that any nation opposing France automatically became an ally of Britain, and that nothing could be more in Britain's self-interest than Spanish success, adumbrating British involvement in the Peninsula (4 June, 4 July, 9 September

1809). Lefebvre-Desnouettes's attack on Saragossa repelled by local forces under Palafox's deputy, Don Vincente Bustamente; siege of Saragossa commenced (23-24 June). In Catalonia, a second attempt to force the Bruch pass by French General Joseph Chabran was repelled (4 June). At Bayonne, the Spanish representative body convened to appoint Joseph Bonaparte king (6 June, 6 July). Murat left his command for health reasons and was succeeded temporarily by General Anne-Jean-Marie-René Savary (2 May).

17 June: Duhesme, with about half his Army of Catalonia, stormed and captured the town of Mataro (20 June).

18 June: popular uprising in Oporto against equivocating leaders; 'Supreme Junta of the Kingdom' formed there, headed by Dom Antonio de Castro (6 June). Insurrection in the Algarve led to the French evacuation of that province.

20 June: Duhesme failed to capture Gerona, defended by Cols. O'Donovan and Daly of the Spanish-Irish Regt. Ultonia (17, 30 June).

21 June: Moncey's advance-guard, advancing on Valencia, swept aside a small Spanish force holding the river-crossing at Pajaso Rio Cabral (8, 24 June).

22 June: French sacked Villa Viciosa.

23-24 June: Col. Jozef Chlopicki from Lefebvre-Desnouettes's force defeated Palafox at Epila (15, 26 June, 1 July).

24 June: advancing on Valencia, Moncey defeated a small Spanish force holding the pass of Cabrillas (21, 28 June).

26 June: Verdier arrived at Saragossa and took command from Lefebvre-Desnouettes (23-4 June, 1 July). French force under Col. Jean-Pierre Maransin sacked the Portuguese town of Beja. General Dominique-Henri Vedel (from Dupont's force) defeated insurgents at Despeña-Perros in New Castile.

28 June: Moncey's attack on Valencia was repelled (24 June, 2 July).

29 June: French General Jean-Gaspard-Pascal René was most horribly murdered by guerrillas in Catalonia.

30 June: Duhesme drove off a Spanish force under Col. Juan Baget at Llobregat, which had been attempting to blockade Barcelona. (20 June, 4 July).

1 July: after defeat at Epila, Palafox returned to lead the defence of Saragossa (23-24 June).

2 July: French assault on Saragossa beaten off; Agostina, 'the Maid of Saragossa', distinguished herself by firing a cannon (4 August). Moncey was ennobled as duc de Conegliano (24 June, 2 January 1809).

2-3 July: Vedel, with a detachment of Dupont's force, sacked Jaen (7 June, 14 July).

4 July: French General Louis-Henri Loison left Almeida for Abrantes, where he arrived a week later, the devastation of his march calculated to terrify the civilian population, for which he was reviled by generations of Portuguese (29 July). In Catalonia, Chabran advanced towards Granollers but was harassed by Col. Francisco Milans, and retired on Mataro. The British government issued an order that hostilities between Britain and Spain should cease (15 June, 12 July).

6 July: the meeting at Bayonne approved a new constitution for Spain, written on Napoleon's orders (15 June).

7 July: Joseph Bonaparte took the oath to

the new constitution.

8 July: Joseph resigned the crown of the Two Sicilies (20 July).

11 July: French General Honoré-Charles-Michel-Joseph Reille, reinforcing the troops in Catalonia, attempted to capture the port of Rosas but was beaten off by local levies under Don Juan Claros and British marines landed from HMS *Montague* (Capt. R.W. Otway) (24 July, 8 November).

12 July: British expedition under Sir Arthur Wellesley set sail for the Peninsula (4 July, 1 August).

14 July: Bessières defeated Cuesta's 'Army of Castile' (General Joachim Blake and 'Army of Galicia' in subordinate command) at Medina de Rio Seco (19 March). Spanish General Theodore Reding attacked a French detachment under General Louis Ligier-Belair at Mengibar, breaking off the action when Vedel came up (2-3 July).

16 July: Reding attacked Ligier-Belair at Mengibar again; General Jacques-Nicolas Gobert arrived to assist the French but was defeated and mortally wounded (he died at Guarroman on the following day); his subordinate, General François-Bertrand Dufour, continued the retreat.

19 July: Dupont was defeated by General Francisco Xavier Castaños at Bailen, and on the following day agreed to capitulate. Prominent among the casualties was the French cavalry general Claude-François Duprès, killed in a charge (2-3, 23 July).

20 July: as a consequence of Rio Seco, Joseph Bonaparte arrived in Madrid (8, 14, 24 July).

23 July: Dupont surrendered his command to Castaños at Bailen. The terms that the French should be sent home by sea were not followed, and they were incarcerated in prison-ships and finally in the Balearic islands (19 July).

24 July: under orders from Dupont, Vedel also surrendered his command. Joseph Bonaparte was officially proclaimed King of Spain and the Indies at Madrid (20 July). In Catalonia, Duhesme and Reille laid siege to Gerona (11 July, 16 August).

27 July: British 10–gun cutter HMS *Pickle* (Capt. Moses Cannadey) was wrecked entering Cadiz with dispatches.

29 July: Loison defeated the Portuguese General Francisco de Paulo Leite's small Spanish-Portuguese force at Evora, and then sacked the town (4 July)

31 July: the castle of Mongat, 10 miles from Barcelona, held by Neapolitans, surrendered to Capt. Lord Thomas Cochrane of HMS *Impérieuse*, to save its garrison from massacre by Spanish local forces under Francisco Barcelo; the castle was blown up. Unrest over events in Spain having spread to the Marquis of La Romana's Spanish corps, serving under French command in Denmark, when assembled to swear loyalty to Joseph Bonaparte, two regiments, Asturias and Guadalajara, broke into open mutiny. La Romana was preparing to act after being contacted by the British intelligence agent James Robertson.

1 August: the mutinous Spanish troops were compelled to surrender by Danish forces and were taken prisoner (9 August). On receiving news of Bailen, Joseph Bonaparte quit Madrid (23 July, 5 August). Wellesley's expedition began to disembark at Mondego Bay (12 July)

2 August: Wellesley and the British naval commander, Admiral Sir Charles Cotton, issued a Proclamation to the People of Portugal assuring them that the British expedition was to help them 'rescue your country, and restore the government of your lawful Prince' (5 August).

4 August: at Saragossa, a major French assault was beaten off, though made a lodgement in the city. (2 July, 14 August).

5 August: reinforcement from Andalusia under Sir Brent Spencer arrived at Mondego Bay to support Wellesley (2 August). Reacting to news of Bailen, Napoleon began to order elements of the *Grande Armée* to Spain (10 August).

9 August: Wellesley prepared to march inland (15 August). Having contacted the British commander in the region, Rear-Admiral Richard Keats, La Romana's Spanish corps in Denmark took possession of the town of Nyborg on Funen island. Two Danish ships (*Fama*, 18-gun cutter, and *Salorman*, 12-gun cutter) resisted and had to be captured by boats under Capt. James Macnamara of HMS *Edgar* (1, 11 August).

10 August: Napoleon ordered the Viceroy of Italy, Eugène de Beauharnais, to send some of his troops to reinforce the French in Catalonia (5, 17 August).

11 August: La Romana's corps embarked from Nyborg and Langeland island in the British fleet; they were landed in northwest Spain to continue the fight against France (9 August, 11 October).

14 August: Verdier raised the siege of Saragossa (4 August, 20 December).

15 August: first British troops in action in the Peninsula, in a skirmish with the rearguard of General Henri-François Delaborde near Obidos; the first British officer fatality of the war was Lieut. Ralph Bunbury of the 2/95th Rifles (9, 17 August).

16 August: French general Christophe-Antoine Merlin, sent by Bessiéres to disperse insurgents around Bilbao, defeated them and sacked the city (14 July, 20 September). A sally by the garrison, and relief by the army of the Conde de Caldagues, broke the French siege of Gerona and forced Duhesme to retreat (24 July, 20 August).

17 August: Wellesley attacked Delaborde's French force and drove it from its position at Roliça, the first British victory of the war (15, 21 August). Napoleon ordered more of the *Grande Armée* from Germany to Spain: Marshal Adolphe-Édouard-Casimir-Joseph Mortier with V Corps, and two dragoon divisions; all in preparation for his personal intervention (10 August, 7 September).

20 August: harassed all the way from Gerona, Duhesme regained the safety of Barcelona (16 August).

21 August: having marched from Lisbon, Junot attacked Wellesley at Vimeiro and was defeated, but the British pursuit was stifled by the arrival of Sir Harry Burrard, who took command when the battle was over (17 August).

22 August: Sir Hew Dalrymple, Burrard's superior, arrived to take command of the British army. Junot sent General François-Etienne de Kellermann to begin negotiations with the British (30 August).

25 August: British reinforcement under Sir John Moore began to disembark in Portugal (6 October).

27 August: tentative Spanish probe along the line of the Ebro, made by the Aragonese force of the Conde de Montijo, was repelled by Lefebvre-Desnouettes at Alfaro.

30 August: Junot and the British concluded the Convention of Cintra, which permitted the French to return home in British transports (13 September).

3 September: Admirals Cotton and Seniavin signed a convention independent to that of Cintra, for the Russian ships in the Tagus to be taken into British custody until six months after the end of hostilities, with the crews to be sent home at British expense (6 December 1807).

5 September: Council of War in Madrid, convened to co-ordinate action against the French, failed to appoint a single commanding general (25 September).

7 September: Napoleon reorganised his forces in Spain into seven *corps d'armée*: I, IV and V new, II Bessières's, III Moncey's, VI Ney's, VII the Army of Catalonia (17 August).

13 September: in accordance with the Convention of Cintra, Junot sailed for France, almost all his army having left Portugal by the end of the month (30 August, 20 September).

18 September: Council of Regency formed to govern Portugal, the Oporto Junta and those of other regions being dissolved.

20 September: Wellesley sailed for home, followed by Dalrymple and Burrard, for an inquiry into Cintra (25 August, 6 October, 14 November). Galician forces under Blake pushed out General François-Gédéon Bailly de Monthion and the French garrison from Bilbao; they retired six days later (16 August, 11 October).

25 September: Spanish Supreme Junta inaugurated to act as the government of 'patriot' Spain, at Aranjuez, with the Conde de Floridablanca as its head; it proclaimed Ferdinand VII king (26 October).

6 October: command of British forces in the Peninsula devolved upon Moore (20 September, 26 October).

11 October: Blake re-occupied Bilbao as French division under Merlin retired (20 September). La Romana landed at Santander (11 August).

13 October: British reinforcement under Sir David Baird began to arrive at Corunna (26 October).

14 October: conclusion of Napoleon's conference at Erfurt with the Tsar and allied states, ensuring that he was in no immediate danger from Austria, permitting him to devote his personal presence to Spain.

25 October: at the Legislative Assembly in Paris, Napoleon declared that he was about to lead his troops into Spain to confirm his brother as king.

26 October: first serious action between Napoleon's army and the Spanish, as the French began to push forward, roughly along the line of the Ebro: Ney routed the Castilian forces of General Pignatelli at Logrono. General Antoine Morlot from Moncey's corps drove part of Grimarest's Andalusian division, under Col. Cruz-Murgeon, into the castle of Lerin, where he was forced to surrender on the following day. The Supreme Junta issued its statement of intent regarding its objectives (25 September, 20 November). Moore began to advance from Lisbon into Spain (6 October, 13 November). After delays in obtaining permission to land from the Supreme Junta, Baird's troops finally began to disembark at Corunna (13 October, 20 December).

31 October: his advance having stalled, Blake was attacked by Marshal François-Joseph Lefebvre at Zornoza (or Durango), and the Spaniards withdrew; Lefebvre took Bilbao (11 October, 5 November).

3 November: Napoleon arrived at Bayonne to take control of the campaign in Spain (25 October, 6 November).

5 November: Blake attacked the division of General Eugène-Casimir Villatte (Lefebvre's corps) at Valmaceda, the French retiring in disorder (31 October, 7 November).

6 November: Napoleon arrived at Vittoria and prepared to launch his great advance (3 November).

7 November: while retiring before Lefebvre, Blake's Army of Galicia fought a brief rearguard action at Guenes (5 November). Marching to the relief of invested Barcelona, General Laurent Gouvion St.Cyr detailed Reille to capture Rosas, held by the Spanish colonel Peter O'Daly.

8 November: French advance drove Blake from Valmaceda (10-11 November). French troops (under Generals Reille and Pino) having entered Rosas the previous day and been fired on by the British ships HMS *Excellent* (Capt. John West) and bomb-vessel *Meteor* (Capt. James Collins), West and a landing party arrived to assist the local miqueletes, but were compelled to take refuge in the fortress (15 November).

9 November: after a long ride, Marshal Jean-de-Dieu Soult arrived to take command of II Corps from Bessières, who was transferred to command Napoleon's cavalry.

10 November: Soult attacked the Conde de Belvedere's Spanish army and routed him at Gamonal (14 November).

10-11 November: Blake was routed by Marshal Claude Victor at Espinosa (8, 14 November).

13 November: advancing into Spain, the leading elements of Moore's army reached Salamanca (26 October, 28 November).

14 November: commencement of the British court of enquiry into the Convention of Cintra (20 September, 22 December). Soult's pursuit cut up part of Blake's baggage, retiring after Espinosa; General Acevedo, the Asturian commander, was killed (10-11 November).

15 November: Blake was ordered to relinquish his command to La Romana, who arrived a short time later. French assault on Rosas beaten off (8, 20 November).

17 November: Soult occupied Santander (14 November).

20 November: his health not sufficient for the task, the head of the Spanish Supreme Junta, Floridablanca, died; he was succeeded by the Marquis of Astorga (26 October). At Rosas, French batteries drove the British ships from the coast (25 November).

23 November: Marshal Jean Lannes, with Moncey's corps and elements of that of Marshal Michel Ney, defeated Castaños and troops from the Armies of the Centre and Aragon at Tudela, though much of the Spanish force managed to escape.

25 November: Moncey resumed command from Lannes, who returned to France to recover his health (20 December). Having arrived on the 21st, Lord Cochrane landed a detachment from HMS *Impérieuse* to reinforce Rosas (30 November).

26 November: French attack on Rosas gained a lodgement (30 November). General Jean-Miguel Vives, Captain-General of Catalonia, attacked the French outposts at Barcelona and drove them into the city (16 December).

28 November: on learning of the defeat at Tudela, Moore ordered the British to retreat from Salamanca to Portugal (13 November, 5 December).

30 November: marching on Madrid,

Napoleon opened the road by defeating General Benito San Juan at the Somosierra Pass. French attack on Rosas was repelled (26 November, 3 December).

1 December: Napoleon's vanguard approached Madrid. French General René-François-Jean Aubrée, brigade commander in III Corps, was killed near Saragossa.

2 December: in the skirmishing before Madrid the French general André-Adrien-Joseph La Bruyère was shot in the throat and died on the following day.

3 December: after a bombardment, Madrid surrendered to Napoleon. At Rosas, a sally by the defenders was beaten back (30 November, 5 December).

4 December: French occupied Madrid (7 December).

5 December: Moore decided to advance again into Spain after a plea from the Supreme Junta and from Madrid, made before the city fell (28 November, 11 December). Rosas fell to French assault; Cochrane was unable to rescue the principal defenders but blew up the outlying fort and evacuated its garrison by sea (3 December).

7 December: upon receiving news of the surrender of Madrid, the Spanish force marching to its relief panicked and fled to Talavera, but when rallied mutinied and murdered its commander, San Juan (4 December).

10 December: British 50-gun ship HMS *Jupiter* (Capt. Hon. E.R. Baker) was wrecked on the reef of Vigo Bay.

11 December: Moore's advance from Salamanca began (5 December).

12 December: first skirmish of Moore's campaign between cavalry vedettes, at Rueda, where the French detachment was dispersed (20 December).

14 December: Sir John Cradock assumed command of British forces in Portugal.

16 December: marching to relieve Barcelona, Gouvion St. Cyr defeated Vives at Cardadieu. A sortie by the French garrison of Barcelona was repelled (26 November).

17 December: Gouvion St. Cyr relieved Barcelona (21 December).

20 December: Moore's army united with Baird's reinforcement, marching from Corunna, at Mayorga (26 October, 11 December). Moncey arrived at Saragossa to renew the siege, assisted by Mortier (14 August).

21 December: Lord Henry William Paget, Moore's cavalry commander, led a raid upon Sahagun and routed the French outpost of General César-Alexandre Debelle. Learning of Moore's advance, Napoleon ordered his forces in the vicinity of Madrid in pursuit, intending Soult to hold Moore until they could arrive: Moore had succeeded in diverting Napoleon's aim from crushing the Spanish before they could reorganise (24 December). Gouvion St. Cyr defeated Reding at Molins del Rey; Reding's second-in-command, the Conde de Caldagues, was captured (17 December, 1 January 1809). The French captured the Monte Terrero heights overlooking Saragossa; an attack on the city's trans-Ebro suburb of San Lazaro was repelled (29 December).

22 December: report issued by the Cintra Inquiry (14 November, 27 December).

24 December: having advanced to Sahagun, Moore learned of the approach of large French forces, abandoned his plans for advancing against Soult, and began to retire (21, 26 December). Lefebvre advanced against the bridge at Almaraz and dispersed

General José Galuzzo's Spanish defenders, but then advanced towards Avila without orders, which led to his replacement (7 November).

25 December: in an action near Tarancon French dragoons of General André-Thomas Perreimond avoided a trap by the Spanish forces of the Duke of Infantado's vanguard of the Army of the Centre, commanded by General Francisco-Javier Venegas (13 January).

26 December: two French squadrons were scattered by Moore's cavalry at Mayorga (24 December).

27 December: disorganisation and destruction becoming evident in the British retreat, Moore issued a harsh order in an attempt to maintain discipline. Termination of the Cintra Inquiry: Dalrymple and Bur-

rard criticised, but Wellesley exonerated (22 December).

29 December: French cavalry attack under Lefebvre-Desnouettes repulsed by Paget at Benavente; Lefebvre-Desnouettes was captured. Moncey was replaced in command by Junot; the first parallel was opened against Saragossa (21 December, 1 January 1809).

30 December: Soult's cavalry under General Jean-Baptiste Franceschi-Delonne dispersed La Romana's rearguard (that had been co-operating with Moore) at Mansilla de las Mulas (2 January 1809).

31 December: Moore detached his two flank brigades to march to Vigo, while the rest of the army continued their retreat to Corunna.

1809

1 January: Pursuing Moore, Napoleon reached Astorga, but then decided to return to France, leaving the pursuit to Soult. In Catalonia, the Marquis de Lazan won a skirmish against a battalion of Reille's division at Castellon, and subsequently checked Reille's advance. The second parallel was opened against Saragossa (29 December, 10 January).

2 January: Franceschi-Delonne cut up the rearguard of La Romana's Army of Galicia, under General Rengel, at Foncebadon, but did not continue the pursuit. Leading Soult's pursuit of Moore, General Armand Lahoussaye's French dragoons cut up many British stragglers left drunk or exhausted at Bembibre. Moncey was recalled from Spain (2 July, 29 December 1808).

3 January: French attack upon Moore's rearguard (commanded by Sir Edward Paget) was repelled at Cacabellos; the French commander, General Auguste-François-Marie de Colbert, was killed by the British sharpshooter Thomas Plunket.

5 January: skirmish at Constantino between Edward Paget's rearguard and Soult's vanguard under Generals Lahoussaye and Merle.

7 January: skirmish at Lugo between Moore's army, which had paused in its retreat, and Soult's vanguard.

10 January: skirmish at Betanzos as British stragglers were gathered by Sergeant William Newman of the 43rd, and repelled an attack by Franceschi-Delonne's pursuing cavalry. At Saragossa, French batteries opened against the outlying fort of San José

(1 January).

11 January: Moore's army reached Corunna. The French successfully stormed the fort of San José at Saragossa (15-16 January).

12 January: Moore's rearguard skirmished with Soult's vanguard at El Burgo, four miles from Corunna. Moore's flank brigades reached Vigo, to be evacuated from there (31 December 1808, 14 January).

13 January: Marshal Victor defeated Venegas's vanguard of Infantado's army at Uclés (25 December 1808, 18 January).

14 January: British transports arrived at Corunna and Moore began to embark his army (12, 16 January).

15-16 January: French captured the outlying redoubt of the Pillar at Saragossa (11, 22 January).

16 January: Soult attacked Moore's position in front of Corunna and was beaten off; Moore was mortally wounded, and a prominent French fatality was brigade-commander General Joseph-Yves Manigault-Gaulois.

18 January: Moore's army, now commanded by Sir John Hope, completed its evacuation from Corunna by sea; the Spanish commander at Corunna, General Alcedo, surrendered to Soult once the British were away. As Infantado retired after Uclés, his artillery (15 guns) was captured by the pursuing cavalry of General Alexandre-Elisabeth-Michel Digeon at Tortola (13 January).

22 January: Lannes replaced Junot in command at Saragossa (15-16 January). Joseph Bonaparte entered Madrid.

23 January: major Spanish sally from Saragossa was repelled.

26 January: French forces established within the defences of Saragossa. French general Pierre Watier de Saint-Alphonse captured the town of Alcañiz and took supplies intended for the relief of Saragossa. The Spanish governor of Ferrol, Admiral Melgarejo, surrendered without resistance to Soult and took service under Joseph Bonaparte.

27 January: French assault on Saragossa captured more territory, street-fighting following daily until the city fell. The commander of Ney's artillery, General Pierre-Marie Bicquilly, died at Villafranca. Sir Arthur Wellesley was present in parliament to receive their vote of thanks for Vimeiro (27 December 1808).

1 February: French chief engineer at Saragossa, General André-Bruno de Frévol, comte de Lacoste, was mortally wounded while reconnoitering.

10 February: at Saragossa a French mine blew up the strongpoint of the San Francisco convent, with immense loss of life (18 February).

16 February: in his attempt to invade Portugal, Soult was repelled from the River Minho by Portuguese defenders (4 March).

17 February: advancing against each other, elements of Gouvion St. Cyr's and Reding's commands engaged near Capellades, the Spaniards retiring.

18 February: Gouvion St. Cyr defeated Reding's subordinate General Castro at Igualada (19 February). At Saragossa, the French captured the San Lazaro suburb (10, 20 February).

19 February: pursuing Reding, Gouvion St. Cyr engaged General Ivanzo's small Spanish force at San Magin; they took refuge in the fortified abbey of Santa Cruces (25 February).

20 February: Saragossa capitulated to the French; Palafox, stricken with fever, opened negotiations but turned over military command to General Saint-March and the civil administration to a temporary junta (18 February).

25 February: retiring on Tarragona, Reding engaged the French division of General Joseph Souham at Valls; Gouvion St. Cyr's arrival turned the action in favour of the French and Reding was defeated and mortally wounded (19 February). The commandant of King Joseph's royal guard, General Charles Saligny, duc de San Germano, died at Madrid.

4 March: in Soult's attempt to invade Portugal, his cavalry under Franceschi-Delonne routed La Romana's rearguard under General Nicolas Mahy at La Trepa (or Monterey) (16 February)

12 March: the town and Portuguese garrison of Chaves surrendered to Soult with little resistance (17 March).

15 March: landing-party from frigate HMS *Arethusa* (Capt. Robert Mends) destroyed the shore-batteries at Lequito (east of Bilbao on the north coast of Spain) and on the following day landed again to destroy two chasse-marées loaded with brandy for the French army.

17 March: La Romana surprised and captured Villafranca, taking prisoner an entire battalion of the 6th *Léger*. Advancing across the Tagus to attack Cuesta's Army of Estremadura, elements of Victor's corps (General Jean-François Leval's division) drove back the Duque del Parque's Spanish division at Mesa de Ibor (21 March).

18 March: Portuguese General Bernardino Freire de Andrade, resisting calls from his army to stand and fight, tried to leave his troops at Braga but was seized, and command of his army passed to Baron Eben; when Eben left, Freire was hauled out of gaol and piked to death by his erstwhile followers.

20 March: Soult routed Eben's army at Braga (26 March).

21 March: Spanish General Henestrosa, covering Cuesta's withdrawal, checked Victor's pursuing cavalry at Miajadas (17, 28 March). The strategically-important fortress of Jaca in the Pyrenean foothills surrendered without resistance to elements of Mortier's corps.

22 March: after serving at Saragossa, French general Antoine Morlot died at Bayonne of a brain fever.

26 March: Soult forced his way across the River Avé at San Justo against Portuguese local forces; this operation was perhaps most noted for the death of the French general Henry-Antoine Jardon, 'the Voltigeur general', brigade-commander under General Julien-Augustin-Joseph Mermet, whose troops had crossed the Avé at Guimaraens (20, 29 March).

27 March: after some minor actions over some days in the vicinity of Ciudad Real, at that place the French general Horace-François-Bastien Sébastiani surprised and routed the Spanish forces of the Conde de Cartaojal, who had taken command of the Army of the Centre earlier in the year; subsequently he was replaced by Venegas. The besieged French garrison of Vigo, commanded by Col. Chalot, surrendered to the Spanish forces without resisting an assault, on condition that the garrison be taken prisoner by the assisting Royal Navy force (HMS *Lively* and *Venus*), so were handed over to Capt. Mackinley of *Lively*.

28 March: Cuesta was routed by Victor at

Medellin and his army destroyed; the province of Estremadura fell to the French (21 March).

29 March: Soult stormed and captured Oporto; its nominal commander, the Bishop Antonio de Castro, escaped, but thousands of defenders and population were slain, and the Portuguese general Lima-Barreto was killed by his own men when he tried to organise a withdrawal (26 March, 18 April).

5 April: General Louis-Gabriel Suchet was appointed to command III Corps of the *Armée d'Espagne* (later the Army of Aragon) in succession to Junot; he actually took command on 19 May (23 May).

12 April: French general Pierre Lapisse, detached from Victor's corps, sacked Alcantara with great brutality.

18 April: Loison, detached from Soult's corps, pushed the Portuguese general Francisco Silveira into the town of Amarante, but failed to capture it (29 March, 2-3 May).

22 April: Sir Arthur Wellesley arrived in Lisbon and took command of British troops in Portugal.

25 April: the French dragoon captain Argenton had his first meeting with Wellesley, in pursuance of the abortive plan of insurrection that later came to bear his name; he was arrested by Soult some two weeks later (11 May).

2-3 May: Loison captured the bridge at Amarante, routing Silveira's Portuguese (18 April).

11 May: Wellesley pushed back Mermet's division of Soult's corps at Grijon (25 April).

12 May: Wellesley crossed the Douro and captured Oporto; Soult was compelled to retire from Portugal (15 May).

14 May: Victor drove a Portuguese detachment under Col. William Mayne of the Loyal Lusitanian Legion from Alcantara.

15 May: Soult forced the bridge at Ponte Nova against Portuguese ordenanza, permitting him to continue his retreat (12, 22 May).

19 May: driving into the Asturias, Ney forced the passage of the River Nora at Gallegos against a small force under La Romana, and went on to sack Oviedo; La Romana escaped by taking a ship at Gihon. The Spanish Col. Perena with local forces, having marched from Lerida and driven the French garrison from Monzon, they withdrew to Barbastro; from there the French General Pierre-Joseph Habert, attempting to recapture Monzon, lost the vanguard of his brigade crossing the River Cinca, which was forced to surrender when he was unable to break through to them.

21 May: collaborating with the Spanish general Francisco Ballesteros, HMS *Amelia* (Capt. Frederick Irby) and HMS *Statira* (Capt. Charles Boys) intercepted some French vessels leaving the harbour of San Andero, the town being captured by the Spanish; five vessels were captured, notably the French 16-gun corvette *La Mouche* (Lieut. de Vaisseau Antoine Allègre), which had been a troublesome commerce-raider.

22 May: Soult relieved the town of Lugo, where General François Fournier had been blockaded by Portuguese forces (15 May). Guerrillas under General Martin La Carrera defeated the outnumbered French force of General Antoine-Louis Maucune at Santiago de Compostelle.

23 May: taking the offensive against Blake in Aragon, Suchet was defeated at Alcañiz (5 April, 15 June).

24 May: Verdier began the siege of Gerona, defended by the governor, General Mariano Alvarez de Castro (6 June).

1 June: Marshal Charles-Pierre-François Augereau was appointed to take command of VII Corps, in place of Gouvion St. Cyr, but took months to arrive (12 October).

6 June: French broke ground at Gerona (24 May, 17 June).

8 June: attempting to ford the Oiteben estuary near Sampayo, Ney was repulsed by Spanish forces under the Conde de Noroña.

10 June: Ballesteros stormed and captured Santander; the French defender, General Jean-Baptiste Noirot, escaped (21 May).

12 June: French general Jean-Pierre-François Bonnet recaptured Santander.

15 June: Suchet was engaged by Blake at Maria de Huerve, and although the Spanish were defeated (partially because General Juan-Carlos Areizaga failed to support Blake), they withdrew in good order (23 May, 18 June).

17 June: major sally by the defenders of Gerona, hindering the progress of the siege (6 June, 5 July).

18 June: Suchet routed Blake at Belchite, ending Blake's invasion of Aragon (15 June). Wellesley instituted a divisional organisation into his British army for the first time.

5 July: Gouvion St. Cyr captured the harbour of Palamos, from where the besieged garrison of Gerona had been receiving succour.

(17 June, 7 July).

6 July: Wellesley was appointed Marshal-General of the Portuguese army.

7 July: Verdier attacked the outlying fort of Montjuich at Gerona, but was repelled; but the position was abandoned on 10 July (5 July).

10 July: relief column for Gerona under the British adventurer Ralph Marshall was intercepted by the French (Pino's Italian division) and surrendered at Castellar (Marshall escaped into Gerona, where subsequently he was killed) (1 September).

26 July: as Cuesta's Spanish army, co-operating with Wellesley's British army, retired on Talavera, Marshal Victor's vanguard defeated the rearguard of General José Zayas at Torrijos.

27 July: Victor made his first attack upon the Anglo-Spanish position at Talavera. As Wellesley's 3rd Division was getting into position, it was surprised and cut up by Lapisse's Division at Casa de Salinas.

28 July: Victor's main attack on Wellesley's position at Talavera was driven off, and the French retired; notable casualties were the commander of the British 3rd Division, Major-General John Randoll Mackenzie, and Brigadier-General Ernst Eberhard von Langwerth, brigade-commander in the 1st Division, both of whom were killed; the French general Pierre Lapisse died two days later.

29 July: Robert Craufurd's Light Brigade joined Wellesley at Talavera, too late for the action, after one of the most famous forced marches in history.

30 July: operating against the Anglo-Spanish forces of Wellesley and Cuesta, Marshal Mortier drove a small Spanish force under the Marquis de Reino from Puerto de Baños.

3-4 August: Cuesta abandoned Talavera in the face of French advance, leaving the British wounded to be captured. Mortier made a probing advance, but drew off to await reinforcement.

8 August: during the pursuit from Talavera, Soult forced the line of the Tagus by driving back the Spanish forces of the Duque de Albuquerque and General L.A. Bassecourt at Arzobispo.

11 August: General Sébastiani engaged the Army of La Mancha under General Venegas at Almonacid; the battle was decided by the arrival of King Joseph and the reserve, but the Spanish got away in reasonable order.

12 August: retiring on Portugal, the small force of Sir Robert Wilson (his Loyal Lusitanian Legion and some Spanish troops), which had been threatening Madrid during the Talavera campaign, made a stand at Puerto de Baños, from where they were driven by Ney's vanguard under General Jean-Baptiste Lorcet; Wilson retired successfully on Portugal.

13 August: Cuesta resigned as commander of the Army of Estremadura after suffering a stroke; temporarily succeeded by General Francisco Eguia.

26 August: Wellesley was created Baron Douro, of Wellesley, Somerset, and Viscount Wellington, of Talavera and Wellington in the same county (1 February 1810, 18 February 1812). A late casualty of the Corunna campaign, Major-General Coote Manningham (brigade-commander in the campaign and one of the founders of the 95th Rifles) died at Maidstone of the exertions of the campaign.

1 September: Verdier interrupted the siege of Gerona, moving away to guard against Blake's manoeuvers towards relief, but a supply convoy got into the city (10 July).

6 September: in tightening the investment of Gerona, Verdier captured the outlying position of Nuesta Señora de los Angeles; a French detachment was beaten nearby at San Gregorio by bands of miqueletes, and the French commander, General Dominique Joba, killed (11 September).

9 September: George Canning relinquished his post as British foreign secretary (15 June 1808).

11 September: Verdier recommenced a full siege of Gerona (6, 19 September).

16 September: Marshal Soult was appointed 'major-general' as chief-of-staff to King Joseph, in succession to Jourdan, who subsequently returned to France, having resigned officially on 31 October.

19 September: French assault on Gerona failed; Verdier quit his command and Gouvion St. Cyr, who had been commanding the covering force, took over (11 September).

26 September: relief-convoy for Gerona, under Henry O'Donnell, was defeated near the defences (12 October). Spencer Perceval became British Prime Minister, replacing Portland (24 March 1807, 11 May 1812).

9 October: General Jean-Augustin Carrié de Boissy, from Kellermann's command, attacked Astorga and was repelled.

12 October: Augereau arrived to command the army besieging Gerona (1 June, 7 December).

18 October: General Jean-Gabriel Marchand, commanding VI Corps, attacked the Duque de Parque's Spanish force at Tamames, was beaten off, and retired.

20 October: Wellington wrote his memorandum to Col. Richard Fletcher, RE, regarding the construction of the Lines of Torres Vedras for the protection of Lisbon.

25 October: detached from Lord Collingwood's fleet blockading Toulon, Rear-Admiral George Martin in HMS *Canopus* and with five other ships-of-the-line, intercepted a French convoy bound to re-supply Duhesme in Barcelona. The French naval escort under Rear-Admiral François-André Baudin in the 80-gun *Robuste* had separated from the convoy, and during the chase *Robuste* and the 74-gun *Lion* ran aground near Cette (Sète) on the French coast; to prevent their capture, Baudin landed his crews and burned the ships. On 23 October five vessels in the convoy had been destroyed by the frigate HMS *Pomone*.

31 October: the remainder of Baudin's convoy – seven merchant and four naval vessels – having sought shelter in Rosas bay, were attacked by boats from five British warships commanded by Captain Benjamin Hallowell, the boats led by Lieutenant John Tailour of HMS *Tigre*. The French commander, Lieutenant de Vaisseau Jacques-Marie Bertaud-la-Bretèche, of the armed storeship *Lamproie*, organised a stout defence, but despite supporting fire from shore all eleven French vessels were burned or captured by the morning of 1 November.

10 November: one of the Bailen prisoners, General Jacques Lefranc, died of fever in prison at Malaga.

18 November: Sébastiani's cavalry defeated a large force of Spanish cavalry under Freire near Ocaña, the largest all-cavalry action of the war; General Antoine-Marie Paris d'Illins, commander of the French IV Corps light cavalry, was killed.

19 November: King Joseph and Soult, with Sébastiani's V and Mortier's VI Corps, routed Ariezaga's Army of La Mancha at Ocaña.

20 November: Del Parque's Spanish Army of the Left occupied Madrid.

23 November: the brigades of French generals Mathieu Delabassée and Pierre-Louis Marcognet attacked Del Parque's advancing vanguard at Medina de Campo, and were driven off.

28 November: retiring after hearing news of Ocaña, at Alba de Tormes Del Parque was attacked by Kellermann's French cavalry; French infantry came up and Del Parque's army partially fell apart as he retired. He was superseded subsequently by La Romana.

7 December: at Gerona, the French stormed the redoubts to the south-east of the city and defeated a sally (12 October).

10 December: Gerona surrendered; because of illness, the governor Alvarez de Castro had turned over command to General Juliano Bolivar.

1810

12 January: pursuing the Spanish Army of Catalonia (in command of which Henry O'Donnell had superseded Blake), the advance-guard of General Joseph Souham of VII Corps was thrown back at the Col de Suspina pass (21-22 January).

13 January: Cadiz was named as the meeting-place of the new national Cortes (29

January).

16 January: French laid siege to Hostalrich, mid-way between Gerona and Barcelona; the governor was Col. Juliano Estrada (12 May).

20-21 January: beginning an assault on Andalusia, Mortier and Sébastiani of King Joseph's army forced the Spanish positions of Puerto del Rey and others, and captured a division at Arquillos (actions sometimes styled 'Sierra Morena') (23 January).

21-22 January: a detachment of Duhesme's garrison of Barcelona, under Colonel Guétry, was cut up near Granollers by part of O'Donnell's Army of Catalonia under the Marquis of Campo Verde (12, 24 January).

23 January: Sébastiani routed Ariezaga's army at Jaen; Ariezana was superseded subsequently by Blake (20, 21, 28 January). In the face of the French advance upon Seville, the Central Junta dispersed (13, 29 January).

24 January: Augereau, commanding VII Corps, relieved Barcelona and subsequently sent Duhesme home (21-22 January, 8 February)

28 January: Sébastiani routed some of Ariezaga's survivors and Freire's cavalry of the Andalusian army at Alcala la Réal (23 January, 5 February).

29 January: the Central Junta abdicated authority at Cadiz, and named a Regency to succeed it (23 January, 5 February).

31 January: Seville surrendered to King Joseph, the ephemeral revolutionary junta which had replaced the fled Central Junta being dispersed (23 January).

1 February: the House of Commons (not unanimously) passed a vote of thanks to Wellington for Talavera; the House of Lords had passed the same on 26 January, when Lords Grenville, Grey and Grosvenor had voted against (28 July 1809, 16 February).

5 February: Marshal Victor's forces arrived before Cadiz to commence a blockade (29 January). Sébastiani opened the passes leading to Malaga, and occupied the city after dispersing its defenders; excepting Cadiz, Andalusia was virtually subdued (28 January).

8 February: Augereau was confirmed officially as commander of the Army of Catalonia (24 October 1809, 24 April).

10 February: first British reinforcements arrived to help garrison Cadiz (5 February, 22 April).

13 February: Marshal Ney, commanding VI Corps, summoned Ciudad Rodrigo to surrender, but withdrew (not having siege artillery) when the governor, Andrès Herrasti, refused (26 April).

14 February: General Bonnet defeated the Asturian forces of General Barcena at Colleto, and occupied Oviedo; possession switched several times and Bonnet was tied up by Spanish activity in the Asturias.

16 February: the House of Commons voted a pension of £2,000 p.a. to Wellington and his two succeeding male heirs, but only by 213 votes to 106; the Court of Common Council passed a petition on 23 February which expressed 'grief and concern' at this payment! (1 February, 26 April 1811).

19-20 February: Ballesteros's division of La Romana's army attacked and defeated the cavalry brigade of Mortier's V Corps at Valverde; the French commander, General Charles-Victor Beauregard, was killed (15 April).

20 February: Souham was attacked by O'Donnell's Army of Catalonia and local miqueletes at Vich; the Spanish were driven off but Souham was wounded in the left temple and had to go home to recuperate (12 January, 20 March).

4 March: advancing against General José Caro's Army of Valencia, Suchet with the Army of Aragon forced the pass of Alventosa against limited resistance.

6 March: Suchet called upon Valencia to surrender, but with no means of taking the city he marched away four days later (13 April).

8 March: General Robert Craufurd was given responsibility, with his Light Division, of the whole outpost line along the Coa by Wellington

19-20 March: French attempt, by the brigade of General Claude-François Ferey of Loison's division, to pierce Craufurd's outpost at Barba del Puerco, was beaten off by Sidney Beckwith's 1st Battn. 95th Rifles (10 July).

21 March: commanding VIII Corps, Junot began the investment of Astorga, defended by the governor, José Santocildes (10 April).

24 March: at Vincennes, the British agent Baron Kolli was betrayed and arrested as he was about to leave for Valençay in his attempt to free Ferdinand VII from detention; Kolli was imprisoned for the remainder of Napoleon's rule.

20 March: General Juan Caro of O'Donnell's army captured Villafranca and its French garrison; Caro was wounded and succeeded by the Marquis of Campo Verde (20 February, 5 April).

31 March: the guerrilla leader Xavier Mina was captured during operations in Aragon.

5 April: Campo Verde captured Manresa,

driving out the Rheinbund forces of General Schwarz (20 March).

10 April: General Echevarria's brigade, intending to help General Nicolas Mahy (commander of the Army of Galicia) in his support for Astorga, was routed near Alcanizas by the cavalry of Junot's VIII Corps (21 March, 21 April).

13 April: Suchet with the Army of Aragon commenced the siege of Lerida, defended by its governor, General Garcia Conde (6 March, 23 April).

15 April: Ballesteros was defeated at Zalamea, and was pursued by elements of Mortier's V Corps (19-20 February, 26 May).

17 April: Napoleon announced the formation of the Army of Portugal, under Massena, principally II, VI and VIII Corps.

21 April: French stormed Astorga through a breach and established a foothold in the city (10 April).

22 April: Spanish attempts to break through to Astorga were repelled, Mahy at Foncebadon and Manzanal, and Echevarria at Penilla; Santocildes surrendered Astorga. Matagorda fort, an outlying work at Cadiz, was abandoned on the orders of Sir Thomas Graham, new commander of British forces at Cadiz, after bombardment rendered it indefensible (10 February, 23-27 February 1811).

23 April: attempting to relieve Lerida, Henry O'Donnell was defeated by Suchet with the division of General Louis-François-Félix Musnier, at Margalef (13, 29 April). Sébastiani entered the city of Murcia unopposed and extracted a contribution from it (5 February).

24 April: Marshal Jacques-Etienne Macdonald was appointed to command in Catalonia, replacing the discredited Augereau, although it was a month before he actually arrived (8 February).

26 April: French began to lay siege to Ciudad Rodrigo (13 February, 30 May).

29 April: French siege-trenches opened at Lerida (23 April, 12-13 May).

12 May: out of supplies, the defender of Hostalrich, Estrada, tried to fight his way out; some of his men got away but he was wounded and captured (16 January).

12-13 May: Suchet stormed the outlying works at Lerida, and on 13 May the town, the garrison retiring into the citadel (29 April).

14 May: Suchet used the civilian population of Lerida as a 'human shield' in front of the French troops attacking the citadel; to prevent further slaughter Garcia Conde surrendered (and subsequently took service under King Joseph).

15 May: Suchet commenced the siege of Mequinenza (governor, Col. Carbon) (5 June).

26 May: Ballesteros was defeated at Araçena, but rallied his forces (15 April).

30 May: Ney arrived at Ciudad Rodrigo to complete the investment (26 April, 15 June).

5 June: the town of Mequinenza was stormed; the garrison retired to the fort (15 May).

8 June: Mequinenza fort being rendered indefensible, it was surrendered to Suchet.

15 June: French opened the first parallel at Ciudad Rodrigo (30 May).

1 July: at Ciudad Rodrigo, the French stormed the outlying positions of San Francisco and Santa Clara, forcing the defend-

ers to withdraw within the main city walls (9 July).

5 July: Anglo-Spanish amphibious raid commanded by Juan Diaz Porlier and Captain R. Mends of HMS *Arethusa* (the British landing-party under Captain Hon. Frederick Aylmer of HMS *Narcissus*) on the Biscay coast, destroyed all the guns at Santona and Laredo and re-embarked on 8 July. Porlier returned in the following month and established himself in the region.

9 July: Ciudad Rodrigo having been battered into indefensibility, Herrasti surrendered to avoid a storm (1 July).

10 July: General Robert Craufurd attempted to cut up some foragers from Junot's corps at Barquilla (or Villar de Puerco); the French infantry stood firm and got away in good order, Captain Gouache and Sergeant Patois of the 22nd Line's grenadiers being especially commended for keeping their square steady. Guerrillas cf 'El Cura' and Tapia engaged French naval battalions at Almazan, near Soria, before being driven off.

25 July: Ney laid siege to Almeida, defended by its governor, Brigadier William Cox.

29 July: General Jean-Mathieu Séras of the Army of Portugal captured Puebla de Sanabria from a Spanish detachment under General Francisco Taboada. (The French detachment left there was forced to surrender to the latter and General Francisco Silveira on 10 August).

3 August: O'Donnell launched a sally from Tortosa against Leval's division (Suchet's command) which was covering this Spanish-garrisoned city; it was repelled (14 September).

8 August: Joseph wrote an impassioned plea

to Napoleon concerning his 'deplorable' position, and asked to be given complete control over the forces in Spain, for his throne was now only 'a seat of punishment, from which I look passively on the devastation of a country which I had hoped to make happy', or he preferred to abdicate. The letter was not answered.

11 August: La Romana, marching to invade Andalusia, was defeated by General Jean-Baptiste Girard from Soult's V Corps at Villagarcia (15 September).

15 August: Ney broke ground at Almeida (25 July).

26 August: the magazine at Almeida blew up, devastating the city.

27 August: with the garrison demoralised and almost out of ammunition, Cox had to surrender Almeida.

4 September: attack by Spanish local forces upon Granada was driven off (4 November).

5 September: Macdonald won a small action at Cervera (24 April).

6 September: one of Suchet's generals, Anne-Gilbert de La Val, died of illness in Catalonia.

7 September: disturbances among Portuguese militia in Lisbon; suspecting that the British were intending to leave, they determined to seize the forts to prevent them. Wellington ordered them to join the army and blamed the general unrest upon the Portuguese government, 'not from evil inclination and design, but from what is worse, probably, in men in public situations in these times – bad heads. If these foolish fellows cannot be kept in order, we must get rid of them . . .'

10 September: General Charles Doyle,

British commissioner in Catalonia, with Spanish troops and the crews of HMS *Cambrian* (Capt. F.W. Fane) and the Spanish frigate *Flora*, raided the port of Bagur, destroyed the battery and captured the garrison before re-embarking.

14 September: with the French commander Schwarz distracted by the raid on Bagur, his brigade was attacked by O'Donnell at La Bispal, and forced to surrender. O'Donnell was wounded in the foot and had to be evacuated in HMS *Cambrian* to Tarragona, ultimately to Majorca, to recover; he was succeeded in command by the Marquis of Campoverde (21 October). In the Asturias, Bonnet won an action against Porlier's command near Oviedo (6 November 1811).

15 September: pursuing La Romana, Mortier cut up the Spanish rearguard at Fuente Cantos, near Monasterio (11 August).

20 September: as Massena advanced in Portugal, Colonel Nicholas Trant with Portuguese militia attacked his siege-train near Sotojal, and was beaten off (27 September).

24 September: opening session of the Cortes at Cadiz, its membership incomplete and selected by unequal means. Doubts were expressed about its democratic leanings; for example, Wellington stated that Spain could only be governed as a monarchy, and that assumption of power and patronage by an assembly 'would immediately deprive them of the confidence of the people, and they would be a worse government, and more impotent, because more numerous than the Central Junta' (28 October, 19 March 1812).

25 September: Brigadier-General Catlin Craufurd, commander of a brigade in Lieutenant-General Rowland Hill's 2nd Division, died of fatigue and the climate at Abrantes.

27 September: Massena attacked Wellington's position at Busaco and was beaten off with heavy loss, temporarily halting the invasion of Portugal; prominent among the casualties was the French general Jean-François Graindorge, who died on 1 October of the wound he received (20 September, 5 October).

28 September: small amphibious raid led by Captain Robert Hall of HMS *Rambler* landed near the mouth of the River Barbate, north-west of Tarifa, marched overland, and captured a French privateer lying three miles upriver, driving off an escort of French dragoons.

5 October: as Wellington withdrew into Portugal, his cavalry (under General George Anson) skirmished with Massena's advance-guard under General Louis-Pierre Montbrun near Pombal (27 September).

7 October: Trant's militia reoccupied Coimbra, which had been occupied and sacked by the French a week earlier.

11-12 October: while reconnoitering the Tagus near Sobral the French cavalry general Charles-Marie-Robert, comte d'Escorches de Sainte-Croix was killed by a shot fired from a British gunboat. As Massena advanced towards the lines of Torres Vedras, Junot drove the British picquets out of Sobral.

12 October: Napoleon instructed Marshal Louis-Alexandre Berthier to inform General Marie-François-Auguste Caffarelli du Falga (commanding the provinces of Biscay and Santander) 'confidentially that I intend to annex Biscay to France', and to inform Reille of the same regarding Navarre; he intended also to annex Aragon, north of the Ebro, and Catalonia, although in the event only the latter was enacted (14 January 1812).

14 October: Massena attempted to pierce the lines of Torres Vedras with Junot's VIII Corps; a sharp skirmish against elements of Wellington's 1st Division convinced him of the futility of trying to storm the position (11 October, 10 November).

15 October: having landed on 13 October with the intention of luring out the French garrison of Malaga to render that city vulnerable, a small Anglo-Spanish expedition under Lord Blayney was besieging Fuengirola when it was surprised, due to Blayney's incompetence, by Sébastiani, and routed; Blayney was captured.

16 October: Spanish amphibious landing commanded by Col. Renovales (from Mahy's army), with British assistance, landed near Gijon on the Biscay coast, to collaborate with Porlier, captured the town, its supplies and some shipping, and was evacuated when French forces under Bonnet came up. Further raiding was prevented by damage sustained during a hurricane.

21 October: Marshal Macdonald, having marched in to co-operate with Suchet, attacked Campoverde near Cardona and was repulsed. (14 September, 12 November).

23 October: two French generals died of illness in captivity at Cartagena: Franceschi-Delonne, captured by the guerrillas of 'El Capuchino' near Toro in June 1809; and the Swiss-born François-Pierre-Félix Vonderweit, captured by irregulars when commanding a brigade in IV Corps in April 1809.

26 October: the famous French artillery commander General Alexandre-Antoine Senarmont was killed by a shell at Cadiz, in the siege of which he was directing the French artillery (22 April, 23-27 February 1811).

28 October: the Cortes deposed the four remaining members of the Regecy (the Bishop of Orense having resigned), and appointed a new three-member Regency (24 September, 19 March 1812).

4 November: advancing towards Granada, Blake was defeated by the French cavalry of General Edouard-Jean-Baptiste Milhaud at Baza (also styled Rio Almanzor), and retired (4 September).

10 November: Massena ordered a withdrawal from the position immediately in front of the lines of Torres Vedras, retiring on Santarem (14 October, 4 March 1811).

12 November: Generals Louis-Jean-Nicolas Abbé and Pierre-Joseph Habert from Suchet's army attacked and defeated the Spanish brigade of General Garcia Navarros at Falcet; he was captured and the Ebro was opened to navigation (21 October, 16 December).

12 December: while becalmed between Malaga and Almeria Bay, the British cutter *Entreprenante* (Lieutenant Peter Williams) was attacked by four French privateers which had been anchored under Faro castle; three attempts to board the *Entreprenante* were beaten off, and one of the privateers was dismasted.

13 December: British amphibious raid on Palamos mounted by a squadron of five ships under Captain Thomas Rogers of HMS *Kent;* a landing under Capt. Thomas Fane of HMS *Cambrian* destroyed the port's artillery, blew up the magazine and captured most of a supply convoy bound for Barcelona; but the arrival of French reinforcements killed or captured one-third of the 600 seamen and marines landed. Fane was among the captured.

16 December: Suchet and his Army of Aragon arrived in front of Tortosa to commence a siege; its governor was General Lilli, the Conde de Alacha (12 November, 19 December).

17 December: the French governor of Pamplona, General Louis-Annibal d'Agoult, died there.

19 December: first parallel opened at Tortosa (16 December).

1811

1 January: at Tortosa, Alacha offered to surrender if not relieved in fifteen days, an offer rejected by the besiegers.

2 January: a breach being opened, Tortosa surrendered.

8 January: Suchet captured the fort of San Felipé de Balaguer with elements of Habert's division, opening the road between Tortosa and Tarragona (3 March). Napoleon created a unified 'Army of the North' under Bessières.

11 January: Soult, with the Army of Andalusia, began the siege of Olivenza; its governor, General Manuel Herck, was old and incapable and its defences were weak (22 January).

15 January: after Macdonald had occupied Valls, his Italian vanguard of General Eugenio (real name Orsatelli) attacked the Spanish division of General Sarsfield north of Valls, at Pla (alternatively styled L'Illa) and was defeated; Eugenio was mortally wounded and the following brigade, of General Palombini, was also scattered (21 October).

19 January: while conducting a reconnaissance in force for Massena, Junot engaged the Portuguese brigade of Denis Pack at Rio Mayor, a minor skirmish in which Junot was slightly wounded (shot in the nose by a member of the 1st King's German Legion Hussars) (10 November 1810, 4 March).

22 January: French opened fire on Olivenza and Herck surrendered (11 January).

23 January: Soult entered Olivenza (28 January). La Romana died unexpectedly; he was succeeded as commander of the Army of Estremadura temporarily by General Gabriel Mendizabel, later by Castaños (19 February).

25 January: attempting to threaten Seville, Ballesteros was beaten by General Honoré-Théodore-Maxime Gazan, comte de La Peyrière, at Villanueva de los Castillejos, but retired without having sustained great damage (2 March).

28 January: Soult opened siege-trenches at Badajoz, defended by its governor, General Rafael Menacho (23 January, 7 February).

1 February: French general Frédéric-Christophe Marizy (known by this, his mother's surname; his real name was Vagnair) was murdered at Talavera.

6 February: George, Prince of Wales, became Prince Regent of Great Britain, his father King George III no longer being able to exercise the role of monarch due to infirmity.

7 February: major sortie from Badajoz, but the siege continued (28 January).

11 February: French assault captured the Pardaleras outwork at Badajoz (19 February).

18 February: the Duque de Albuquerque, serving as Spanish ambassador to London, died of 'a most alarming paroxysm of mental derangement'.

19 February: Soult attacked and routed Mendizabel's Army of Estremadura, which had been supporting Badajoz, at the River Gebora (28 January, 3 March).

23-27 February: Anglo-Spanish landing at Algesiras and Tarifa under General Manuel de la Peña (British contingent under General Thomas Graham), intended to threaten the French siege-lines at Cadiz (22 April 1810, 3-4 March).

2 March: marching from Portugal, Ballesteros engaged and defeated General Victor-Urbain Rémond on the Rio Tinto (25 January, 9 March).

3 March: during a Spanish sortie from Badajoz, its governor, Menacho, was killed; he was succeeded by the less able and determined General José Imaz (19 February, 11 March). Campoverde attempted to recover the fort of San Felipé de Balaguer, and was repelled (8 January, 3 May).

3-4 March: Marshal Victor attacked and captured a position established by General Zayas, near Santa Petri, in a sally from Cadiz, intending to collaborate with de la Peña (23-27 February, 5 March).

4 March: having exhausted supplies in the region, Massena began to retire from Santarem (10 November 1810).

5 March: Victor attacked de la Peña's army as it marched on the coast road toward Cadiz, at Barossa (or Chiclana); the French were beaten off by Graham's British contingent, the Spanish part of the army playing little part. Despite the victory, de la Peña's hesitancy lost the opportunity of driving the

French from their siege-lines in front of Cadiz. Prominent among the fatalities was the French general Pierre-Guillaume Chaudron-Rousseau (8 August, 24 August 1812).

6 March: in support of de la Peña, two amphibious landings were made between Rota and Santa Maria, by British and Spanish seamen and marines commanded by Captains Spranger and Kittoe of HMS *Warrior* and HMS *Milford* respectively; they dismantled some of the defences and re-embarked.

9 March: Ballesteros again engaged Rémond and the French had to retire into Seville (2 March, 12 April).

10 March: pursuing Massena, Wellington's cavalry (Frederick von Arentsschildt's brigade) skirmished successfully with Montbrun's dragoons at Pombal (4 March).

11 March: opposed by Wellington's Light Division (the detachment led by Colonel George Elder of the 3rd Caçadores), Ney's rearguard (VI Corps) withdrew from Pombal. A breach having been opened, Badajoz was surrendered to the French (3 March).

12 March: opposed principally by Wellington's Light, 3rd, 4th and 5th Divisions, Ney's VI Corps held up the British pursuit at Redinha and withdrew in good order.

14 March: Wellington's Light Division (under Sir William Erskine) engaged Marchand's division of Ney's rearguard at Casal Novo, and although the French continued to withdraw, the British suffered heavier casualties. Mortier, with elements of V Corps, opened the siege of Campo Mayor; its governor was Major José Talaya (21 March).

15 March: Ney's rearguard was engaged principally by Wellington's Light and 3rd Divisions at Foz do Arounce (or Foz d'Arouce), and was mauled before continuing to retire (23 March).

16 March: the fortress of Albuquerque (governor General José Cagigal) surrendered without resistance to General Marie-Victor-Nicolas de Latour-Maubourg with two regiments of Soult's cavalry (25 March).

19 March: expecting help from within (which did not materialise), Campoverde attacked the fortress of Monjuich, near Barcelona, and was repelled (3 March).

21 March: Campo Mayor being rendered indefensible, it surrendered (14 March).

23 March: Massena dismissed Ney for insubordination; command of VI Corps passed to Loison (15 March, 3 April).

25 March: Beresford's army, approaching Campo Mayor, engaged Latour-Maubourg as he was withdrawing; a cavalry charge overthrew the French but failed to capture their siege-train; yet Campo Mayor was recaptured. A notable casualty was Vital-Joachim Chamorin, colonel of the French 26th Dragoons, who had just (5 March) been promoted to *général de brigade;* he was killed in single combat by Corporal Logan of the 13th Light Dragoons (21 March, 9 April).

3 April: combat at Sabugal when Erskine's outnumbered Light Division (principally Beckwith's brigade) was sent across the Coa and engaged II Corps of General Jean-Louis-Ebénézer Reynier, which withdrew as more British troops came up. Wellington commented (without blaming Erskine openly, who was at fault) that 'Although the operations of this day were . . . not performed in the manner in which I intended they should be, I consider the action that was fought by the Light Division to be one of the most glorious that British troops were ever engaged in' (23 March, 3 May).

9 April: Beresford advanced to Olivenza and commenced a siege (25 March, 15 April).

9-10 April: the guerrilla Francisco Rovira with miqueletes gained entry to the citadel of San Fernando at Figueras by means of help from within; the governor, General François-Gilles Guillot, was captured. General Peyri had insufficient forces in Figueras itself to attempt to re-capture the citadel, so withdrew, subsequently returning with reinforcements (17 April).

12 April: General Maransin (from Soult's army) defeated Ballesteros at Frenegal, but retired because of the proximity of Beresford's army (4 September).

15 April: being rendered indefensible, Olivenza surrendered (9 April, 6-7 May).

17 April: General Louis Baraguay d'Hilliers having come up, it was possible for the French to blockade the San Fernando citadel at Figueras, now commanded by General Martinez (9-10 April, 3 May).

26 April: unanimous vote of thanks in both Houses of Parliament to Wellington for the preservation of Portugal against 'the flower of the French Army, commanded by Officers of the first-rate talents' (16 February 1810, 10 February 1812).

3 May: Suchet with the Army of Aragon arrived at Tarragona to commence its siege; it was defended by Generals Caro and Courten (8 May). At Fuentes de Oñoro there was a preliminary engagement as Massena attacked Wellington's position (3 April). Campoverde's relief force under General Sarsfield beaten off from Figueras by Baraguay d'Hilliers, though some reinforcement did get through. Macdonald subsequently took command of the investment (17 April, 16 August).

5 May: Massena's main attack at Fuentes de Oñoro was repelled; the French withdrew on 8 May (7 May).

6-7 May: Beresford began the siege of Badajoz; its governor was General Armand Philippon (15 April, 13 May).

7 May: Marshal Marmont superseded Massena as commander of the Army of Portugal, according to Napoleon's order of 20 April.

8 May: Suchet's siege of Tarragona began in earnest (3 May).

10 May: Campoverde reinforced Tarragona by sea and in person (18 May). The French garrison of Almeida, commanded by General Antoine-François Brennier, evacuated the city safely due to the laxity of British commanders, notably General Erskine; although Colonel Charles Bevan of the 4th Foot was blamed unjustly, and shot himself.

13 May: siege of Badajoz was raised as Beresford turned to meet Soult, advancing to its relief (6-7, 16 May).

15 May: a late, prominent casualty of Barossa was the French general François-Amable Ruffin, who had been wounded and captured at Barossa and who died of his injury at sea, off Portsmouth, while being conveyed to England as a prisoner (5 March).

16 May: marching to relieve Badajoz, Soult attacked Beresford and Blake at Albuera, and was repelled after a desperate fight, success turning upon a counter-attack without orders by General Galbraith Lowry Cole and his 4th Division. Prominent fatalities were the British major-general Daniel Hoghton and the French generals Joseph Pépin and François-Jean Werlé; General Jean-André Praefke was mortally wounded and died on the following day (13 May).

18 May: British blockade of Badajoz was resumed. The garrison made a serious sortie at Tarragona (one had been made on 14 May, a third on 20 May) but the siege continued (10, 27-8 May).

25 May: as Soult withdrew, his pursuers were engaged by Latour-Maubourg's cavalry at Usagre; General Hon. William Lumley caught them crossing the bridge at that town and destroyed the brigade of General André-François Bron de Bailly for hardly any loss (27 May).

26 May: cruising on the Cadiz station, the brig-sloop HMS *Sabine* (Capt. George Price) mounted a raid by boats on the port of Sablona, cutting-out three French privateers that had been causing destruction to commerce (*Guardia de Via* under Lieutenant de Vaisseau Graw, *Canari* and *Medina*).

27 May: Wellington took command of Beresford's army, henceforth the (enlarged) main field army (25, 29 May). HMS *Sabine*, and the sloop *Papillon*, capured another privateer near Sablona after a stalwart defence.

27-28 May: in the operations before Fort Olivo at Tarragona, on this night the French general Jean-Baptiste Salme was shot through the head and killed (18 May).

29 May: Suchet carried the outlying Fort Olivo at Tarragona; a Spanish counter-attack failed. Full siege of Badajoz recommenced (27 May, 6 June).

31 May: Campoverde left Tarragona by sea, to command the forces intended for its relief; command passed to General Juan Contreras (11 June).

6 June: British assault on Fort Cristobal, an outwork of Badajoz on the opposite bank of the Guadiana, was beaten off (29 May).

9 June: second attack on San Cristobal failed.

10 June: Wellington raised the siege of Bada-

joz before Marmont and Soult could come up; it had failed due to shortages of engineers and siege artillery.

11 June: further sally by the defenders of Tarragona (and on 14 June), but the siege continued (31 May, 16-17 June).

14 June: Reille fought a sharp action against Francisco Espoz y Mina near Sanguenza, but the guerrillas were able to withdraw.

16-17 June: French assault captured the outlying work of the Prince lunette at Tarragona (11 June).

21 June: Suchet stormed and captured the lower city of Tarragona (24 June).

22 June: minor cavalry skirmish near Elvas, in which Latour-Maubourg cut up an inferior British force; the capture of Captain Benjamin Lutyens's troop of 11th Light Dragoons was later cited by Wellington as a criticism of making British uniforms resemble those of the French, confusion of national identity seeming to have been a factor in the reverse (25 September).

23 June: General Santocildes with elements of the Army of Galicia (which he was commanding in the absence of Castaños) was engaged by General Jean-André Valletaux from Bonnet's command of Bessières's Army of the North, at Cogoredos (also known as Quintanilla de Valle or Quintina del Rey); the French were defeated and Valletaux killed, but despite this success Santocildes was superseded subsequently by General Francisco Abadia (8 July).

24 June: Campoverde's attempt to relieve Tarragona was abandoned after manoeuvering, without combat (21 June).

26 June: small reinforcement to Tarragona arrived by sea, including a British force under Colonel John Skerrett, in conjunction with Captain Edward Codrington of HMS *Blake;* after reconnoitering it was decided not to land the British as Tarragona was deemed no longer defensible (28, 30 June).

27 June: British brig-sloop HMS *Guadeloupe* (Captain Joseph Tetley) engaged the French brig-corvette *Tactique* and xebec *Guêpe* off Cape Cerus (at the north-east corner of the Spanish coast); the French ships went for shelter under the shore-batteries at Saint-André and *Guadeloupe* broke off the action.

28 June: Tarragona fell to a French assault; Contreras was wounded and captured, and more than 2,000 civilians perished (26, 30 June, 8 July).

30 June: Skerrett's planned landing to reinforce Campoverde was aborted when the French seized the Spanish base at Villanueva de Sitjes, upon Campoverde's retirement; the British expedition returned to Cadiz. Campoverde was subsequently superseded by General Luis Lacy (11-12 September). Blake laid siege to Niebla, Andalusia, weakly garrisoned, but the siege was raised upon the approach of a relief force (16 May).

8 July: General Suchet was promoted to Marshal, for the capture of Tarragona; he was the only French commander to win his bâton in the Peninsula (28 June). Marshal Jean-Baptiste Jourdan was appointed governor of Madrid, and returned to the Peninsula to advise Joseph (28 October). General Jean-Marie-Pierre-François Lepaige Dorsenne took over command of the Army of the North from Bessières (23 June, 27 July).

25 July: Suchet stormed the Spanish positions on the mountain of Montserrat, near Barcelona, which deprived the Spanish of any stronghold on the road from there to Lerida (28 June, 23 September, 11 October).

27 July: advancing against Abadia in Galicia, Dorsenne forced the passes of Manzanal and Fuencebadon (8 July, 25 August).

8 August: Thomas Graham arrived from Cadiz to replace Brent Spencer as Wellington's deputy (5 March).

9 August: advancing against the Army of Murcia, General Deo-Gratias-Nicolas Godinot's division of Soult's army defeated General Joseph O'Donnell's division at Zujar (18 October).

10 August: advancing against Freire's Army of Murcia (of which Blake was officially commander), Soult dispersed it at Las Vertientes.

14-15 August: Porlier raided Santander, driving out the garrison of General Claude-Pierre Rouget, and retired on the approach of French reinforcements.

16 August: with rations exhausted in Figueras, Martinez attempted to break out, but failed (3 May).

19 August: Figueras was starved into surrender.

25 August: advancing into Galicia, Dorsenne engaged Abadia near Astorga (San Martin de Torres) and occupied that town (27 July).

29 August: Dorsenne sacked Villafranca but subsequently retired, followed by the Spanish.

4 September: Ballesteros landed at Algesiras to operate in that region (12 April, 18 October).

11-12 September: Lacy, with British naval

assistance, captured the Medas Islands at the mouth of the River Ter (mid-way between Rosas and Palamos) to provide a base from which to co-operate with the British navy (30 June, 4 October).

23 September: invading Valencia, Suchet with the Army of Aragon commenced a siege of Saguntum, or Murviedro, defended by Colonel Luis Andriani (25 July, 28 September).

25 September: as Marmont advanced to relieve Wellington's blockade of Ciudad Rodrigo, General Watier fought a small skirmish at Carpio against elements of the 6th Division and Anson's light cavalry brigade: the French were repelled. At El Bodon, Marmont's cavalry (under Montbrun) engaged General Thomas Picton's 3rd Division and were repulsed as the British withdrew (10 June, 27 September).

26 September: in Aragon, the guerrillas Duran and El Empecinado attacked Calatayud, and drove the French and Italian garrison into their citadel, the convent of La Merced (3 October).

27 September: Marmont's advancing vanguard, commanded by General Paul-Charles-François-Adrien-Henri Thiébault, engaged elements of Wellington's 4th Division at Aldea da Ponte; they secured the village but declined to attack Wellington's main position, and retired (25 September, 15 October).

28 September: French assault on Saguntum was repelled, and the siege continued (23 September, 16 October).

1 October: Suchet, with the division of General Jean-Isidore Harispe, defeated General Charles O'Donnell's division at Benaguacil

(10-11 October).

3 October: Duran breached the citadel wall at Calatayud, and the garrison surrendered (26 September).

4 October: Lacy raided Igualada (on the Barcelona-Lerida road) at night, surprised the garrison by pretending to be French, then retired after driving them into a fortified convent (11-12 September).

7 October: detached by Lacy, Baron Eroles captured an important convoy near Iorba (11 October).

10-11 October: Suchet captured Oropesa; part of its garrison was evacuated by sea by HMS *Magnificent* and Spanish gunboats (1, 16 October).

11 October: in course of eliminating French garrisons, Lacy captured Cervera; subsequently the French evacuated Montserrat (25 July, 7 October).

12 October: Eroles captured the castle of Bellpuig near Lerida, clearing the French from the Barcelona-Lerida road (11, 29 October).

15 October: Julian Sanchez's guerrillas raided Ciudad Rodrigo, capturing the garrison's cattle and governor, General Hilaire-Benoît Reynaud, who was replaced by General Jean-Léonard Barrié (27 September, 8 January 1812).

16 October: Suchet's siege artillery began to batter Saguntum (28 September). Small Italian column under Colonel Ceccopieri, marching from Saragossa to relieve Ayerbe, was annihilated by Espoz y Mina near that place.

18 October: storm of the breach at Saguntum, led by General Habert, was beaten off (25 October). General Godinot, marching on Tarifa while attempting to pursue and trap Blake, was bombarded by the British fleet and forced to withdraw (4 September, 27 October, 5 November).

18-19 October: guerrillas of El Pastor made an amphibious landing from fishing boats, with marines from HMS *Surveillante* (Captain Sir George Collier commanding) and HMS *Iris* near Bermeo on the Biscay coast; the town was taken, its defences destroyed and shipping carried off before the raid re-embarked, and on 19 October the guerrillas put to flight a small relief-force sent from Bilbao.

25 October: Blake, attempting to relieve Saguntum with his own troops and Mahy's Murcians, was routed at that place by Suchet (18 October).

26 October: Saguntum surrendered (26 December). Wellington received permission from the Prince Regent to accept the title of Conde do Vimeiro from the Prince Regent of Portugal (26 April, 10 February 1812).

27 October: after a reprimand from Soult, General Godinot shot himself (18 October).

28 October: pursuing Girard's Division of V Corps, Rowland Hill with the British 2nd Division, cavalry and Portuguese, surprised and defeated Girard at Arroyo dos Molinos: the French cavalry commander, Bron de Bailly, and the Prince of Aremberg, CO of the 27th Chasseurs à Cheval, were among those captured (29 December). Jourdan was appointed as Joseph's chief of staff and commander of the Army of the Centre (8 July). Macdonald was recalled from Catalonia, command passing to General Charles-Mathieu-Isidore Decaen (21 October 1810).

29 October: Lacy sent Eroles over the border from Catalonia to raid into France, which infuriated Napoleon and made it necessary to improve security along the Pyrenees (12 October, 18 January 1812).

5 November: withdrawing from its pursuit of Ballesteros, the column of General Jean-Baptiste-Pierre Semellé (or Sémelé) was surprised at Bornos by Ballesteros and suffered losses before continuing its retreat (18 October, 13 April 1812).

6 November: on his re-occupation of the Asturias, Bonnet entered Oviedo without opposition (14 September 1810, 17-18 May 1812).

27 November: having left Gijon on the approach of the French moving through the Asturias, Gaspar de Jovellanos died at Vega.

15 December: in preparation for the approaching war against Russia, Napoleon began withdrawing troops from the Peninsula.

20 December: Victor began a siege of Tarifa, defended by General Francisco Copons and a British contingent under Skerrett (29 December).

26 December: Suchet completed the encirclement of Blake's army at Valencia, only a small part of the Spanish force being able to escape (26 October). The British brig-sloop HMS *Ephera* (Captain Thomas Everard) was wrecked near Cadiz, but the crew was saved.

28-29 December: Blake's attempt to break out of Valencia failed (9 January 1812).

29 December: advancing in Estremadura to distract the French from Ballesteros and Tarifa, Rowland Hill's cavalry engaged a small French foraging column from General Jean-Baptiste Drouet, comte d'Erlon's division of the Army of the Centre at Navas de Membrillo; the French remained steady and got away in good order (28 October, 3 January 1812). A breach was opened in the wall of Tarifa (20 December).

31 December: French storm of Tarifa was repelled (4-5 January 1812).

1812

3 January: a detachment of Hill's force under Major-General John Abercrombie, pursuing d'Erlon, won a small cavalry skirmish at Fuente del Maestre (29 December).

4-5 January: French abandoned the siege of Tarifa (31 December, 9 February).

8 January: Wellington commenced the siege of Ciudad Rodrigo, defended by General Barrié; on the night of 8-9 January a detachment of the Light Division, commanded by Lieutenant-Colonel John Colborne, captured the outwork on the Greater Teson hill (15 October, 13-14 January).

9 January: Valencia surrended; Blake was sent as a prisoner to France (28-29 December 1811, 20 January).

11 January: Espoz y Mina defeated a French detachment under General Abbé at Rocaforte; Abbé withdrew to Pamplona (Mina's superior Mendizabel was present but not in command).

13-14 January: the besiegers of Ciudad Rodrigo stormed the outwork of the Santa Cruz convent, and made a lodgement (8 January).

14 January: French sortie at Ciudad Rodrigo re-occupied Santa Cruz until a British counter-attack drove them back. Writing to Berthier, Napoleon ordered the finalisation of plans for the annexation of Catalonia and its division into four French *départements* (12 October 1810, 7 February).

14-15 January: a British detachment (40th Foot) captured the outwork of the convent of San Francisco at Ciudad Rodrigo (19 January).

15 January: General Pablo Morillo, with a brigade of Castaños's Army of Estremadura, raided La Mancha and took Ciudad Real without resistance; he retired when French reinforcements approached.

16 January: detached from the Army of Portugal, Montbrun demonstrated before Alicante but was unable to capture it.

18 January: a small relief-force under General Jacques-Mathurin Lafosse, governor of Tortosa, heading for Tarragona (blockaded by Lacy), was surprised and captured by Eroles at Villaseca (or Col de Balaguer) although Lafosse was among those who escaped (29 October 1811, 24 January).

19 January: Ciudad Rodrigo was stormed and captured; Major-General Henry Mackinnon was killed when one of the garrison's expense magazines blew up (14-15, 24 January, 10 February, 16, 30 March).

20 January: General Harispe, of Suchet's army, occupied the port of Denia, mid-way between Valencia and Alicante, a Spanish base for supplies (9, 28 January).

24 January: Eroles was defeated at Altafulla by General David-Maurice-Joseph Mathieu, governor of Barcelona, marching to the relief of Tarragona (18 January, 5 March). Major-General Robert Craufurd, wounded at the storm of Ciudad Rodrigo, died and was buried on 25 January in the breach where he had suffered his wound (19 January). Marshal Suchet was created duc d'Albufera.

26 January: General Pierre-Benoit Soult, with cavalry from his brother's army, entered the city of Murcia unopposed and drove off a counter-attack by Spanish cavalry under General Martin La Carrera, who was killed. Soult withdrew next day.

28 January: Suchet opened trenches before the reputedly impregnable fortress of Pensicola, defended by the governor, General Garcia Navarro (20 January).

3 February: Navarro surrendered Pensicola without mounting a defence, and took service under King Joseph, stating that his change of sides was in the cause of unity and 'to render our country less unhappy'.

7 February: in accordance with the annexation of Catalonia this month, to emphasize the union of Catalonia with France, Napoleon ordered the formation of a Catalonian Regiment; it was never fully organised and was disbanded in the following month (14 January). El Empecinado was defeated by a detachment of Joseph's army at Siguenza, but escaped.

9 February: Marshal Victor left his command, having been ordered to return to France in the previous December (4-5 January).

10 February: Wellington received the thanks of Parliament for Ciudad Rodrigo (19 January).

18 February: Wellington was created Earl of Wellington (26 August 1809, 21 February).

19 February: Richard, Marquess Wellesley (Wellington's elder brother) resigned as British Foreign Secretary, ostensibly over the ministry's unwillingness to support his plans for aiding his brother and the Penin-

sular army; he was succeeded by Lord Castlereagh.

21 February: Wellington was voted an additional £2,000 p.a. by the House of Commons; only Sir Francis Burdett voted against (16, 21 February, 27 April)

5 March: marching with a detachment of Reille's new 'Army of the Ebro', General Jean-Raymond-Charles Bourke was defeated by Eroles at Roda (24 January).

16 March: Napoleon appointed Joseph commander-in-chief of all forces in Spain, with Jourdan as chief-of-staff, with Soult and Marmont being informed that they were to obey Joseph's orders, 'so as to prevent discordant action'. Wellington invested Badajoz, defended by its governor, General Armand Philippon (19 January).

17 March: first trenches opened at Badajoz.

19 March: French sortie from Badajoz, but the siege continued; the British chief engineer, Lieutenant-Colonel Richard Fletcher, was wounded and incapacitated for a fortnight. The Cortes published the Constitution of 1812 (24 September 1810).

25 March: batteries opened against Badajoz.

25-26 March: the outlying Fort Picurina at Badajoz was stormed and captured (6 April).

30 March: Marmont advanced to Ciudad Rodrigo and called upon it to surrender; he moved off when the commander of the Spanish garrison, General Vives, declined (19 January, 14 April).

6-7 April: Badajoz was stormed and captured, the assault on the breaches failing but the 'diversionary' attacks by escalade succeeding; the city was sacked after its fall (25-6 March).

7 April: having escaped to the outwork of

San Cristobal on the far bank of the Guadiana, Philippon surrendered at dawn. The British troops continued to run wild, looting the city (11 April).

9 April: Espoz y Mina destroyed a huge French convoy and escort in the Salinas pass (or Puerte de Arlaban).

11 April: British cavalry under General Sir Stapleton Cotton defeated d'Erlon's cavalry rearguard at Villagarcia near Llerena; the French continued to withdraw (7 April, 18 May).

13 April: Ballesteros attacked the French garrison of Osuna; they were driven into the citadel but the Spanish retired when French reinforcements approached (18 October 1811).

14 April: Ballesteros engaged General Jean-Pierre-Antoine Rey at Alhaurin or Alora (1 June). Marmont surprised and routed Colonel Trant's Portuguese militia division at Guarda (30 March).

27 April: Wellington received a vote of thanks in parliament for the capture of Badajoz (21 February, 7 April, 3 December).

29 April: the French (actually Italian) garrison of Calatayud was besieged by the guerrilla Gayan; it was relieved on 9 May (3 October 1811).

3 May: General Luis Lacy began to bombard the fort of Mataro, on the coast north of Barcelona, using guns loaned by the British navy, into which fortification the garrison of the town had retired some days before; after three days the siege was lifted upon the approach of French reinforcements (16 July).

11 May: Prime Minister Spencer Perceval was assassinated by the madman John Bellingham in the lobby of the House of Commons; he was succeeded as Prime Minister by Lord Liverpool, but the prosecution of the war continued (26 September 1809).

14 May: a small Spanish force under Col. Alveor, sent by General Manuel Freire (second-in-command of the Murcian army to Joseph O'Donnell, Mahy's successor), and transported by the Royal Navy (HMS *Invincible*, Captain Adam), landed and captured Almeria, where the defences were destroyed (21 July).

17-18 May: having evacuated the region in early 1812, re-entering the Asturias, General Bonnet once more occupied Oviedo; he was to be called away by Marmont for the Salamanca campaign, however (6 November 1811).

18 May: to cover the southern flank of Wellington's advance, Hill stormed the forts of Almaraz, whose governor, Colonel Aubert, was mortally wounded. The crossing over the Tagus was secured, although the French pontoon bridge was destroyed (11 April, 11, 17 June).

1 June: demonstrating to deflect French attention from Wellington's advance, Ballesteros attacked General Nicolas-François Conroux's force, covering the siege-lines at Cadiz, at Bornos, and was repelled (14 April, 14 July).

11 June: as Hill advanced in Estremadura, General John Slade's cavalry was beaten by General François-Antoine Lallemend's French cavalry at Maguilla (or Valencia de Torres), by not preserving their order; this prompted Wellington to write his famous criticism of 'the trick our officers of cavalry have acquired of galloping at every thing . . . I do not wonder at the French boasting of it; it is the greatest blow they have struck' (18 May, 1 July).

17 June: Wellington's army began the siege of the forts at Salamanca, beginning with that of San Vincente, defended by chef de bataillon Duchemin of the 65th Line (18 May).

19 June: Wellington's artillery opened against San Vincente at Salamanca (23 June).

20 June: advancing towards Salamanca, Marmont skirmished with Wellington's outpost at Morisco, which was withdrawn, but neither commander initiated a general action (22 June).

20-21 June: a force from the British squadron under Captain Sir Home Popham (HMS *Venerable*) landed on the Biscay coast at Lequeitio and assisted the guerrillas of El Pastor to capture the French defences (a fort was stormed and the fortified convent surrendered by chef de bataillon Gillort of the 119th Line). The British squadron moved along the coast, destroying defences, including those at Bermeo (23 June), Plencia, Galea, Algorta, Begona, el Campillo las Queras and Xebiles (24 June) (2 July).

22 June: Wellington probed towards Morisco with the 7th Division, and Marmont withdrew (20 June).

23 June: ceasing the attack on San Vincente for shortage of munitions, Wellington attempted to storm the San Cayetano fort at Salamanca with elements of the 6th Division; the assault was repelled and brigade-commander Major-General Barnard Bowes was killed.

27 June: San Cayetano fort surrendered as a second assault went in, followed by the surrender of San Vincente (18 July).

1 July: D'Erlon carried out a reconnaissance in force under Pierre Soult, and skirmished with Hill's cavalry near Albuera (11 June).

2 July: Popham landed two companies of Royal Marines near Guetaria, but with the local guerrillas being engaged elsewhere, had to re-embark (20-21 June). Castaños's Army of Galicia, which had been blockading Astorga, began a regular siege (18 August).

7-8 July: Popham's squadron drove the French from the town of Castro Urdiales, and on 8 July a landing from the ships, reinforcing General Francisco Longa and an earlier British landing made by Sir George Collier from HMS *Surveillante*, whereupon the fort of Castro surrendered (18 July).

11 July: British gun-brig HMS *Encounter* (Captain James Talbot) was wrecked while attempting to cut out enemy shipping at San Lucar.

14 July: Ballesteros captured Malaga (minus the citadel, into which the garrison withdrew), and then evaded French attempts to catch him (1 June, 20 October).

16 July: Lacy attempted to capture Lerida by having the magazine blown up by saboteurs; the explosion did great damage but the French governor, General Jean-François Henriod, held firm and a storm was not attempted (3 May).

18 July: advancing against Wellington, Marmont's vanguard engaged Wellington's cavalry at Castrejon; the British retired, Wellington being in personal danger and having to draw his sword. There was skirmishing in the subsequent retreat over the River Guarena, and General Bertrand Clausel attacked with his and Brennier's divisions, at Castrillo, and was beaten off (27 June, 22 July). Popham landed seamen and marines from HMS *Venerable*, HMS *Medusa* and HMS *Rhin* near Guetaria, and began to bombard the town; he had to re-embark upon the approach of French rein-forcements (7-8, 22 July). The Polish-born French general Louis-Mathieu Dembowski died at Valladolid.

21 July: Joseph O'Donnell, Captain-General of Murcia, advanced upon and was routed at Castalla by Generals Jean-Isidore Harispe and Jacques-Antoine-Adrien Delort from Suchet's army (14 May, 31 July).

22 July: Wellington routed Marmont at Sala-manca, one of the most decisive actions of the war; the Army of Portugal was effective-ly wrecked for some time. Marmont was wounded; command passed first to Bon-net, who was them himself wounded, and then to Clausel. Other generals became casualties: the commander of Wellington's heavy cavalry, John Gaspard Le Marchant, was killed leading a charge; on the French side, General Jean-Guillaume-Barthélemy Thomières was killed, and mortally wound-ed were Generals Claude-François Ferey (died 24 July) and François-Desgraviers Berthelot (died 26 July) (18 July, 3 Decem-ber). Popham arrived off Santander to besiege the port, in conjunction with one of Porlier's guerrilla commanders, Campil-lo; it was defended by the commandant of Santander province, General Jean-Louis Dubreton (18 July, 30 July-1 August).

23 July: although Wellington did not pursue the retreating French with any great vigour, as they retired General Eberhard von Bock with the Dragoons of the King's German Legion broke some squares of the division of General Maximilien-Sébastien Foy at Garcia Hernandez, one of the few genuine cases of infantry in square being over-thrown by cavalry .

25 July: in a small but celebrated skirmish during the French retreat, Corporal William Hanley of the British 14th Light Dragoons, with a reconnaissance patrol of seven men, captured a troop of Juramentado chasseurs at Blasco Sancho (11 August).

30 July-1 August: the siege of Santander con-tinued: an attack by Royal Marines from HMS *Magnificent* (Captain Willoughby Lake) and HMS *Surveillante* (Captain Sir George Collier), and Porlier's guerrillas, captured the castle but failed to take the town, and both British naval captains were wounded (22 July, 3 August).

31 July: General Frederick Maitland arrived off Palamos with an expedition from Sicily, organised by the British commander there, Lord William Bentinck, plus General Samuel Ford Whittingham's Spanish Divi-sion from the Balearic Islands (21 July, 7 August).

2 August: French general Gabriel-Joseph Clé-ment was killed at Barcelona in a duel with commissaire-ordonnateur Larpin.

3 August: General Gabriel Mendizabel hav-ing come up on 2 August, the French evac-uated Santander, joining Caffarelli who was marching up to its assistance; as they with-drew the Allies took possession of the important port (30 July-1 August, 13 August).

7 August: Maitland's force landed at Alicante (31 July, 5 October).

11 August: as Wellington advanced towards Madrid, his vanguard under General Ben-jamin D'Urban was attacked at Majalahon-da (also styled Las Rosas) by General Anne-François-Charles Treillard's French cavalry, 'a devil of an affair' according to Wellington; D'Urban's Portuguese cavalry broke but his KGL cavalry and light infantry held firm and the French broke off the action as British supports came up (25 July).

12 August: Wellington entered Madrid to scenes of wild rejoicing. Learning of Marmont's defeat at Salamanca, Soult began to evacuate Andalusia (1 July, 24 August). While blockading three French privateers in the harbour of Benidorm, north of Alicante, Lieutenant Michael Dwyer and seven seamen from HMS *Minstrel* (Captain John Peyton) drove off some 80 largely Genoese privateersmen from a shore battery, but were then counter-attacked by the French garrison; one man was killed and all but one wounded, Dwyer receiving one bullet and 17 bayonet-wounds. They were taken as prisoners to the local commander, General Pierre-César Gudin des Bardelières, who was so impressed by their courage that he invited Capt. Peyton to dinner and released all the prisoners (29 September).

13 August: Wellington captured the outer line of fortifications of the Retiro at Madrid, where the French garrison was holding out, under the governor, General Guillaume-Joseph-Nicolas de Lafon-Blaniac. Attacked by Spanish columns under Mendizabel and Colonel Renovales, with a diversionary raid from Popham's British fleet, the French abandoned Bilbao (3 August).

14 August: the Retiro at Madrid surrendered (1 November). General Rouget, commanding French forces in the province, attempted to capture Bilbao, but was repelled by Mendizabel and Renovales (27-29 August).

17 August: as Clausel advanced with the Army of Portugal, Foy raised the siege of Toro, the Spanish besiegers retiring upon his approach (19 September).

18 August: Astorga surrendered to Castaños's Army of Galicia (2 July, 15 June 1813). Wellington was advanced in the peerage to the rank of Marquess (18 February 1812, 3 July 1813).

19 August: Espoz y Mina inflicted a reverse upon General Abbé, governor of Navarre, at Tiebas capturing a cargo of grain destined for Pamplona.

24 August: the French siege-lines at Cadiz were destroyed as Soult withdrew (4 March 1811, 12 August, 9 October).

27 August: an Anglo-Spanish force under General Juan Cruz Murgeon, the British detachment under Colonel Skerrett, attacked Seville, from where the French were withdrawing; the garrison was driven out.

27-29 August: Caffarelli having reinforced Rouget, the French recaptured Bilbao (14 August, 14 January 1813).

6 September: Major-General Richard Hulse died (senior officer of Wellington's 5th Division since its head, General James Leith, was wounded at Salamanca).

19 September: as Clausel retired, Wellington invested the citadel of Burgos, defended by its governor, General Jean-Louis Dubreton.

19-20 September: the outwork of San Miguel at Burgos was stormed and captured principally by Pack's Portuguese Brigade and elements of Wellington's 1st Division.

22 September: attempt to storm the outer defences of Burgos by escalade failed (29-30 September). The Cortes accorded Wellington the rank of Generalissimo of the Spanish armies (he received the news on 2 October, and was granted permission to accept by the Prince Regent on 21 October) (30 October).

29 September: at Valencia harbour, boats under Lieutenant George Thomas, sent by Captain John Peyton of HMS *Minstrel*, cut out four ships carrying munitions for Pensicola; a fifth ran aground and was recaptured, as were the three British seamen aboard (12 August).

29-30 September: a mine containing 1,080lbs. of powder was exploded under the Burgos defences; five members of the storming-party got into the breach but were not supported and the garrison held the position (22 September).

4 October: a second mine was exploded under the outer defences at Burgos and a lodgement was gained by the 2/24th Foot. Having returned from leave, General Joseph Souham replaced Clausel as commander of the Army of Portugal (18 September is also quoted as the date of official supercession) (21-22 October, 14 January 1813).

5 October: a French sally from Burgos carried off many of the besiegers' tools. At Alicante, Maitland being ill, command passed to General John Mackenzie, who sent a small expedition under General Rufane Donkin to capture Denia, on the coast to the north; it failed and the troops were evacuated by sea (7 August, 25 October).

8 October: a second sally from Burgos interrupted the siege-works; among those killed was Major Hon. Edward Somers Cocks, who had been regarded as one of the British Army's most capable officers and brightest prospects (18 October).

9 October: the fortress of Chinchilla, in Murcia, was set alight, and the Spanish gover-

nor, Colonel Cearra, disabled, by a strike of lightning, whereupon the garrison surrendered to Soult (24 August, 25 October).

18 October: a storm of the second line of Burgos defences failed (8 October).

21-22 October: the siege of Burgos was abandoned and Wellington retired as Souham advanced to its relief.

23 October: as Wellington retired, Souham engaged his rearguard at Venta del Pozo and Villadrigo (the former one of the most fiercely-contested cavalry fights of the period), but the actions were inconclusive and Wellington continued to withdraw (29 November).

25 October: in pursuit of Wellington, Foy took Palencia, routing the Galician troops there. Maucune, with his own division and others, was stopped at Villa Muriel by elements of Wellington's 5th Division. As Soult advanced against Hill, the French won a cavalry skirmish near Ocaña (9, 30 October). On the east coast, Mackenzie was superseded by General William Clinton (5 October, 2 December).

28 October: in the pursuit of Wellington, an audacious crossing by 11 officers and 44 other ranks, led by Captain Guingret of the 6th Léger, secured the passage over the Douro at Torsedillas (10-11 November).

30 October: Soult attacked Hill's rearguard under Skerrett at Puente Larga (or Tajuna); unable to force the bridge (over the River Jarama) Soult declined to press the assault (25 October, 10-11 November). At Granada, the Cortes arrested Ballesteros (Captain-General of Andalusia and commander of the Fourth Army) in reaction to his protests over the appointment of Wellington as generalissimo; he was imprisoned, and the Duque de Parque took over Fourth Army

(14 July, 22 September).

1 November: the French re-entered Madrid (14 August).

8 November: Joseph abandoned Madrid to keep all available troops with the field army (2 December).

10-11 November: Soult attacked Wellington's bridgehead at Alba de Tormes, held by Howard's brigade of the 2nd Division, and Hamilton's Portuguese brigade, but was unable to force the position (30 October).

15 November: Wellington offered to fight on the old Salamanca battlefield, but Soult declined and Wellington withdrew.

16 November: Soult's light cavalry vanguard skirmished with Victor Alten's light cavalry brigade in front of the position of Wellington's 2nd Division at Matilla, the French withdrawing.

17 November: Soult's vanguard (division of General Augustin Darricau) skirmished with Wellington's Light and 7th Divisions at San Muñoz, as the British were crossing the River Huebra, but the action was not pressed home (3 January 1813). Having just taken over Wellington's 1st Division (and acting as Wellington's second-in-command), General Sir Edward Paget was captured by the French during the retreat.

29 November: General Reille took command of the Army of Portugal in succession to Souham.

2 December: Joseph Bonaparte returned again to Madrid, El Empecinado having left upon his approach (4 January, 27 May 1813). On the east coast, Clinton was superseded by General James Campbell (25 October, 25 February 1813).

3 December: Parliament voted thanks to Wellington for Salamanca; Burdett commented that it was an inferior victory to Blenheim and that final success was as distant as ever (22 July).

7 December: Parliament voted £100,000 to Wellington to purchase an estate; stating that 'He had foiled and defeated all the most celebrated Marshals of France, who had taken the field against him', including Soult, 'who was himself an host'(4 March 1813).

1813

3 January: Soult was recalled from Spain, for which Joseph had been urging as relations between them had become strained, especially since Soult had implied that Joseph was considering treason against the French cause (17 November 1812, 2 March).

4 January: Clarke wrote to Joseph conveying Napoleon's instruction that the capital should be moved from Madrid to Valladolid, to shorten communication with France and permit a concentration to be made against enemy activity in northern Spain. Further reductions were ordered from all six French armies in Spain, to provide troops for Napoleon's war in Germany (2 December 1812, 14 February, 23 March).

14 January: Napoleon ordered Caffarelli to be superseded by Clausel as commander of the Army of the North; the actual change occurred on 18 January (4 October 1812).

8 February: General Abbé, governor of

Navarre, attempting to relieve Espoz y Mina's siege of Tafalla, engaged the Spanish at Tiebas, some 18 km. south of Pamplona, but had to retire (11 February, 31 March).

10-11 February: the HQ of General Palombini's Italian Division was attacked by Longa at Poza de la Sal, near Briviesca; the Spanish withdrew as the remainder of the division approached (24 March).

11 February: Tafalla surrendered to Espoz y Mina (8 February).

13 February: Major-General William Erskine killed himself at Lisbon by leaping from a window 'in a fit of delirium'.

14 February: Joseph Bonaparte received a despatch, written 3 January, from his ADC Francois-Alexandre Desprez who had just returned from the Russian campaign, which gave a true picture of the extent of Napoleon's defeat, and if this were not sufficiently damaging to morale, he noted that Napoleon commented on a despatch from Soult that implied mistrust of Joseph, 'shared by many generals belonging to the army of Spain, who think that your Majesty prefers Spain to France' (4 January, 23 March).

20 February: from his base at Avila, Foy mounted a minor raid on Hill's outpost at Bejar; it was repelled after a skirmish .

25 February: Sir John Murray succeeded Campbell as commander of British forces on the east coast of Spain (2 December 1812, 15 March).

2 March: having been ordered back to France, Soult took his leave of Joseph (3 January, 14 February, 23 March).

4 March: Wellington was appointed a Knight of the Garter (7 December 1812, 3 July).

11 March: guerrillas under Leguia captured and burned the castle of Fuenterrabia, on the Bidassoan estuary, and withdrew before French reinforcements arrived.

15 March: Whittingham's Spanish division of Murray's army seized the pass of Albeyda from General Habert's division (25 February, 11 April).

23 March: Joseph transferred his headquarters from Madrid to Valladolid (4 January, 2-3 June).

24 March: Palombini repelled an attack by Mendizabel upon his camp at San Pelayo, south of Castro Urdiales (10-11 February, 5 April).

31 March: two battalions (from 25th Léger and 27th Line) from the division of General Marie-Etienne Barbot of the Army of Portugal were wiped out by Espoz y Mina on a foraging expedition, at Lerin (8 February).

2 April: Baron de Eroles's Spanish and a landing party from HMS *Invincible* (Captain Charles Adam) captured the post of Ampolla, near the mouth of the Ebro, south of Tarragona, and on 3 April Eroles's troops, with British naval artillery under Lieutenant Corbyn of *Invincible*, captured the town and fort of Perello, thus severing communications between Tortosa and Tarragona (7 June).

5 April: having been repulsed on 2 April, Palombini defeated Spanish local forces around Guernica, seat of the Biscayan junta (24 March).

10 April: Mendizabel attacked General Rouget at Bilbao, but retired when French support under Palombini approached.

11 April: taking the offensive against the Allied forces based on Alicante, Suchet with Harispe's division defeated General Francisco Mijares's Murcian Division at Yecla;

half the Spanish force was destroyed by Harispe's two cavalry regiments, the 4th Hussars and 24th Dragoons (15 March).

12 April: Suchet captured the castle of Villena virtually without resistance, and then attacked Colonel Frederick Adam's light brigade at Biar; this force, largely of British 'foreign corps', fought a creditable rearguard action and retired upon Murray's main body.

13 April: Suchet engaged Murray at Castalla, was defeated and retired; the scale of the victory was disputed, as Wellington noted when receiving a full account, 'I do not think the success appears so decided as it did upon the perusal of the Alicante Gazettes of the 15th', especially as Suchet had then taken up a position at Biar, only two miles from the battlefield (3 June).

6 May: General Foy (from the Army of Portugal) laid siege to Castro Urdiales, the Biscayan port, the governor of which was Colonel Pedro Alvarez from Longa's command.

11-12 May: Foy captured Castro Urdiales; on the 11th part of the civilian population went aboard British ships in the harbour (brigsloops HMS *Lyra*, *Royalist* and *Sparrow*, commanded by Captain Robert Bloye of the former), the place being no longer defensible. On 12 May most of the garrison was evacuated similarly. A detachment was left in the castle to blow up the magazines; although the walls were scaled (led by the heroic Captain Guingret of the 6th Léger), most of this last party escaped. The town was ransacked by the French (30 May, 22 June).

22 May: having ordered his advance to begin on 18 May, Wellington left his headquarters at Frenada and arrived at Ciudad Rodrigo on 22 May. It was presumably on this day that he was reported to have taken off his hat and declared, 'Farewell, Portugal! I shall never see you again', where he had spent the previous five years.

26 May: as Wellington advanced, the cavalry brigades of Victor Alten and Henry Fane engaged the retiring French of Villatte's division near Aldea Lengua, having just left Salamanca; there was some skirmishing but the British did not attempt to attack the steady French infantry.

27 May: in reaction to Wellington's advance, the French abandoned Madrid for the last time (2 December 1812, 2 June).

30 May: Foy defeated a Spanish local battalion at Lequeitio (11-12 May).

2 June: as Wellington advanced, the hussar brigade of Colquhoun Grant routed the dragoon division of General Alexandre-Elisabeth-Michel Digeon at Morales (27 May, 10 June).

2-3 June: Joseph Bonaparte evacuated his new capital, Valladolid (23 March).

3 June: Murray's force from Alicante landed near Tarragona and with general Francisco Copons, Captain-General of Catalonia and elements of his First Army, invested Tarragona, which was defended by General Bertolotti with a Franco-Italian garrison of two battalions (13 April).

6 June: siege artillery opened against Tarragona.

7 June: the fort of San Felipe de Balaguer, 20 miles south of Tarragona, blocking the coast road, surrendered to a British force under Lieutenant-Colonel William Prevost and Captain Charles Adam of HMS *Invincible*, detached by Murray, after four days' siege (12 June).

10 June: Wellington ordered a convoy of biscuit, flour, artillery and ammunition to proceed from Corunna to Santander by sea, and if the latter were occupied by the enemy, 'I beg [the naval commander] to remain off the port till the operations of this army have obliged the enemy to abandon it'; this seems the first evidence of his plan to move his base from Lisbon to Santander and thus drastically shorten his line of communication (2, 13 June).

12 June: fearing the arrival of French reinforcements, Murray re-embarked his expedition before he had taken Tarragona, abandoning his artillery, for which he was court-martialled; ironically, Suchet also retired (7, 13-15 June).

13 June: in course of their withdrawal, the French blew up the castle of Burgos, but although great damage was done to the city and casualties caused to the French troops who were leaving, Wellington reported that 'it is possible to put it in a state of repair at a reasonable expense' (10, 18 June). A Spanish offensive in eastern Spain made little progress; Del Parque's advance (Third Army) was defeated by Harispe at Carcagente.

13-15 June: Murray landed his expedition at the Col de Balaguer (12, 18 June).

15 June: the Spanish Regency decided to replace Castaños as Captain-General of Galicia, Estremadura and the Castiles, and superseded his nephew Giron as commander of Fourth Army, replacing them with Lacy and Freire respectively, on account of them being thought insufficiently 'liberal'; these changes took some time to effect, and Giron subsequently replaced Henry O'Donnell as head of the Army of Andalusia (13 June).

18 June: Lord William Bentinck, having arrived to supersede Murray, re-embarked the expedition (13-15, 28 June). Reille, with three divisions, skirmished inconclusively with Graham's column of Wellington's army at Osma, and retired. Maucune's Division encountered Alten's Light Division at San Millan; the French escaped after a running fight but lost their baggage (13 June).

20 June: as Joseph's army prepared to face Wellington, his cavalry skirmished with Longa's troops along the River Zadorra; the Spanish were reluctant to charge until William Hay of the British 12th Light Dragoons, present reconnoitering, was asked to lead them, proving, he remarked, that despite the poor quality of officers, 'the Spanish soldiers . . . are a brave a set of men as need be'.

21 June: Wellington defeated Joseph and Jourdan, with troops from the Armies of the South, Centre and Portugal, at Vittoria (or Vitoria), and captured immense baggage and almost all the French artillery; but the victory could have been even more comprehensive had the French route of withdrawal been cut (24 June).

22 June: a blockade by sea having been imposed upon Castro Urdiales, the French evacuated the town and retired to Santona. The British brig-sloop HMS *Sparrow* (Captain Joseph Tayler) arrived off the port at that time, and garrisoned the castle (11-12 May).

24 June: pursuing the French, Wellington's vanguard from the Light Division skirmished with the French rearguard, the division of General Jean-Barthélemy-Claude-Toussaint Darmagnac from the Army of the Centre, near Yrurzun; the French continued to withdraw. Graham engaged Maucune at Villafranca, but the plan to trap them failed (21 June).

25 June: Graham with the 1st Division, Giron's Galicians and Pack's Portuguese, later supported by Longa and Mendizabel, engaged Foy at Tolosa, but the French continued to retreat. Henry O'Donnell's Andalusian army laid siege to the Pancorbo forts, which dominated the road to the Ebro; their commandant was Lieutenant-Colonel Charles-Auguste Durand of the 55th Line (28 June).

26 June: Wellington's army invested Pamplona; it was originally blockaded by British forces but they were relieved subsequently by Spanish. The city's governor was General Louis-Pierre-Jean-Aphrodise Cassan (27 July). A late, prominent casualty of Vittoria was the French general Jacques-Thomas Sarrut, wounded and captured at the battle, who died of his injury in hospital at Vittoria.

28 June: Spanish troops under Mendizabel established a blockade of San Sebastian, defended by the governor, General Emanuel Rey; an attempt to capture the outwork of San Bartolomé was unsuccessful (7 July). Joseph Bonaparte established his new headquarters in France, at St. Jean de Luz (2-3 June, 12 July). Spanish élite companies stormed and captured the fort of Santa Marta at Pancorbo (25 June). All Bentinck's force concentrated at Alicante (18 June, 5, 30 July).

30 June: the remaining fort at Pancorbo, Santa Engracia, surrendered to O'Donnell. Graham attacked the crossing-point of the Bidassoa at Behobie and Hendaye; Foy had the bridge burned (26 June, 7 July).

3 July: Wellington was promoted to Field-Marshal, backdated to 21 June (18 August 1812, 7 July, 3 May 1814).

5 July: Suchet evacuated Valencia as a result of Vittoria; he commented that it had undone five years of hard work (28 June, 8 July).

6 July: Napoleon ordered Soult to take overall command of French forces in Spain, finally placing their troops under a unified command (12 July).

7 July: Wellington probed the positions of General Honoré-Théodore-Maxime Gazan at Maya; the French retired (30 June, 12 July). British and Portuguese troops took over the siege of San Sebastian; Graham was to command (28 June, 17 July). Wellington received a vote of thanks in parliament for Vittoria, a victory which Castlereagh declared 'would shake to its base French domination in Germany' (21 June, 3, 22 July).

8 July: Decaen having planned an offensive on Vich, against Copons' Army of Catalonia, abandoned it after receiving news of Vittoria; but his second column, under General Jean-Maximilien Lamarque, from Gerona, attacked Eroles, was outnumbered and almost destroyed at La Salud, Decaen sending reinforcements to rescue him (5 July).

10 July: the French commander at Saragossa, General Marie-Auguste Paris, after fighting Espoz y Mina's advance, quit the city; his retreat involved a running fight and instead of joining Suchet he had to retire into France (5 August).

12 July: Soult arrived and took command from King Joseph, was who effectively dismissed. Napoleon ordered that he should not go beyond Bayonne upon pain of arrest, and subsequently he had to be prevented from breaking this injunction, until Napoleon relented and permitted him to settle on his own estate (6 July).

15 July: Soult announced the reorganisation of the forces under his command, no longer Armies of the North, Centre, South and Portugal, but a unified command with three lieutenant-generals under him: the lieutenant-generalcy of the Right, Reille; Centre, d'Erlon, and Left, Clausel (25 July).

17 July: an attempt having failed two days earlier, Portuguese troops captured the outwork of San Bartolomé at San Sebastian (7, 25 July).

22 July: on the suggestion of the Cortes, the Regency offered Wellington (as Duque de Ciudad Rodrigo) an estate in Granada, to express the gratitude of the Spanish people (7 July, 8 October).

25 July: Soult launched a major attack in the Pyrenees. At Roncesvalles, Clausel attacked Generals Sir John Byng and Pablo Morillo around the hill of Leiçar Atheca, but not much progress was made. Reille attacked towards the Linduz hill; it was held off. Lowry Cole was in overall command at Roncesvalles and he evacuated the position overnight. At Maya, d'Erlon attacked the 2nd Division of William Stewart who, with his superior Hill, was temporarily absent, so General William Pringle was in command. The French forced the pass but were stopped and then thrown back by a counter-attack from General Edward Barnes's brigade of the 7th Division. As Cole had retired, Hill also ordered a withdrawal during the night. An attempt to storm San Sebastian was beaten off, and in response to Soult's advance, Wellington ordered Graham to lift most of the siege and to embark most of his siege artillery (17, 26-27 July).

26 July: as Soult advanced, Clausel skirmished with Lowry Cole's 4th Division; he was supported by Sir Thomas Picton's 3rd Division, but the British retired at nightfall.

26-27 July: Graham raised the siege of San Sebastian as ordered; Rey made a sortie on 27 July that took some prisoners (24 August).

27 July: Soult made a minor probing advance against the Allied positions at Sorauren, and was repulsed. At Pamplona, Cassan's garrison made a sally against O'Donnell's blockading division and did some damage to the siege-lines (26 June, 9 September).

28 July: Soult made a major attack upon Wellington's positions at Sorauren, and was beaten off in some of the most bitter fighting of the war; Wellington remarked that 'I never saw such fighting . . . it began on the 25th, and, excepting the 29th . . . we had it every day till the 2nd. The battle of the 28th was fair *bludgeon* work', and of the 28th he wrote, 'upon the whole I never saw the troops behave so well'.

30 July: Wellington attacked Clausel at the 2nd Battle of Sorauren, where the brigades of Generals Maucune and Nicolas-François Conroux were virtually crippled. Simultaneously, Wellington's 7th Division attacked the divisions of Generals Lubin-Martin Vandermaesen and Eloi-Charlemagne Taupin near Olabe. Having lost heavily, Clausel retired. D'Erlon's corps attacked Hill at Beunza and forced him back, but the approach of reinforcements caused the French to halt. Overall, despite d'Erlon's success, Soult's advance had been defeated, and he retired. Bentinck blockaded Tarragona (28 June, 5 July, 15 August).

31 July: as d'Erlon retired, Hill attacked at

Venta de Urroz, causing the French to retire more rapidly, though the 2nd Division sustained heavy losses.

1 **August**: Wellington's 4th Division pressed the retreating French (Clausel) at Sumbilla, causing them to retire in some disorder. Retreating, Reille's troops forced the bridge at Yanzi against a sterling defence by element's of Longa's command and General Barcena's Galician Division; the Light Division arrived, took the bridge and hastened the French retreat.

2 **August**: Wellington's Light, 4th and 7th Divisions attacked the French rearguard near Echelar, and hastened their retreat (24 August).

5 **August**: after bombardment by General José Duran, the French garrison of the citadel of Saragossa surrendered (10 July).

15 **August**: on Suchet's advance, Bentinck fell back from Tarragona (30 July).

18 **August**: Suchet evacuated Tarragona and blew up its fortifications; at the end of the month the city was occupied by Bentinck (13 September).

19 **August**: the French garrison of Tortosa under General Louis-Benoît Robert made a sally as Del Parque's army was withdrawing across the Ebro, and at Amposta caused some casualties against the last unit to cross, Berenguer's Division.

24 **August**: the trenches at San Sebastian were re-occupied, and the siege recommenced (26-7 July).

26 **August**: having received new artillery, Wellington opened the bombardment of San Sebastian (31 August).

30 **August**: Wellington wrote to the Spanish war minister, General Juan O'Donoju, offering to resign command of the Spanish armies, over the treatment he was receiving, notably the ignoring of his advice over the appointment and dismissal of officers. The decision was postponed for the new Cortes (1 October, 8 November).

31 **August**: San Sebastian was stormed and the city captured, the garrison retiring to the citadel; Wellington's chief engineer, Sir Richard Fletcher, was killed (26 August, 5 September). Soult launched a major attack; against Freire at San Marcial he was beaten off, Wellington claiming that he withheld British reinforcements so that the Spanish could have a victory ('I made them win'). A notable casualty was French general Thomas Mignot, baron de Lamartiniere, mortally wounded (he died at Bayonne on 6 September). Similar attacks against the British to the east were also unsuccessful, near Salain de Lesaca, Sare and Santa Barbara. As Clausel retired from his attack, Vandermaesan's Division and part of Clausel's other two divisions were isolated on the enemy bank of the rising Bidassoa. To escape they had to fight their way across the bridge at Vera, held by Captain Daniel Cadoux and his company of 2/95th Rifles. The nearest British reinforcement was withheld by its commander (Skerrett), so instead of the French being trapped, they overpowered Cadoux's party and escaped; Cadoux and Vandermaesan were killed (2 August).

3 **September**: Wellington received news of the Austrian declaration of war upon Napoleon, so with the conflict continuing

in central Eurooe he realised that his own operations could continue safely (19 September).

5 September: at San Sebastian a council of war informed Rey that the citadel was not defensible, but despite all his unit-commanders urging him to seek 'an honourable capitulation as possible', he refused to surrender (31 August).

8 September: after a heavy bombardment, Rey surrendered the citadel of San Sebastian (8 October).

9 September: Adjutant-Commandant Baron Maucune (Cassan's chief-of-staff) led a major sortie from Pamplona; General Carlos de España, now in command of the besiegers, was wounded as he led the counter-attack (27 July, 10 October).

13 September: Suchet surprised and defeated Bentinck's Anglo-Spanish advance-guard under Colonel Frederick Adam, at Ordal, in a night attack (5 July).

14 September: as Suchet pursued Bentinck, a running fight occurred at Villafranca (22 September),

19 September: Wellington declared that although 'I acknowledge that I feel a great disinclination to enter the French territory under existing circumstances', he appreciated the Allied pressure, and would 'if it can be done with safety to the army, notwithstanding that I acknowledge I should prefer to turn my attention to Catalonia, as soon as I shall have secured this frontier' (3 September, 7 October).

22 September: Bentinck returned to Sicily, leaving William Clinton in command (14 September, 16 January 1814).

27 September: the tiny French garrison of Monzon, commanded by Captain Boutan of the 81st Line, a company of gendarmerie

and five gunners, and a skilled engineer NCO, Saint-Jacques, was besieged by Espoz y Mina (18 February 1814).

1 October: the new Spanish Cortes, much more representative than its predecessor, was scheduled to meet, but was delayed by an outbreak of fever, and in the following month re-located to Madrid (10-11 May 1814).

7 October: Wellington's army crossed the River Bidassoa, pushing back the French; the hardest task was that of the Light Division, assaulting positions above Vera, notably the forts on the Bayonette Ridge. The 5th Division's advance on the extreme west of the line is sometimes styled the action at Hendaye (19 September).

8 October: continuing to advance, Wellington manoeuvred the French out of their position on the Great Rhune; in consequence, Maucune was dismissed, but re-employed under Eugène de Beauharnais in Italy by mid-November (12 October). Wellington received a vote of thanks from parliament for San Sebastian and the operations subsequent to Vittoria (22 July, 8 September, 24 March 1814).

10 October: Adjutant-Commandant Maucune (not to be confused with the above) again led a major sortie from Pamplona; the siege continued, and it convinced Cassan of the impossibility of breaking out (9 September, 24 October).

12 October: Clausel, with Conroux's Division, recaptured the redoubt of Sainte Barbe near the French lines, which had been held by Spanish troops; when their counter-attack failed, Wellington refused to attempt its recapture due to its exposed and hazardous position (8 October).

13 October: having recaptured Sainte Barbe, the French attacked other positions taken from them on 8 October, now held by Giron's Army of Andalusia, but they were repelled (10 November). The French brig-corvette *Flibustier* (Lieutenant de Vaisseau Jean-Jacques-Léonore Daniel), carrying munitions and provisions from St. Jean de Luz to the garrison of Santona, was engaged (within sight of the British and French armies on the Adour) by the British schooner HMS *Telegraph* (Lieutenant Timothy Scriven). Upon the approach of the British ships HMS *Challenger* and *Constant*, the French set their ship ablaze and escaped to shore in their boats; *Flibustier* blew up.

24 October: Cassan opened negotiations for the surrender of Pamplona (10 October).

31 October: Cassan surrendered Pamplona, Wellington having written to Carlos de España on 20 October authorising him to shoot Cassan, his officers and NCOs and one-tenth of his soldiers, if as he had threatened Cassan blew up the place before surrendering, contrary to all the laws of war.

8 November: the Spanish Council of State confirmed that Wellington should remain in command of the Spanish armies, and that the conditions originally granted to him were confirmed; the war minister O'Donoju, who had never enjoyed good relations with Wellington, was dismissed subsequently (30 August). On this night boats of HMS *Revenge* (Captain Sir John Gore), commanded by Lieutenant William Richards, cut out a French felucca privateer from the harbour of Palamos.

10 November: Wellington attacked Soult and defeated him at the Battle of the Nivelle, despite the French having fortified their positions; Soult withdrew in disorder (13 October, 9 December).

11 November: French general Nicolas-François Conroux, commander of the 4th Division at the Nivelle, died of a wound sustained on the previous day.

17 November: Napoleon's representative presented the captive Ferdinand VII with a plan for restoring him to the throne; this was formalised on 22 November when the draft of the Treaty of Valençay was presented (10 December).

9 December: Wellington forced the line of the Nive; there was considerable fighting between Hill and d'Erlon at Villefranque, and Sir John Hope's force was engaged at Anglet (10 November).

10 December: Soult counter-attacked in the 1st Battle of the Nive, but was checked; Clausel (largely) and d'Erlon attacked at Arcangues, but were held off by the Light Division. Soult's secondary attack, by Reille, almost broke through, but was repelled at Barouillet. Ferdinand VII assented to the proposed Treaty of Valençay, although he had no intention of abiding by it (17 November, 10 January 1814).

10-11 December: three battalions of Rheinbund troops (2nd Nassau Regt. and Frankfurt Battn.) defected to the Allies, as a consequence of the course of the war in Germany and the collapse of the Rheinbund.

11 December: an attack by Soult at Barouillet, less intense than before, was repulsed.

12 December: a probe by Pierre Soult's light

cavalry involved some largely indecisive skirmishing at Hasparren.

13 December: Soult attacked Hill at St. Pierre, or the 2nd Battle of the Nive: Hill held out and Soult retired on Bayonne before British reinforcements arrived (3 January 1814).

16 December: Espoz y Mina raided over the French frontier towards St. Jean-Pied-du-Port, without authorisation (10 January 1814).

18 December: Morillo raided over the French border without orders, provoking Wellington's furious retort of 23 December: 'I did not lose thousands of men to bring the army under my command into the French territory, in order that the soldiers might plunder and ill treat the French peasantry, in positive disobedience of my orders . . .'

1814

3 January: Soult drove Buchan's brigade of General Le Cor's Portuguese Division from La Bastide-Clarence (13 December).

6 January: with the 3rd, 4th and Le Cor's Divisions, Wellington drove back the French incursion of three days previously (15 February).

10 January: Wellington wrote to Bathurst concerning the Treaty of Valençay, which was supposed to bring peace between Napoleon and Ferdinand VII; it was a delusion on Napoleon's part but even Wellington was uncertain: 'I have long suspected that Buonaparte would adopt this expedient; and if he had had less pride, and more common sense, and could have carried his measure into execution as he ought to have done, it would have succeeded. I am not certain that it will not succeed now . . .' (10 December, 2 February). Believing that the Treaty would be honoured, Napoleon issued orders for the withdrawal of substantial numbers of Soult's army to bolster his own front; they were dispatched before the end of the month. Espoz y Mina raided over the French frontier again, without orders; Wellington stated that it was motivated by the need to gather supplies. On 12

January Harispe collected troops and moved against Mina, who retired (16 December 1813).

16 January: Clinton and Copons attacked Suchet at Molins del Rey; after some skirmishing Clinton declined to engage after French reinforcements arrived (22 September 1813, 18 February, 4 March).

2 February: the Treaty of Valençay was presented to the Cortes, which declared it invalid, having been negotiated under duress (while Ferdinand VII was imprisoned) (10 January, 24 March). The Duke of Angoulême arrived incognito at St. Jean de Luz, in preparation for raising a Royalist rebellion in southern France (12 March).

15 February: as Wellington advanced, Pringle's Brigade of the 2nd Division took the position of Garris from Harispe's Division (6 January).

16 February: following Harispe's defeat, Soult had to abandon the line of the Bidouse.

17 February: as Wellington advanced, Hill with the 2nd Division forced the crossing over the River Saison at Arriverayte, against Harispe (23-24 February). The French garrison of Jaca surrendered (east of Pamplona, near the Franco-Spanish border), having been besieged by Espoz y Mina for some months.

18 February: the French governor of Lerida, General Jean-Baptiste-Isidore Lamarque d'Arrouzat, being deceived by a traitor on Suchet's staff, Juan Van Halen, that an armistice had been signed, was taken prisoner with his garrison at Martorell, en route to Barcelona (16 January, 13 April). At the same time, the tiny garrison of Monzon was also deceived into surrendering (27 September 1813).

23 February: the governor of Barcelona, Habert, made an ineffective sally against the besieging Spaniards of General Pedro Sarsfield (16 April).

23-24 February: as Wellington advanced, Hope crossed the Adour; a weak French attack was repelled (17 February).

25-26 February: Wellington's engineers constructed a bridge over the River Adour.

26 February: as Wellington advanced, the forward elements of Hussey Vivian's light cavalry brigade (18th Hussars) drove back the French vedettes at Puyoo.

27 February: Wellington defeated Soult in the Battle of Orthez; prominent among the fatalities was the French brigade-commander General Jean-Pierre Béchaud. The Allied investment of Bayonne was completed by Hope's capture of the suburbs of St. Etienne; the defending French governor was General Pierre Thouvenot, who was wounded by a shot in the thigh in this action.

2 March: as Wellington advanced, Hill defeated Clausel at Aire (12, 19 March).

4 March: Wellington ordered Clinton to break up his army, in the expectation that news of Orthez would compel Suchet to evacuate Catalonia; some to join Wellington, some to return to Sicily to aid Bentinck in Italy, and the Spanish to transfer to their own command. He assured Clinton that 'if it should be agreeable to you to come and command a division with this army, I will, with pleasure, give you the command of one', but Clinton delayed until he was sure that Suchet was no longer a threat (16 January).

12 March: Beresford, with the 7th Division (and accompanied by the Duke of Angoulême) entered Bordeaux unopposed, the citizens having declared for King Louis XVIII (2, 21 March).

14 March: on about this day a brigade of three provisional battalions of Militia embarked at Portsmouth for the campaign; they arrived in the Garonne in early April (too late to see action) but the event is significant for being the first occasion that militia (albeit units assembled for the purpose from the existing county corps) had been sent abroad after volunteering for active service.

19 March: as Wellington advanced, he engaged d'Erlon's rearguard at Vic-en-Bigorre; the French retreated. A notable casualty there was the engineer Major Henry Sturgeon of the Royal Staff Corps, killed while reconnoitering (2 March).

20 March: continuing to advance, Wellington engaged the French at Tarbes, notably the Light Division against Harispe's Division, involving what was described as some of the fiercest fighting of the war; the French continued to retire (22 March).

21 March: as requested by Wellington on 17 March, Rear-Admiral Charles Penrose, aboard HMS *Egmont*, anchored in the Gironde preparatory to clearing French naval forces in the estuary (commanded by

Contre-Amiral Louis-Leon Jacob, flagship the 74-gunner *Régulus*), to secure Bordeaux (12 March, 2 April).

22 March: as Wellington advanced, a minor cavalry action occurred near St. Gaudens between Hill and Soult's rearguard, in which the 13th Light Dragoons routed the 10th Chasseurs à Cheval (22 March, 4 April).

24 March: released by Napoleon, Ferdinand VII returned to Spain (2 February, 18 May). Parliament passed a vote of thanks to Wellington for Orthez (8 October 1813, 3 May).

25 March: General Decaen took command in the Bordeaux region as commander of the Armée de la Haute-Garonne (12 March, 11 April).

2 April: in Penrose's efforts to clear the Gironde, boats from HMS *Porcupine* (Capt. Coode), under Lieutenant Robert Dunlop, attacked a French flotilla near Blaye, which ran ashore; Dunlop landed, drove off the French soldiers trying to protect the vessels, captured twelve of the craft and burned four others (21 March, 6 April).

4 April: the first of Wellington's units crossed the Garonne by pontoon bridge, near La Capelette (22 March). Napoleon abdicated at Fontainebleau, albeit tentatively.

6 April: General the Earl of Dalhousie, with part of the 7th Division, defeated General François L'Huillier de Hoff, who was retiring from Blaye, at Etauliers. Admiral Penrose in HMS *Egmont*, with the 74-gunner HMS *Centaur*, made to rush up the Gironde to attack the French 74-gunner *Régulus* and the three brig-corvettes and other vessels attending her, but at midnight the French burned their ships (2 April). Napoleon abdicated fully, renouncing the rights of his family; the delay in the news reaching southern

France and Spain led to the continuance of the war beyond this date.

7 April: Admiral Jacob, commanding at Blaye since the destruction of his ships, repelled an Allied attempt to enter the town; but the collapse of the empire led him to declare for the new government a few days later.

7-9 April: French batteries overlooking the Gironde were entered and destroyed by landing-parties from HMS *Belle-Poule*, under Captain George Harris (6 April).

8 April: as Wellington advanced, Hussey Vivian and the 18th Hussars captured the bridge over the River Era at Croix d'Orade, defeating Pierre Soult's two regiments of chasseurs à cheval (4 April).

10 April: Wellington defeated Soult at the Battle of Toulouse; a notable fatality was French general Eloi-Charlemagne Taupin, killed after sustaining eight wounds.

11 April: Soult evacuated Toulouse. General Decaen declared for the new government (25 March).

12 April: Wellington entered Toulouse, which had declared for the king. At 5 p.m. came news of Napoleon's abdication; allowing his reserve to drop for a moment, Wellington spun on his heels and clicked his fingers, saying 'Hurrah!'. At dinner that evening Alava proposed a toast to him as 'Liberador del'España', whereupon those present cheered him for ten minutes. Wellington was rather embarassed: 'Lord Wellington bowed, confused, and immediately called for coffee'. He immediately sent the news to Soult via his aide Colonel Henry Cooke and his French counterpart Colonel St. Simon (17 April).

13 April: Suchet received news of Napoleon's abdication (18 February).

14 April: despite having received news of

Napoleon's abdication, albeit unofficially, Thouvenot in Bayonne made a huge sally against Hope's army besieging the city; Major-General Andrew Hay was killed, Hope captured, but the sortie was repelled. Sir Henry Clinton of the 5th Division took command of the besiegers. The whole exercise was pointless, and Thouvenot was much condemned for causing such useless loss of life (27 February, 26 April).

16 April: another sortie was made by the garrison of Barcelona, news of Napoleon's abdication not arriving until two days later. It was the last action of the Peninsular War (23 February, 28 April).

17 April: Soult received official confirmation of Napoleon's abdication and the end of hostilities; immediately he sent his chief-of-staff, General Gazan, to Toulouse to conclude an official armistice (12 April).

18 April: hostilities were concluded by the Convention of Toulouse, Generals Sir George Murray and Luis Wimpffen for the Allies, Gazan for the French being the signatories; it was confirmed by Wellington, Soult and Suchet.

26 April: having finally received the news officially, Thouvenot in Bayonne accepted the end of the war. The Duke of Angoulême entered Toulouse in ceremony; he was welcomed by all the civic dignitaries, with Wellington and Clausel riding side by side (12, 14 April).

28 April: in Barcelona, Habert finally accepted the end of hostilities, and marched out of the city (16 April).

3 May: Wellington was created Marquess of Douro and Duke of Wellington (3 July 1813, 24 March).

4 May: Wellington entered Paris (24 May).

10-11 May: on behalf of Ferdinand VII, General Francisco Eguia arrested leading Liberals in Madrid, overturning the Regency and Cortes, and ending the 1812 Constitution (1 October 1813).

18 May: Ferdinand VII returned to Madrid in triumph (24 March).

24 May: having returned to Madrid, Wellington was invested by Ferdinand VII with all the honours and rewards conferred in the king's name by the Regency and Cortes (4 May).

14 June: on the eve of his quitting the army, leaving Dalhousie to supervise its final withdrawal from the Peninsula, Wellington issued his valedictory General Order, in which he 'takes this opportunity of congratulating the army upon the recent events which have restored peace to their country and the world. The share which the British army has had in producing these events, and the high character with which the army will quit this country, must be equally satisfactory to every individual belonging to it, as they are to the Commander of the Forces . . . [who] once more requests the army to accept his thanks . . . he assures them that he will never cease to feel the warmest interest in their welfare and honor; and that he will be at all times happy to be of any service to those to whose conduct, discipline, and gallantry, their country is so much indebted'.

28 June: taking his seat in the House of Lords, Wellington was welcomed with a speech of gratitude by the Lord Chancellor; he replied that such was the support he had received from the government, the officers and the whole army, 'he could not but be sensible that, whatever difficulties he had to encounter, the means were adequate to the end'.

1 July: Wellington thanked the House of Commons in person for their support, and to declare his admiration for 'the great efforts made by this House and Country, at a moment of unexampled pressure and difficulty, in order to support the great scale of operation by which the contest was brought to so fortunate a termination'.

Chronology: sources of direct quotations

The following are the sources of the quotations which appear in the chronology:

16 February 1810: *Gentleman's Magazine*, March 1810, p. 275.

8 August 1810: *The Confidential Correspondence of Napoleon Bonaparte with his Brother Joseph, Sometime King of Spain*, London 1855, Vol. II p. 135 (hereafter quoted as *Confidential Correspondence*).

7 September 1810: *Dispatches of Field-Marshal the Duke of Wellington*, ed. J. Gurwood, London 1834-38, Vol. VI p. 424 (hereafter quoted as 'WD').

24 September 1810: WD Vol. VI, p. 587.

12 October 1810: *Confidential Correspondence* Vol. II, p. 152.

18 February 1811: *Gentleman's Magazine*, February 1811, p. 197.

3 April 1811: WD Vol. VII, p. 432.

3 February 1812: Belmas, J., *Journaux des Sièges faits ou soutenus par les Français dans la Péninsule de 1807 à 1814*, Paris 1836-37, Vol. IV p. 248.

16 March 1812: *Confidential Correspondence* Vol. II, p. 225.

11 June 1812: WD Vol. IX, p. 240.

11 August 1812: WD Vol. IX, p. 347.

7 December 1812: *Gentleman's Magazine*, December 1812, p. 572.

13 February 1813: *Gentleman's Magazine*, June 1813, p. 595.

13 April 1813: WD Vol. X, p. 354.

22 May 1813: Maxwell, Sir Herbert, *Life of Wellington*, London 1899, Vol. I, p. 310.

20 June 1813: Hay, W., *Reminiscences 1808-1815 under Wellington*, ed. Mrs. S.C.I. Wood., London 1901, p. 108.

28 July 1813: WD Vol. X pp. 602, 572.

31 August 1813: Stanhope, Earl, *Notes on Conversations with the Duke of Wellington*, London 1888, p. 22.

5 September 1813: Belmas, Vol. IV, p. 738.

19 September 1813: WD Vol. XI, p. 124.

18 December 1813: WD Vol. XI, p. 391.

10 January 1814: WD Vol. XI, p. 433.

4 March 1814: WD Vol. XI, p. 546.

12 April 1814: Larpent, F.S., *The Private Journal of Judge-Advocate Larpent*, London 1854, p. 487.

14 June 1814: WD Vol. XII, p. 62.

28 June 1814: *Gentleman's Magazine*, August 1814, p. 164.

1 July 1814: *Gentleman's Magazine*, August 1814, p. 166.

PARTICIPANTS IN THE PENINSULAR WAR

The following brief biographical notices concern some of the most significant personalities involved in the war. The concentration is upon the role of each participant in the war, nor upon their previous or subsequent career, and the ranks quoted are those held at the time of their participation in the war; for example, although Clausel ultimately became a Marshal of France, and Hardinge a Field-Marshal and Viscount, they appear here as General and Lieutenant-Colonel respectively.

Abispal (or La Bispal), conde de: see O'Donnell.

Abrantes, duc de: see Junot.

Adam, Colonel Frederick (1781-1853) Adam served as commander of a light brigade in eastern Spain in 1813. Under Murray he performed with great credit in his rearguard action at Biar in April 1813, but under Bentinck was badly surprised at Ordal, largely the consequence of his own carelessness. He was wounded quite severely in the left arm early in that action. Major-General from 4 June 1814, he played a significant role in the Waterloo campaign.

Alava, General Miguel Ricardo (1770-1843) Although not a commander, Alava was one of the best-known Spanish officers of the war, by virtue of his position as Spanish attaché at Wellington's headquarters. He served at Trafalgar (where his uncle, Vice-Admiral Don Ignacio Maria Alava, was second-in-command of the Spanish fleet), and at Tudela, Ucles and Medellin (he remarked to Wellington that until appointed to the British HQ he had always been on the losing side, against the British at sea and the French on land!). He became one of Wellington's closest friends, at his side for most of the war, and was a useful advisor. Internal unrest in Spain after the war led to his alternating between acting as a Spanish ambassador and living in exile, when Wellington's friendship and support helped repay him for his assistance during the war.

Albuquerque, General José Maria de la Cueva, Duque de (1774-1811)

One of the most distinguished Spanish generals, Albuquerque was a man of great honour and personal courage, and one of the few with whom Wellington could work without trouble (Albuquerque was something of an Anglophile and a friend of John Hookham Frere), but was militarily ungifted; Wellington noted that 'although he does not want spirit, [he] is deficient in other qualities for a commander'[1]. He was an uneasy subordinate, quarrelling with his superiors and intriguing against Cuesta. He led the troops from the Army of the Centre at Medellin, the 2nd Cavalry Division at Talavera, and was defeated at Arzobispo; but his most crucial service was early in 1810, commanding the Army of Estremadura, when he secured Cadiz as the base for Spanish resistance in southern Spain. Appointed governor, he quarrelled with the Cadiz Junta, which cast unjustified aspersions upon his honour; so he quit his command and in March 1810 became ambassador to London, where he published a vindication of his conduct, *Manifiesto del Ducque de Albuquerque* . . . The comments about him were said to have brought on 'a most alarming paroxysm of mental derangement' and he died on 13 February 1811, shortly after the Cortes had recommended his re-employment in command of an army. His funeral was conducted at Westminster Abbey; as a British obituary remarked, he should have been lamented 'by Spain, as an ardent Patriot and gallant Soldier; by England, as a firm Friend and ally; and by Mankind, as an honest Man'[2].

[1] *Dispatches of Field-Marshal the Duke of Wellington*, London 1834-3-8, Vol. V p. 292.
[2] *Gentleman's Magazine*, February 1811, pp. 197-98.

Alorna, General Pedro de Almeida, marquis de (1755-1813)

One of the best-known Portuguese soldiers of the period, Alorna served with the Spanish army against France in 1793-95 and in 1796 commanded the 'Experimental Legion', raised at his behest and sometimes styled as bearing his name, which introduced 'light' tactics into the Portuguese army. In 1807 he was charged with the defence of Elvas but surrendered on the orders of the Prince Regent and, essentially pro-French, commanded the Portuguese army re-formed for service with the French; Alorna became a *général de division* in the French army. He became commander of the French Portuguese Legion but remained in the Peninsula to assist Massena, who blamed him for not anticipating the construction of the lines of Torres Vedras: Massena described him and Pamplona as, *ce sont deux mauvais coquins*[1]. Alorna left the Peninsula in 1811, served with the *Grande Armée* in the invasion of Russia, and died at Königsberg on 26 January 1813.

[1] Stanhope, Earl, *Notes on Conversations with the Duke of Wellington*, London 1888, p. 162.

Alvarez de Castro, General Mariano (1749-1810) An experienced veteran who had been in command of the castle of Barcelona at the time of its capture in 1808, he was appointed governor of Gerona, which he defended with ability, courage and resolution. A severe, determined and devout man, he conducted the defence heroically until, towards the end, he fell seriously ill. Although he exhorted his successor, General Juliano Bolivar, to hold out to the last, the council of war capitulated and Alvarez was sent as a prisoner to France. He was then returned to Spain, apparently for trial as a traitor (it was alleged that he had accepted Murat's provisional administration), but he died after his arrival at Figueras, probably of ill-treatment and neglect.

Angoulême, Louis-Antoine de Bourbon, duc de (1775-1844) One of the most prominent of French royalists, Angoulême was the son of the comte d'Artois (later King Charles X), and nephew of Louis XVI and Louis XVIII. Incognito, calling himself the comte de Pradel, he joined Wellington's army in early 1814 with the intention of raising a royalist insurrection in southern France. Nicknamed 'the Royal Tiger' by the British, he did not impress Larpent, who described him as 'the little Duke [whose] figure and manners are by no means imposing, and his talents appear not very great. He seems affable and good-tempered . . .'[1]. On 12 March 1814 he made a triumphal entry into Bordeaux, although Wellington made it quite clear that he could not use the presence of the Allied army to impose royal control, the population being more anti-Bonaparte than pro-Bourbon. Nominally commander of the French army sent to Spain in 1823 to restore the absolutist rule of Ferdinand VII, upon the abdication of his father Angoulême renounced his claim to succession and went into exile.

[1] Larpent, F.S., *The Private Journal of Judge-Advocate Larpent*, London 1854, p. 385.

Augereau, Marshal Pierre-François-Charles, duc de Castiglione (1757-1816) One of Napoleon's oldest companions, Augereau came from a humble background and remained unpolished, though punctilious in his dress (hence his nickname, *'le grand Prussien'*). In June 1809 he was appointed to lead VII Corps in Spain, and took command of the army at Gerona in October. In February 1810 he was appointed commander of the Army of Catalonia and established himself in Barcelona, but was checked before Tarragona, failed to support Suchet when required and abandoned central Catalonia on the grounds of shortage of provisions. In April he was replaced by Macdonald, officially on health grounds but actually because of Napoleon's displeasure with his conduct of the war: a brave commander on the battlefield, he was plainly unsuccessful in independent command, and was known as a looter. His half-brother, General Jean-Pierre Augereau, succeeded to command Souham's Division of VII Corps after Souham was wounded at Vich, and the Marshal gave him much responsibility thereafter, virtually putting him in command of operations in Catalonia, with little success. He retired from the Peninsula on health grounds in August 1810.

Bailen, Duke of: see Castaños.

Baird, Lieutenant-General Sir David (1757-1829) A tough and experienced Scottish soldier (who had survived a traumatic imprisonment in Seringapatam), Baird was appointed second-in-command to Moore in the Peninsula, leading the reinforcement which landed at Corunna in October 1808. He marched inland and united with Moore at Mayorga, shortly before the beginning of the retreat to Corunna and Vigo. At the Battle of Corunna Baird should have succeeded to command when Moore was wounded, but at almost the same moment was himself hit by a grapeshot, which resulted in the loss of his left arm. Sir John Hope conducted the remainder of the battle, though Baird was nominally in command and wrote a covering letter to Hope's dispatch. Baird's eighty-odd days in the Peninsula were his last active command, though he received a baronetcy in April 1809 and became a full general in 1814.

Ballesteros, General Francisco One of the most active Spanish commanders of the first part of the Peninsular War, Ballesteros's first major exploit was the capture of Santander in June 1809, followed almost immediately by his expulsion. Something similar occurred in March-April 1810 when a success against Mortier at Valverde was followed by defeat at Zalamea and Araçena. Early in 1811 he conducted a fighting retreat into Portugal with some skill, and at Albuera held the left of the Spanish line which fought so well. Later based in southern Andalusia as commander of the fourth Army and Captain-General of Andalusia, and entertaining a high opinion of his own (rather modest) talents, he was not happy taking orders from a British colleague so failed to distract Soult during the Burgos operation, and his opposition to Wellington as generalissimo turned into outright mutiny. He threatened to resign if the appointment were made, which he regarded as dishonourable to Spain; the Cortes reacted by having him arrested by his own subordinates, General Virues and the Prince of Anglona, at his headquarters at Granada on 30 October 1812. Ballesteros was sent as a prisoner to the African fortress of Ceuta, and command of the Fourth Army passed to the Duque de Parque.

Bathurst, Henry, 3rd Earl (1755-1841) Earl Bathurst features in the Peninsular War as British Secretary for War and the Colonies from June 1812 until 1827, having earlier occupied a number of important posts, including briefly that of Foreign Secretary. He did much towards aiding Wellington's campaigns, and it was to him that Wellington addressed many of his most important dispatches.

Beauharnais, François, Marquis de (1756-1847) Brother-in-law of the Empress Josephine, the Marquis was appointed ambassador to Spain by Napoleon, despite having emigrated during the Revolutionary Wars and having served in the *Armée de Condé*. He was the French contact with Escoiquiz and Ferdinand, Prince of the Asturias, in the so-called 'Escorial conspiracy' of 1807, but declined to recognise Ferdinand as king after the abdication of Charles IV.

Beckwith, Colonel Thomas Sidney (1772-1831) Described by William Napier as a man equal to rally an army in flight, Sidney Beckwith (as he was known) was one of the British army's finest regimental officers. He joined the 95th Rifles in 1800 and helped Moore formulate the light infantry tactics that had great influence upon the operations of the British army in the Peninsula, where he served from the beginning of the war. In February 1810 he stepped up from commanding the 1/95th to lead a brigade of the Light Division, but was invalided home by August 1811; subsequently he became a lieutenant-general and C-in-C at Bombay, and died in India. He was admired universally as one who put efficiency on the battlefield before the parade-ground, and his care for his men led them to 'follow him cheerfully through fire and water'[1].

[1] Leach, J., *Rough Sketches of the Life of an Old Soldier*, London 1831, p. 121.

Bellune, duc de: see Victor.

Benevente, prince de: see Talleyrand.

Bentinck (or Cavendish-Bentinck), Lieutenant-General Lord William Henry (1774-1839) Son of the 3rd Duke of Portland (Prime Minister 1783 and 1807-09), he served as British military representative at Madrid at the beginning of the war, and led a brigade of the 1st Division in the Corunna campaign. Lieutenant-General from June 1811, he was appointed to command British forces in Sicily, and when his plans for a descent onto the Italian mainland were not accepted, he proposed the expedition to eastern Spain. He joined it in person in June 1813, replacing the ineffectual Murray, but having been checked by Suchet at Ordal and Villafranca, sailed for Sicily on 22 September, leaving Clinton in command. The invasion that he finally mounted to Italy achieved only minor success. His brother, Lieutenant-Colonel Lord Frederick Bentinck (1781-1828) of the 1st Foot Guards (colonel from June 1813) acted as Lord William's liason officer with Wellington in early 1812 and commanded Murray's advance-guard in the expedition to Tarragona.

Beresford, Marshal William Carr (1768-1854) The driving force, and indeed largely the creator of the Portuguese army that fought in the Peninsula, Beresford was a natural son of the 1st Marquess of Waterford who, after considerable service in the British Army (including a period as commander and governor of Madeira in the name of the Portuguese monarchy, and command of a brigade in the Corunna campaign), was a British major-general from 25 April 1808. On 2 March 1809 he was appointed to command and reorganise the Portuguese army. In this task he was conspicuously successful, though was less capable as a field commander; his limitations were demonstrated at Albuera, although William Napier's comments were somewhat unjust, to which Beresford responded in a pamphlet war. Beresford never lost Wellington's trust, however, and provided valuable advice (for example in cancelling the premature attack of the 1st Division at Salamanca), and indeed Wellington stated that he was the best man to succeed him in command of the army - 'the only person capable of conducting a large concern', even though this was based mostly upon Beresford's administrative skills. His aide William Warre wrote of his 'unremitted exertions, and Herculean labour. There exists not a more honourable firm man or a more zealous Patriot. His failings are mere foibles of a temper naturally warm and hasty, and great zeal to have everything right, without much patience'[1]. Beresford left Portuguese service in 1819 upon the dismissal of British officers after the revolution; awarded a viscountcy in 1823, he remained a loyal supporter of Wellington and was Master-General of the Ordnance during the Duke's premiership (1828-30).

[1] Warre, W., *Letters from the Peninsula 1808-1812*, ed. Revd. E. Warre, London 1909, p. 106.

Berg, Grand Duke of: see Murat.

Berthier, Marshal Louis-Alexandre, Prince de Neuchâtel (1753-1815) Napoleon's invaluable chief of staff served only briefly in the Peninsular War; appointed 'major-general of the Army of Spain' on 3 November 1808, he acted as Napoleon's principal staff officer during the Emperor's personal intervention in the war, before returning to central Europe for the campaign against Austria.

Bessières, Marshal Jean-Baptiste, duc d'Istrie (1768-1813) The famous cavalry commander was one of the marshals to whom Napoleon was most friendly, and repaid him with great loyalty. Bessières was appointed commander of the Corps of Observation of the Western Pyrenees on 19 March 1808, initially demonstrating decision and activity, winning the Battle of Medina de Rio Seco, and on 7 September was confirmed in command of II Corps of the Army of Spain. Subsequently Napoleon thought his conduct somewhat lethargic and transferred him to command the reserve cavalry on 9 November 1808; appointed governor of northern Spain on 17 January 1809, in March he was recalled to France for the Austrian campaign. In January 1811 he was sent back to Spain as commander of the Army of the North, but was allocated insufficient forces for the task in hand. On 6 June 1811 he wrote a perceptive report to Berthier, criticising the whole strategy with regard to the Peninsula: 'We are short of everything, because it is only with great difficulty that we can be fed from day to day . . . we are too widely spread; we use up our resources with neither profit nor necessity . . . we should concentrate, establish safe bases for our magazines and hospitals, and regard two-thirds of Spain as a vast battlefield . . .'[1] His urging that large swathes of Spain should be abandoned to concentrate upon the pacification of the north found no favour with Napoleon, his relations with Joseph were not good, and Massena regarded him as unco-operative (though he was present at Fuentes de Oñoro). He returned to his own region and repelled an attack on Leon, but Napoleon was unhappy with his conduct and his assessment of the situation in Spain, and recalled him to France in July 1811. Bessières never again exercised independent command; he led the Guard cavalry in Russia and was killed at Rippach on 1 May 1813. His brother, General Bertrand Bessières (1773-1854) served as a cavalry commander in Spain, notably in Catalonia 1808-10.

[1] Belmas, J., *Journaux des Sièges faits ou soutenus par les Français dans la Péninsule, de 1807 à 1814*, Paris 1836-37, Vol. I pp. 560-61.

Blake, General Joaquin (Joachim) (1759-1827) The grandson of a Jacobite, Blake was one of a number of Spanish commanders of foreign birth or descent. One of the best Spanish generals - personally brave and neither over-cautious nor reckless - he was inexperienced in high command when first appointed as Captain-General of Galicia, in succession to Filanghieri, murdered for not supporting the popular will. An able administrator, Blake was unlucky in the field: he was replaced by La Romana after defeats at Medina de Rio Seco, Zornoza and Espinosa. In 1809 he was given command of the forces of Aragon, Valencia and Catalonia, defeated Suchet at Alcañiz, but was routed at Belchite, and resigned after failing to relieve Gerona. In April 1810 he took command of the Army of the Centre at Cadiz, but was defeated at Baza and was undistinguished at Albuera. Commanding the forces of Valencia, Murcia and Aragon he was defeated by Suchet at Saguntum, was besieged in Valencia, and upon the surrender of that city was sent as a prisoner to Vincennes, where he remained in close confinement for the remainder of the war.

Bock, Major-General Eberhardt Otto Georg von (d. 1814) Celebrated for a single, outstanding action, this Hanoverian general arrived in the Peninsula on 1 January 1812 with a brigade composed of the 1st and 2nd Dragoons of the King's German Legion, Bock being colonel of the 1st. At Garcia Hernandez on 23 July 1812 these troops did what many thought virtually impossible, breaking squares of regularly-formed infantry. Bock himself was probably not responsible for this triumph: described as being a short, slender man with a hump on one shoulder, he was also extremely short-sighted, and at Garcia Hernandez had to ask the direction in which the enemy stood. He charged off at the head of one squadron, leaving two others to attack the infantry; it was the commanders of these - Captains Gustavus von der Decken (who was killed) and Augustus von Reizenstein - who broke the squares. Bock led his brigade until early 1814 (less a period April-June when he seems to have commanded all the cavalry during Cotton's absence) and on leaving the Peninsula was drowned when his transport, *Bellona*, was wrecked on the coast of France.

Bonaparte, Joseph, King of Naples and Spain (1768-1844) Although Joseph's installation as king of Spain was the catalyst for the Peninsular War, it was not a consequence of his own desires. The eldest of the Bonaparte brothers, he lived in Napoleon's shadow and was used as a pawn in Napoleon's plan for European domination. Napoleon made him King of Naples in 1806, and then transferred him to the throne of Spain; in both places Joseph genuinely tried to be a good king and care for his subjects, and even in Spain his opponents did not portray him as a figure of hate, like Napoleon, but more as a figure of fun, mocking his mistresses (his wife did not accompany him to Spain as queen-consort) and his fondress for strong drink, hence nicknames like 'Pepe Botellas' ('Joe Bottles'). Joseph declared that the crown would not lose dignity while he wore it; but a popular saying stated that although he might put the crown in his pocket, he could not put it on his head. Although an instrument of his brother's policies, Joseph tried to be so considerate to his subjects that rumours suggested that he preferred Spain to France, to the extent of turning against the French; clearly wrong, but indicative of how his humane policies might be misinterpreted. Joseph often complained about the role thrust upon him, and the fact that Napoleon persisted in sending him instructions and accorded him neither civil nor military authority, and more than once threatened to abdicate: 'I am King of Spain only through the force of your arms; I might be so through the love of the Spanish people, but for that purpose I must govern them in my own way . . . I will be such a king as the brother and friend of your Majesty ought to be, or I will return to Mortefontaine [his French estate], where I ask for no happiness but to live without humiliation and to die with a good conscience. Only a fool remains long in a false position'[1]. Although generally regarded as a decent man, Joseph had no great talent for administration, less for military affairs, and was unable to inspire great confidence, so could not fulfill the task required of him by Napoleon, whose own assessment was probably accurate: 'Joseph . . . is a very good man [but] his qualities are only suited to private life . . . in the discharge of the high duties which I confided to him, he did the best he could. His intentions were good; and therefore the principal fault rested not so much with him as with me, who raised him above his proper sphere'[2]. Following his exit from Spain, in January 1814 Joseph was appointed Lieutenant-General of the Empire, and headed the Council of Ministers during the Hundred Days; after Waterloo he went into exile, and died in Florence.

[1] *The Confidential Correspondence of Napoleon Bonaparte with his Brother Joseph*, London 1855, Vol. II p. 47.
[2] Las Cases, E.A.D.M.J., *Memoirs of the Life, Exile and Conversations of the Emperor Napoleon*, London 1834, Vol. II p. 192.

Bonnet (or Bonet), General Jean-Pierre-François, comte (1768-1857)

An experienced soldier who had joined the French army before the Revolution, Bonnet served in the Peninsula from 1808, originally as a divisional commander under Bessières and Soult, and from early 1810 commanded in the Asturias and at Oviedo. His forces were never sufficient to subdue the region, and twice in 1811-12 he was ordered to withdraw, only for Napoleon to disapprove and send him back both times. Marmont called him up before Salamanca, and when Marmont was wounded at that battle, as senior general Bonnet took command of the Army of Portugal. This role as army commander was fleeting; within an hour he was also wounded, and command passed to Clausel. Regarded as one of the best commanders in the army, upon his recovery Bonnet was employed in Germany.

Brennier (or Brenier) de Montmorand, General Antoine-François, comte (1767-1832) Having begun his military career in Spanish service, Brennier had been eight years a general when he led a brigade of Delaborde's division in the Peninsula in 1807. Wounded and captured when his brigade was routed at Vimeiro, after his exchange he returned to Spain with a brigade command in February 1810, and in that August he was appointed governor of Almeida. When that city was blockaded by Wellington, Massena ordered him to break out (three messengers were sent: at a time when ordinary soldiers were largely anonymous, it is satisfying to be able to identify the courier who got through, one André Tillet of the 6th Léger). Thanks to laxity in the British blockade, Brennier not only broke out and rejoined the Army of Portugal with almost 1,000 of his 1,300 men, he also blew up part of the defences. Promoted to *général de division* on 26 May 1811, in October he took command of the 6th Division of the Army of Portugal. In July 1812 he was defeated at Castrillo and his division was routed at Salamanca; he relinquished his command in August 1812 and the remainder of his service was in Germany, until wounded at Lützen. Wellington added a curious footnote to his great exploit of the escape from Almeida; when a prisoner-of-war, Brennier had asked Wellington for a loan, and had received £500; Wellington commented that had he been captured again at Almeida, he would have had to repay the loan, but 'I heard no more of the money'![1].

[1] Stanhope, Earl, *Notes on Conversations with the Duke of Wellington*, London 1888, p. 89.

Burrard, Lieutenant-General Sir Harry, Bt. (1755-1813) Having been second-in-command in the expeditions to Ostend and Copenhagen, 'Betty' Burrard (as he was known) was sent to the Peninsula as Dalrymple's deputy, Wellesley at that stage not being trusted with supreme command. He arrived off Portugal in the frigate HMS *Brazen* just before the Battle of Vimeiro, and although he permitted Wellesley to conduct the battle, he forbade any pursuit of the defeated French, much to Wellesley's and the army's disgust. His command in the Peninsula lasted only a few hours,

until Dalrymple's arrival, whose concurrence with Burrard's caution lost the opportunity of a decisive victory. Both subsequently approved of the Convention of Cintra (with Wellesley an unwilling signatory), which permitted the French to leave Portugal with all their booty. All three generals were recalled for an inquiry, from which Wellesley was exonerated, but it was made clear that neither Burrard nor Dalrymple would again hold field commands. Burrard was not a bad officer, merely over-cautious, which may have been partly the result of experiencing the débâcle of the Ostend expedition.

Cabarrus, François, count (1752-1810) This French entrepreneur is best remembered as an advocate of the 'enlightenment' in eighteenth-century Spain, where he greatly assisted the reform of finances during the reign of Charles III. Imprisoned for two years under the reactionary reign of Charles IV, his knowledge and experience led to his appointment as Joseph Bonaparte's minister of finance. His abilities were undoubted, but there was never sufficient revenue to carry out the reforms Joseph advocated, and Cabarrus died at Seville in 1810 probably from a combination of hard work and a surfeit of strong drink; he received a state funeral. His daughter Thérèse is perhaps better-known than her father by virtue of her second marriage to the French revolutionary Jean Tallien.

Caffarelli du Falga, General Marie-François-Auguste (1766-1849) The younger brother of Napoleon's engineer general mortally wounded at Acre, his Peninsular service began at Saragossa in February 1810. He returned to Spain in September 1810, leading the 'Division of Reserve of the Army of Spain' and commanding in the regions of Biscay and Santander, and succeeded Dorsenne as commander of the Army of the North. Much troubled by guerrilla activity and amphibious landings on the north coast of Spain, he failed to assist Marmont as he had promised and was unable to prevent the capture of Santander. He did recover Bilbao, however (August 1812) and operated in pursuit of Wellington from Burgos, but was considered to lack energy and method, though his resources were insufficient for the task he had been set, and depleted by the need to provide garrisons. His inability to keep order in the Biscay region led to his replacement by Clausel in January 1813.

Canning, George (1770-1827) One of the great British statesmen of his generation, Canning was Foreign Secretary under Portland, from 25 March 1807 until 9 September 1809, during which time he gave early support to the nascent Spanish opposition to Napoleon. On 15 June 1808 he made a notable speech in the House of Commons in which he declared that any state opposed to Britain's enemy became Britain's ally, and that in aiding Spain, the British national interest was being served. This cemented Britain's involvement in the Peninsular War, but his own part ended in his resignation when his manoeuvering to succeed Portland and discredit Castlereagh failed (subsequently he was shot by Castlereagh in a duel). Apart from accepting a mission to Lisbon in 1812 - where he was going in the interests of the health of his eldest son - he remained out of government until 1816.

Carlos Maria Isidro, Don (1788-1855) The eldest brother of Ferdinand, Prince of the Asturias, in April 1808 he was sent by Ferdinand as his emissary to meet Napoleon at Bayonne. He was detained there with Ferdinand, and spent the war under virtual house arrest with his brother and uncle, Don Antonio, at Talleyrand's château at Valençay. A pious individual, he took little subsequent role in the governance of Spain until he asserted his claim to the throne after Ferdinand's death, which sparked the Carlist Wars; forced to flee from Spain in September 1839, he died at Trieste.

Castaños, General Francisco Xavier, Duque de Bailen (1756-1852) Probably the leading Spanish commander of the war, he gained the first great victory over the French by forcing Dupont to surrender his command at Bailen, which won for Castaños a great reputation and a dukedom. Subsequently he enjoyed less good fortune; defeated at the Tudela, he gave up command of the Army of the Centre, but in January 1810 saved the principal members of the Central Junta from a mob at Jerez, and on 29 January was named one of the five-man Regency, a position held until he was deposed with the others by the Cortes on 28 October of that year. In February 1811 he succeeded La Romana as Captain-General of Estremadura, and aided Beresford at Albuera. In 1812 Castaños was given command of the forces of Galicia and Castile as well, as advocated by Wellington, by whom he was trusted completely, though his military talents were considered limited. Some in the Spanish establishment mistrusted Anglophiles, as Castaños was perceived, one of the more absurd rumours suggesting that Castaños had offered to make Wellington king of Spain if he became a Roman Catholic (Wellington commented, 'What can de done with such libels and such people, excepting despise them, and continuing one's road without noticing them?'[1]). In June 1813 Castaños was replaced in command, ostensibly for not being at the head of his army (Fourth); this aroused Wellington's anger.

Calling the decision 'harsh and unjust', he praised Castaños's previous service and noted that it was his decision that Castaños be occupied elsewhere: 'we should have neglected our duty to the State if we had not chalked out for General Castaños the performance of those duties for which he is now punished and disgraced'[2]. Castaños was told that his recall was to enable him to take his seat in the Council of State, but it was plainly motivated by a desire of the Liberals to exclude pro-Royalists (Serviles) or moderates from positions of influence; after the war, however, Castaños served in a variety of significant posts.

[1] *Dispatches of Field-Marshal the Duke of Wellington*, ed. J. Gurwood, London 1834-38, Vol. XI p. 199.
[2] *Ibid.*, Vol. X p. 493.

Castiglione, duc de: see Augereau.

Castlereagh, Robert Stewart, Viscount (1769-1822) One of the foremost statesmen of the age, Robert Stewart adopted the title of Viscount Castlereagh when his father became Earl of Londonderry in August 1796, and thus was able to serve in the House of Commons. A stalwart supporter of the war against France, he advocated maintaining the British effort in the Peninsula, aided by Wellesley's positive assessment of the situation, when serving as Portland's secretary of state for war and the colonies. His reputation was undermined by the Walcheren expedition and his duel with Canning, and he resigned; but in March 1812 returned as foreign secretary, and led the House of Commons after Perceval was assassinated. His influence upon Liverpool's government, its determination to prosecute the war and to support the continuing struggle in the Peninsula, was immense, as Wellington acknowledged. Still serving as foreign secretary, suffering from fatigue and perhaps mental illness, he cut his throat in 1822. His half-brother was Charles Stewart, Wellington's adjutant-general.

Cavendish-Bentinck, Lieutenant-General Lord William Henry: see Bentinck.

Charles (Carlos) IV, King of Spain (1748-1819) One of the most ineffective of European monarchs, Charles IV was the second son of Charles III and succeeded him on account of the mental incapacity of his older brother, Don Philip. He possessed great physical strength but not an intellect to match; indeed, he has been described as dull-witted, good-natured but concerned primarily of the

dignity of his position, and ignorant of the true nature of the kingdom and those who manipulated him, notably his wife (and first cousin), Maria Luisa of Parma, and her 'favourite', Manuel Godoy. Charles was opposed to any form of liberalism and prevented any progression of Charles III's reforms, and was so blindly trustful of Godoy that both he and the queen took the minister's part against their own son and heir, Ferdinand. So inept a ruler was he that he had effectually abdicated all responsibility long before his official first abdication, in favour of Ferdinand, in March 1808, which decision he then withdrew and abdicated again in May in favour of Napoleon, which enabled Joseph Bonaparte to become king. Charles accepted a pension from Napoleon and lived the remainder of his life in exile, dying in Rome on 20 January 1819.

Chlopicki, General Jozef Gregorz (1771-1854) Probably the most prominent Polish officer to serve in the Peninsula, he came to prominence as colonel of the 1st Regt. of the Vistula Legion during the operations around Saragossa, defeating Palafox's relief-force at Epila on the night of 23-24 June 1808. Wounded in the assault on Saragossa on 4 August 1808, he became a *général de brigade* on 18 July 1809. He led a brigade under Suchet, and at Saguntum was detached with one of his regiments to join the flank-guard from Musnier's Division, and being senior to its brigadier, Louis-Benoît Robert, took command, and led the vital charge that won the battle. In January 1812 he was withdrawn from Spain for the Russian campaign, and is also noted for his service during the Polish rebellion of 1830-31, during which he was briefly in command of the Polish forces.

Clarke, General Henri-Jacques-Guillaume, duc de Feltre (1765-1818) A descendent from an English baronet, Clarke became Napoleon's war minister (in succession to Berthier) on 9 August 1807, and held the position until 3 April 1814. Although he never served in the Peninsula, he was the author of many of the dispatches sent from France to King Joseph and to commanders in the field, and so his name is found frequently in correspondence concerning the war in Spain. He was ennobled as duc de Feltre on 15 August 1809, and having accepted the Bourbon restoration, served as war minister 1815-17 and became a marshal in 1816.

Clary, Julie, Queen of Naples and Spain (1771-1845) Daughter of a prosperous Marseilles silk merchant, she married Joseph Bonaparte in 1794 and thus subsequently became Queen of Spain. She did not act as Joseph's consort, however, preferring to remain in France, and at times Joseph wrote to her asking that she intercede with Napoleon. Often her letters to Joseph were intercepted and delivered to Wellington; when they contained information that Wellington preferred Joseph not to know, he could not forward the actual documents, 'but as they also constantly referred to the health, which was rather delicate, of the two daughters, Princess Charlotte and Princess Zenaide, the Duke never failed to send a flag of truce to the French outposts with the tidings about the young ladies'[1], and as late as 1840 Joseph stated that he would never forget such kindness from an enemy.

[1] Stanhope, Earl, *Notes on Conversations with the Duke of Wellington*, London 1888, p. 225.

Clausel (or Clauzel), General Bertrand, comte (1772-1842) First serving in Spain under Junot, Clausel was one of only two divisional commanders retained upon Marmont's reorganisation of the Army of Portugal in 1811, in which he was appointed to lead the 2nd Division. At Salamanca he succeeded to command of the army after both Marmont and Bonnet were wounded; Clausel was also wounded, in the right foot, but not so seriously as to force him to retire. He conducted the retreat after the battle and retained command until replaced by Souham in early October 1812. After convalescent leave, he replaced Caffarelli as commander of the Army of the North in January 1813, but with insufficient resources for his task, was unable to join Joseph before Vittoria. He evaded Wellington's pursuit with some skill, and upon Soult's reorganisation was given command of the 'lieutenancy of the Left' and served in the Pyrenees with distinction. He was regarded as among the best of the second rank of French generals, Foy remarking that he always supported the boldest course of action, even if unwise (at Sorauren he was notably upset with Soult for going to sleep after lunch, instead of attacking immediately!). He became a marshal in 1831 but his career ended with his repulse at Constantine in 1836.

Clemencin, Diego (1765-1834) The experience of this noted scholar (probably best-known for historical works and a commentary on *Don Quixote*) shows how all aspects of life could be affected by the Peninsular War. In 1807 he became editor of the *Gaceta de Madrid* (Madrid Gazette) but had to flee to Cadiz in the following year after Murat condemned him to death for publishing an article not supportive of French rule; subsequently he was employed by the Central Junta. He was a minister in the liberal government 1820-23, and after a period in exile was restored to favour as royal librarian.

Clinton, Lieutenant-General Sir Henry (1771-1829) Son of General Sir Henry Clinton (1738?-95), he served as Moore's adjutant-general in the Corunna campaign, and was one of the first to defend Moore's reputation in print. Major-General from July 1810, he requested to return to the Peninsula and in February 1812 was given command of the 6th Division, which played a prominent role at Salamanca, for which in February 1813 he received the thanks of the House of Commons, of which he was a member (MP for Boroughbridge 1808-18). Absent in early 1813, he received the local rank of lieutenant-general that April, returned to the 6th Division briefly, just missed Vittoria and left again on health grounds in late July; but returned to serve at Nivelle, Nive, Orthes and Toulouse. Though a fairly reliable divisional commander, he was unsuited for higher authority, and was criticised by those under his command, notably for his insistence on formality and discipline; Sir George Bingham of the 53rd described him as 'one of the greatest fools I ever met with . . . he makes no allowance for weather, fatigue, or any other cause'[1].

[1] 'The Bingham Manuscripts', ed. T.H. McGuffie, *Journal of the Society for Army Historical Research*, Vol. XXVI (1948) p. 108.

Clinton, Lieutenant-General Sir William Henry (1769-1846) Elder brother of the foregoing, and a major-general from 1808 (lieutenant-general June 1813), he was sent by Bentinck to command at Alicante. His period in command was brief - in early December 1812 he was superseded by Campbell - but during that time caused trouble by taking command of the Alicante defences from the perfectly capable Spanish governor, much to Wellington's unease. He led a division at Castalla, was censorious of Murray's conduct at Tarragona, and in September 1813 was left in command on the east coast by Bentinck, who reported to Wellington that although there was no more honourable man, he was so fearful of responsibility and full of anxiety that he was unfit for the task, even Clinton requesting another be appointed in his stead. Wellington, however, left him in place, though Clinton was so fearful of Suchet that he declined to break up the Catalonian army as rapidly as Wellington requested. Subsequently he commanded British troops in Portugal 1826-28.

Colbert, General Auguste-François-Marie de (1777-1809) 'A very interesting man, one of the flower of the army on account of his fine figure, his courteous bearing, and his chivalrous courage'[1] according to Lejeune, he was one of the French Army's most famous light cavalry commanders. In Spain from 1808, he served at Medina del Rio Seco and Tudela, and from November commanded the cavalry of Ney's VI Corps (Ney stated that he always slept soundly when Colbert commanded his outposts). On 3 January 1809, rather unwisely he tried to charge the bridge at Cacabellos, and was killed by a shot through the head fired by the British sharpshooter Thomas Plunket of the 95th. Auguste de Colbert was the brother of two other French cavalry generals, Louis-Pierre-Alphone (1776-1843) and Edouard (1774-1853).

[1] Lejeune, L.F., *Memoirs of Baron Lejeune*, trans. Mrs. A Bell, London 1897, p. 115.

Colborne, Lieutenant-Colonel John (1778-1863)

Acknowledged as one of the finest regimental officers in the British Army, and an expert in light infantry service, Colborne was Moore's military secretary in the Corunna campaign, and as British attaché to the Spanish army was present at Ocaña. He commanded the 2/66th at Busaco and stepped up to command their brigade at Albuera, the disaster which befell it being caused by factors outside his control. In July 1811 he took command of the 52nd, one of the best regiments in the service and a mainstay of the Light Division, where his skills found full expression: Harry Smith thought these abilities superior to those of any other officer, to which Colborne added 'coolness and animation, under fire, no matter how hot'[1]. George Napier concurred, remarking that 'except the Duke of Wellington, I know no officer in the British Army his equal. His expansive mind is capable of grasping anything'[2]. Colborne was wounded severely at Ciudad Rodrigo by a shot near the shoulder joint, but though he could only move his right army from below the elbow he rejoined his regiment in July 1813, and from September 1813 led a brigade in the Light Division. At Waterloo he executed a vital manoeuvre that helped defeat the last French attack, and, ennobled as Baron Seaton in 1839, he became a field-marshal in 1860.

[1] Smith, Sir Harry, *The Autobiography of Sir Harry Smith 1787-1819*, ed. G.C. Moore Smith, London 1910, p. 130.
[2] Napier, Sir George, *Passages in the Early Military Life of General Sir George T. Napier*, ed. W.C.E. Napier. London 1884, p. 220.

Cole, Lieutenant-General Sir Galbraith Lowry (1772-1842)

Second son of the 1st Earl of Enniskillen, Lowry Cole was one of Wellington's most reliable divisional commanders. Major-General from 1808, he was appointed to lead the 4th Division in the Peninsula in October 1809, and remained in that position throughout the war, less a period from late 1811 to July 1812, and three months' convalescence following a wound through the body at Salamanca. Personally brave and with a temperament as 'hot as pepper' according to Harry Smith, he was reliable when following orders but somewhat uncertain when operating on his own: Colborne recalled him rather flustered at Orthes, and his most famous service, advancing without authorisation to save the day at Albuera, was only after prompting by Hardinge and others. Due to his concern for the ordinary soldiers, he was very popular; promoted to lieutenant-general with local rank in September 1811 (permanently in June 1813), he became a full general in 1830.

Colville, Major-General Charles (1770-1843) A younger son of the 8th Lord Colville of Culross, he was promoted to major-general in 1810 and was given a brigade command in the 3rd Division in the Peninsula in October of that year. Distinguished at El Bodon, he commanded the 4th Division in Cole's absence from December 1811. Wounded at Badajoz (shot through the thigh and losing part of a finger), upon his return from convalescence he commanded the 3rd Division January-May 1813 and at the Nivelle when Picton was absent, otherwise leading a brigade, until appointed to lead the 5th Division in December 1813. After Hope's capture he commanded the force that besieged Bayonne in 1814.

Conegliano, duc de: see Moncey.

Cotton, Admiral Sir Charles, Bt. (1753-1812) In his flagship HMS *Hibernia*, Cotton commanded the British squadron that cruised off the Tagus in 1808, watching the Russian squadron of Vice-Admiral Seniavin. In July 1808 Cotton sent a report urging British intervention in Portugal, which grossly under-estimated the number of French troops there; but it helped the government to decide to act. Jointly with Wellesley he signed the proclamation to the People of Portugal, dated 2 August 1808, which announced the British arrival; and he opposed the Convention of Cintra and repudiated the articles which bound the Royal Navy to treat with the French and allow the Russians to escape. Instead, he arranged a separate convention with Seniavin much more favourable to Britain, by which the crews were sent home but the ships held until six months after the conclusion of peace.

Cotton, Lieutenant-General Sir Stapleton, Bt. (1773-1865) Major-general from October 1805, Stapleton Cotton went to the Peninsula in 1808 as deputy to William Payne, the cavalry commander. Between April and June 1810 Cotton led the 1st Division, but on 3 June he succeeded to command of the cavalry, Payne having gone home with gout. Having succeeded to the family baronetcy in 1809, and becoming a lieutenant-general in January 1812, Cotton remained in command of Wellington's cavalry for the remainder of the war, less absences beginning with that of January-April 1811. Although Wellington stated that he was 'not exactly the person I should select to command an army'[1], equally he acknowledged that Cotton was his best cavalry commander, and praised him especially for his handling of the cavalry at Salamanca. On the night of that battle he was shot accidentally by a sentry whose challenge he failed to answer, returning to command in October 1812 but being invalided home in December, and not returning until June 1813. Upset at not having received a peerage (which he only attained in May 1814, Baron Combermere of Combermere, Cheshire), he delayed his return to the Peninsula and did so only on condition that he should not be expected to serve under Beresford, his junior in British service. He was advanced to a viscountcy after his capture of Bhurtpore in 1826, and became a field-marshal in 1865.

[1] *Dispatches of Field-Marshal the Duke of Wellington*, ed. J. Gurwood, London 1834-38, Vol. IX p. 279.

Cradock, General Sir John Francis (1762-1839) Recently withdrawn from his position as C-in-C at Madras after his insensitivity had contributed towards the incitement of the Vellore mutiny, in 1808 Cradock was appointed to command British forces in Portugal; he sailed in HMS *Lavinia*, which was returning the Galician deputies to Spain. He was never confident that Portugal could be held, and was both unenterprising and despondent, but still bitterly resented his supersession by Wellesley in April 1809. Cradock was then sent to Seville to confer with Frere, and served briefly as governor of Gibraltar. Subsequently he altered his name to 'Caradoc', and was granted an Irish peerage in 1819 and in 1831 the English barony of Howden and Grimston.

Craufurd, Brigadier-General James Catlin (1776-1810) Catlin Craufurd (as he was generally known) commanded a brigade under Wellesley at Vimeiro, and under Moore in the Corunna campaign, and returned to the Peninsula with Wellesley, his brigade being added to the 2nd Division in September 1809. He died in September 1810 from fatigue and the climate: 'he had given in difficult situations the fairest promise of talents as an officer; he was beloved by all those with whom he served; his zeal was ardent and continued, his humanity conspicuous. The whole tenour [sic] of his private life was most meritorious; his character discreet, sincere, and manly; his heart grateful and affectionate'[1]. His name is often mis-spelled, in contemporary sources and later, as 'Crawford' or 'Crawfurd'.

[1] *Gentleman's Magazine*, October 1810, p. 391.

Craufurd, Major-General Robert (1764-1812) 'Black Bob' Craufurd was one of the hardest and most competent of Peninsular War generals. Although an officer of great experience, and not without influence (he was a friend of William Windham and sat in Parliament himself), his promotion had been slow, perhaps on account of his temper and habit of speaking his mind. He held his light brigade together by sheer force of will during the retreat to Vigo, and returned to the Peninsula to lead Wellesley's light brigade, arriving just too late for Talavera after a legendary forced march. From February 1810 he led the Light Division with exemplary skill (despite causing Wellington some alarm by his unwillingness to retire at the Coa), and his abilities were fully recognised: with the exceptions of Hill and Beresford, to no other general did Wellington explain his orders, and even authorise to act on his own discretion, as he did with Craufurd. (Larpent claimed that once Wellington asked him, 'You are going into a delicate situation; what orders do you wish for? I will write what you think best'[1]). Craufurd's style of command involved draconian punishment and incurred unpopularity among some officers, but he was respected by all and trusted by the ordinary soldiers. Benjamin Harris's comments are familiar: 'He seemed an iron man; nothing daunted him - nothing turned him from his purpose. War was his very element, and toil and danger seemed to call forth only an increasing determination to surmount them'[2]. While directing the Light Division's stormers at Ciudad Rodrigo he was shot through the lungs and died four days later; his death was one of the most severe blows suffered by the Peninsular army. Londonderry commented that 'he was a man, to know whom in his profession without admiring was impossible . . . whilst the memory of the brave and skilful shall continue to be cherished by British soldiers, thou wilt not be forgotten'[3].

[1] Larpent, F.S., *The Private Journal of Judge-Advocate Larpent*, London 1854, p. 85.
[2] Harris, B.R., *The Recollections of Rifleman Harris*, ed. H. Curling, London 1970 edn. ed. C. Hibbert, p. 93.
[3] Londonderry, Marquess of, *Narrative of the Peninsular War*, London 1828, pp. 646-7.

Cuesta, General Don Gregorio Garcia de la (1740-1812) An experienced Spanish soldier who had first fought the French in 1793, at the beginning of the war Cuesta was Governor-General of Old Castile. Coerced to take up arms (by the erection of a gallows outside his house), he led his followers to disaster at Cabezon, insisted on taking precedence over the vastly more able Blake and was defeated at Medina de Rio Seco, and was obstructive towards rival generals and local administrations. Though once removed from command, he was given charge of the Estremaduran army and was defeated at Medellin; and in the Talavera campaign Wellesley found him an impossible ally. Although he never doubted the old man's courage (though noted he travelled in a six-horse coach, never reconnoitered and only mounted a horse for a battle), Wellesley found him 'as obstinate as any gentleman at the head of any army need be'; 'It is impossible for me to say what plans General Cuesta entertains' (though it was believed in the army that he was planning to depose the Central Junta!); 'I find General Cuesta more and more impracticable every day. It is impossible to do business with him, and very uncertain that any operation will succeed in which he has any concern'[1]. Consequently the British fought almost unaided at Talavera, Cuesta refusing to supply them or protect their wounded from capture, and if loud complaints about him were made by Spanish officers, those of the British were vitriolic. On 13 August 1809 Cuesta suffered a stroke and resigned his command to Francisco Eguia, and William Warre reflected a universal view: 'This obstinate surly old fellow is, thank God, removed. He was, to say the best of him, quite superannuated, and so violent and obstinate that everbody feared him but his enemies'[2].

[1] *Dispatches of Field-Marshal the Duke of Wellington*, ed. J. Gurwood, London 1834-38, Vol. IV pp. 430, 506, 526.

[2] Warre, W., *Letters from the Peninsula*, ed. Revd. E. Warre, London 1909, p. 74.

Dalhousie, Lieutenant-General Sir George Ramsay, 9th Earl of (1770-1838)

A major-general from 1808 (lieutenant-general June 1813), he joined the staff of the Peninsular army in September 1812, and on 25 October was appointed to lead the 7th Division. He was generally competent but at times disobedient, causing severe delays by failing to take the prescribed route both in the retreat from Burgos and Vittoria. After the Bidassoa he went home, but returned after Orthez, and was victorious at Etauliers, shortly before the surrender of the Bordeaux region.

Dalmatie (Dalmatia), duc de: see Soult.

Dalrymple, Lieutenant-General Sir Hew Whiteford (1750-1830)

Having been appointed governor of Gibraltar in 1806, he was appointed to command British forces in Portugal in 1808 partly because of his knowledge of Spain, and partly because he was more acceptable politically than Wellesley or Moore. Arriving just after Vimeiro, to replace Burrard in command, he was very over-cautious and from the outset seemed prejudiced against any opinions advanced by Wellesley, who declared that Dalrymple was ignorant of even the word 'plan', and that both he and Burrard were the stupidest and most incapable individuals he had ever met - harsh comments but justified, given the opportunity missed after Vimeiro. Dalrymple concluded the Convention of Cintra, and although not disciplined after the subsequent enquiry, for which he took leave of the Peninsula, he received no further employment. He became a full general in 1812 and upon petitioning for recompense for having been criticised, in 1814 was given a baronetcy.

Danzig, duc de: see Lefebvre.

Decaen, General Charles-Mathieu-Isidore, comte (1769-1832)

Probably best known for commanding in the French East Indian colonies, of which he had been appointed captain-general in 1802, Decaen had been permitted to return to France after the surrender of Ile-de-France (Mauritius) in 1810, and on 3 October 1811 was appointed to lead the Army of Catalonia in succession to Macdonald. In December 1811 he led the operation to relieve Barcelona, but the failure to attack Vich in July 1813 led to criticisms of irresolution, and in November 1813 he was recalled to France. In March 1814 he was appointed to lead the Army of Haute-Garonne, and as such concluded the armistice with Dalhousie in the following month.

Delaborde, General Henri-François (1764-1833) Having joined the French army as a private and risen from lieutenant to general in two years (1791-93), Delaborde entered Spain in October 1807 as a divisional commander under Junot. Governor of Lisbon from that December, he was the first French commander to engage the British in the Peninsula, being defeated at Roliça, though he fought a creditable rearguard action. He served at Vimeiro, with Soult's II Corps at Corunna, and in September 1809 was appointed to succeed Soult in command of the corps, but returned to France the following month. Subsequently he served throughout the campaigns of 1812-13 in Russia and Germany, and rallied to Napoleon in 1815.

D'Erlon, General Jean-Baptiste Drouet, comte (1765-1844) One of the most reliable French commanders of the war, d'Erlon's Peninsular service began in mid-1810, as commander of IX Corps, then under Massena in the Army of Portugal, including service at Fuentes de Oñoro. In April 1811 he was appointed to lead V Corps in Soult's Army of the South; commander of the Army of the Centre (October 1812) he replaced Souham in command of the Army of Portugal (November) and served at Vittoria. He was one of the lieutenant-generals in Soult's unified command, leading the 'Centre' from July 1813 until the end of the war, and commanding the

French left at the Nivelle and Nive. He rallied to Napoleon in 1815, when his ineffectual manoeuvering on 16 June tended to overshadow his previous good service; proscribed after the second Restoration, he only recovered his standing after the 1830 Revolution, and became a marshal in April 1843.

Dickson, Lieutenant-Colonel Sir Alexander (1777-1840) Although only a captain in the Royal Artillery (where promotion was dependent upon seniority), Dickson was able to hold the position of Wellington's chief of artillery from Vittoria onwards by virtue of his lieutenant-colonelcy in the Portuguese artillery. He had seen extensive Peninsular service before being selected by Wellington to command the artillery, a post in which all his predecessors had been found wanting; probably the most competent British gunnery commander of his generation, he was trusted completely by Wellington and accepted by his superiors in rank-precedence, and always wore his Portuguese uniform to avoid giving offence by emphasizing his low British rank. KCB in 1815, regimental precedence precluded his leading the artillery at Waterloo (he commanded the siege-train instead), and finally attained the rank of major-general.

Dorsenne, General Jean-Marie-Pierre-François Lepaige (1773-1812) One of the most celebrated officers of the Imperial Guard, and commander of the Grenadiers of the Old Guard, as a *général de division* (from June 1809), he went to Spain in April 1810 to command the Guard serving there; he was appointed governor of Burgos province in June, and Old Castile in December. In July 1811 he replaced Bessières as commander of the Army of the North, numerically a larger command than that of any of the marshals serving in Spain at the time. Though less capable than Bessières, 'le Beau Dorsenne' (as he was known) was more prepared to assist other commanders (for example helping Marmont relieve Ciudad Rodrigo), but in 1812 his command and responsibilities were reduced, and he declined to obey orders issued by Jourdan in the belief (or pretence) that he was not responsible to any central command. He returned to France in May 1812 and died on 24 July after a trepanning operation to treat an old wound, sustained at Essling.

Dubreton, General Jean-Louis (1773-1855) One of the most resourceful commanders of the war, and one of very few who could claim a success over Wellington, having commanded the 5th *Léger*, Dubreton was appointed a *général de brigade* in August 1811. Appointed commandant of Santander in November

1811, he defended the port against Popham and his Spanish allies (July 1812) until on the night of 2-3 August he broke out and led his garrison to safety. Almost immediately he was installed in an even more hazardous position, as commandant of Burgos; there he frustrated all Wellington's attempts to capture the place, demonstrating skill, quick decision and resolution, holding on for 35 days (and including five successful sorties) until Wellington withdrew. His superior Caffarelli commended the garrison but added that success had depended upon the devotion of the commandant, and as Belmas noted, it covered him with glory. In December 1812 he was deservedly promoted to *général de division*, and left Spain in the following month.

Duhesme, General Philibert Guillaume (1766-1815) Although a brave, experienced and capable divisional commander, Duhesme earned from himself a very bad reputation; for despite great physical presence and intelligence, he seems to have been motivated largely by self-interest. Commanding the Eastern Pyrenees Division he was among the first to cross into Spain (February 1808) and despite some success (two actions at Llobregat, June 1808) he failed abysmally to capture Gerona. As governor of Barcelona his regime was characterised by unbridled corruption, violence and looting; which, together with an unnecessary defeat at Granollers and Augereau's hostility, led to his dismissal. (Despite his cruel and rapacious conduct at Barcelona, Napoleon declined to discipline him lest it gave satisfaction to the Spanish!). Duhesme lived in well-merited disgrace until called back to service in December 1813, and was killed at Waterloo, exhibiting the bravery that formed the best part of his character.

Dupont de l'Etang, General Pierre (1765-1840) Perhaps the most notorious French commander of the war, Dupont was appointed to lead the 2nd Corps of Observation of the Gironde in November 1807. Victorious in the first real action of the war - Alcolea on 7 June 1808 - he met utter catastrophe at Bailen in July. Despite his difficulties - he had few seasoned troops - his surrender was such a humiliation that when permitted to return home (he arrived at Toulon in September) he was arrested. Napoleon was furious: 'Dupont has dishonoured our flag. What incapacity, what cowardice!'[1]. Though released from imprisonment after nine months, when the investigation cleared him of all charges except ineptitude, he was re-arrested in February 1812. A secret trial before a military commission found him not guilty of treason or cowardice, but Napoleon was not satisfied and

kept him confined until the end of the Empire; only after the Bourbon restoration
was he rehabilitated.

[1] *The Confidential Correspondence of Napoleon Bonaparte with his Brother Joseph*, London 1855, Vol. I
p. 343.

D'Urban, Major-General Benjamin (1777-1849) An experienced British
officer, D'Urban was selected by Beresford to be Quartermaster-General of the Portuguese Army; a colonel in British service, he was a Portuguese major-general, and
served throughout the Peninsular War from Busaco to Toulouse. At Medellin he
helped drag Cuesta to safety after he had been ridden over, and his principal personal
action was at Majalahona (11 August 1812) when he was lucky to survive: refusing to
emulate his bravery, his Portuguese cavalry broke off their advance and left him to
charge the French virtually alone. Lieutenant-General from 1837, he is best remembered for his service at the Cape (1834-38) as governor and C-in-C, where he gave his
name to the city of Durban.

Eblé, General Jean-Baptiste, baron (1758-1812) Known especially for
his contribution to saving the *Grande Armée* in 1812, by improvising pontoon
bridges over the river Berezina, Eblé also served with distinction in the Peninsula.
Artillery commandant of the Army of Portugal from April 1810, he served at the sieges
of Ciudad Rodrigo and Almeida, and (adumbrating his exploit at the Berezina) impro-
vised a pontoon train for Massena from wood and ironwork scavenged from houses
around Santarem, which in December 1810 he established at Punhete. He returned
to France in May 1811, commanded the pontoon train in the Russian campaign and
died of exertion at Königsberg on 31 December 1812. Acknowledged as a most
upright man, it was said that he once remarked that there were only two honest men
in the army, Latour-Maubourg and himself!

Elchingen, duc de: see Ney.

Erskine, Major-General Sir William, Bt. (1777-1813) Sir David Dundas (Commander-in-Chief 1809-11) entertained a high opinion of Erskine, and thus
he was sent to the Peninsula; Wellington queried the appointment on the grounds
that Erskine was believed to be insane. Henry Torrens (secretary to C-in-C)
responded by remarking that although he *was* a little mad, 'in his lucid intervals he
is an uncommonly clever fellow; and I trust he may have no fit during the campaign,

though he looked a little wild before he embarked'[1]. In February 1811 Erskine was appointed to command the 5th Division, then both the cavalry and the Light Division, and then the 2nd Cavalry Division. On a number of occasions he demonstrated incompetence, notably at Sabugal and in allowing the escape of the French from Almeida, and Wellington was duly critical. Erskine's mental instability seems to have been proven when in February 1813 he was killed by throwing himself from a window in Lisbon, 'in a fit of delirium'[2].

[1] Fortescue, Hon. Sir John, *History of the British Army*, London 1899-1920, Vol. VII p. 419.
[2] *Gentleman's Magazine* June 1813, p. 595.

Escoiquiz, Juan (1762-1820)

Escoiquiz, Juan (1762-1820) Son of a Spanish general and a page at the court of Charles III, Escoiquiz entered the church and became tutor to Ferdinand, Prince of the Asturias. He encouraged Ferdinand's opposition to Godoy, but was sent from court (to be canon of Toledo) when his intriguing became known; he maintained his contact with Ferdinand and was a major influence in the 'Escorial conspiracy' when Ferdinand attempted to enlist Napoleon's help against the king. Escoiquiz was arrested over the affair, but released, and remained a major influence on, and a trusted confidant of Ferdinand, supporting him in his trip to meet Napoleon at Bayonne and negotiating in an attempt to secure Ferdinand's position as king. He accompanied Ferdinand in exile at Valençay (when he worked on literary endeavours, including a translation of *Paradise Lost*), and returned to Spain with Ferdinand, who subsequently lost confidence in him, and he died in internal exile.

Espoz y Mina, General Francisco (1781-1836)

Espoz y Mina, General Francisco (1781-1836) One of the greatest guerrilla leaders, Francisco Espoz Ilundain came from yeoman stock in Navarre, joined the guerrilla band of his nephew, Xavier Mina, and succeeded to its command after Mina's capture in 1810, commemorating him by changing his name to Espoz y Mina. Operating principally in Navarre and Aragon, he ranged into the provinces of Biscay, Soria and Burgos, his force up to 3,000 strong, and collaborating with other leaders, for example with Longa and Porlier in the Burgos area in 1811, and with Longa, 'El Pastor' and Home Popham along the Biscayan coast in 1812. His operations were considerably effective (at one point he boasted that no fewer than six French generals were chasing him), and when defeated always rallied and returned to the fray; among his successes were the defeat of Abbé near Pamplona early in 1812, and the annihilation of two battalions at Lerin in March 1813. He earned Wellington's trust, proved most useful in the Pyrenees and even raided into France;

his force became regularly organised and financed by a levy he imposed upon goods entering Spain. By espousing the liberal cause he was forced into exile more than once after the war, and it was during his exile in London that he wrote his memoirs (published 1825).

Essling, Prince de: see Massena.

España, General Carlos d'Espignac (1775-1839) One of the best-known Spanish commanders, he was a French royalist who had emigrated to Britain during the French Revolution. Entering Spanish service in 1792, he led a brigade under La Romana, and his brigade was the only infantry from Castaños's army present at Albuera. His failure to hold Alba de Tormes had serious consequences after Salamanca, not least in his failure to inform Wellington; but was made governor of Madrid and was zealous in apprehending supporters of the French. With his Castilian division he took command of the blockade of Pamplona, and was wounded leading a charge against a sally on 9 September, characteristic of the reckless courage he often exhibited. It was to España that Wellington sent his authorisation for the draconian punishment of the garrison had Cassan carried out his threat to blow up the place, and few would have doubted his willingness to comply had the occasion arisen. Subsequently he served at the blockade of Bayonne. After the war he was invited to return to France, but he declared that all his French blood had been shed while fighting for Spain. Subsequently he fought against his erstwhile 'liberal' colleagues in defence of the king, and while governor of Catalonia became known for the brutality of his repression of those who opposed the king. After such a career it is perhaps not surprising that he was finally thrown into a river with a millstone around his neck by mutinous troops.

Ferdinand (Fernando) VII, King of Spain, Prince of the Asturias (1784-1833) Napoleon stated that although King Charles IV and his queen were 'the objects of the hatred and contempt of their subjects', their son Ferdinand, Prince of the Asturias and heir to the throne of Spain, 'united in his own person the love and hopes of the nation'[1]. That was true: during the Peninsular War Ferdinand represented the legitimate kingship of Spain to both ultra-royalists and liberals, though it was unfortunate that he was not more worthy of that hope and trust. Between him and his parents there existed mutual hatred, and in October 1807 Ferdinand sought Napoleon's help; he was arrested when the correspondence was discovered and duly betrayed his fellow-conspiritors, but became king when Charles was forced to abdicate. When Charles withdrew his abdication and assigned disposal of the throne to Napoleon, Ferdinand acceded to his own deposition. For the course of the war he was kept under house arrest - with his brother Don Carlos and uncle Don Antonio - at Talleyrand's château of Valençay, amusing himself with such intellectual pursuits as cutting out paper patterns. Napoleon stated that it appeared as if Ferdinand did not wish to escape: 'he spontaneously wrote me letters of congratulation upon every event that occurred in my favour. He had addressed proclamations to the Spaniards recommending their submission . . . a son could not write more cordially to his father'[2]. Late in 1813 Ferdinand agreed to the Treaty of Valençay which would have restored him to his throne, but with every intention of repudiating it, even if it had been ratified by the Cortes. When he finally did return to Spain the war was all but over, and his determination to rule as an absolute monarch plunged the country into another round of bloodshed, the resulting civil war only being resolved by the intervention of another French army. Even in his chosen succession, favouring his daughter over his brother, Ferdinand was the cause of even more conflict.

[1] Las Cases, E.A.D.M.J., *Memoirs of the Life, Exile and Conversations of the Emperor Napoleon*, London 1834, Vol. II p. 292.

[2] *Ibid.*, Vol. II pp. 293-94.

Fletcher, Lieutenant-Colonel Sir Richard, Bt. (1768-1813)

One of the most distinguished engineers of the war, Fletcher served as Wellington's chief engineer from 1809. He was the recipient of Wellington's letter of 20 October 1809, which set out the essentials of the lines of Torres Vedras, of which Fletcher was a principal designer. He conducted the three great British sieges of the war, Ciudad Rodrigo, Badajoz and San Sebastian, and continued to supervise the work at Badajoz even when incapacitated by a wound received during the French sortie of 19 March 1812, when a musket-ball drove a dollar from his purse into his thigh. Wellington recognised and praised his talents, and when Fletcher was killed by a shot through the spine at the storm of San Sebastian his loss was felt keenly.

Floridablanca, José Monino y Redondo, conde de (1728-1808)

Having achieved great distinction as Charles III's chief minister, Floridablanca fell from grace under Charles IV, in part due to the opposition of the Queen. After some years of eclipse he emerged in 1808 as a guide to the Murcian junta, of which he was a member, and it was under his influence that the junta issued a proclamation in favour of a central government, and when that was formed he was one of the representatives for Murcia (the other being the Marquis del Villar). When the Supreme Junta convened on 25 September 1808, Floridablanca was elected president (being its most distinguished statesman), but his health was broken, and he died on 20 November.

Fournier, General François, comte (1773-1827) One of the most flamboyant of French light cavalry leaders, Fournier was also one of the most unpleasant, in trouble more than once for political intrigue and for shirking his duty; Lejeune described him as 'a noted duellist and bully, the terror of all peaceable men'[1]. He led a brigade in Lorges's dragoon division in autumn 1808, served in the Corunna campaign and was blockaded by Portuguese forces when holding Lugo, from where he was relieved by Soult on 22 May 1809. Later in the year he was relieved of command, but in September 1810 was appointed to lead the cavalry of IX Corps, served in the Army of Portugal under Massena, but his transfer in late 1811 to the Army of Aragon was prevented by ill-health, and he returned to France at the end of the year.

[1] Lejeune, L.F., *Memoirs of Baron Lejeune*, trans. Mrs. A. Bell, London 1897, Vol. II p. 289.

Foy, General Maximilien-Sébastien, comte (1775-1825) Marked by Napoleon as one of the next generation of marshals, Foy was one of the most able divisional commanders. He served in the early Peninsular War, commanding the artillery reserve at Vimeiro, where he was wounded. *Général de brigade* from November 1808, he led a brigade under Delaborde at Corunna; captured at Oporto in March 1809, he was almost lynched, being mistaken for Loison, saving himself by holding up two hands to prove that he was not the hated one-armed general. Wounded seriously at Busaco, he was sent by Massena to explain to Napoleon the position of the army outside the lines of Torres Vedras, and at the conclusion of the interview was promoted to *général de division*. Leading the 1st Division of the Army of Portugal, he served at Salamanca, and while covering the retreat his command was severely battered at Garcia Hernandez on the following day. He commanded the 1st Division under Reille in the Pyrenees with distinction, and was wounded by a shrapnel-ball in the shoulder at Orthez. After service at Waterloo he entered politics, where his honesty and sincerity were recognised universally, but this career, and the writing of his history of the Peninsular War, were curtailed by his early death from a heart complaint. A curious story concerned his sending for English newspapers while outside the lines of Torres Vedras; Wellington enquired the reason, and was told that Foy was anxious to check his investments in British government stock. Wellington permitted the transmission of this information to continue, but not the remainder of the papers, lest they prove a source of information to the enemy.

Freire (or Freyre), General Manuel (1765-1834) The early experience of this Spanish general in the Peninsular War was as a cavalry commander - he was defeated in the largest cavalry fight of the war near Ocaña on 18 November 1809, and at Alcala de Real in January 1810 - but later that year he took command of the Army of Murcia from Blake, until replaced by Mahy in autumn 1811. In autumn 1813 he replaced Giron in command of the Army of Galicia, with which he won the action at San Marcial (Wellington deliberately withholding British assistance to prove to the Spanish that they could win unaided). At the invasion of France Wellington sent Freire's troops away, fearing their looting would antagonise the population, and wrote a sharp letter to Freire on the subject; but they were brought up for the blockade of Bayonne, and they fought with courage at Toulouse, Freire bravely leading from the front.

Freire de Andrade, General Bernardino (1764-1809) An experienced officer who had fought the French in the Roussillon campaign of 1793, he was given command of the Portuguese forces in 1808, although incapable of holding so important a post. He refused to co-operate with Wellesley, so that the British were virtually unsupported in their first campaign, and complained that he was not consulted over the Convention of Cintra, though he had done nothing to oppose the French. Faced with them in March 1809 he showed timidity when his army assembled at Braga, which led to open mutiny when they thought him insufficiently aggressive. Freire fled but was apprehended and committed to Braga gaol, and command given to his deputy, Baron Eben. It was suspected that Eben had not done his utmost to prevent what then occurred: Freire was dragged from the prison and piked to death by a mob of militiamen, 'raging, like savage beasts' according to Napier[1]. The ease with which his ill-disciplined troops were defeated subsequently, however, makes Freire's timidity seem less unreasonable.

[1] Napier, W.F.P., *History of the War in the Peninsula*, London 1828-40, Vol. I p. 187.

Frere, John Hookham (1769-1846) A friend of Canning and MP (for West Looe, 1796-1802), Frere held a number of posts in the British diplomatic service, including envoy to Lisbon (1800) and Madrid (1802-04). It was as plenipotentiary to the Spanish Central Junta that his influence was felt upon the Peninsular war, his romantic zeal in supporting the 'patriots' bringing him into conflict with Moore, whom he tried to undermine by sending a secret letter for consideration by Moore's subordinates. His comments must have had some effect upon Moore's decision to advance into Spain, and although this had a positive effect in drawing away Napoleon's forces, Frere surely exceeded his authority. Subsequently he pressed the claims of his friend Albuquerque, and urged that Wellesley be made generalissimo, neither of which were particularly popular with parts of the Spanish establishment. He was replaced as minister by Marquess Wellesley and undertook no further diplomatic duties, spending the rest of his life in literary pursuits.

Freyre de Andrade, General Gomez (1764-1817) One of the best-known Portuguese generals, he was born in Vienna, where his father was Portuguese ambassador, and spent his early military service in Portuguese, Russian and Prussian service. A Portuguese lieutenant-general in 1807, he sided with the French after the invasion of Portugal, and from August 1808 was a French *général de division*. At the first siege of Saragossa he commanded Verdier's 2nd Division (two of his brigades being weak Portuguese units), and commanded the Portuguese troops with Junot in late 1808. With the Portuguese Legion in 1809, for the rest of the war his career was spent away from the Peninsula (he was taken prisoner at Dresden), but after the war returned to Portugal and was shot for complicity in the military revolt at Lisbon.

Gazan, General Honoré Theodore Maxime, comte de La Peyrière (1765-1845) Distinguished in earlier campaigns, notably at Durren-stein, he entered the Peninsula as a divisional commander under Mortier in autumn 1808, and became comte de La Peyrière (from his family property in Provence) in November 1808. He commanded the 2nd Division of V Corps at the second siege of Saragossa, and won the action at Villanueva de los Castillejos against Ballesteros in January 1811. In the following month he was wounded at Badajoz, and again at Albuera when leading his division in the great attack on 'the heights'. In January 1813 he succeeded Soult as commander of the Army of the South, and was justifiably criticised by Jourdan for retiring without orders at Vittoria, leaving other French formations in difficulty. (His wife was captured by the British on this occasion: she was entertained by them and Wellington sent her back to her husband in her own carriage). In July 1813 Gazan was appointed as chief of staff to Soult, in which capacity he signed the armistice on 17 April 1814.

Girard, General Jean-Baptiste, baron (1775-1815) Girard went to Spain in September 1808 with a brigade of V Corps, in which he led the 1st Division April-September 1809 in a provisional capacity, and at Ocaña (where he was wounded), before he was confirmed in command in December. He defeated La Romana at Villagarcia (11 August 1810) and led V Corps at Albuera, but is best-remembered for his surprise and defeat by Hill at Arroyo dos Molinos. Shortly afterwards he was appointed as governor of Seville and commander of the reserve division of the Army of the Centre, but in some disgrace after his late defeat was recalled to France at the end of 1811, leaving Spain in February 1812. He was mortally wounded at Ligny.

Giron, General Pedro Agostin (1788-1842) One of the best-known Spanish commanders, he was Castaños's nephew, and is sometimes referred to by his later title, Duque de Ahumada. Subordinate to Venegas in 1809, he commanded against Sébastiani at Aranjuez and led Venegas's reserve at Almonacid, but his most significant service was as commander of Fourth Army in 1813, when he collaborated closely with Wellington, who had requested him, knowing his abilities. With his uncle, Giron was removed from command shortly after Tolosa by the Regency, much to Wellington's disgust (he reported that Giron had been dismissed 'without trial or even cause assigned, from a situation in which he had been placed by General Castaños by my desire, and in which he had conducted himself entirely to my satisfaction, as I had already reported to Government'[1]). Giron instead took command of the Andalusian Army of Reserve in the place of Henry O'Donnell, which he led for the remainder of the war.

[1] *Dispatches of Field Marshal the Duke of Wellington*, ed. J. Gurwood, London 1834-38, Vol. X pp. 493-94.

Godoy, Alvarez de Faria, Rois Sanchez y Zaragoza, Manuel de, duque de Alcudia, Prince of the Peace (1767-1851) Although removed from the scene almost before the war had begun, Godoy was a major factor in its origin. From a family of minor aristocracy and not without talent, he became the 'favourite' of Queen Maria Luisa, wife of Charles IV (none of the rumours concerning their relationship were proven beyond question). With her support he came to dominate both the king and Spanish national policy, though was unfit for the positions he held, including prime minister 1792-98 until removed as a consequence of French opposition. For his role in negotiating the Peace of Basle in 1795 he was given the title 'Prince of the Peace' (sometimes rendered as 'Prince of Peace' though the definitive article should strictly be present: Principe de la Paz) and previously had been ennobled as duque de Alcudia. Hugely ambitious, he became extremely rich through royal favours and frauds, and his reputation was undermined by a profligate lifestyle; but though his policies helped ruin national finances, he did attempt to institute some reforms. He returned to office in 1801 and pursued the disastrous alliance with France, and when Napoleon exploited the hostility between the king and his heir Ferdinand, so highly regarded was Godoy that the king and queen took his part against that of their own son. Godoy was finally driven from office by the popular rising at Aranjuez in March 1808; arrested upon the instigation of Ferdinand, Napoleon had him released, and he accompanied Charles IV into exile; he lived in considerable poverty thereafter and died in Paris.

Gordon, Colonel James Willoughby (1773-1851) Selected by the Duke of York to be Wellington's Quartermaster-General in 1812, in the place of the invaluable George Murray, Gordon was sent to the Peninsula without prior consultation with Wellington. He proved not only incapable but sent despondent letters, containing confidential information, to his friends in the government's political opposition, which found its way into the popular press. This most reprehensible conduct was discovered by Wellington, who reported it to Bathurst, and declared that Gordon should no longer see his reports. Wellington indicated that he was incapable of doing his duty, and he was recalled, but not punished; a very ambitious man with an inflated idea of his own abilities, subsequently he became a general, baronet, and MP for Launceston.

Gouvion St. Cyr, General Laurent, comte (1764-1830) Known as 'le hibou' ('the owl') from his aloof, morose and unsociable behaviour, Gouvion St. Cyr served relatively briefly in Spain, but unlike many of his colleagues, he was 'everywhere accounted, and especially in Spain, an honourable and upright man, who scorned to violate the humanities of civilized warfare'[1]. He was not popular with Napoleon (believing that soldiers should not be involved in politics, he had declined to sign a proclamation supporting Napoleon's elevation to emperor), but was sent to Spain in 1808 as commander of the Army of Catalonia. Though unwilling to co-operate with others - he despised looters like Massena - he was a very able commander; Marbot stated that he knew no general more skilled at handling troops, and that 'It was impossible to find a calmer man; the greatest danger, disappointments, successes, defeats, were alike unable to move him. In the presence of every sort of contingency he was like ice'[2]. He had some successes in Spain, including the capture of Rosas and relief of Barcelona, but was unco-operative with Verdier in the operation which failed to take Gerona, and then absented himself on the grounds of ill-health before his successor, Augereau, had arrived, a dereliction of duty which led to temporary disgrace. He was re-employed in the Russian campaign of 1812 and there won his marshal's baton.

[1] Anon., *The Court and Camp of Bonaparte*, London 1831, p. 270.
[2] Marbot, J.B.A.M., *The Memoirs of Baron de Marbot*, trans. A.J. Butler, London 1913.

Goya y Lucientes, Francisco (1746-1821) One of the greatest of Spanish artists, he was appointed principal painter to the Spanish court in 1786; but never attempted to glamourise the subjects of his portraits, which are staggeringly truthful. For most of the Peninsular War he lived in Madrid (though for a period as Saragossa, where he had been brought up), and was confirmed as court painter to Joseph Bonaparte. He executed portraits of some of the leading personalities of the war, from the royal family to Wellington; and more notably, his 82 etchings 'The Disasters of War' are the most horribly realistic images of the inhumanities of war ever portrayed, and still have the capacity to shock. In 1814 he painted two historical works showing the Madrid uprising of 1808 and its suppression, 'The Second of May 1808 at the Puerta del Sol' and 'The Firing Squad: The Third of May 1808', which are among his most famous works. Despite having worked for Joseph, Goya kept his position as court painter after Ferdinand's return, though was not patronised to the same degree as before, and as a liberal left Spain following the renewed French invasion; he died at Bordeaux.

Graham, Lieutenant-General Sir Thomas (1748-1843) A Scottish country gentleman, Thomas Graham of Balgowan had no military aspirations until French troops desecrated the coffin of his wife, being taken home to Scotland, in their search for contraband. This fired him with a hatred for French republicanism; at his own expense he raised the 90th Foot, and accompanied his friend Moore to the Peninsula as a volunteer aide. He attained his first regular rank as major-general after Corunna, and as lieutenant-general was sent to command British forces at Cadiz. There he won his great victory of Barossa, but criticism of his Spanish allies was so great as to preclude his further service there, and he transferred to Wellington's army. He led the 1st Division from August 1811 until he went home in July 1812 for treatment on an eye, returning in 1813 virtually as Wellington's second-in-command. He led the left wing of Wellington's army, executed the vital flanking movement at Vittoria, and commanded at San Sebastian. He retired in 1814 after less success in the Netherlands, was ennobled as Baron Lynedoch, and became a general in 1821. If not the greatest strategist, he was renowned and admired throughout the army as a brave and honest man, and genuinely adored by all ranks.

Grant, Major Colquhoun (1780-1829) The most outstanding intelligence officer of his generation, Grant was a captain in the 11th Foot (not until May 1814 did he attain the rank of lieutenant-colonel), but was one of the most valuable of Wellington's assets. The best of the 'observing officers', he roamed behind French lines and via a network of agents transmitted vital intelligence to headquarters. His knowledge of Spain and its dialects was unrivalled, and Wellington declared him worth a brigade. In April 1812 he was betrayed and captured at Idanha Nova near the Portuguese-Spanish border, but escaped at Bayonne, gathered intelligence in France and returned home in a fishing boat. He should not be confused with another Colquhoun Grant (c. 1764-1835), who led the 15th Hussars in the Corunna campaign and in the Peninsula again from April 1813; he led the 'hussar brigade' April-June 1813 and a light dragoon brigade September-November 1813.

Hardinge, Lieutenant-Colonel Henry (1785-1856) Later a distinguished governor-general of India, field-marshal, viscount and commander-in-chief (1852-56), Hardinge served in the Peninsula as a staff officer. At Vimeiro he was wounded as deputy assistant quartermaster general; he was ADC to Moore at Corunna, and as a Portuguese lieutenant-colonel was deputy quartermaster general at Albuera. It was there that he, among others, urged Lowry Cole to make his crucial advance, without orders, that saved the day; as Cole admitted, 'the merit of originating the movement rests with you, but the credit for having incurred the responsibility is mine'[1]. Hardinge continued in the Portuguese army and was severely wounded at Vittoria; as British commissioner to the Prussian army in 1815, he lost his left hand at Ligny.

[1] *United Service Journal* 1840, Vol. III p. 248.

Harispe, General Jean-Isidore, comte (1768-1855) Harispe served as chief-of-staff to the Corps of Observation of the Ocean Coasts, to Murat in 1808, and to III Corps until promotion to *général de division* in October 1810. He succeeded Laval in command of the 2nd Division of III Corps in October 1811; he was wounded by a shell at Tarragona, served prominently at Benaguasil (1 October 1811) and defeated Mijares at Yecla (11 April 1813). In December 1813 he transferred to lead the 8th Division under Soult, in the hope that he could inspire support from the inhabitants of his native Basque region. He served at Orthez under Clausel, at Tarbes, and had a foot shot off by a roundshot at Toulouse, where he was captured. He became a marshal in December 1851.

Harris, Benjamin Randall (1781-1858) The memoir of 'Rifleman Harris' is one of the most famous Peninsular War accounts, even if the book were dictated to, and edited by, Lieutenant Henry Curling. A private soldier in the British 95th Rifles, Harris served in the Corunna campaign and left a most memorable account; and although it has been suggested that he may have been illiterate, he had letters published in the *United Service Journal* under his own name. After his discharge he took up the occupation he had followed in the army, running a shoemaking shop in Soho; he died in a workhouse in Westminster.

Hay, Major-General Andrew (1762-1814) Notable mainly for his death in action, Hay commanded the 1/1st Foot in the Corunna campaign, and led a brigade in the 5th Division from September 1810, becoming a major-general in June 1811. Absent for the second half of 1812, he commanded the division in the first three months of 1813 and at the Bidassoa. Another brigadier, Frederick Robinson, described him as 'a fool and I verily believe . . . an arrant Coward. That he is a paltry, plundering old wretch is established beyond doubt'[1], but Hay was killed in the sortie from Bayonne, attempting to hold the church in the village of St. Etienne. His eldest son, Captain George Hay of the 1st Foot, was killed as his ADC at Vittoria.

[1] quoted in *Journal of the Society for Historical Research*, Vol. XXXIV (1956), p. 168.

Hill, Lieutenant-General Sir Rowland (1772-1842) For much of the Peninsular War Rowland Hill filled the position of Wellington's second-in-command, even if not officially thus nominated. He led brigades in the Corunna campaign and at Vimeiro, and from June 1809 commanded the 2nd Division, including the exercise of a considerable degree of independence when operating in Estremadura. His skill as a divisional commander was proven, for example, at Arroyo dos Molinos and Almaraz; it was from the latter victory that Hill received the title of his barony, of Almaraz and Hawkestone, Shropshire, on 17 May 1814. In March 1813 Stewart took command of the 2nd Division, under Hill's direction, Hill becoming virtually a corps commander, leading the army's right wing at Vittoria and after. He was distinguished especially at the Nive and Nivelle, and Wellington declared that St. Pierre was his victory alone. Although he never enjoyed complete independence of command, he did have Wellington's complete trust; the Duke remarked that nothing ever interrupted the 'friendly and intimate relations which subsisted between us'[1], and the level of trust is shown by a letter of May 1810, which Wellington began, 'I am convinced that whatever you decide on will be right'[2]. Colborne recalled that the victory of Busaco 'was gained solely in consequence of Hill's precise attention to Wellington's orders, for which he was always remarkable, so much so, that the Duke once remarked to me, "The best of Hill is that I always know where to find him"'[3] Hill was renowned for his kindness and concern for those under his command, and was nicknamed 'Daddy' by the ordinary soldiers. Subsequently he became a viscount and commander-in-chief of the British Army.

[1] Griffiths, A.J., *The Wellington Memorial*, London 1897, p. 295.
[2] *Dispatches of Field-Marshal the Duke of Wellington*, ed. J. Gurwood, London 1834-38, Vol. VI p. 124.
[3] Moore Smith, G.C., *The Life of John Colborne, Field-Marshal Lord Seaton*, London 1903, p. 140.

Hope, Lieutenant-General Sir John (1765-1823)

Hope led one of Moore's columns in the advance into Spain, and succeeded to command of the army at Corunna. From October 1813 he was back in the Peninsula as commander of the 1st Division, and replaced Graham as leader of the army's left wing. His reckless bravery, as demonstrated at Nive, led Wellington to remark: 'I have long entertained the highest opinion of Sir John Hope . . . we shall lose him, however, if he continues to expose himself in fire as he did in the last three days; indeed his escape was then wonderful. His hat and coat were shot through in many places, beside the wound in the legs . . .'[1]. Wellington was right: Hope was wounded and captured during the sortie from Bayonne. He succeeded his half-brother as 4th Earl of Hopetoun in May 1817 and became a full general in 1819. He should not be confused with Major-General Sir John Hope (1765-1836), who led the 7th Division from May to September 1812, including Salamanca. He was so unimpressive that when he complained of rheumatism Wellington took the opportunity to order him to go home for a cure.

[1] *Dispatches of Field-Marshal the Duke of Wellington*, ed. J. Gurwood, London 1834-38, Vol. XI p. 371.

Hugo, General Joseph-Léopold-Sigisbert (1773-1828) One of Joseph Bonaparte's closest aides, Hugo had been his ADC in Naples and followed him to Spain, running the royal household, serving as governor of Avila and later Guadalajara, and commanding the infantry of the Royal Guard. He served in a number of actions (he was ennobled as Count of Siguenza after an engagement against El Empecinado on 6 July 1810), in 1811 was Jourdan's chief of staff, and accompanied Joseph at Vittoria. He returned to French service in September 1813, becoming a general in 1814, as he had been in the Spanish Army. He is best known as the father of the French literary celebrity Victor Hugo, who spent part of his childhood with his father in Spain.

Inglis, Major-General William (1764-1833) One of the iconic figures of the Peninsular War, he had become lieutenant-colonel of the 57th Foot in 1804 and led the 1st Battalion in the Peninsula, commanding a brigade of the 2nd Division at Busaco. His fame was achieved at Albuera by his call to his men, when lying injured, to 'Die hard, 57th, die hard!'. One of the most famous of all battlefield exhortations, it was used to inspire succeeding generations of his regiment, and was the origin of the nickname 'Diehards' accorded to the Middlesex Regiment (formed by the amalgamation of the 57th and 77th Foot in 1881). Inglis continued to serve in the Peninsula and became a major-general on 4 June 1813.

John (João), Prince of Brazil, Regent of Portugal (1769-1826) Prince John of Portugal, who held the title 'Prince of Brazil' from 1788, was the second son of Queen Maria I, and had assumed the governance of the country in 1792 after his mother had become insane following the deaths of her husband and eldest son; he was officially titled as Regent in 1799. Although somewhat weak and indecisive, he had the great problem of preserving Portuguese integrity from the combined pressures of France and Spain, while maintaining friendly relations with a traditional ally, Britain. He attempted to placate Napoleon without succumbing entirely to the Continental System, while assuring the British that he was acting under compulsion; this could never have been satisfactory to Napoleon, who declared the House of Braganza deposed, whereupon John took the entire royal family, court and much of the national treasury to Brazil, leaving the country to be governed by a Council of Regency (he beat Junot's entry into Lisbon by a single day, 29-30 November 1807). For the remainder of the war he remained in Brazil, hardly interfering except for drawing money from Portugal (when the wealth of Brazil was at his disposal); his wife, the Spanish princess Carlotta, interfered via her supporters in the Cortes, but was discouraged from making a claim in person to be Regent of Spain during the absence of her brother Ferdinand. John remained in Portugal even after his accession as King John VI in 1816, returning to Portugal only after the 1820 revolution had established a constitutional monarchy.

Jones, Lieutenant-Colonel John Thomas (1783-1843) As a captain in the Royal Engineers, he went to Spain in 1808 as assistant British commissioner to the Spanish armies; in the Corunna campaign he served first as Leith's ADC and then as an engineer. He returned in spring 1810 as chief engineer in Portugal and worked on the lines of Torres Vedras, of which he wrote a valuable account; he performed much of the engineering work at Badajoz after Fletcher's injury, but was wounded severely at Burgos by a shot through the ankle. He was an invalid for eighteen months, during which time he wrote his *Journals of the Sieges undertaken by the Allies in Spain* (1814), a leading work on the subject.

Jourdan, Marshal Jean-Baptiste, comte (1762-1833) One of the most experienced of Napoleon's marshals, he had been Joseph Bonaparte's advisor at Naples and followed him to Spain as chief of staff. He had great difficulties of lack of co-operation by other marshals, and was blamed, somewhat unfairly, for the defeat at Talavera; he returned home on health grounds before he could be recalled. He was back in the Peninsula in 1811 with the relatively lowly role of governor of Madrid (July), and from October as Joseph's chief of staff and commander of the Army of the Centre. Not until March 1812 was he appointed chief of general staff over all the French forces in the Peninsula, but the old problems of non-co-operation remained, his advice was ignored, and when he was defeated (with Joseph) at Vittoria he was again made a scapegoat, and in July 1813 left his command under a cloud. Subsequently Napoleon recognised how badly he had been treated, and praised Jourdan for maintaining his honour and showing no resentment despite all his tribulations.

Jovellanos, Gaspar Melchor de (1742-1811) Statesman, author and economist, Jovellanos had held ministerial office in Spain but had become disillusioned with Godoy and had been imprisoned in Majorca in 1801. A proponent of enlightened absolutism rather than of the more radical form of liberalism, with a reputation for wisdom and patriotism, he refused Joseph Bonaparte's offer of employment (who wished him to be minister of the interior) and instead joined the patriot party, joining the Central Junta as one of two members for the Asturias (the other being the Marquis of Campo Sagrado). He became the leader of the supporters of his principles after the death of Floridablanca; helped reorganise the Cortes but was involved in the fall of the Junta, whose defence he undertook. In 1811 he returned to his native Gijon, but had to leave upon the approach of the French; bad weather forced the ship in which he was sailing to put into Vega, where he died (27 November 1811).

Junot, General Jean-Andoche, duc d'Abrantes (1771-1813) One of Napoleon's earliest comrades, he had served as ambassador to Portugal and as commander of the Army of Observation of the Gironde led the first French army into Portugal, of which he was appointed governor-general (1 February 1808) and ennobled as duc d'Abrantes. Defeated at Vimeiro, he returned to France under the terms of the Convention of Cintra, but later in the year replaced Moncey in command of III Corps. He commanded briefly at Saragossa (where only with difficulty was he dissuaded from ordering a suicidal assault intended to bring him personal glory before he could be superseded, Lejeune suggesting signs of mental instability), and in mid-1809 he was posted to Germany. He returned again as commander of VIII Corps of Massena's Army of Portugal (which formed the reserve at Busaco), and in January 1809 was shot in the nose in a skirmish at Rio Mayor. After Fuentes de Oñoro he was recalled to France, receiving no further field command after performing badly in Russia in 1812, his abilities having declined notably since his successful march through Spain in 1807. His dissolute lifestyle was probably the ultimate cause of his death in July 1813 after leaping from a window in his father's house, where he had been sent in a state of derangement.

Kellermann, General François-Etienne, comte (1770-1835) Son of Marshal François-Christophe Kellermann, duc de Valmy, he went to the Peninsula with an illustrious reputation as a cavalry commander, notably for making a vital charge at Marengo. He commanded Junot's cavalry in 1807-08 and negotiated the Convention of Cintra. On his return he led the Army of Reserve and VI Corps temporarily (1809), accompanied Ney in his operation in the Asturias, defeated Del Parque at Alba de Tormes and in June 1810 was appointed governor of the provinces of Valladolid, Toro and Palencia. He gained a reputation for ferocity and unrestrained looting, and ferocity. Unwilling to co-operate with King Joseph, he treated his governorship as a kind of viceroyalty, his officials having to take an oath of allegiance to

Napoleon, as if the Kingdom of Spain did not exist. In September 1810 he was appointed commander of the Army of the North but returned to France on sick leave in 1811. Aymar de Gonneville described him as 'a little man, of unhealthy and insignificant appearance, with a clever look, but false', and stated that the church he constructed as an act of piety near his home in France was, like the house, 'very likely . . . the result of exactions committed in Spain'[1]. He was, though, one of Napoleon's best cavalry generals.

[1] Gonneville, A. de, *Recollections of Colonel de Gonneville*, ed. C.M. Yonge, London 1875, Vol. I pp. 250-1.

Kruse, Colonel August von (1779-1848) Born at Wiesbaden in Nassau, Kruse began his military career in the Hanoverian guards, but transferred to Nassau service in 1803. He led the 2nd Nassau Regiment in the Peninsula, and (as colonel from December 1808) led the brigade in which they served following the invaliding home of its original commander, Conrad von Schäffer. In December 1813 Kruse received news from the Duke of Nassau that the state had left the Confederation of the Rhine (*Rhein-bund*) and joined the Allies, so on 10 December Kruse led three battalions (two of the 2nd Nassau and the Frankfurt Battalion) out of the French lines and defected to the British, where they were welcomed readily. Wellington reported that Kruse 'appears to me to have conducted himself with great judgment, decision, and firmness, in the whole of the delicate transaction'[1], and had acted entirely upon his sovereign's instructions; indeed, to defend his honour he even wrote to Soult to explain, and to emphasize that so long as his sovereign had been with the French, he had done his duty. Kruse became a major-general in August 1814 and served with the Allies at Waterloo.

[1] *Dispatches of Field-Marshal the Duke of Wellington*, ed. J. Gurwood, London 1834-38, Vol. XI p. 360.

La Bispal (or Abispal), conde de: see O'Donnell.

Lallemand, General François-Antoine, baron (1774-1839) One of the lesser French cavalry commanders, Lallemand went to Spain in September 1808 as commander of the 20th Dragoons, went home to recover his health after a year, returned in January 1810 and became *général de brigade* in August 1811, commanding a cavalry brigade in the Army of the Centre from November 1811 until recalled to France in February 1813. His fame rests upon his victory at Maguilla in June 1812, where his maintenance of a reserve overturned the British cavalry of the incompetent Slade.

Lannes, Marshal Jean, duc de Montebello (1769-1809) One of Napoleon's few real friends and most capable subordinates, Lannes went to Spain in 1808 and on 18 November was given command of Moncey's III Corps, the cavalry and half the infantry from Ney's VI Corps, and a dragoon division from the cavalry reserve, with which he defeated Castaños at the Tudela on 23 November. Still suffering from an earlier fall from his horse, Lannes left this command on 2 December, but on 20 December was appointed to lead the besieging forces at Saragossa. Following his convalescence, he arrived in mid-January 1809 and took overall command of III and V Corps, and brought the siege to a satisfactory conclusion. Leaving Saragossa in late March, he was called to lead a corps in the war against Austria, and was mortally wounded at Essling on 22 May.

La Peyrière, comte de: see Gazan.

Lapisse, General Pierre Bellon, baron de Sainte-Hélène (1762-1809) He went to the Peninsula in September 1808 as commander of the 2nd Division of Victor's I Corps, and is probably best remembered for executing the decisive attack at Espinosa. Sent to subdue southern Leon and then advance into Portugal, he had insufficient resources and behaved with some timidity; retiring to re-join Victor, he took Alcantara and committed great brutality during the sacking of the town. He was mortally wounded at Talavera.

La Romana, General Pedro Caro y Sureda, Marquis of (1761-1811) The Spanish general perhaps most esteemed by his British allies, he had commanded the Spanish expeditionary force in French service in Denmark and northern Germany, and was instrumental in its defection, evacuation in British ships, and landing in Spain to help the fight against Napoleon. Late in 1808 he took command of the Army of Galicia, collaborating with Moore, and pursued the war with vigour if not much skill. When he found the Oviedo junta unco-operative in April 1809, he dismissed them and appointed his own, an example of his political manoeuvering which cannot have assisted the patriot cause. Early in 1810 he joined the Seville junta and was named commander of the Army of the Left; commanding in Estremadura he was defeated at Villa Garcia in August 1810, and in October joined Wellington in the lines of Torres Vedras. Although involved in some intrigue, he remained a committed patriot, and must have been stung by libels against him, published in Cadiz, which may even have hastened his death, which occurred on 23 January 1813, apparently of an aneurism of the heart. Though Wellington had little opinion of La Romana's military skills, he found him 'a good-natured excellent man' of knowledge and intelligence, and his public statement was probably heartfelt: that 'the Spanish Army has lost their brightest ornament, his country their most upright patriot, and the world the most strenuous and zealous defender of the cause in which we are engaged'[1].

[1] *Dispatches of Field-Marshal the Duke of Wellington*, ed. J. Gurwood, London 1834-38, Vol. VII p. 190.

Lasalle, General Antoine-Charles-Louis, comte (1775-1809) Per-
haps the finest of Napoleon's light cavalry leaders, whose flamboyant behaviour and rough manners were thought to be part of the hussar ethos yet concealed a supremely professional commander, in February 1808 Lasalle was appointed to a divisional command under Bessières. He served with distinction at Torquemade, Cabezon, Medina de Rio Seco and notably at Medellin, but was recalled in March 1809 and left in the following month, to take up a command against Austria; he was killed leading a charge at Wagram.

Latour-Maubourg, General Marie-Victor-Nicolas de Fay, vicomte de (1768-1850) This aristocratic French cavalry general went to Spain in late 1808 leading the 1st Dragoon Division. He served at Medellin, Talavera and Ocaña, and captured Albuquerque in March 1811, but although a reliable divisional commander, when Mortier's departure later in that month left him in command on the Guadiana, he was undistinguished in the enhanced role. He is probably most famous for the devastating charge made by elements of his cavalry at Albuera, and in August 1811 mauled the retiring Murcian army at Las Vertientes, but in March 1812 he was recalled to France to lead a corps in the Russian campaign.

Lefebvre, Marshal François-Joseph, duc de Danzig (1755-1820)
A brave but very unpolished, plain-spoken officer, Lefebvre went to the Peninsula following command at the siege of Danzig, from where he took the title of his dukedom (September 1808). In the same month he took command of IV Corps in Spain, his first experience of real independent command. He defeated Blake at Zornoza (or Durango) and Valmaceda, and had a hand in the victory of Espinosa, but caused Napoleon dissatisfaction by not following orders. In January 1809 the Emperor complained that he 'commits nothing but follies; he cannot read his instructions. It is impossible to intrust him with the command of a corps, which is a pity, as he shows

great bravery on the field of battle'[1], and in that month was relieved of his command. He should not be confused with his son, General Marie-Xavier-Joseph Lefebvre, comte de Danzig (1785-1812), who served on the staff of the Army of Portugal in 1810 and died as a consequence of the Russian campaign; nor with General Simon Lefebvre (1768-1822), who was wounded commanding a brigade of Mermet's division at Corunna, and served in Catalonia 1810-14.

[1] *The Confidential Correspondence of Napoleon Bonaparte with his Brother Joseph*, London 1855, Vol. II p. 11.

Lefebvre-Desnouettes, Charles, comte (1773-1822)

One of Napoleon's most favoured generals (he was married to Napoleon's second cousin), he served as Bessières's chief of staff from March 1808, initiated the siege of Saragossa but in late August 1808 was recalled to France. Later in the year he returned to Spain at the head of the Chasseurs à Cheval of the Imperial Guard (of which he was colonel), served at the Tudela and Somosierra but made an injudicious advance at Benavente and his command was handled severely by Moore's cavalry. He was wounded and captured, traditionally by Corporal Levi Grisdale of the 10th Hussars, although apparently Johann Bergmann of the 3rd Hussars of the King's German Legion also had a hand in the capture. Lefebvre-Desnouettes was sent on parole as a prisoner to Cheltenham, but escaped in 1812 and resumed his military career; after the fall of Napoleon he fled France under sentence of death, and upon receiving a pardon was drowned when his ship sank off Ireland when returning from exile in America.

Leith, Lieutenant-General Sir James (1763-1816)

One of the most reliable of Wellington's subordinates, as a major-general from April 1808 he led a brigade in Hope's Division in the Corunna campaign, and in 1810 was the first commander of the newly-organised 5th Division. He served at Busaco but was absent for most of 1811; he was wounded at Salamanca and went home again, returning as a lieutenant-general on 30 August 1813. On the following day he suffered a broken arm and severe contusions to the breast while conducting the attack on San Sebastian.

Lejeune, Colonel Louis-François, baron (1776-1848)

Renowned as one of the outstanding battle painters of the period, Lejeune was also a trained engineer and staff officer. He served at Somosierra and at the siege of Saragossa (where he was wounded), and returned to Spain in 1810 to gather information on behalf of Napoleon. Near Toledo in April 1811 he was wounded and captured by the guerrillas of El Medico, and almost hanged; but was transferred to British custody. He stayed as a prisoner near Portsmouth and at Ashby de la Zouche. He escaped and returned to France at the end of July 1811. He became a general in 1812, and his memoirs provide a valuable record of service in important positions of the staff, and of experiences while a prisoner in Spain.

Le Marchant, Major-General John Gaspard (1766-1812) Le Marchant was one of the British Army's most intelligent and progressive officers, who had realised the need for reforms as a consequence of observing the failings in the Netherlands. He was responsible for the re-designed cavalry sabres of 1796 pattern, and the army's instructional manual on swordsmanship; and his plan for the education of officers led to the establishment of the schools at High Wycombe and Marlow, which were the foundation of the academy at Sandhurst. Le Marchant was in control himself from 1799 until his promotion to major-general in June 1811, from that August commanding a brigade of heavy cavalry in the Peninsula. Acknowledged as an excellent theorist, it was thought that he would have become a cavalry general of the first rank, but having led a decisive charge at Salamanca he was killed by a shot through the body while harrying some retreating French infantry (demonstrating bravery as well as ability, he had engaged in hand-to-hand combat and was probably unduly conspicuous by wearing, for reasons of economy, his old blue uniform of the 7th Light Dragoons, which contrasted fatally with the red of his brigade). Although his career was thus curtailed, his importance as an educator and reformer was of great significance.

Liverpool, Robert Banks Jenkinson, 2nd Earl of (1770-1828) After a long political career, and after inheriting his father's peerage in 1808, in 1809 he was appointed secretary for war and the colonies by Perceval. A noted supporter of Wellington, the army and British presence in the Peninsula, he became prime minister following Perceval's murder in May 1812, and under his superintendence Britain continued to pursue the war until Napoleon was defeated. He remained in office until he retired for reasons of ill-health in 1827, and during the Peninsular War, as Lord Warden of the Cinque ports, was himself colonel of the Cinque Ports Local Militia (formed 1808).

Loison, General Louis-Henri (1771-1816) Known as 'Maneta' - 'one-arm' - to the Portuguese, Loison was disliked by his own side and detested by his enemies, becoming one of the most reviled personalities of the war by virtue of his appalling conduct. He commanded the 2nd Division under Junot in 1807, won the victory of

Evora and sacked that city with dreadful brutality, and led his division at Vimeiro. After the Cintra repatriation he returned to lead the 2nd Division of VIII Corps under Junot, and in January 1809 became governor of Leon. He served under Soult, whom he hated and may have suspected of treason at the time of the Argenton plot, while Soult regarded Loison with equal distaste. From January 1810 he commanded the 3rd Division of Ney's VI Corps, which he led at Busaco, and in March 1811 took command of the corps in place of Ney. He led it at Fuentes de Oñoro, where he was blamed for the casualties incurred by the Hanoverian Legion, refusing them permission to wear their greatcoats, and thus their red jackets caused them to be mistaken for British and to be attacked by their own side. Immediately after the battle Loison was sent back to France as Marmont reorganised his army; the remainder of his service was in Germany and eastern Europe.

Longa, General Francisco (1770-1831) One of the guerrilla leaders whose commands were transformed into valuable elements of the regular forces, Longa led his irregulars in the Cantabrian region until they took on the organisation of regular troops; he was commissioned a colonel in the regular army and by 1813 his troops had become so proficient as to overshadow Porlier's reputation. They fitted in to the regular organisation of the allied forces, serving with Graham at Vittoria, where they were especially praised. Longa's men served well at Tolosa; he captured the French garrison of Passages, and served at San Marcial and at the Nivelle, but the disciplinary record of his troops was such that Wellington dare not let them participate in the invasion of France.

Lowry Cole, Galbraith: see Cole.

Lumley, Major-General Hon. William (1769-1850) Seventh son of the 4th Earl of Scarborough and a major-general from 1805, he was sent to the Peninsula upon the recommendation of Sir Henry Bunbury, although Torrens stated that 'I never thought him a clever man, but he is zealous, active, obedient, and brave as a lion'[1], if only suited to lead a brigade. On 30 September 1810 he was given command of Catlin Craufurd's old brigade of the 2nd Division, but at Albuera it was led by the senior battalion-commander, while Lumley commanded the cavalry, with considerable skill. He had even greater success at Usagre, a notable victory, but in August 1811 he went home ill, ending his Peninsular service.

[1] Fortescue, Hon. Sir John, *History of the British Army*, London 1899-1920, Vol. VII p. 419.

Lynedoch, Baron: see Graham.

Macdonald, Marshal Jacques-Etienne-Joseph-Alexandre, duc de Tarente (1765-1840) The son of a Jacobite exile from South Uist, Macdonald had fallen from favour in the wake of the accusations against Moreau in 1803, and was re-employed by Napoleon only out of necessity in 1809, when he won his marshal's bâton at Wagram and his dukedom of Taranto. In April 1810 he was named as commander of the Army of Catalonia in place of Augereau; it was not a command he relished, and indeed he made some critical remarks about the nature of the war being waged in Spain. He won a small engagement at Cervera (5 September) but elements of his command suffered a reverse at Valls. Although Figueras was taken, in October 1811 he was recalled to France, having enjoyed little more success in Catalonia than his predecessors.

McGrigor, Sir James (1771-1858) Described by Wellington as one of the most able, industrious and successful public servants that he had ever known, McGrigor was one of the great medical practitioners of his generation. Appointed Inspector-General of the Medical Department in August 1809, from January 1811 he served as head of the Medical Department with Wellington's army. Energetic and a great moderniser, he made much progress in the treatment of the injured, most notably in the evacuation of casualties and by the introduction of prefabricated, portable hospitals. Although Wellington gave him a severe admonition for diverting commissariat resources without authority after Salamanca, the Duke never doubted his abilities or commitment. McGrigor was knighted in 1814 and made many important reforms as Director-General of the Medical Department from 1815 to 1851.

Marbot, Major Jean-Baptiste-Antoine-Marcellin (1782-1854) Perhaps the most famous of all French military memorialists of the Napoleonic Wars (though his memoirs have been criticised for accuracy in places), he first went to Spain as ADC to Murat, witnessing the uprising of 2 May, but left the Peninsula in the following month. He returned on Lannes's staff, was wounded by a slug fired from a blunderbuss at Saragossa, and went home with Lannes. Finally he served on Massena's staff, leaving a graphic account of the friction between the Marshal and his subordinates, and leaving the Peninsula in mid-1811 when Massena was recalled. His career formed the inspiration for Sir Arthur Conan Doyle's 'Brigadier Gerard'.

111

Marchand, General Jean-Gabriel, comte (1765-1851) One of the best of Napoleon's divisional commanders, he led the 1st Division of Ney's VI Corps in Spain in 1808; from that September he commanded the corps in Ney's absence, and on 18 October 1809 was defeated by Del Parque at Tamames. Reverting to his divisional command in December, he led it at Busaco, commanded the rearguard of Massena's retreat in March 1811, and with VI Corps under Loison, fought at Fuentes de Oñoro. Shortly after he left Spain and led a division under his old chief, Ney, in the Russian campaign of 1812.

Marmont, Marshal Auguste-Frédéric-Louis Viesse de, duc de Raguse (1774-1852) The youngest marshal to serve in the Peninsula, Marmont was an early companion of Napoleon's. Having been responsible for major reforms in the artillery, he had served as governor-general of Dalmatia (hence his title), and (largely as a consequence of his friendship with Napoleon) in July 1809 was appointed as a marshal. In April 1811 he was given command of VI Corps in the Peninsula, in place of Ney, and on 7 May of the same year succeeded Massena as commander of the Army of Portugal. He was popular with his men, who admired his ostentation, and was an excellent organiser and not a bad strategist, but on the battlefield seemed to lack resolution, and probably over-estimated his own talent. Wellington commented upon his military weakness: 'Marmont was a great tactician. Very clever in handling his troops; but he was too theatrical. It was *Pas en avant! Pas en arrière!* And while he was manoeuvering he lost his opportunities, and I caught him'[1]. At Salamanca he was wounded severely in the right arm by the explosion of a shell quite early in the battle, and took no further part in the Peninsular War. (Later he asked Wellington at what point he had decided to attack; 'As soon as I perceived the extension of your left' said the Duke. Characteristically Marmont replied, 'Ah, that was after I was wounded'[2], though it was his own actions which had lost the day). Having surrendered his corps in 1814 and permitted the Allies to enter Paris, he was ever after regarded as a traitor by the French.

[1] Bunbury, Sir Henry, *Memoirs and Literary Remains of Lieutenant-General Sir Henry Edward Bunbury*, Bt., ed. Sir Charles Bunbury, London 1868, p. 295.

[2] Ellesmere, Earl of, *Personal Reminiscences of the Duke of Wellington*, London 1904, p. 127.

Massena, Marshal André, duc de Rivoli, prince d'Essling (1758-1817) One of the finest of Napoleon's marshals - Wellington regarded him as 'the ablest after Napoleon'[1] - Massena had reached the high point of his career before he ever entered the Peninsula. At Aspern-Essling (May 1809) his spirit and leadership had proved inspirational, and it was for this that he received his princely title in January 1810. In April 1810 he was appointed to lead the Army of Portugal, though by that time he was past his peak. Although an insatiable plunderer, at times he displayed a lack of energy, appeared distracted by his mistress (who accompanied his headquarters dressed as an officer), and enjoyed poisonous relations with some of his senior subordinates. (His aide Marbot, for example, recalled a luncheon party which ended with Ney and Junot, and to a lesser extent Reynier and Montbrun, expressing their displeasure in the most unmistakable terms). In September 1810 he was defeated at Busaco, and was compelled to withdraw from Portugal by the impenetrable nature of the lines of Torres Vedras. His retreat was followed by further defeat at Fuentes de Oñoro (May 1811), and he was replaced by Marmont, although the decision to supersede him had been made in mid-April, before his last defeat. It was the end of his active career, and so disappointed was Napoleon that upon his first audience after Massena's recall, he remarked that the Prince of Essling was no longer Massena. That was harsh: Wellington was more realistic, remarking that of all his opponents, 'I found him oftenest where I wished him not to be'[2], and that when opposed to Massena he had to be perpetually in a state of alert.

[1] Stanhope, Earl, *Notes on Conversations with the Duke of Wellington*, London 1888, p. 20.
[2] Bunbury, Sir Henry, *Memoirs and Literary Remains of Lieutenant-General Sir Henry Edward Bunbury, Bt.*, ed. Sir Charles Bunbury, London 1868, p. 295.

Matarossa, vizconde de: see Toreno.

Maucune, General Antoine-Louis Popon, baron de (1772-1824)

From March 1807 Maucune led a brigade in VI Corps, including its service in Spain; he suffered a broken thigh in action at Santiago in May 1809, was shot in the right thigh at Busaco and in the right heel and groin at Fuentes de Oñoro. In May 1811 he was promoted to *général de division* and given command of the 5th Division of the Army of Portugal, which he led at Salamanca. Though a tough fighter, he was somewhat rash and in June 1813 was surprised and roughly handled at San Milan, and in July 1813 led the 7th Division under Reille. In October Soult held him negligent in failing to prevent the crossing of the Bidassoa - not entirely his fault - but he was removed from command, though soon received employment with the Army of Italy.

Milhaud, General Edouard-Jean-Baptiste, comte (1766-1833) A friend of Marat and a member of the most extreme faction within the National Convention (he voted for the death of Louis XVI), Milhaud became a noted cavalry leader. From September 1808 his dragoon division joined the French forces in Spain, served at Talavera and made a vital charge at Oçana. His greatest success was the defeat of Blake at Baza in October 1810, accomplished with his own division, some Polish lancers and a small force of infantry, which was hardly involved. He left Spain in mid-1811.

Mina y Larrea, Xavier (1789-1817) Xavier Mina achieved almost legendary status as one of the early guerrilla leaders, based in Navarre and Aragon. Not only one of the most skilled, he achieved fame when one of the youngest guerrilla commanders, hence his nicknames 'El Mozo' ('the Youth') and 'El Estudiante' ('the Student'). His command undertook major operations but would disperse when pressed, then reassemble, in classic guerrilla mode; but on 31 March 1810 he was trapped between two French forces, to be imprisoned at Vincennes until 1814. His forces were rallied by his uncle, Francisco Espoz Ilundain, who took the name Mina to capitalise upon its fame, and achieved even greater successes. As a supporter of constitutional government, Xavier Mina had to leave Spain, and was shot as a rebel when he tried to raise a revolt in Mexico.

Miot de Melito, André François, comte (1762-1841) Having occupied important posts in Napoleon's diplomatic service, he was a close friend of Joseph Bonaparte, had served as his interior minister in Naples, and moved to Spain as head of Joseph's household. As such he was a close observer of events; like Joseph, he was almost captured in the flight from Vittoria, when the arrival of a cavalry detachment under General Jean-Baptiste-Auguste-Marie Jamin, Miot's son-in-law and commander of the cavalry of Joseph's guard, helped them to escape. He recorded the story of how on the evening of the battle Jourdan joined their supper, remarking that they *would* have a battle, and now had lost it!. Consequently, Miot is best remembered for the memoirs he wrote in retirement, having been created comte de Melito in 1814.

Moncey, Marshal Bon-Adrien-Jeannot de, duc de Conegliano (1754-1842) One of Napoleon's lesser-known, but most honest and honourable marshals, Moncey went to Spain in 1808 (where he had campaigned 1794-95). Initially he commanded the Corps of Observation of the Ocean Coast, and in June 1808 was repelled when he attempted to attack Valencia. Ennobled as duc de Conegliano in the following month, in September he took command of III Corps. He won a minor victory at Lerin in October, but was subordinated to Lannes at the Tudela, and having commenced the siege of Saragossa, was replaced by Junot in command of his corps on 2 January 1809. Thereafter he held only commands in the reserve, until the last days of the Empire when he led the defence of the Clichy Gate at Paris. Never a favourite with Napoleon, he was recalled from Spain partly as a consequence of his fairly unimpressive record in command, and perhaps partly because of the consideration he showed his enemies, unlike the conduct of some other French commanders. Even his enemies praised him: Palafox, who declined his generous terms of surrender at Saragossa, remarked that his wisdom and character were exemplified by his name 'Bon', while the junta of Oviedo remarked that 'We know that this illustrious general detests the conduct of his companions', and that even if 'the respect which he pays to the mandates of nature' did not permit him to change sides and assist the Spanish 'against his unworthy companions, yet he shall be considered by us as a just and honourable man, and our love and esteem shall follow him'[1], a remarkable tribute to an honourable foe.

[1] *The Court and Camp of Bonaparte*, London 1831, p. 332.

Montbrun, General Louis-Pierre, comte (1770-1812) Commander of the cavalry of the French I Corps in September 1808, he was relieved of duty for overstaying a leave of absence (to protect his wife-to-be); but given the chance to redeem himself by Bessières, he was distinguished leading the Polish Chevau-Légers in their attack at Somosierra. After the war against Austria, he returned to the Peninsula as cavalry commander of the Army of Portugal, and was one of those subordinates who were hostile to Massena. He was distinguished at El Bodon, but in January 1812 failed to capture Alicante; Marbot blamed him for being so anxious to distinguish himself in independent command that he fatally diverted resources from the relief of Ciudad Rodrigo, though it would be unfair to blame that city's fall upon Montbrun. In the same month he was recalled to France, and was killed leading II Cavalry Corps at Borodino.

Montebello, duc de: see Lannes.

Moore, Lieutenant-General Sir John (1761-1809) A near legend in the British Army, Moore was the most famous British soldier of his generation after Wellington, though is remembered as much as a theorist as a field commander. A thoughtful, experienced soldier, he was responsible to a considerable degree for the formulation of light infantry tactics, upon which he worked while commanding at Shorncliffe; though not a complete innovator, he developed theories already expressed by others such as de Rottenberg, and added an intellectual dimension, which marked him as one of the founders of 'modern' infantry tactics. His influence was immense, and he was revered by those who knew him; as George Napier commented, they regarded him as 'a model for everything that marks the obedient soldier, the persevering, firm, and skilful general; the inflexible and real patriot who sacrified all personal feeling to his country's weal; the truly virtuous and honourable man; the high-minded, finished, and accomplished gentleman'[1]. Like Wellington, Moore had political affiliations, though his were in the Whig interest, and cannot have aided his career. He was sent to the Peninsula as deputy to Burrard and Dalrymple (he ignored this slight to one who had already held independent command) and after Cintra succeeded to command of the British forces. He advanced into Spain in what became the Corunna campaign, and by so doing deflected Napoleon's attention from crushing the Spanish military, though compelling his own army, in his own words, to 'run for it'. His fighting retreat to Corunna led to the evacuation of the army but to his own death, dreadfully injured by a roundshot which struck his shoulder during the Battle of Corunna. Initially he received some posthumous criticism for his conduct of the campaign - William Napier originally commenced his great history to vindicate Moore's reputation - but his situation had been very difficult, and the attempts by political opponents to damage his reputation were ultimately unsuccessful.

[1] Napier, Sir George, *Passages in the Early Military Life of General Sir George T. Napier*, ed. W.C.E. Napier, London 1884, pp. 77-8.

Morillo, General Pablo, conde de Cartagena (1778-1837)

Although best known for commanding a division under Wellington, he had served at St. Vincent, Trafalgar and Bailen. In the later Peninsular war he led flying columns under Castaños's direction, including a remarkable march in La Mancha (December 1811-January 1812) during which he captured Ciudad Real. His troops were the first to make contact with the enemy at Vittoria (where Morillo was wounded), and in subsequent operations under Wellington they served with some distinction. His division was the only one retained by Wellington after the other Spanish forces were sent back to Spain to prevent them looting in France, though even Morillo had to be reminded sharply to look to the discipline of his command. In the final stage of the war he was left to invest the fortress of Navarrenx, which was quite a loss to the field army.

Mortier, Marshal Edouard-Adolphe-Casimir-Joseph, duc de Trévise (1768-1835) Napoleon's half-English marshal was one of the few of his rank who left the Peninsula without having suffered a serious reverse. Commanding V Corps in October 1808, he assisted in the siege of Saragossa; he permitted Cuesta to get away after Talavera, but received a note from Wellington which thanked him for his kindness shown to the enemy wounded who had fallen into his hands. At Oçana he was slightly wounded in the arm, in January 1810 he participated in the invasion of Andalusia, in that September he won a small victory at Fuente Cantos over La Romana's rearguard; he participated in the siege of Badajoz and made a major contribution to the victory of the Gebora. In March 1811 he captured Campo Mayor, but in the following month was recalled to France. After a distinguished career he was killed by the terrorist Fieschi's explosive device when attending a review with Louis-Philippe on 28 July 1835.

Murat, Marshal Joachim, Grand Duke of Berg (1767-1815) One of the greatest cavalry leaders, and probably the most flamboyant personality of the age, Napoleon's old comrade and brother-in-law served in the Peninsula for only a short period. On 20 February 1808 he was appointed 'Lieutenant of the Emperor' and commander of all French forces in Spain, but his service there was as much diplomatic as military, in the dealings which led to the removal of the existing monarchy. On 2 May 1808 he was appointed 'Lieutenant-General of the Kingdom' and on the same day had to suppress the Madrid insurrection, which was accomplished without mercy. Unwell for some time, Murat vacated his post on 15 June 1808 and, having hinted that he might himself be an appropriate new king for Spain, was actually appointed King of Naples on 15 July 1808, in succession to Joseph Bonaparte, who took the Spanish crown. Murat's kingship ended in October 1815 with his execution by firing-squad when attempting to re-possess his kingdom.

Murray, Major-General Sir George (1772-1846) A very professional staff officer, Murray went to the Peninsula as quartermaster-general with Burrard, held the same post in Moore's army, and as a colonel from March 1809 was the same under Wellesley, with whom he had served in Denmark. His influence increased as the war progressed and he became one of Wellington's most valuable subordinates, but following a broken collar-bone sustained by falling when hunting, in December 1811 he took home leave; promotion to local rank of major-general earlier that month may also have increased his desire for a more active command. He was so missed, however, that pleas for him to return led to him reassuming his duties as quartermaster-general in March 1813, and for the remainder of the war he proved invaluable as virtual chief of staff, undertaking much important business (including campaign planning) that Wellington, with increasing responsibilities, could no longer do himself. After Waterloo he was appointed chief of staff to Wellington as commander of the allied occupation forces in France, and became a full general in 1841.

Murray, Lieutenant-General Sir John, Bt. (1768?-1827) One of the least effective Peninsular War generals, he led a brigade of King's German Legion in the Oporto campaign, declining to take a risk when he had the opportunity to cut off, or at least severely harass, the retreating French army. Following this unimpressive performance he left the army rather than take orders from Beresford, his junior in terms of British rank. In February 1813 he succeeded James Campbell in command of the Anglo-Sicilian expedition on the east coast of Spain, though quite unsuited for the task. Despite success at Castalla, he prevaricated and was timid; his hesitant attempt on Tarragona was a miserable failure, and he abandoned 18 siege-guns in his haste to get away, which Wellington condemned: 'not only does he think he was wrong in so doing, but he writes of it as being rather meritorious'[1]. Superseded by Bentinck's arrival, he was court-martialled in 1814 but acquitted on all charges save abandoning his guns, for which he was reprimanded; that he had abandoned his Spanish ally Copons was not mentioned. He should not be confused with his namesake, John Murray, Wellington's Commissary-General 1809-10.

[1] *Dispatches of Field-Marshal the Duke of Wellington*, ed. J. Gurwood, London 1834-38, Vol. X p. 616.

Napier, Lieutenant-Colonel William Francis Patrick (1785-1860) The author of the first great history of the Peninsular war, he had joined the 43rd Light Infantry in 1804, and served in the Corunna campaign. On the march to Talavera he suffered an attack of pleurisy, was wounded in the side at the Coa, and at Casal Nova had a bullet lodge near the spine, which gave him pain for the rest of his life. Brigade-major with the Portuguese in the Light Division, in autumn 1811 he went home to recover from an attack of fever; he returned to lead the 43rd in the Salamanca campaign, at the Nivelle, and was wounded at the Nive. Promoted to lieutenant-colonel in 1813, he went on half-pay in 1819 and rose to general in 1859. His *History of the War in the Peninsula and the South of France*, begun to vindicate the reputation of his friend Moore, established him as the greatest British military historian of the war but produced some controversy, including a fierce dispute with Beresford, but despite failings its importance can hardly be over-estimated for its time. His brothers served with distinction in the Peninsula: Sir Charles James Napier (1782-1853) notably with the 50th at Corunna, and Sir George Thomas Napier (1784-1855), who lost an arm at Ciudad Rodrigo, with the 52nd and 71st.

Napoleon I (Bonaparte), Emperor of the French, King of Italy (1769-1821)

No other personality exerted so great an influence upon the Iberian Peninsula at the time than did Napoleon; it was his policy alone that caused the French invasion and the replacement of the Spanish royal dynasty with his brother Joseph, and thus initiated the Peninsular War. His personal presence in the war was of brief duration: he arrived at Bayonne to take command of French forces in Spain on 3 November 1808, and on 1 January 1809 he broke off his pursuit of Moore to return to France to organise the war against Austria. Nevertheless, his personal campaign was the most successful episode of the war for the French: he defeated the Spanish armies and although Moore's march into Spain caused him to turn aside from consolidating his success against the Spanish, when Napoleon departed the French cause seemed to be in the ascendent. For the remainder of the war, Napoleon provided much more than a general direction of policy: despite the fact that often he had no certain knowledge of the exact state of affairs, complicated by drastic delays in the transmission of correspondence, he interfered with the conduct of the war in ways that undermined the commanders in the region, including his brother Joseph. Certainly none of his commanders possessed Napoleon's military talents, but it was an impossible task to attempt to run a campaign with such precision at so great a distance. Long after the war, Gurwood remarked to Wellington 'how strange it was that Napoleon would send orders from Paris for the movement of single divisions in Spain, without reference to the circumstances of the moment'. The Duke replied that 'Nothing was too great or too small for his proboscis'[1]. The whole of what Napoleon described as his 'Spanish ulcer' was a miscalculation on his part, and his interference only compounded the problem. The war cost him dearly; but its effect upon the Peninsula and its inhabitants was even more profound.

[1] Stanhope, Earl, *Notes on Conversations with the Duke of Wellington*, London 1888, p. 98.

Neuchâtel, Prince de: see Berthier.

Ney, Marshal Michel, duc d'Elchingen (1769-1815) One of the most stalwart of Napoleon's marshals, Ney was recently ennobled as duc d'Elchingen (from his victory in 1805) when he went to Spain in autumn 1808 as commander of VI Corps. He enjoyed some successes, but proved unco-operative as a colleague, both with Soult and especially Massena, whom he actively disliked and was downright insubordinate to him. He supervised the sieges of Ciudad Rodrigo and Almeida, served at Busaco, and led Massena's rearguard in his retreat; in March 1811 he held up Wellington's pursuit at Redinha but three days later was mauled at Foz d'Arouce. On 22 March 1811 Ney wrote to Massena flatly refusing to obey a movement order, giving cogent reasons and ending, 'I realise that in formally opposing your intention, I take on great responsibility; but were I to be dismissed or lose my head, I could not execute the march ordered by Your Excellency on Coria and Plasencia, unless, of course, it has been ordered by the Emperor'[1]. This utter insubordination Massena could not ignore, and he dismissed Ney immediately. Some of Ney's supporters urged him to replace Massena by force - which would probably have received wide support - but Ney would not contemplate open mutiny, and he left for France, to win greater laurels in Russia in 1812. Ney's conduct was not held against him, but in assessing his abilities, Napoleon remarked in 1814 that 'he was a man who lived on fire, that he would go into the cannon's mouth if he were ordered, but that he was not a man of talent or education'[2]. Ney's nickname was 'bravest of the brave', and he met his end - executed by royalist firing-squad - with the same courage.

[1] Belmas, J., *Journaux des Sièges faits ou soutenus par les Français dans la Péninsule, de 1807 à 1814*, Paris 1836-37, Vol. I p. 508.
[2] *United Service Journal* 1840, Vol. III p. 167.

O'Donnell, General Henry Joseph (Enrique José), conde de Abispal (or La Bispal) (1769-1834) One of the leading Spanish commanders, Enrique O'Donnell (often referred to by the English version of his name, Henry Joseph) was, like a number of others, a product of the Jacobite diaspora. An officer of the (Irish) Regiment Ultonia, in October 1809 he made his first mark in the war when attempting to re-supply Gerona and then breaking out of the French siege-lines when that proved impossible; for that he was promoted to major-general. Commanding the Army of Catalonia from January 1810, he suffered some reverses (notably an attempt to relieve Lerida) but in September defeated Schwarz's Rheinbund contingent at Abispal, from which he took his title. After retiring to recover from a wound in the foot, in January 1812 he became a member of the Council of Regency, and succeeded Ballesteros as commander of the Army of Reserve of Andalusia. In June 1813 he took the Pancorbo forts and was ordered by Wellington to take over the siege of Pamplona, but quarrelled with Wellington by suggesting he be given command of the whole of the Spanish forces present. Wellington declared O'Donnell the most difficult person with whom he had ever had to deal, with 'the most impracticable temper that I have yet met with in any country'[1], and O'Donnell promptly went on sick leave, but returned to command in December 1813, for the last stage of the war. He should not be confused with his brothers: José, who when leading a division was beaten at La Cuadra in August 1811 and as captain-general of Murcia was defeated at Castalla in July 1812; and Carlos, later conde O'Donnell, who overthrew his superior, the Marques de Casa Cagigal, captain-general of Tenerife, even though he had declared for Ferdinand VII, led a division under La Romana, became captain-general of Valencia and was defeated at Saguntum.

[1] *Dispatches of Field-Marshal the Duke of Wellington*, ed. J. Gurwood, London 1834-38, Vol. XI p. 5.

O'Donoju, General Juan (1762-1821)

O'Donoju was appointed to the post of Spanish Minister of War in early 1813, which did not bode well for Wellington's relationship with the Spanish government (O'Donoju had been Cuesta's chief of staff in the Talavera campaign). He proved to be obstructive and hostile to Wellington, and their correspondence was sometimes acrimonious; matters came to a head in November 1813 over the question of Wellington's command of the Spanish forces. In the wake of the Council of State's censure of the Regency and their war minister, the Cortes decreed that the terms originally granted to Wellington should be upheld, and that O'Donoju should be dismissed. This removed a considerable obstruction to Wellington, but to show their disagreement over O'Donoju's enforced resignation, the Regency immediately promoted him from major- to lieutenant-general!

Paget, Lieutenant-General Hon. Sir Edward (1775-1849)

One of the unluckiest of commanders, he was the fourth son of the 1st Earl of Uxbridge, and brother of Henry William Paget (below). Under Moore he proved a stalwart leader of the rearguard, as commander of the Reserve Division, in the retreat to Corunna, and returned to the Peninsula as deputy to Wellesley. In May 1809, days after his arrival, he was entrusted to lead the crossing of the Douro, but was severely wounded by a shot in the arm, which necessitated amputation. Lieutenant-general from 4 June 1811, he returned to the Peninsula and was posted to command the 1st Division on 11 October 1812, but his misfortune continued and on 17 November he was taken prisoner. Subsequently he rose to the rank of full general and served as C-in-C India.

Paget, Lieutenant-General Hon. Henry William, Lord (1768-1854)

Best-known for his command of the Anglo-Allied cavalry in the Waterloo campaign, in the Peninsular War Paget established his reputation as one of the finest cavalry commanders. A lieutenant-general from 1808, he led the cavalry of Moore's army and demonstrated his abilities in the Corunna campaign, most notably in his audacious raid at Sahagun, and subsequently at Benevente, though he missed the Battle of Corunna because of suffering from opthalmia. Despite his ability, he saw no further Peninsular service: having eloped with the wife of Henry Wellesley, Wellington's brother, the family quarrel thus engendered made it impossible for him to serve under the Duke until the 1815 campaign. He was known as Lord Paget until he succeeded his father as 2nd Earl of Uxbridge in 1812, and for Waterloo (where he lost a leg) he became the 1st Marquess of Anglesey, subsequently rising to the rank of field-marshal.

Pakenham, Major-General Sir Edward Michael (1778-1815)

Wellington's brother-in-law, he served at Fuentes de Oñoro but only became a general officer in January 1812. His most outstanding service was at Salamanca; having been appointed to command one of its brigades in late June, he led the 3rd Division at that battle, Picton having fallen ill. As Wellington stated, 'he made the manoeuvre which led to our success . . . with a celerity and accuracy of which I doubt that many are capable . . . Pakenham may not be the brightest genius, but . . . he is one of the best we have'[1]. He retained command until the end of the year, and in January 1813 was appointed to lead the 6th Division in Clinton's absence; in June 1813 he became adjutant-general, but with the renewed absence of Clinton and the wounding of his successor Sir Denis Pack at Sorauren, Pakenham filled in again before Colville took over in early August. As commander of the British expedition to New Orleans, he was killed there in 1815.

[1] *Dispatches of Field-Marshal the Duke of Wellington*, ed. J. Gurwood, London 1834-38, Vol. IX p. 395.

Palafox y Melzi, General José de (1780-1847)

One of the most famous Spanish personalities of the war, Palafox came to represent national resistance by his defence of Saragossa. An aristocrat devoted to the monarchy and an ex-member of the royal bodyguard, he was appointed Captain-General of Aragon in May 1808, and organised resistance to the French from Saragossa. His military abilities were limited, and he was more of a politician: Wellington claimed that 'there was nothing in him - all parties agreed that he was a poor creature [who] allowed everything to *laisser aller* very much in that resistance'[1], and William Napier thought him a figurehead for the leaders of the populace, but these are harsh views. Initially he met with defeat: his brother Luis, Marquis of Lazan, was beaten at Tudela (8 June 1808) as was Palafox at Alagon; wounded in the arm, he withdrew to Saragossa but left again when the French appeared, ostensibly to gather reinforcements. He returned when it was clear that the French attack had failed, and characterised the defence of Saragossa as a beacon for the whole of Europe. Subsequently he collaborated (uneasily) with Castaños, but the siege was resumed after the defeat at Tudela in November 1808. Although Palafox's conduct of the defence was unenterprising - he never tried to send out a large force to harry the besiegers - his leadership was a major factor in enabling the city to hold out so resolutely for so long. He fell ill and thus the surrender was negotiated by others, and he was imprisoned in France for the remainder of the war. He was released in time to welcome the king into Saragossa upon his return in 1814, and subsequently was rewarded with the title of Duke of Saragossa.

[1] Stanhope, Earl, *Notes on Conversations with the Duke of Wellington*, London 1888, p. 10.

Pamplona, General Emmanuel-Ignace (1766-1831)

Born in the Azores, Pamplona began his career in the Portuguese cavalry, returned to Portuguese service in 1792 after a period in the Russian army, and served in Alorna's Legion of Light Troops from its creation. A Portuguese *marechal de campo* from March 1808, he became a *général de brigade* in French service that August, commanding the chasseurs of the Portuguese Legion. Like Alorna he served as an advisor to Massena, who was unimpressed, describing them as *'deux mauvais coquins'*. He commanded a division in Napoleon's invasion of Russia and became a naturalised French subject in 1818, but died in his native country, at Elvas.

Peace, Prince of the: see Godoy.

Pelet-Clozeau, Chef de Bataillon Jean-Jacques-Germain (1777-1858)

Pelet's reputation was made largely after his Peninsular service: he became a colonel only in April 1811, and a *général de brigade* not until April 1813. As ADC to Massena from 1805, he advised the marshal during his command of the Army of Portugal (not altogether successfully according to Marbot, who stated that only Pelet was permitted to submit suggestions to him directly), and it was Pelet whom Massena sent to Napoleon to explain the dismissal of Ney, before that marshal could advance his side of the argument. After the war Pelet wrote a number of histories, notably one on the Peninsula, an English translation of which is *The French Campaign in Portugal 1810-1811*, trans. & ed. D.D. Horward, Minneapolis 1973.

Perceval, Rt. Hon. Spencer (1762-1812) British prime minister during the earlier part of the Peninsular war, he was the fourth son of the Earl of Egmont, and had held a number of government appointments before succeeding Portland as prime minister in September 1809. He pursued the war in the Peninsula, though received some criticism for providing insufficient support; and his career was cut short when on 11 May 1812, in the lobby of the House of Commons, he was shot dead by John Bellingham, a bankrupt, who had been unable to gain redress when he had sought the prime minister's assistance. Perceval was succeeded by the Earl of Liverpool.

Philippon, General Armand, baron (1761-1836) Colonel of the French 54th Line from October 1803, he served in Spain from 1808, with Lapisse's Division of Victor's I Corps, at Talavera and in the siege of Cadiz, and was promoted to *général de brigade* in June 1810, *de division* in July 1811. On 11 March 1811 he was appointed governor of Badajoz, where he made his name; for although not especially distinguished as a field commander, his defence of that city was exemplary. He resisted Allied attempts to capture it in 1811, and conducted a heroic defence in 1812, the obstacles he constructed in the path of the attackers making the breaches in the wall impregnable and costing dreadful casualties, so that the city only fell to the unexpected success of a diversionary escalade. When the city fell, Philippon retired to the San Christobal fort across the Guadiana, where he surrendered on the following day (he and his two daughters being escorted to safety by British officers, through the drunken mob of Allied soldiers). He was attacked by another mob when sent as a prisoner to Lisbon, was taken to England but in July 1812 broke his parole, escaped from his place of residence at Oswestry and returned home with the aid of two smugglers. He served briefly in Germany in 1813, but soon retired.

Picton, Lieutenant-General Sir Thomas (1758-1815) 'A rough foulmouthed devil as ever lived, but he always behaved extremely well; no man could do better in the different services I assigned to him'[1] was Wellington's comment on his eccentric Welsh subordinate. A brigadier-general from 1801, Picton had served as governor of Trinidad, where an accusation that he had permitted the interrogation of a Mulatto woman under duress caused problems for him long after his return to England in 1803, the case casting a shadow over his subsequent career even after the technically guilty verdict was overturned in 1808. Invalided home from Walcheren, upon the recommendation of the Spanish fighter for South American independence, Francisco Miranda, his services were requested by Wellington. A hard and uncompromising soldier, Picton took command of the 3rd Division and led it with distinction, and his personal style. An early incident was his quarrel with Robert Craufurd, equally uncompromising, when Picton refused to risk his men by supporting Craufurd's Light Division at the Coa. Napier wrote of this 'sharp altercation' and described Picton's 'short thick figure, dark flashing eyes, quick movements and fiery temper'; both, he claimed, were 'ambitious and craving of glory' and 'possessed decided military talents, were enterprising and intrepid, yet neither were remarkable for skill in handling troops under fire'[1]. Nevertheless, Picton proved a stalwart character, especially distinguished at Fuentes de Oñoro and Badajoz (where a wound caused his absence in command until May 1813). Although promoted to lieutenant-general in June of that year, Picton received no peerage, perhaps a legacy of his Trinidad reputation. He was killed leading his division at Waterloo. He was an acknowledged eccentric, eschewing uniform in favour of civilian dress: at Busaco, for example, he wore his nightcap, and at Vittoria Kincaid described him wearing a 'round hat' but swearing as if he had two cocked ones.

[1] Stanhope, Earl, *Notes on Conversations with the Duke of Wellington*, London 1888, p. 69.
[2] Napier, W.F.P., *History of the War in the Peninsula*, London 1828-40, Vol. III p. 294.

Popham, Captain Home Riggs (1762-1820) An expert in amphibious warfare, Popham had devised the disastrous raid on Ostend in 1798, and commanded its naval contingent, and survived a court-martial for initiating the unauthorised expedition to South America while leading the naval part of Baird's force at the Cape in 1806. An advocate of the offensive power of the navy, and of army-navy co-operation, he harried the Biscay coast to great effect from mid-1812, seamen and marines from the fleet collaborating with guerrillas like Longa, Porlier and El Pastor. Such raids alarmed the French and diverted troops from more necessary duties, but the greatest significance was the capture of Santander for use as a base, drastically shortening Wellington's line of communications. The diversionary operations on the coast were planned by Wellington, but Popham was considerably responsible for their success. He became a rear-admiral on 4 June 1814.

Porlier, General Juan Diaz (1783-1815) Originally an officer of the Spanish navy who had fought at Trafalgar, Porlier was one of the guerrilla commanders whose forces were originally based upon, and continued to resemble, regular troops. A nephew of La Romana - hence his nickname 'El Marquesito', 'the little Marquis' - he was authorised in 1809 by La Romana and the Oviedo junta to begin irregular warfare in the Asturias. An effective commander, he was known for dogged perseverence, courage and audacity, and proved a major problem for the French in the northern provinces. He collaborated with the British navy (notably Home Popham) and made daring raids like his capture of Santander in 1811, withdrawing to safety when French reinforcements arrived. His troops were notable in the capture of Santander in August 1812 (under his deputy Juan Lopez Campillo: at the time Porlier himself was besieging Santoña), which provided a base for the Spanish Seventh Army, and a route for supplies. This Seventh Army was a combination of the forces of Porlier, Longa and Espoz y Mina, under the command of Gabriel Mendizabel, and if his fame came to be somewhat overshadowed, Porlier's forces remained an important asset in the area and he collaborated in the actions around Tolosa (June 1813) and at San Marcial. In September 1815 he led the liberal insurrection at Corunna but was captured and executed.

Portland, William Henry Cavendish Bentinck, 3rd Duke of (1738-1809) British prime minister at the commencement of the Peninsular War, Portland was a somewhat nominal (and ineffectual) head of government. Having been nominal prime minister in the Fox-North coalition of 1783, and later Pitt's home secretary, in March 1807 he again accepted the nominal post of prime minister, until he resignation following a stroke shortly before his death (30 October 1809), being replaced on 26 September by Spencer Perceval.

Ramsay, Major William Norman (1782-1815) One of the most celebrated junior officers of the Peninsular War, Norman Ramsay (as he was known) came to prominence with Bull's Troop of Royal Horse Artillery when at Fuentes de Oñoro he rescued two guns that had been cut off, by charging through the French cavalry. William Napier made much of the exploit in his history (though some veterans thought that it had been rather embroidered), but perhaps of more consequence was a misunderstanding on the day after Vittoria when Ramsay was arrested and threatened with court-martial by Wellington himself, for having moved his guns without orders. Ramsay had the sympathy of the entire army, and though his excellent services at Vittoria were not praised officially, he was soon restored to duty and received a brevet-majority a short while later (22 November 1813). He was killed at Waterloo, but his reputation as the perfect horse artillery-man was not forgotten, nor his encounter with Wellington; one officer admitted that his actions in the Crimean War were influenced by what had happened to Ramsay, the circumstances of his arrest still overshadowing the corps more than forty years later.

Reding, General Theodore de (1755-1809) One of the most prominent Swiss officers of the Peninsular War, as a general in the Spanish Army he served under Castaños and played a major role in the campaign of Bailen. In October 1808 he was sent to take command of the Granadan troops in the Army of Andalusia; sent to assist the forces in Catalonia, he suffered defeats at Caradeu and Molins de Rey. He replaced Juan Miguel de Vives as captain-general of Catalonia but in February 1809 he engaged Souham at Valls, the action being decided by the arrival of Gouvion St. Cyr. Though acknowledged as a brave and honest man, Reding was undistinguished as a general, his handling of the battle was considerably at fault, and his army, stated by some to be the best of the Spanish forces at the time, was defeated severely. Wounded several times, Reding reached Tarragona with the remnant of his army, but subsequently succumbed to his injuries.

Reille, General Honoré-Charles-Michel-Joseph, comte (1775-1860) One of the most reliable French divisional commanders, Reille was an imperial aide from May 1807, and was sent to Madrid in April 1808, becoming involved in the intrigues which led to the detention of Ferdinand VII. He was then sent to Catalonia to assist Duhesme, took command of the 1st Division of VII Corps, captured Rosas in December but in March 1809 was recalled for the campaign against Austria. He returned to Spain in May 1810 as governor of Navarre, subsequently served under Suchet in Aragon, in January 1812 was named commander of a new 'corps of the Ebro', and in October was appointed commander of the Army of Portugal in succession to Souham, taking command on 29 November 1812. He made an orderly retreat from Vittoria and upon Soult's return as overall commander was given command of the 'lieutenancy of the Right'. Relations with Soult were not easy and came to a head when he objected to sharing command at Bayonne with its governor, Thouvenot, and Reille duly resigned on 15 February 1814. His insubordination was overlooked, Clarke (minister of war) ordered him back to the army, and he led a couple of divisions from Orthez until the end of the war, without great opportunity for distinction. He commanded II Corps in the Waterloo campaign and rose to the rank of marshal in 1847.

Rey, General Louis-Emmanuel, baron (1768-1846) Gouvion St. Cyr's chief of staff in the Peninsula, and then a brigade commander in Caffarelli's division from October 1810, Rey was appointed governor of San Sebastian. He improved the defences and made sorties against the besiegers in the first siege, but his position was without much hope in the second siege, especially after the explosion of a magazine on 31 August 1813. Having insufficient troops to hold his internal defence-line, he withdrew into the castle until his defences were destroyed on 8 September, three days after his subordinates had declared the position indefensible. The besiegers so admired his stalwart defence that they allowed him to send a last despatch to Soult, but his person did not impress them: Augustus Frazer described him as 'a great fat man, not pleasing, at least in appearance' and recorded how, when discussing the terms of surrender, he used 'an opprobrious and vulgar term'[1]. As a tribute to his defence, Rey was promoted to *général de division* on 6 November 1813, even though he was then a prisoner in England. He should not be confused with General Jean-Pierre-Antoine Rey (1767-1842), who served in the Peninsula from June 1808, leading a brigade of Conroux's Division at Vittoria and commanding the division after Conroux received his mortal wound.

[1] Frazer, A.S., *Letters of Colonel Sir Augustus Simon Frazer*, ed. Maj.Gen. E. Sabine, London 1859, pp. 265, 267.

Reynier, General Jean-Louis-Ebenézer, comte (1771-1814) An officer of Swiss birth, Reynier was one of Napoleon's most loyal subordinates, despite a reputation for insubordination and taciturnity. He is perhaps best remembered for his defeat at Maida, but from April 1810 led II Corps of the Army of Portugal, including Busaco, Sabugal and Fuentes de Oñoro, and like his fellow corps-commanders was highly critical of Massena. In June 1811 he was named second-in-command to Marmont in the Army of Portugal, but in January 1812 was recalled by Napoleon for the Russian campaign. Captured at Leipzig, he was exchanged and returned to France, but died of exhaustion on 27 February 1814.

Ricard, General Etienne-Pierre-Sylvestre, baron (1771-1843) Having served as his ADC, Ricard was Soult's chief of staff from November 1808. He is noteworthy for the curious incident of circulating a letter to all French generals,

Above: Fusilier of French infantry.

Left: Joseph Bonaparte, King of Spain (engraving after Picart).

Left: Fusilier-Chasseur (left) and Fusilier-Grenadier of the French Imperial Guard (right); the loose trousers worn by the latter were commonly used on campaign (print by Vilain).

ilier Chasseur | Fusilier Grenadier.

grande tenue. | tenue de route.

Left: Arthur Wellesley, 1st Duke of Wellington (print after Sir Thomas Lawrence).

Right: Infantry of the Vistula Legion; Polish troops were among the best of the foreign contingents employed by Napoleon (print after 'Job').

OFFICER OF ENGINEERS.   OFFICER OF INFANTRY.

Above: Officers of the Portuguese Army: Engineers (left) and infantry (right) (engraving by I Clark after H Michel).

Above: Regiments of the French Army: left, 4th Dragoons, right, 94th Line. Both saw considerable service in the Peninsular War: the 4th Dragoons at Talavera, Albuera and Usagre, the 94th at Talavera, Barrosa, Fuentes de Onoro, Vittoria and in the Sortie from Bayonne (print by Goddard & Booth).

Below: Wellesley's quarters at Vimeiro, 1808 (engraving by I C Stadler after Col. George Landmann); a good reference to the architecture of this part of Portugal.

Top: The Battle of Corunna (aquatint by M. Dubourg after William Heath).

Bottom: The Battle of the Pyrenees (aquatint by T Sutherland after William Heath).

Top: Wellington's Bivouac in the Pyrenees (aquatint by J C Stadler after William Heath).

Bottom: The Battle of Salamanca: Wellington and staff in left foreground (print by G Lewis after J A Atkinson)

Above: Wellington's army crosses the Douro (print by H L'Eveque from *Campaigns of the British Army in Portugal*, published 1813).

Left: Sir John Moore (engraving by Turner after Sir Thomas Lawrence).

Above: 'Steady the Drums and Fifes': the 57th Foot at Albuera, one of the most famous paintings of a Peninsular War scene (exhibited by Lady Elizabeth Butler at the Royal Academy in 1897).

Below: Sir John Moore mortally wounded at Corunna (print by T Sutherland after William Heath).

Left: Members of the Portuguese forces; left, Lisbon Police Guard; right, Algarve volunteer (engraving by I Clark after H Michel).

Below: Dupont's surrender at Bailen - the greatest Spanish victory of the war (print after Maurice Orange).

Left: Spanish Hussar officer (print by Goddard & Booth).

Right: Members of the Spanish Army: left, light infantry; right, artillery (engraving by I Clark).

Left: French infantry engaging Spanish irregulars (print after Maurice Orange).

Below: Vimeiro: Piper George Clarke of the British 71st continues to play his pipes even though wounded; in recognition of his heroism he was presented with a set of silver pipes (print by Clark & Dubourg after Manskirch).

Above: French grenadiers skirmishing with Spanish troops, c. 1808 (engraving after Hippolyte Bellangé).

Below: Marshal Jean-de-Dieu Soult (engraving by E Findon after R Grevedon).

Below: Busaco: a depiction of the characteristic tactic of French attacks being repelled by the fire of a British line, seconded by rapid counter-attacks (print after St Clair).

Above: 'The Defence of Saragossa'; a very romanticized version of the deeds of Agostina, 'the Maid of Saragossa' (engraving by Lizars after Sir David Wilkie).

Left: Marshal Auguste-Frederic-Louis Viesse de Marmont (engraving by T Johnson after J B P Guérin).

Right: Marshal André Massena.

Left: Marshal Louis-Gabriel Suchet (engraving by R A Muller after J B P Guérin).

Above left: Sir Rowland Hill, Wellington's senior deputy.

Above right: Major-General Robert Craufurd, commander of the Light Division.

Left: Lieutenant-General Sir Thomas Picton, a divisional commander (engraving by W L Colls).

Right: A group representative of the British Army in the Peninsula, c. 1811: left to right, infantry, dragoon and Highlander (print by Goddard & Booth).

Right: The first great historian of the Peninsular War: William Napier in the uniform of the 43rd Light Infantry (engraving after 'Miss Jones').

Above: General Jean-Andoche Junot (engraving by T Read).

Above right: William Carr Beresford, as Marshal of the Portuguese Army (print after Thomas Heaphy).

Right: Marshal Jean-Baptiste Jourdan (print after A Tardieu).

inviting their co-operation, and stating that if Soult were to assume royal powers it would not be disloyal to Napoleon; he also solicited support from towns in northern Portugal, where it was suggested that Soult might establish his kingdom. Napoleon's reaction was immediate: Ricard was recalled for a reprimand and Soult was criticised for allowing him to become involved in such intrigue. Ricard's disgrace was not permanent: in May 1811 he was appointed ADC to Suchet but left the Peninsula for service in Russia in 1812. He led a division of the French expedition to Spain in 1823.

Riego Nunez, Rafael del (1784-1823) The legacy of the Peninsular War is perhaps exemplified by the career of Riego. A native of the Asturias, he was educated for the law at Oviedo but entered the royal guard in 1807, and in 1808 was given command of a battalion by the Asturias junta. He was captured at Espinosa and imprisoned in France, where before his escape (eventually he reached Britain) he absorbed liberal philosophies. He returned to the military in Spain in 1814 and in January 1820 led a mutiny, proclaiming the 1812 constitution, and he became a popular leader of the most extreme elements. He continued to intrigue, in 1822 was chosen as deputy for Oviedo in the Cortes, and in February 1823 was elected president of the chamber. After the French invasion to restore the authority of the king, he was captured by the royalists and hanged at Madrid in November 1823.

Rogniat, General Joseph, baron (1776-1840) One of the most prominent French military engineers of the period, he went to Spain as a colonel on the general staff in February 1808, succeeding to command the engineers after the death of General André-Bruno Lacoste at Saragossa. *Général de brigade* from March 1809, he served against Austria before returning to the Peninsula when appointed to command the siege-train in December 1809. Subsequently chief engineer of the Army of Aragon under Suchet, he directed the sieges of Mequinenza, Tortosa, Tarragona, Saguntum, Murviedro and Valencia, but in January 1813 was appointed chief engineer of the *Grande Armée* and left the Peninsula, having become *général de division* on 9 July 1811. Among his subsequent writings was *Relation des Sièges de Saragosse et Tortose par les Français*, Paris 1814.

Rosily-Mesros, Vice-Amiral François-Etienne (1748-1832) Probably the most prominent French naval officer of the Peninsular War, Rosily was an experienced seaman who in 1805 had been sent to take command from Villeneuve at Cadiz, but arrived only after the defeat of the Franco-Spanish fleet at Trafalgar. He reorganised what remained of the fleet, which was attacked by the Spanish, after the declaration of war, on 9 June 1808. On the following day he called for a truce and offered to sail away if the watching British fleet would permit him; but this being unacceptable, the Spanish threatened to renew hostilities, leading to the surrender of the French ships on 14 June. Rosily returned to France, where he held a number of administrative posts.

Rovigo, duc de: see Savary.

Ruffin, General François-Amable, comte (1771-1811) *Général de divsion* from 3 November 1807, on the same day he took command of the 1st Division of Victor's I Corps in place of Dupont, and in September 1808 led it into Spain. He served at Somosierra, Ucles, Medellin and Talavera, and commanded the force that occupied the Cerro del Puerco at Barossa. As his troops were defeated by Graham's counter-attack, he was shot through the neck by a rifle-ball, which struck his spine and caused paralysis. He fell into British hands and was treated with great humanity, Graham sending him dishes from his own table every day; sent to England, he appeared to be recovering but on 15 May suffered a relapse and died aboard the transport *Gorgon*, within sight of the Isle of Wight. Three days later he was buried at Portsmouth with full military honours. William Surtees described him as 'an immense and fine-looking man, about six feet two inches or six feet three inches high, and ate enormously'[1]. He is depicted in Lejeune's painting of Barossa.

[1] Surtees, W., *Twenty-Five Years in the Rifle Brigade*, London 1833, pp. 126-7.

Sainte-Hélène, baron de: see Lapisse.

San Juan, General Benito (d. 1808) The unfortunate San Juan was the Spanish commander ordered to defend Madrid in late 1808. His superior, General Francisco Eguia, instructed him to hold the Somosierra pass; but having divided his forces unwisely, they were thrust aside by Napoleon on 30 November, San Juan being wounded twice by sword-cuts to the head as he bravely tried to rally his reserve. He gathered some troops and marched towards Madrid, whose junta was known to be considering surrender; when he paused on 3 December his men mutinied and demanded they continue. News of the surrender of the capital, however, caused them to bolt, and when San Juan attempted to reassert his authority at Talavera on 6 December, they again mutinied, accusing him of leading them to surrender (he was evidently unpopular for having commanded Godoy's bodyguard). In what William Napier described as 'intolerable villainy', San Juan was shot as he tried to escape, and then hanged from an elm tree outside the town.

Savary, General Anne-Jean-Marie-René, duc de Rovigo (1774-1833)

A diplomat, politician and soldier known for his devotion to Napoleon, he was sent to Spain, helped persuade Ferdinand VII to go to Bayonne, and on 15 June 1808 temporarily succeeded Murat as commander of all French forces in the Peninsula. He left the following month but returned with Napoleon, commanding the Fusiliers of the Imperial Guard, and served at Somosierra. He returned to France with Napoleon, served against Austria in 1809 and succeeded Fouché as minister of police in June 1810.

Scovell, Lieutenant-Colonel George (1774-1861)

One of the most significant, albeit junior, members of Wellington's staff, Scovell served in the quarter-master-general's department while an officer of the 57th Foot, at Corunna, and with Wellington's headquarters 1809-14. He acted largely as an intelligence officer, and was responsible for breaking the French cyphers, the ability to read captured messages sent in code being a huge advantage to Wellington's strategy. He became commandant of the Staff Corps of Cavalry (1813) and by 1854 attained the rank of full general.

Sébastiani, General Horace-François-Bastien, comte (1772-1851)

A diplomat as well as a soldier, the Corsican Sébastiani had served as ambassador to the Ottoman Empire immediately prior to commanding the 1st Division of Lefebvre's IV Corps in Spain from September 1808. He replaced Lefebvre in command of IV Corps on 21 February 1809, led it at Talavera and helped defeat Venegas at Almonacid on 11 August 1809. He served at Ocaña, participated in the conquest of Andalusia, on 28 January 1810 won the action at Alcala la Réal, and in October 1810 defeated Blayney's landing at Fuengirola. Soult left him and his corps in the region of Granada to watch the Spanish Army of Murcia and to check guerrilla activity in the mountains and eastern coast of Andalusia, but in May 1811 he was replaced as head of IV Corps by Leval, the remainder of his service being spent in Russia and in subsequent campaigns; he attained the rank of marshal in 1840.

Senarmont, General Alexandre-Antoine Hureau, baron de (1769-1810)

The son of an artillery general, he became one of the most distinguished gunners of his generation. *Général de brigade* from July 1806, he won great renown by his artillery 'charge' at Friedland, a clasic example of massed-battery fire as an offensive weapon instead of just as a support. He was appointed artillery commander of Victor's I Corps in August 1808, and ennobled as a baron in the previous month; he served at Somosierra, became *général de division* on 7 December 1808, and in March 1809 succeeded Lariboisière as artillery commander of the Army of Spain. He was distinguished again at Ocaña - where he again employed a massed battery formed of the artillery of IV and V Corps - but when commanding the artillery at the siege of Cadiz, on 26 October 1810 he was killed by the explosion of a howitzer-shell.

Sherbrooke, Major-General Sir John Coape (1764-1830) An old associate of Wellington (second-in-command of Wellington's 33rd Foot in the Netherlands), he commanded the 1st Division in the Peninsula from June 1809 to April 1810, and was second-in-command of the army, until he went home on health grounds. He was not an especially effective commander if a good regimental officer, and had a notoriously bad temper: 'the most passionate man I think I ever knew', Wellington stated. He recalled how on the day after the capture of Oporto, Sherbrooke had got into a 'terrible rage before me about nothing with my Portuguese interpreter. He was standing with his hands behind his back, and said at last to the man: It is lucky for you, Sir, I can tell you, that I am now in the presence of the Commander of the Forces and with my hands behind me; and I can tell you, you had better not wait until I bring them into the advanced guard! I laughed, but the interpreter thought it best upon the whole to take himself off'[1]. Subsequently Sherbrooke served as governor and C-in-C Canada, where the town of Sherbrooke was named after him.

[1] Stanhope, Earl, *Notes on Conversations with the Duke of Wellington*, London 1888, p. 190.

Smith, Captain Henry George Wakelyn (1787-1860) Especially distinguished in South Africa (1828-52) and in the First Sikh War, 'Harry' Smith (by which name he was known universally) served throughout the Peninsular War and wrote a noted autobiography. An officer of the 95th Rifles, a shot through the ankle at the Coa inhibited his regimental service and led to staff appointments, as ADC and brigade-major. His Peninsular service is probably best remembered for surely the most remarkable love story of the period: after the storm of Badajoz, he was approached by two Spanish ladies, seeking protection. With the younger - Juana Maria de los Dolores de Leon (1798-1872) - he fell in love, married her, and she accompanied him throughout his subsequent campaigning, becoming admired and respected throughout the army. It was for her that the town of Ladysmith was named (and Harrismith from Harry, also in southern Africa); Smith rose to the rank of lieutenant-general and was rewarded with a baronetcy for his victory at Aliwal over the Sikhs.

Souham, General Joseph, comte (1760-1837) *Général de division* from 1793, Souham had recovered from a period of disgrace arising from his association with Moreau, when in September 1808 he was appointed to lead the 2nd Division of V Corps of the Army of Spain (subsequently 4th, then 1st Division, of VII Corps). He served at Molins del Rey, Valls and the siege of Gerona; he won a considerable victory over O'Donnell at Vich (20 February 1810) but was wounded in the head, and returned to France in the following April. Ennobled as a *comte*, he returned to Spain with a divisional command in August 1811, and from December led the 7th Division of the Army of Portugal. On leave in France at the time of Salamanca, he returned in September 1812 and took over the Army of Portugal from Clausel. Although he relieved Burgos, he was regarded as somewhat over-cautious and in November was relieved of command; his subsequent service was on the German front.

Soult, Marshal Jean-de-Dieu, duc de Dalmatie (1769-1851) Styled by Napoleon as the ablest tactician in the empire, Soult (often known as Nicolas Soult though it was not his real name) was among the most trusted of Napoleon's subordinates and one of the principal commanders of his generation. Rushed into action in great haste in late 1808 to take command of II Corps in Spain, he was left by Napoleon to deal with Moore, by whom he was defeated at Corunna. In May 1809 he was out manoeuvred at Oporto by Wellesley, but was appointed as Joseph's major-general in place of Jourdan in September, and on 19 November defeated Ariezaga at Ocaña. Somewhat damaged by rumours that he had designs upon becoming king of Portugal, relations with other French commanders were poor, leading to mutual lack of co-operation, and although he wielded considerable influence as Joseph's senior subordinate and commander of the Army of the South, an attempt to relieve Badajoz led to defeat at Albuera. In August 1812 he had to raise the siege of Cadiz and was ordered by Joseph to evacuate Andalusia, against which he protested, and relations with the king collapsed when Joseph discovered the contents of a letter to Clarke in which Soult implied that Joseph was attempting to negotiate with the enemy, to Napoleon's disadvantage. Soult was recalled from

Spain, leaving in March 1813 and taking with him the loot he had accumulated. The situation in the Peninsula deteriorated so rapidly that shortly after Napoleon had told Joseph's aide that 'Marshal Soult's was the only head in Spain'[1]. Soult was sent back to take overall command from Joseph (12 July 1813). Excluding Suchet's command, all French forces were unified under Soult, intended to prevent the mutual lack of co-operation that had so bedevilled French operations, but by then the situation was beyond recovery. Nevertheless, Soult performed with distinction in the actions in the Pyrenees and south of France. William Napier claimed that Soult was respected by every British officer who fought against him, though Wellington commented that although Soult was excellent at bringing up his troops, he was not as confident about how to use them: 'in the field he is apt to doubt and hesitate, and lose the proper moment for acting'[2], such opinions also being entertained by his subordinates. After his retirement in 1847 Soult was accorded the rare appointment of Marshal-General of France, held previously only by Turenne, Saxe and Villars. From his dukedom (of Dalmatia, awarded June 1808) he was nicknamed by the British as the 'Duke of Damnation', or 'Old Salt'.

[1] *The Confidential Correspondence of Napoleon Bonaparte with His Brother Joseph*, London 1855, Vol. II, p. 244.

[2] Bunbury, Sir Henry, *Memoirs and Literary remains of Lieutenant-General Sir Henry Edward Bunbury, Bt.*, ed. Sir Charles Bunbury, London 1868, p. 296.

Soult, General Pierre-Benoît, baron (1770-1843) The marshal's younger brother had served as his ADC prior to becoming a general in July 1807, and from November 1808 was with the staff of the Army of Spain, serving as commandant of Santander before replacing Franceschi-Delonne as cavalry commander of II Corps under his brother. His promotion probably owed more to this relationship than to his talent; indeed, Joseph Bonaparte suggested that the marshal was unwilling to let him operate without close supervision. He served at Arzobispo in August 1809, was hit by a grapeshot in the left leg at Busaco, and in August 1811 provisionally took command of the 3rd Dragoon Division of IV Corps, in February 1812 the 3rd Cavalry Division of the Army of the South. Shot in the right arm at Alba de Tormes, he led the 2nd Dragoon Division from October 1812, and as *général de division* from March 1813, commanded the light cavalry of the Army of the Centre (April) and in July the 1st Cavalry Division of his brother's army, until the end of the war (being blamed by the marshal for the loss of the bridge at Croix d'Orade).

Spencer, Lieutenant-General Sir Brent (1760-1828) In early 1808 Spencer was sent with a small British force to Sicily, from where he sailed to Andalusia in June; from there he took his troops to reinforce Wellesley upon the latter's landing in Portugal, and served as Wellesley's deputy at Roliça and Vimeiro. He returned to the Peninsula to lead the 1st Division from June 1810 to July 1811, and was promoted to lieutenant-general in June 1811. Though a competent administrator, and very brave, even one well-disposed towards him admitted that he was 'a zealous, gallant officer, without any great military genius; anxious and fidgety when there was nothing to do, but, once under fire, looking like a philosopher solving a problem, perfectly cool and self-possessed'[1]. As a second-in-command, Wellington wrote, he was 'very unfit for his situation. He is a good executive officer, but has no mind and is incapable of forming any opinions of his own; and he is the centre of all the vulgar and foolish opinions of the day . . . I cannot depend upon him for anything'[2]. Spencer went home in 1811 on health grounds but privately confided that it was 'in consequence of Sir Thomas Graham's appointment to this army as second in command . . . he could not reconcile to his feelings to accept a lower post [and] had therefore determined to resign and return to England'[3].

[1] Cowell, J.S., *Leaves from the Diary of an Officer of the Guards*, London 1854, p. 80.
[2] Fortescue, Hon. Sir John, *History of the British Army*, London 1899-1920, Vol. VII p. 499.
[3] Cowell, p. 135.

Stewart, Major-General Hon. Charles William (1778-1854) Castlereagh's half-brother, he served as Wellington's adjutant-general from 1809 to 1813, and proved to be a valuable staff officer, but such duties were not entirely to his liking; as a cavalry officer, he lobbied for a field command, for which Wellington thought him unfit, having such bad sight and hearing that he had difficulty knowing what was going on around him. More than once he was scolded by Wellington for becoming too involved in the fighting. In 1813 he was sent as British representative to Allied headquarters in Europe. In 1822 he succeeded as 3rd Marquess of Londonderry, under which name he published his noted *Narrative of the Peninsular War from 1808 to 1813* (London 1828).

Stewart, Lieutenant-General Hon. Sir William (1774-1827) One of the founders of the British rifle corps (95th), as a major-general William Stewart went to the Peninsula in 1810. Present in an unofficial capacity at Busaco, in August 1810 he was given command of a brigade in the 2nd Division, and to lead the division itself, which he did with great impetuosity at Albuera, resulting in its near-destruction. Wounded there, he went home to recuperate, returning in November 1812 to lead the 1st Division, transferring to the 2nd Division in March 1813, which he commanded until the end of the war. Although his zeal and courage were unquestionable, his overall performance was not good; during the withdrawal in late 1812 he led three divisions astray, and as Wellington observed, for all his good intentions, he could not obey an order. Wounded in the leg at Maya on 25 July 1813, he returned to command within days, cost his division unnecessary casualties and was wounded yet again. Popular with his men, he was nicknamed by them 'Auld Grog Willie' from his issuance of extra rum.

Suchet, Marshal Louis-Gabriel, duc d'Albufera (1770-1826) Of all the marshals who served in the Peninsula, Suchet was the among the most successful. He was sent to Spain as a general in October 1808 in command of the 1st Division of V Corps, under Mortier, and in April 1809 replaced Junot as commander of III Corps of the Army of Spain, later known as the Army of Aragon. Thereafter he was in virtually independent command, acting in both military and civil capacities, his success (at least by his own account) at least partly the result of an administration more humane than practiced by some of his fellows, tending to reduce the amount of opposition to French rule. (It was, however, a qualified benevolence: exactions were still made, and opponents still crushed, but his impositions were less than others might have made). He defeated Blake at Belchite (18 June 1809) and captured Lerida, Tortosa and Mequinenza, the former by the unusual expedient of using the civilian population as a 'human shield' in front of his attack, which was criticised severely as 'scarcely to be admitted within the pale of civilised warfare'. 'Suchet justifies it, on the ground, that he thus spared a great effusion of blood . . . But this is to spare soldiers' blood at the expense of women's and children's, and had Garcia Conde's [commander of the garrison] nature been stern, he , too, might have pleaded expediency, and the victory would have fallen to him who could longest have sustained the sight of mangled infants and despairing mothers'[1]. Suchet's capture of Tarragona in June 1811 led to his promotion to marshal, and in that October he defeated Blake at Saguntum (where he was wounded in the shoulder); following his capture of Valencia in June 1812 he was ennobled as duc d'Albufera. Defeated at Castalla, he forced the allies to lift the siege of Tarragona, and in 1813 he was appointed governor of Catalonia as well as head of the Armies of Aragon and (from April 1813) Catalonia. When Soult was appointed to command all

French forces in Spain, Suchet alone retained his independence, but his own successes ultimately made no difference to the outcome of the war. Napoleon remarked that if he had had two such marshals as Suchet in Spain, 'he should not only have conquered, but kept the Peninsula. His sound judgment, his governing, yet conciliating spirit, his military tact, had procured him astonishing success. It is a pity that a sovereign cannot *improvise* men of his stamp'[2].

[1] Napier, W.F.P., *History of the War in the Peninsula*, London 1828-40, Vol. III p. 157.
[2] Anon., *The Court and Camp of Bonaparte*, London 1831, p. 419.

Talleyrand-Perigord, Charles-Maurice de, prince de Benevente (1754-1838)

One of the greatest statesmen of the age, Talleyrand had only a peripheral role in the Peninsular war. He disapproved strongly of Napoleon's policy in Spain, but had relinquished his post as French foreign minister in August 1807. It was at his magnificent château of Valençay, south-east of Tours, which he had purchased in 1805, that Ferdinand VII, his brother and uncle were interned during the Peninsular war. The title conferred upon him by Napoleon in July 1806, 'prince de Benevente', was taken from Benevento, a papal fief in Neapolitan territory, not from Benavente in northern Spain, the site of the cavalry action during the Corunna campaign.

Tascher de la Pagerie, General Jean-Henry-Robert, comte (1785-1816)

A cousin of the Empress Josephine, he had joined the French Army in 1803, and served Joseph Bonaparte in both Naples and Spain, becoming a colonel in April 1808. He is perhaps best remembered as the commandant of the 1st Provisional Chasseurs, the unit so badly cut up at Sahagun that it had to be disbanded. In 1813 he became a general in Joseph's service and subsequently returned to the French Army, serving as Joseph's aide in 1815.

Thomières, General Jean-Guillaume-Barthélemy, baron (1771-1812)

In the first French army in Spain, Thomières led a brigade of Loison's 2nd Division under Junot, and was wounded at Vimeiro. In Soult's army he led the 1st Brigade of Merle's Division at Corunna, and in January 1810 was head of the 2nd Brigade of the 2nd Division of VIII Corps in the Army of Portugal. Provisionally he stepped up to command the 7th Division, and led it in his most famous engagement, at Salamanca. There he was surprised and his division was driven from the field in disorder; mortally wounded, Thomières died within the British lines.

Thouvenot, General Pierre, baron (1757-1817) Having rehabilitated his reputation in France - he had deserted with Dumouriez in 1793 - in May 1808 Thouvenot was appointed commandant of Guipuzcoa, with headquarters in San Sebastian. From June to October 1813 he held several brief commands with the field army, and in October was appointed commandant at Bayonne, which brought to a head the conflict between Reille and Soult, the former objecting to Thouvenot's command of some of the troops there, by virtue of his governorship, though junior to Reille. Thouvenot performed poorly when opposing the Allied advance over the Adour, and was condemned by his enemies for the last act of the war. On 14 April 1814 he mounted the sortie from Bayonne, almost the last action of the war, when he must have realised that the war was over. For it and the useless loss of life that resulted, he was roundly denounced as a blackguard by Allied officers, including Wellington (though Colville thought him a well-intentioned, gentlemanly individual, and suspected that sortie had been forced upon him by subordinates). Nevertheless, Thouvenot refused to yield Bayonne until proof of the armistice had been delivered to him by his own side.

Toreno, José Maria Quiepo de Llano Ruiz de Saravia, conde de (1786-1843) Author of a noted, Spanish early history of the Peninsular war, and a leading liberal politician, he was born into one of the most ancient noble famililies of the Asturias. As Vizconde de Matarossa (the title he bore until his father's death in 1808), he was one of the Asturian delegates who journeyed to London in May-June 1808 to seek British assistance. He returned to Spain at the end of the year and saw some military service, but was mainly concerned with the Cortes: his uncle was a member of the Central Junta, and he led the party which compelled the Regency to summon the Cortes, to which he was elected in 1811, though short of the qualifying age of 25 (his election was opposed by some of his own relatives, who found his sympathies too advanced). As a leader of those who framed the 1812 Constitution, he thought it prudent to go into exile upon the return of Ferdinand VII (he was doubly suspect to the ultra-royalists for both his liberal views and for his family connection with his brother-in-law Porlier, who led the insurrection at Corunna). He served in the Cortes again after the 1820 revolution, but went into exile on the French invasion, and remained abroad until 1833; he was briefly prime minister in 1834, but went into exile again and died in Paris.

Trant, Brigadier-General Sir Nicholas (1769-1839) One of the most prominent and audacious (even reckless) commanders of the Portuguese Army, Nicholas Trant was an officer of the British Royal Staff Corps, and one of the first to help reorganise the Portuguese forces. He served at Roliça and Vimeiro, and from April 1809 led a Portuguese force, largely militia, and was appointed governor of Oporto in that year. He harried Massena's artillery reserve at Sotojal near Vizeu (20 September 1810) but was unable to capture it, and found his troops wanting at Sardão on 30 September. A week later he recaptured Coimbra, and during Massena's retreat in the following year audaciously engaged Claparede's Division and might have been handled roughly had not reinforcements arrived. In 1812 he covered Almeida with his militia division, formed an impractical plan to raid Marmont's head-quarters but was himself surprised and routed at Guarda (14 April 1812). Although a general officer in Portuguese service, his regimental rank at the end of the war was still captain; his knighthood was by virtue of the award of the Portuguese Order of the Tower and Sword.

Trévise, duc de: see Mortier.

Vandeleur, Major-General John Ormsby (1763-1849) Best-known for command of a cavalry brigade at Waterloo, Vandeleur became a major-general on 4 June 1811 and on the following 30 September was appointed to command a brigade of the Light Division in succession to George Drummond, who had died from a 'malignant fever'. Wounded at the storm of Ciudad Rodrigo (in the shoulder), Vandeleur resumed command in mid-April, and in July 1813 was transferred to command a cavalry brigade (12th and 16th Light Dragoons) which he led to the end of the war (and at Waterloo). He became a KCB in 1815 and rose to the rank of general. George Napier thought him 'a fine, honourable, kind-hearted, gallant soldier, and an excellent man'[1].

[1] Napier, Sir George, *Passages in the Early Military Life of General Sir George T. Napier*, ed. Gen. W.C.E. Napier, London 1884, p. 218.

Vedel, General Dominique-Honoré-Antoine, comte de (1771-1848) Born in Monaco, of noble birth, Vedel attained the rank of *général de division* in November 1807, after much active service and several wounds, but his career was undone in the Peninsula. He was sent to reinforce Dupont with a division largely of untried troops (six battalions of Légions de Reserve and the 1/3rd Swiss) and, operating independently of Dupont's main body, was slow to respond when he heard the cannonade of Bailen. After he finally got into action he was ordered by Dupont to cease hostilities, an armistice having been agreed. Initially Dupont told Vedel to extricate his command, but recalled him upon discovering that his troops had been included in the articles of capitulation. As Dupont was a prisoner under duress, Vedel should have ignored this order and saved his command; but he returned to surrender and even called in outlying detachments to capitulate, though they had not been included in the negotiations. In November 1808 Vedel returned to France, was arrested, imprisoned for a time and court-martialled; not until December 1813 was his disgrace overlooked and another command given him.

Verdier, General Jean-Antoine, comte (1767-1839) Appointed to command the 2nd Division of Bessières's Corps of Observation of the Pyrenees in March 1808, Verdier won one of the earliest actions in the war, at Logroño in June. Later in the month he superseded Lefebvre-Desnouettes in command of the forces besieging Saragossa, and was wounded by a ball in the left thigh in the attack of 4 August. In November he was appointed to command the Bilbao province, but in the following year replaced Reille in Catalonia and took on the siege of Gerona. He had little success, attacked without caution, and, dissatisfied with support from Gouvion St. Cyr, on 21 September 1809 announced that he was going home, declaring himself unfit, even though he had officially been denied permission. Subsequently he served in Russia and Italy.

Victor Perrin, Marshal Claude, duc de Bellune (1764-1841) A marshal from July 1807, Claude Victor (as he called himself) was appointed to command I Corps in Spain in September 1808. He defeated Blake at Espinosa, Venegas at Uclès and, most notably, Cuesta at Medellin; but in July 1809 was defeated at Talavera. In 1810 he participated in the conquest of Andalusia, received the surrender of Seville and laid siege to Cadiz, but in March 1811 was beaten by Graham at Barossa, despite displaying his customary bravery. At the end of the year he was recalled to France and left his command early in the following year, to be re-employed immediately for the invasion of Russia. On 10 September 1808 he had been ennobled as duc de Bellune, a title apparently not much to his liking, and supposedly a pun on his nickname '*le beau soleil*' (handsome sun, supposedly from his pleasant disposition; hence *belle-lune*, beautiful moon!).

Waters, Lieutenant-Colonel John (1774-1842) Described by Rees Gronow as one of those extraordinary individuals who seemed to have been designed by nature for a special purpose, this Welsh officer was one of the most remarkable intelligence agents of the period. In Portuguese service from February

1809 until the end of the war, he was an expert at roaming behind enemy lines in disguise, and gathering invaluable intelligence for Wellington. He had a complete command of all Spanish dialects and spoke French with a deliberate German accent so as to impersonate an Alsatian. Even when captured (at Sabugal), he escaped. One of the most valuable of Wellington's subordinates, he rose to the rank of lieutenant-general by 1841.

Wellesley, Hon. Henry (1773-1847) Wellington's youngest brother (known as Baron Cowley from 1828), he had held a number of political and diplomatic appointments (including that of First Secretary to the Treasury 1808-09) when he was appointed as British ambassador to Spain, a position he retained until 1822. His influence provided considerable support both to his brother and to the Spanish patriot cause, for example in helping facilitate large loans to the Regency despite the disapproval of others in the ministry. It was his wife with whom Lord Paget eloped, thus preventing this skilled cavalry leader from serving under Wellington's command until 1815.

Wellesley, Richard Colley, Marquess (1760-1842) Wellington's eldest brother achieved his greatest fame as governor-general of India (1797-1805), but played a small role in the Peninsular War when appointed British ambassador to Spain in 1809, in succession to Frere; but he held this post only a few months, when he was appointed British foreign secretary. He resigned from this office in 1812, partly over a perceived lack of support for Wellington, and partly over the vexed question of Catholic Emancipation.

Wellington, Field Marshal Arthur Wellesley, 1st Duke of (1769-1852) Although the most profound effects of the Peninsular War were those experienced by the nations and inhabitants of the Peninsula, arguably its dominant personality was Arthur Wellesley, who the war established as one of the greatest of commanders. Having experienced a successful career in India, and as subordinate to Cathcart in the Danish expedition, and with the great advantage of being connected closely (and a one-time member of) the British ministry, he was selected to command British forces in the Peninsula, but originally was subordinate to both Burrard and Dalrymple. They prevented the exploitation of his victory at Vimeiro, and concluded the Convention of Cintra; recalled for the inquiry into the latter, Wellesley was the only one exonerated entirely, and returned to Portugal in April 1809. From then until the end of the war his army formed one of the primary opponents of the French, and without it - and probably without Wellesley himself - it is unlikely that the French would ever have been expelled from Spain. After Talavera he became Viscount Wellington, successive steps in the peerage taking him through Earl (February 1812) and Marquess (October 1812) to Duke (May 1814), and his rank rose to field-marshal in June 1813 (he was also marshal-general of Portugal and ultimately generalissimo of Spain). He never enjoyed complete freedom of command, being responsible to his masters at home, and did not even have the ability to appoint his preferred subordinates, yet he coupled his military command with diplomatic concerns; nothing about his army or its campaigns was beneath his gaze, his grasp being all the more remarkable by virtue of the shortage of competent subordinates (though having total confidence in himself, it might be argued that he stifled the development of some capable deputies). He has been characterised as a defensive general: but though his strategy had to be defensive at first, in establishing a secure base in Portugal, his increasing forays into Spain enabled him to demonstrate that he was a master of opportunity (as at Salamanca) and manoeuvre (1813). Within the confines of a 'defensive battle' - in which his tactics of shielding his army with skirmishers and establishing his position on the reverse slope of high ground entirely frustrated the French system of manoeuvre - his tactics could be quite aggressive, and his caution was to a large extent forced upon him by the knowledge that he commanded the only British army capable of taking the field in so large an undertaking (in which his Portuguese troops formed an integral part). To his army he appeared aloof and austere, though he could be moved to tears by casualty-returns; yet though never adored by his followers in the way of a Napoleon or a Marlborough, he had their complete and utter trust, that he would not expend their lives without purpose and would see them fed and clothed wherever possible (he appreciated the importance of logistics more than many commanders of the era). John Kincaid spoke for the whole army when he remarked that they would rather see his long nose in a fight than a reinforcement of 10,000 men; or, as Lieutenant John Bainbrigge of the 20th recalled rather more respectfully, on the day before he lost his arm in the Pyrenees, when the British had suffered a rough day, 'I can never forget the joy which beamed in every countenance when his Lordship's presence became known; it diffused a general feeling of confidence through the ranks'[1].

[1] Smyth, B., *History of the XX Regiment 1688-1888*, London 1889, p. 396.

White, Joseph Blanco (1775-1841) A significant contemporary commentator, José Maria Blanco y Crespo was born at Seville and trained for the Roman Catholic priesthood, but his doubts led him to study in Britain, where he entered the Anglican Church. Though best-known as a theologian and poet (notably for his sonnet *Night and Death*), he remained in Spain until 1810, observing the beginning of the uprising and the Peninsular War, upon which he commentated. Very much a political liberal, he went into exile in England in 1810, adopting the name of Joseph Blanco White, and from 1810 until 1814 edited the Spanish monthly magazine *El Español*, which commented upon current affairs; he received a pension of £250 from the civil list. His later writings were largely theological, and he translated the Book of Common Prayer into Spanish.

York, Field-Marshal Frederick Augustus, Duke of (1763-1827) The second son of King George III, the Duke of York had commanded the British expeditions to the Netherlands in 1793-95 and 1799, and during the Peninsular War was commander-in-chief of the British Army (less a period 1809-11, when Sir David Dundas held that post, the Duke having been forced to resign over the scandal of his mistress accepting money for military and other preferments, although the Duke was proved to have been entirely innocent). As commander-in-chief he was in general supportive of Wellington, but his actions were not entirely in Wellington's best interests, as in the case in 1813 when York insisted that under-strength units be replaced, whereas Wellington preferred to retain experienced men inured to the hardships of campaigning, even if not so numerous as the planned replacements. The Duke of York's concern for the army was genuine, and was recognised in his popularity with the ordinary soldiers, who styled him 'the Soldiers' Friend'.

Zaragoza, Agostina (1788-1857) Taking her surname from her native city, Agostina 'the Maid of Saragossa' was undoubtedly the greatest popular heroine of the war, and an incarnation of Spanish resistance to French invasion. She came to prominence in the defence of Saragossa when, it was said, she crewed a cannon at which her lover or fiancé had been killed. She appears in the literature of the war under various names: 'Maria Agostina', 'Augustina Sarzella', 'Agustina Zaragoza Domenech', while Belmas calls her 'Augustina d'Aragon'. Her bravery became an icon for the war and later: Goya portrayed her in his print *Que Valor!*, she was the subject of a painting of her serving the gun by Sir David Wilkie, and Byron eulogised her beauty and 'fairy form'; though others (including William Napier) seem to have thought her exploits - and those of other heroines of the war - perhaps had been over-stated. Palafox was said to have witnessed her firing the cannon, and commissioned her as a sub-lieutenant of artillery; certainly, she appeared in uniform at Cadiz, where she acted as a symbol for national patriotism. Sir John Carr, who met her, remarked that Spain would have been happier if most of her generals 'had acted with the undaunted intrepidity of this young female'[1].

[1] *Gentleman's Magazine*, December 1811, p. 549.

THE ARMIES

ORGANISATION AND ESTABLISHMENTS

Details of the military and naval forces of the various national armies which served in the Peninsular War are arranged here in alphabetical order of the names of the states involved in the war.

FRANCE

The experience of the French Army in the Peninsula was a succession of difficulties. Although until 1812 it could reasonably be claimed that they were winning the war, posting there was generally unpopular, except for those in the higher ranks who might take advantage of the opportunities for personal enrichment.

Probably many French soldiers would have held a similar opinion to Marshal Macdonald (although it was written after the event when the outcome of the war was known): 'I had a very strong objection to the manner in which war was carried on in Spain; my objection had its root in the dishonesty – or what in high places is called policy – which caused the invasion of the country; however, the noble and courageous resistance of its inhabitants triumphed over our efforts and our arms. I obeyed, nevertheless, and . . . led a very active life, that was as odious as it was exhausting'[1].

Ultimately, the task of subduing the Peninsula proved impossible and led to defeat; indeed, a realistic assessment of the situation of the French in trying to accomplish too much with insufficient resources was given by Marshal Bessières, writing to Berthier in June 1811: 'we hold on to dreams'[2]. Many of those who survived their period of duty in the Iberian peninsula might well have agreed with Albert de Rocca, upon his departure from Spain: 'I was glad, at any price, to quit an unjust and inglorious war, where the sentiments of my heart continually disavowed the evil my arm was condemned to do'[3].

---

[1] Macdonald, Marshal J.E.J.A., *Recollections of Marshal Macdonald*, ed. C. Rousset, trans. S.L. Simeon, London 1892, Vol. II p. 16.

[2] Belmas, J., *Journaux des Sièges faits ou soutenus par les Français dans la Péninsule de 1807 à 1814*, Paris 1836-37, Vol. I p. 562.

[3] De Rocca, A.J.M., *Memoirs of the War of the French in Spain*, London 1815 (modern edition entitled *In the Peninsula with a French Hussar*, London 1990, p. 170).

Imperial Guard

Upon the creation of the Empire, in May 1804 the existing *Garde des Consuls* was re-titled as the *Garde Impériale*; the military formation most closely connected to Napoleon, in subsequent years it grew to become an army within an army, the empire's military élite, encompassing all 'arms of service'.

Elements of the Guard preceded Napoleon's personal intervention in the war in Spain: the junior regiments of Fusiliers, the Seamen of the Guard, and nine squadrons of cavalry including Dragoons, Chasseurs à Cheval with attached Mameluke squadron, Polish Chevau-Légers, Gendarmerie d'Elite and the Chevau-Légers de Berg (the latter from Murat's duchy and attached to the Guard); which together with artillery numbered in excess of 6,400 men. Although the battalion of Seamen was lost at Bailen, the number of Guard deployed in the Peninsula virtually doubled with Napoleon's arrival, to about 8,000 infantry, 3,500 cavalry and 600 gunners by November 1808, the reinforcements including the two regiments of Grenadiers à Pied and the two of Chasseurs à Pied (four battalions each of Grenadiers and Chasseurs).

The two Fusilier regiments numbered six battalions, and the cavalry regiments included the Chasseurs à Cheval with Mameluke squadron, Dragoons, Grenadiers à Cheval, Polish Chevau-Légers and Gendarmerie d'Elite; with 36 guns. These troops returned with Napoleon for the 1809 campaign against Austria, but in late 1809 a further Guard formation was sent to Spain, including three provisional regiments of cavalry (formed from the various regiments) and two divisions of Young Guard infantry (8 regiments), which with artillery and supporting services numbered some 17,300 men in January 1810. Subsequently they received reinforcements, and served principally with the Army of the North, until withdrawn with other units to bolster Napoleon's forces in central Europe. The Young Guard regiments had some changes of title during this period: in December 1810 the Tirailleurs-Chasseurs and Tirailleurs-Grenadiers were re-titled as Voltigeurs and Tirailleurs respectively, and in February 1811 the Conscrits-Chasseurs and Conscrits-Grenadiers similarly became Voltigeurs and Tirailleurs respectively; hence in mid-1811 the two Young Guard divisions with the Army of the North included four regiments each of Voltigeurs and Tirailleurs.

Infantry

Representing the most numerous part of the French army deployed in the Peninsula, at the beginning of the war the infantry included some 90 line regiments, numbered from 1 to 112 (22 numbers were vacant); before the end of the war the number of regiments had risen to 156, with two of the vacant numbers being filled in addition. Of these, at least 72 of the original regiments, and twelve of those newly-raised, spent some time in the Peninsula, which exemplifies the resources that the war demanded. Of the regiments raised during the period of the Peninsular War, some were formed from Provisional, Reserve or Auxiliary units deployed in Spain (see below). The 135th to 156th Regiments were formed from the National Guard, elements of which did participate in the Peninsula; the 143rd Line, for example, was formed in January 1813 from the 28th-31st Cohortes of National Guard, and served in Catalonia.

Each infantry regiment consisted of a number of battalions, and it was quite usual for a number of battalions of the same regiment to serve together. In the French army in Spain in late 1808, for example (excluding the foreign corps), some 42 regiments had three of their battalions in the same division, 16 had four battalions, 10 had two battalions, and 27 battalions were serving independently, though eight of the latter were transferred from VIII Corps in December to join other battalions of their regiment in different formations. In the Army of Portugal at the beginning of 1810, eight regiments were present with four battalions each, eleven had three battalions, three had two battalions, and eight had only a single battalion present (of the latter, seven were in VIII Corps, six being so weak that their cadres were subsequently sent back to France and the men distributed among the regiments of II Corps).

The official establishment of each battalion was originally of nine companies, seven of fusiliers and two élite companies, one of grenadiers and one of voltigeurs, each company of three officers and 137 other ranks. A decree of 18 February 1808 confirmed a change in establishment which may have been in motion already: henceforth each regiment was to comprise four *bataillons de guerre* (service battalions), and one depot battalion commanded by the senior captain, with a major in command of the depot itself. Each *bataillon de guerre*, commanded by a *chef de bataillon*, comprised four fusilier companies and one each of grenadiers and voltigeurs, each company of three officers, fourteen NCOs, two drummers and 121 privates. With a staff (including officers) of 50 for each battalion, and regimental staff, a regiment of four battalions plus depot battalion should have numbered 108 officers and 3,862 other ranks. Subsequently some regiments raised a 5th, 6th or even 7th field battalion. Actual strength on campaign was often very much weaker than the official establishment: for example, in the Army of Portugal at the beginning of 1811 average battalion strength (all ranks) seems to have been, in II Corps 373, VI Corps 450, and VIII Corps 334. In the same army in mid-1812, before the Battle of Salamanca, average battalion-strength was 574; at Fuentes de Oñoro

512; at Albuera (including the combined grenadiers) 528; at Toulouse 478.

At the beginning of the Peninsular War there were 25 regiments of light infantry (*Infanterie Légère*), numbered 1 to 31 (with five numbers vacant). During the period of the war the number increased to the 37me *Léger*, with three numbers remaining vacant. They followed the line regiments in establishment, and although the convention persisted of distributing the light regiments throughout the divisions, to provide an enhanced skirmishing capacity, in effect they were similar to the line regiments: all were able to skirmish and act in a light infantry role if required. The light regiments had some differences in uniform and often an enhanced *esprit de corps*, but unlike the light units of some armies, no rifled firearms were used. There was also a difference in terminology: the ordinary companies were styled chasseurs rather than fusiliers, and the 'grenadiers' of light infantry were designated as carabiniers, though the light companies were voltigeurs, as in the line regiments.

Other infantry units were deployed in Spain, including *régiments de marche:* provisional regiments, composed of drafts, to be broken up when reaching their parent formations. *Ad hoc* formations could be created on campaign, such as the battalions of *Grenadiers réunis* ('combined grenadiers') which served at Albuera, in this case evidently drawn from four regiments, none of which were otherwise present at the battle. A number of 'Provisional Regiments' were sent to Spain, formations composed of elements of various units: for example, the 6th Provisional Regiment that fought at Bailen had four battalions (of four companies each), drawn from (1st-4th Battns. respectively) the 76th, 27th, 111th and 95th Line Regiments, comprising some 1,850 men. In July 1808 the Provisional Regiments in Spain were converted to the

114th-117th, 119th and 120th Line, and the 118th Line was formed from the 11th Provisional Regiment and three depot battalions at Bayonne. Another formation was the five *Légions de Réserve*, formed from conscripts in 1807-08, each of four infantry battalions of eight companies each, and an artillery company. They were sent into Spain, eleven battalions from the 1st, 3rd and 4th Legions being captured at Bailen; the remainder were formed into the 121st and 122nd Line Regiments on 1 January 1809. Another type of temporary unit was the Auxiliary Battalions (*Bataillons Auxiliares*), formed in 1810 from the depots of regiments not already serving in Spain. They were sent to the Peninsula and in March 1811 the 1st, 3rd and 6th Auxiliary Battalions were formed into the new 130th Line Regiment, and the 2nd, 4th, 5th and 7th Auxiliary Battalions into a new 34th Light Infantry.

Foreign regiments composed a small but significant part of the French army, apart from the line regiments that were originally foreign in composition (the 113th Line, for example, which served in Spain, was formed in May 1808 from Tuscan troops). Pre-eminent among the foreign regiments were the four Swiss Regiments, each of four battalions, formed 1805-06; the 2nd, 3rd and 4th Regiments all served in the Peninsula, where their red coats on occasion caused confusion with the British, both in and out of battle. Other Swiss corps deployed to the Peninsula were the *Bataillon du Prince de Neufchâtel* (Berthier's Neufchâtel – or Neuchâtel – Battalion, formed 1807 with an establishment of one artillery and six infantry companies, Marshal Berthier being the prince of the state; it served in the Army of the North from early 1810 to March 1812); and the *Bataillon Valaisan* (Valais Battalion), formed 1805, of five companies, serving in Catalonia from July 1808 until 1811.

Four of Napoleon's foreign regiments were re-titled as the 1st-4th *Régiments d'Etrangers* in August 1811; all served in the Peninsula. The 1st, raised in 1805 as the *Régiment de la Tour d'Auvergne*, was initially German in composition; its 4th Battalion, formed in 1809 largely from Austrian prisoners, served in Spain (latterly Catalonia) until recalled in June 1811. The 2nd, originally the *Régiment d'Isembourg*, largely German in composition, sent its 4th Battalion (of nine companies, mostly Austrians captured in 1809) to Spain in 1810, where it suffered some desertion to the guerrillas, and returned to France early in 1811. The 3rd was originally the *Légion Irlandaise*, sending a detachment to Spain in January 1808, which in that December was designated as the 2nd Battalion, being joined by the 3rd Battalion in the following year. Early in 1811 the battalions were amalgamated because of the attrition of campaign, and the survivors withdrawn from the Peninsula in the following year. The 4th was originally the *Régiment de Prusse*, raised from Prussian deserters; the 1st Battalion went to Spain in 1808, the 2nd in 1810, subsequently being amalgamated; plagued with desertion, it was withdrawn from Spain in 1812.

Among the best-known foreign corps was the *Légion de la Vistule*, (Vistula Legion), formed from Poles in March 1808, comprising lancers (see below) and three infantry regiments, each of two, six-company battalions, and a depot battalion. All three served in Spain from 1808, and a new 4th Regiment from 1810; all were withdrawn early in 1812 for the Russian campaign. Other foreign units included the *Légion Hanovrienne*, five companies of light infantry and three of chasseurs à cheval, formed from Hanoverians in 1803. The infantry entered the Peninsular war with Junot in 1807, returning in 1808 after the Cintra evacuation, and expanded to two battalions from September 1809. Losses (including at Fuentes de Oñoro where their red coats led to confusion and cost casualties from 'friendly fire') resulted in the consolidation of the unit into one battalion, and the incorporation in it of the *Régiment de Westphalie*, a light infantry corps raised in north Germany in 1806, and in Spain from 1808. In late 1811 the Legion was broken up. Another was the *Légion du Midi*, of Piedmontese origin, which served in the Peninsula with Junot and consolidated its two battalions into one in 1810, which was disbanded in August 1811 and its personnel incorporated into the 31st *Léger.*

Cavalry

The French cavalry comprised 'heavy' regiments, Cuirassiers and Carabiniers; 'light', Chasseurs à Cheval, Hussars and (from 1811) Chevau-Légers-Lanciers; and Dragoons, which were sometimes described as intermediate between the two.

There were originally twelve cuirassier regiments, rising to fourteen by 1810, and two carabinier regiments. Authorised in October 1807, two Provisional Heavy Cavalry regiments were sent to Spain, the 1st composed of detachments from the 1st-3rd Cuirassiers and both Carabinier regiments, and the 2nd (which served at Bailen) from the 5th, 9th and 10th-12th Cuirassiers. In October 1808 the 13th Cuirassiers was formed from the 1st Provisional Heavy Cavalry; it was the only cuirassier regiment to serve as a regiment in the Peninsula (neither of the carabinier regiments served there as regiments, only detachments); the 13th served under Suchet until 1813. The establishment for cuirassier regiments was four squadrons of two companies each, increased to five squadrons with a total of 1,040 men in March 1807; in December 1809 they reverted to four squadrons, but the 13th remained with five. A 3rd Provisional

Cuirassier Regiment was formed in January 1808 from the 4th and 6th-8th Cuirassiers, and served in Spain until disbandment in 1810.

From 1807 the other cavalry regiments had an establishment of four squadrons of two companies each, the company comprising four officers and 128 other ranks; a 5th squadron acted as a depot, although some light regiments were increased to six, seven or even eight squadrons. Strength on campaign was often very different from the establishment: for example, at the beginning of 1809, the average strength of 'corps cavalry' (regiments attached to a *corps d'armée*) was about 480 per regiment, in the cavalry reserve 420; at Albuera the average regimental strength was less than 350. Statistics of regimental strength can be deceptive, however, as squadrons could be detached so that a regiment might be represented in a formation or at an action by only one or two squadrons. For example, at the second siege of Saragossa, III Corps had two cavalry regiments of four squadrons each (average squadron-strength 113) plus four other regiments represented by detachments, and a *régiment de marche*; and V Corps had two regiments, each of three squadrons, average squadron-strength 251. At the French siege of Badajoz in 1811, two of the seven French regiments had four squadrons each, the remainder only two each, with an average squadron-strength of almost 200; Suchet's cavalry at Tarragona in 1811 included two French regiments of three squadrons each and one with two, average squadron-strength 148. In Dupont's 'Army of Observation of the Gironde', his five provisional regiments had an average strength of 660, or 220 per squadron; in September 1810 VIII Corps of the Army of Portugal had a dragoon division of twelve squadrons, drawn from six regiments, with an average squadron-strength of 155.

It was not always possible to attain the ideal of having brigades composed of only one type of cavalry (heavy, light, etc.); in the case of Tarragona quoted above, for example, Suchet's single cavalry brigade was composed of the 13th Cuirassiers, 24th Dragoons, 4th Hussars and an Italian dragoon regiment. The numbers of cavalry available, as well as circumstances, affected the proportions of an army that the cavalry represented; at Albuera, for example, some 16 per cent of Soult's army was cavalry, whereas in September 1810 cavalry comprised some 12.5 per cent of the Army of Portugal, and only 6.5 per cent of the army at Toulouse.

Of thirty dragoon regiments, no less than 26 served in the Peninsula, the most numerous part of the cavalry in Spain and Portugal, and the most versatile. Armed with the Dragoon Musket, much more effective than the carbines carried by the other cavalry, while retaining all the abilities of cavalry, they were also able to skirmish as effectively as infantry. Combining firepower with mobility, they were ideally suited for anti-guerrilla operations, as well as patrolling and escort duty; though formations of permanently-dismounted dragoons (*Dragons à Pied*), deployed elsewhere, were not utilised in the Peninsula, despite their ability to fight on foot. Some Provisional Regiments were deployed early in the war; for example, three were at Bailen: the 1st (drawn from the 11th, 13th, 14th, 18th, 19th and 22nd Dragoons), 2nd (from the 8th, 12th, 20th, 21st, 25th and 26th Dragoons) and the 6th (drawn entirely from the 6th Dragoons).

At the beginning of the war there were 24 regiments of Chasseurs à Cheval, the most numerous type of light cavalry, numbered 1-26 (nos. 17 and 18 were vacant). Five more regiments were formed between 1808 and 1811, bearing numbers 27-31. Some sixteen regiments served in the Peninsula, plus detachments which formed part of the Provisional Regiments sent to Spain early in the war. (Of the two which served at Bailen, for example, the 1st Provisional Chasseurs comprised detachments from the 1st, 2nd, 7th, 13th and 21st Regiments, the 2nd Provisional from the 5th, 11th, 12th, 16th and 20th). Four of the new regiments served in Spain: the 27th Chasseurs, formed in May 1808 from the existing Chevau-Légers d'Aremberg or Chevau-Légers Belges, which left for Spain in the following month; the 28th, formed at the same time from the Tuscan Dragoons; the 29th, formed August 1808 from the 3rd Provisional Regiment (itself formed in the previous March); and the 31st, formed in Spain in September 1811 from the 1st and 2nd Provisional Regiments.

There were ten regiments of hussars at the beginning of the Peninsular War, of which seven served in Spain; subsequently the number was raised to fourteen, of which two served in the Peninsula: the 11th Hussars was formed in December 1810 from the 2nd Dutch Hussars, and the 12th was formed in February 1813 from the *9me bis Hussards*, which had been created in January 1812 from three squadrons of the 9th Hussars which had been detached in Spain. The Chevau-Légers-Lanciers were created in June 1811, six regiments converted from the 1st, 3rd, 8th-10th and 29th Dragoons, two from the lancers of the Vistula Legion, and one from the 30th Chasseurs à Cheval. Most of these had served in the Peninsula, but all were present in the Russian campaign of 1812 and the subsequent campaigning in Germany.

The most notable of the foreign cavalry which served in the French army in the Peninsula were the lancers of the Vistula Legion, the mounted part of the infantry corps mentioned above. There was initially one regiment of four squadrons and a depot, which served in Spain from 1808 (with one squadron being detached, which served subsequently as Suchet's escort); a second regiment was authorised in February 1811. It was the Vistula Lancers which with the 2nd Hussars executed probably the most devastating charge of the war, against Colborne's Brigade at Albuera. In June 1811 the two regiments became the 7th and 8th Chevau-Légers-Lanciers respectively, Soult retaining most of the 7th (ex-1st Vistula) in Spain until late 1812. The Hanoverian Legion included three squadrons of Chasseurs à Cheval, which served in Spain from 1808 until disbanded in 1811, being incorporated into the 30th Chasseurs à Cheval (later 9th Chevau-Légers-Lanciers).

Artillery

At the beginning of the war there were eight regiments of Foot Artillery (Artillerie à Pied), and six of Horse Artillery (Artillerie à Cheval); 9th and 7th Regiments respectively were formed from the ex-Dutch artillery in 1810, the latter disbanded in 1811. Each foot regiment originally comprised twenty companies, 22 from 1803, rising to 28 by 1813; the horse regiments had three squadrons of two companies each, some increasing to seven companies by 1813. Each company acted as a separate entity, so that regiments did not serve entire, or even in the same army. Each company was normally equipped with six guns of one 'nature' and two howitzers, horse companies with six or eight guns and two howitzers. The ordnance was originally of the Gribeauval system, in which the field guns were of 4-, 6- and 8-pdr. 'nature', the former eventually being withdrawn from the artillery and used instead as 'battalion guns' for the infantry regiments, when this form of fire-support was introduced. A new design, the 'System of Year XI' was introduced, in which

the 4- and 8-pdrs. were intended to be replaced by a new 6-pdr., but the army in Spain seems to have retained the Gribeauval System, which was re-introduced generally in 1818 when the new system was recognised as being less effective. (An example may be quoted concerning the ordnance captured at Vittoria: 28 12-pdrs., 42 8-pdrs., 43 4-pdrs., together with howitzers of four calibres and two mortars.) When the 4-pdrs. were relegated to regimental artillery, it was usual for the 8-pdrs. to be deployed at brigade or divisional level, with the 12-pdrs. for corps or army reserves. The horse artillery, equipped with 6- or 8-pdrs., was intended to provide fire-support for the cavalry, though in general the artillery was deployed where and when required. The heavier guns of the siege-train were generally deployed as corps or army reserve.

Drivers were members of the Artillery Train (Train d'Artillerie), of which 13 battalions existed in 1808, a number doubled in 1810 (with the new battalions numbered 1-13 *bis*); personnel were attached to horse and foot batteries irrespective of their company or battalion. There were also battalions of artillery 'ouvriers' (lit. 'workmen'), to assist; the Pontoneers also formed part of the artillery, detachments being distributed throughout the army.

An example of how the various units were deployed is provided by the artillery present at the siege of Gerona in 1809. VII Corps's artillery comprised No. 11 Company of the 7th Foot Artillery, No. 2 Company of the 2nd Horse Artillery, detachments of Italian Foot and Horse Artillery, No. 3 Company of the 2nd Battalion of Pontoneers, a detachment (13 men) of ouvriers, detachments from the 4th and 6th, and 4th and 6th *bis* Battalions of Train, and an Italian Train company. The siege-train was crewed by Nos. 2, 5 and 12 Companies of the 3rd Foot Artillery, Nos. 10,

12 and 13 Companies of the 4th Foot Artillery, Nos. 4 and 16 Companies of the 6th Foot Artillery, a detachment of the 2nd Horse Artillery, two companies of Westphalian artillery and a detachment from Berg, two ouvrier detachments, and elements from the 12th and 2nd, 4th and 13th *bis* battalions of Train. Excluding staff, VII Corps's artillery numbered 11 officers and 961 other ranks, the siege-train 36 officers and 1,239 other ranks (plus 3 officers and 123 pioneers not part of the artillery establishment).

Engineers

The engineer service consisted of a corps of officers, battalions of sappers (*sapeurs*), eight by 1812, and companies of miners (*mineurs*); the latter were formed into two battalions of five (later six) companies each in 1806. An Engineer Train was established in 1806, formed into a battalion of seven companies in 1811. *Sapeur* and *mineur* companies were deployed as required, and supported by units of pioneers, for example the *Pioniers Blancs* ('White Pioneers'), elements of which were deployed in Spain. Originally formed in February 1806, primarily from Austrian prisoners of war, they were titled thus presumably to distinguish them from the *Pioniers Noirs*, which in August 1806 passed into Neapolitan service; in September 1810 the *Pioniers Blancs* were transformed into the *Pioniers Volontaires Etrangers*.

Taking as an example the above case of the supporting services deployed at Gerona to demonstrate a typical organisation, VII Corps contributed eight French and two Italian engineer officers, while the siege-train had 19 French and two Italian officers of the engineer staff, No. 5 Company of the 1st Battn. *Mineurs*; No. 7 Company of the 2nd Battn., and No. 2 Company of the 3rd Battn. of *Sapeurs*, and an Italian *sapeur* company;

with the 1st Company of *Pioniers Blancs* attached to the artillery. (Of a total of 33 officers with the engineer siege-train, three were killed, 17 wounded and six fell ill during the siege, a casualty-rate of almost 79 per cent).

Auxiliaries

A number of what might be termed 'auxiliary' units were employed in the Peninsula, including the *Garde de Paris.* This was raised in October 1802 as the *Garde Municipale de Paris*, initially for the security of the capital, and re-titled *Garde de Paris* in May 1806; its two regiments had two battalions each. The 2nd Battalions of both regiments served in Dupont's 1st Division and were captured at Bailen; another detachment went to Spain in June 1808 and joined the Army of the North. 182 members participated in the defence of Burgos. The *Garde* was disbanded in 1812.

National Guard units existed inside France, the principal unit being the *cohorte* of ten companies, grouped into 'legions' normally of four *cohortes*; from 1812 the force was reorganised to encompass virtually all able-bodied men aged between 20 and 60 (most duty fell on those aged 20-26), with *cohortes* consisting of one artillery and six infantry companies and a depot. At times the National Guard of the *départements* adjoining the Spanish frontier were used to secure that boundary, or even to serve in garrisons on the Spanish side of the border. There were also 'Departmental Reserve Companies', created in each *département* in 1805 to perform civic duties within their own area, which could be mobilised for service along and over the border. In mid-1808, for example, when Reille was ordered to relieve Figueras with an army assembled at Perpignan, it included a battalion of National Guard from the Pyrénées Orientales.

Another formation intended to protect the Pyrenees was the *Chasseurs de Montagne*, established in August 1806, originally planned as 34 companies. Recruited primarily from the local National Guard, in 1811 the force was reorganised in three battalions, the 1st in the *départements* of Hautes-Pyrénées, Haute-Garonne and Pyrénées Orientales, the 2nd from l'Ariège, and the 3rd from Basses-Pyrénées. They were involved in some skirmishes with guerrillas, and some 255 members of the 3rd Battn. formed part of the garrison of San Sebastian during the siege. In 1814 the three battalions were absorbed by the 116th Line, 4th and 25th *Léger* respectively.

The *Gendarmerie Impériale* operated throughout the Empire, organised in 'legions' (29 in 1808, 34 by 1811), units both mounted and on foot, a militarised force of ex-soldiers. In 1810 20 squadrons of *Gendarmerie d'Espagne* were created for service in Spain, from experienced gendarmes and selected soldiers, each of 7 officers, 80 mounted and 120 dismounted men, some stationed along the road from the frontier to Madrid to secure communications, with a separate legion for Catalonia. In November 1810 the best were concentrated into a mounted legion of six squadrons, with headquarters at Burgos, styled the *Légion à Cheval de Burgos*. Gendarmes armed with the lance were distinguished by a chasseur-style uniform and titled *Lanciers-Gendarmes* or *Gendarmes Chevau-Légers*.

In December 1811 the *Gendarmerie d'Espagne* was reorganised in six legions: the 1st was the Burgos *Légion à Cheval*, the 2nd was based at Saragossa, the 3rd at Pamplona, the 4th in the Vittoria region and the 5th at Burgos; the 6th was the legion in Catalonia. Not all their service was against guerrillas: the Burgos Legion, for example, participated in the great cavalry mêlée against Anson's Brigade at Venta del Pozo/Villadrigo in October 1812; a company of the 12th squadron (2 officers and 90 men), with five gunners, the commandant, surgeon and Saint-Jacques the engineer, formed the entire garrison of Monzon fort in 1813-14; and a squadron of the 3rd Legion formed the whole of the garrison's cavalry at the siege of Pamplona.

A number of auxiliary units were formed in Spain during the war. In Aragon, a company of *Gendarmes Aragonais* was formed at Jaca in January 1810, rising to three companies in strength; in March 1811 four companies of *Fusiliers Aragonais* (one of which deserted to the guerrillas); and an ephemeral company of *Chasseurs à Cheval Aragonais*, formed in November 1811. These corps were united in July 1812, and after losses and desertion were disbanded and interned in France in October 1813.

Catalonia provided a number of Spanish auxiliary units, including the *Régiment de Catalogne*, created in February 1812 to demonstrate the new status of the territory annexed to France; it was never fully formed and was disbanded in March 1812. In September 1810 a unit of *Chasseurs de l'Ampurdam* or *Miqueletes de Don Pujol* (named from the area, around Figueras, or from the commandant, José Pujol) was formed, from guerrilla deserters; they had a dreadful reputation for pillage and in late 1813 were absorbed into a unit entitled *Chasseurs Etrangers*, together with another counter-guerrilla unit, the *Miqueletes Catalans*, two companies regulated in 1812 although existing earlier. Suchet formed a company of *Gendarmes Catalans*, increasing to three companies before being disbanded by Decaen in December 1811, in which month two companies of *Guides Catalans* were formed, being disbanded in France in May 1814. Spanish deserters were formed into two companies of *Chasseurs Catalans* in spring 1812, disbanded in

January 1814.

In April 1813 Clausel created eight *Compagnies Franches Cantabres* (Companies of Cantabrian Volunteers) in the Basque provinces; one company in each of the maritime provinces (Guipuzcoa and Vizcaya) doubled as coastguards.

Other Spanish units of the French Army served only in northern and central Europe, not in the Peninsula. These included the *Régiment Joseph-Napoléon*, authorised in February 1809 and recruited from those members of La Romana's force that had not been able to escape from Denmark; also formed from Spanish prisoners were units of *Pioniers Espanols* and *Sapeurs Espanols* (1811-13), and a company of *Ouvriers Espanols* attached to the artillery. In March 1812 Napoleon ordered that battalions of Spanish prisoners be raised to reinforce the disciplinary regiments of Walchen, Ile-de-Ré and Belle-Ile, but in the event only a battalion was formed for the former, which became the 131st Line.

Mention should also be made of the Spanish Swiss regiments Reding and Preux, which were forced to change their allegiance to Napoleon early in the war, and which formed a brigade of Dupont's army at Bailen. Many of them defected during the action, and others with Moncey at the same time also deserted.

Command and higher formations

The French forces in Spain were organised in the conventional manner: the basic element was the division, composed of two or more brigades, each of which comprised a number of infantry battalions and was usually led by a *Général de Brigade*, with a *Général de Division* in command of the division (although these were ranks rather than necessarily representing the particular appointment). Two or more divisions could be combined to form a *corps d'armée*, to which a brigade of cavalry might be attached, and which possessed its own artillery and supporting services, so as to be able to operate as a self-contained army (an example is given in the appendix). The remainder of the cavalry was concentrated into a Reserve, divisions and brigades which might be deployed independently if required. A *corps d'armée* could be commanded either by a Marshal or a *Général de Division*.

Beyond the *corps d'armée* there was no permanent structure to cover the entire war, as individual armies were created to serve in various regions, each with their own commander. Whatever the official chain of command, there was continual bickering between army and corps commanders, some at times officially under the control of King Joseph and his chief of staff (but sometimes ignoring him), with others reporting directly to Napoleon who, being far removed from the campaign, issued orders without knowledge of the circumstances of the moment, and often without a full disclosure by his subordinates of the actual situation. The difficulties of commanding from a distance were exascerbated by the slowness of communications, and their frequent interruption by guerrillas.

For example, when Napoleon wrote from Paris on 16 March 1812, announcing that Joseph was to take overall command of the armies in Spain, the message reached Madrid on 28 March, but Soult apparently only received it in late April and Suchet perhaps as late as the second week of May. The famous 29th Bulletin of the *Grande Armée* (which announced the defeat in Russia) was written before Napoleon left the army on 5 December 1812 and reached Paris on the 16th; it took a further 21 days for the news to reach Madrid (though London had it only five days after Paris!). There was much concerned correspondence on such delays, even messages sent in triplicate sometimes failing to reach their destination, and such was the problem that a considerable proportion of the French resources in Spain had to be allocated to maintaining a channel of communication. In February 1813, for example, Clarke wrote to Joseph: 'The interruption of our communications is always mischievous, sometimes alarming, and may become fatal. It is necessary that it be seriously attended to, and made not only safe but expeditious, by making the couriers, escorted by infantry, travel between Bayonne and Valladolid at least a league per hour'[4], acknowledging that dispatches could only travel at the speed of an infantry escort illustrates the problem. Even some strategy was determined by the trouble with communications: for example, it was the reason why Napoleon ordered Joseph to transfer his headquarters from Madrid to Valladolid.

Under such circumstances, Napoleon's attempts to control the war from a distance could be extremely unhelpful, even if motivated in part by his doubts over the competence of his commanders in Spain. Orders which might in theory have been perfectly feasible could be impractical without the necessary knowledge of prevailing local conditions. For example, by his order of May 1812 which forbade the relinquishing of territory, Napoleon prevented Joseph and Jourdan from concentrating their forces into the strongest field army possible; and Napoleon might be held responsible, to a considerable degree, for the loss of Badajoz in 1812, by forbidding Marmont from marching to its support until too late, the consequence of attempting to run a campaign without knowledge of local conditions and from so great a distance.

The first French 'Army of Spain' was composed of formations assembled for the purpose outside the Peninsula: the 1st and 2nd Corps of Observation of the Gironde (the 1st styled the Army of Portugal), the Corps of Observation of the Ocean Coast, of the Pyrenees and of the Eastern Pyrenees, plus the Imperial Guard. In September 1808 Napoleon reorganised his forces in Spain into numbered *corps d'armée*; Bessières's command formed II Corps, Moncey's III, and Ney's VI; the Army of Catalonia was VII, and I, IV and V were new, brought from central Europe. Some of these, in fact, kept their previous identities: Ney's VI Corps, for example, had exactly the same infantry regiments, in the same divisions, as had fought against Prussia in 1806. Not all troops in the area of operations were in such formations, however, some divisions and garrisons remaining independent; for example, of about 230,000 troops present in Spain in early 1809 (not including the sick), the seven *corps d'armée* accounted for only about 149,000 of them.

Organisation in *corps d'armées* or armies was neither constant nor permanent. For example, in April 1810 Napoleon announced the formation of the Army of Portugal under Massena, comprising principally II, VI and VIII Corps; in December 1810 it was joined by IX Corps, but when Marmont took over after Massena's departure he reorganised the army so that the corps structure was replaced by numbered divisions, with almost all previous corps and divisional commanders replaced as well.

The absence of a unified command was fatal to French plans, for except for the short time Napoleon was present, there was no universal commander-in-chief in the Peninsula. Indeed, Napoleon deliberately fractured any hope of unified command; with Massena allocated

[4] *The Confidential Correspondence of Napoleon Bonaparte with his Brother Joseph*, London 1855, Vol. II pp. 249-50.

only the Army of Portugal, Suchet with III Corps in Aragon and Augereau with VII Corps in Catalonia were removed from the authority of King Joseph and ordered to report directly to Paris. The same applied to the 'Military Governments' of Navarre, the Basque provinces, Burgos, and Valladolid, Palencia and Toro, whose governors were given autonomy under Napoleon's direct authority (although the Valladolid, Palencia and Toro viceroyalty was later placed under Massena). With Massena commanding in Leon and parts of Old Castile and Estremadura; and Soult with I, IV and V Corps virtually autonomous in Andalusia (though not officially a viceroyalty), King Joseph was left with authority only over his Army of the Centre and New Castile. This system would have been fraught with difficulty and potential confusion even had the various commanders been prepared to co-operate with one another, but there was constant bickering. For example Soult (reported Lejeune), 'was especially bitter at having to command men of equal rank with himself, and said he was often very much worried by being obliged to show so much consideration for them. "Of course", he said, "I feel greatly flattered at having Marshals de Treviso and de Belluno under my orders, but I should much prefer generals on whose passive obedience I could rely'[5].

So bad was co-operation between commanders that in March 1812 Napoleon appointed Joseph to overall command, 'to prevent discordant action'[6], but Joseph's first attempt to co-ordinate the operations of the armies failed, as neither Soult, Marmont nor Suchet decided to obey him!

Organisation continued to fluctuate; in January 1811, for example, Napoleon created the Army of the North, initially under Bessières, to unify command in that region; while in that autumn corps-designations in the Army of the South were abolished. Six principal armies existed: those of the North, South (or Andalusia), Portugal, Aragon, Centre, and Catalonia, and reinforcements were sent regularly, in the form of new units, drafts for existing battalions, and notably in 1810, 4th Battalions of regiments already serving in Spain.

The process of reinforcement, however, gave way to one of reduction. Early in 1812, in preparation for the war against Russia, Napoleon recalled significant forces, including the Guard infantry and the Vistula Legion, depriving the Army of the North of its best divisions, and reducing significantly the Armies of the South and Aragon. More were withdrawn to replace troops lost in Russia: drafts were requisitioned from each regiment to reconstitute the Imperial Guard, and regiments with three or four battalions or squadrons each lost one, the cadres being sent home to recruit, with remaining personnel distributed among the battalions or squadrons that remained. Armies whose regiments mostly had two battalions were not affected greatly, but the Army of the South lost 21 battalions, and the Army of Catalonia six.

In July 1813 Soult was recalled and implemented the most fundamental reorganisation of French forces. With the exception of Suchet's command (in April 1813 he had been named commander for both Catalonia and Aragon), Soult unified the remainder under his own command, and abolished the Armies of the North, South, Centre and Portugal, whose names were meaningless after the loss of territory. Soult was ordered to create divisions of two brigades and about

---

[5] Lejeune, L.F., *Memoirs of Baron Lejeune*, trans. Mrs. A. Bell, London 1897, Vol. II p. 58.
[6] *Confidential Correspondence*, Vol. II p. 225.

6,000 men each (strength varied) and to dispose of them as he wished. He created three 'Lieutenancies' of the Right, Centre and Left, under three 'lieutenant-generals', Reille, d'Erlon and Clausel respectively, which were virtually *corps d'armée* in all but name; plus a reserve. Each lieutenancy had three divisions: Right, 1st, 7th and 9th; Centre, 2nd, 3rd and 6th; Left, 4th, 5th and 8th. Of the 16 Light and 50 Line regiments therein, including the reserve, 24 were represented by two battalions, one by three, and the remainder by just a single battalion.

In the later stages of the war the level of experience of the troops declined, as regiments were reinforced by drafts of conscripts (many – known as *réfractaires* – declined to be conscripted or deserted immediately), and even National Guards were thrown into action. Nevertheless, the new soldiers often fought as stoutly as the old, but were less able to maintain their morale when retreating, and desertion became prevalent. After Orthez Francis Larpent observed that 'the conscripts are all running home as fast as they can', and that 'One feels now quite strange in an enemy's country, meeting deserters around on the road, gens-d'armes [sic], the same conscripts going home, and a stout peasantry with great Irish bludgeons, all very civil and friendly'[7]. In December 1813 Napoleon wrote to Joseph that 'I do not want Spain either to keep or give away. I will have nothing more to do with that country, except live in peace with it, and have the use of my army'[8]. Had he realised that earlier, there might not have arisen such disillusionment with the war, as exemplified by the lines of graffiti which stated, 'This war in Spain means death for the men, ruin for the officers, a fortune for the generals'[9].

Navy

The French navy did not play a major role in the Peninsular War; there was no attempt to bring about a fleet action as a way of interrupting the British conveyance of supplies by sea to the Peninsula. During the entire period of the Peninsular War, France lost only sixteen ships of the line: six surrendered to the Spanish at Cadiz and Vigo; four were destroyed in the British attack on Basque Roads; two were destroyed to prevent capture while escorting a convoy attempting to re-supply Barcelona, and one (the last loss, *Regulus*, in April 1814) in the Gironde; and three in other regions. Many smaller vessels were involved in coastal activity, conveyance by sea being a convenient and often more rapid method of delivery of supplies to coastal garrisons; such vessels were not infrequently attacked by British naval forces.

Naval personnel saw some service on land; small numbers of the *Artillerie de la Marine*, for example, served in Spain. In March 1808 Napoleon 'militarised' the navy by organising it in numbered battalions, later styled *Equipages*, some of which served in Spain, notably the 44th and 45th *Equipages*. Two of these battalions of sailors – the 44th *Equipage* and the *Bataillon d'Espagne* – while en route to join Massena's army and the French forces before Cadiz respectively, fought the action at Almazan on 10 July 1810, against 'El Cura's' guerrillas. Some 22 seamen were counted among the defenders of San Sebastian in 1813.

---

[7] Larpent, F.S., *The Private Journal of Judge-Advocate Larpent*, ed. Sir George Larpent, London 1854, pp. 421, 423.

[8] *Confidential Correspondence*, Vol. II pp. 255-56.

[9] Parquin, C., *Charles Parquin: Napoleon's Army*, trans. & ed. B.T. Jones, London 1969, p. 126.

GREAT BRITAIN

The presence of a British army in the Peninsula was one of (but not the only) factors which ultimately proved decisive in the war against France. It is difficult to conceive how Napoleon's forces could have been expelled without the efforts of Wellington and his troops; but conversely the Anglo-Portuguese army could surely not have prevailed had the French been able to concentrate all their resources against them, as could have happened had there been no Spanish resistance. The maintenance of a large field army in Portugal and Spain was extremely costly in financial terms, but despite some dissenting voices among the political opposition and others, the will to maintain the fight in the Peninsula hardly faltered, and the efforts of British forces bolstered the influence of the British government in negotiations with their continental allies. Notably, the successes of the war greatly enhanced the reputation of British arms, and provided the individual regiments with a fund of history and tradition that inspired succeeding generations and enhanced the regimental spirit which has been, and remains, such an important part of the British military ethos.

The internal organisation of the component parts of the British Army remained reasonably constant throughout the war, although the higher formations did become more sophisticated.

Infantry

At the beginning of the Peninsular War the infantry comprised three regiments of Foot Guards and 101 line regiments, the number of the latter increasing to 104 by 1810. About 65 of these served in the Peninsula (the exact number can be disputed: a small number of regiments contributed only detached companies for service in the Peninsula, for example the 21st, which sent its grenadier company from Sicily to eastern Spain in 1812). From 1782 most line regiments had borne a county title, an affiliation that in many cases was illusory: very often regiments recruited outside their official county, and the situation was further altered when members of the militia were permitted to volunteer for regular service, which had the effect of bringing in many more recruits with no connection to a regiment's specified county. This enrolment of militiamen was also of great consequence in providing the regular army with a supply of men already familiar with the handling of arms, drill, and with experience of military discipline.

The principal tactical element was the battalion. Some regiments only ever had one battalion, others two; at the commencement of the war, 61 line regiments had two battalions, two had three, the 1st Foot four and the 60th six; subsequently seven of the single-battalion corps raised a second, and the 56th a third. Each battalion comprised ten companies, eight 'battalion' or 'centre' companies and two 'flank' (named from their position in the line when the battalion was drawn up), one of grenadiers and one of light infantry. There was no permanently-regulated establishment in terms of numbers: each company was intended to contain about 100 'other ranks' but in practice the number was usually considerably less.

Unlike the practice in some continental armies, it was extremely unusual for two battalions of the same regiment to serve together. In theory, when a 1st Battalion was sent on active service, it exchanged its ineffective men (invalids, etc.) with fit men from the 2nd Battalion; so that if the 2nd Battalion were then itself ordered abroad, it left behind at the regimental depot not only its own ineffectives, but those of the 1st Battalion, so that 2nd Battalions were generally considerably weaker than 1st Battalions. Strengths on campaign thus varied markedly: for example, excluding the Foot Guards (habitually stronger than line battalions) and individual rifle companies, at Talavera the average battalion-strength was 633; at Busaco 623; at Salamanca 543. The prevailing difference in strength between 1st and 2nd Battalions is exemplified by the latter action: excluding two strong 3rd Battalions, the 1st Battalions averaged 561 men and the 2nd Battalions 371.

Drafts were sent to reinforce battalions during the war (such was the attrition that in 1814 it was remarked that of the 1/61st, only three officers and seven other ranks who had begun their Peninsular career in 1809 were still present), a process made easier when a 1st Battalion could call upon men from a 2nd Battalion at home. Sometimes, however, numbers dropped below a level at which battalions could operate effectively; the Duke of

York's solution was to recall them and replace them with new battalions from home. Wellington protested in 1812 at the withdrawal of some 2nd Battalions: 'some of the best and most experienced soldiers in this army, the most healthy and capable of bearing fatigue, are in the 2nd battalions. The 2nd battns. 53rd, 31st, and 66th, for instance, are much more efficient, and have always more men for duty in proportion to their gross numbers, and fewer sick than any of the 1st battalions recently arrived which had been in Walcheren; and it is certain that this army will not be so strong by the exchange of new for old soldiers'[1]. Wellington's solution was to amalgamate two weak battalions into a 'Provisional Battalion', sending home only the surplus cadres to recruit; four of these were formed from 1811, the 1st Provisional Battalion (comprising the 2/31st and 2/66th, and originally the 29th); 2nd (2nd and 2/53rd); 3rd (2/24th and 2/58th); and 4th (2/30th and 2/44th). Early in 1813 the Duke of York again tried to recall the weak battalions, to which Wellington replied, 'It is better for the service here to have one soldier or officer . . . who has served one or two campaigns, than it is to have two or even three who have not'; and of the Provisional Battalions, 'I will never part with them so long as it is left to my discretion'[2], and having seen them in action some time later, 'it is impossible for any troops to behave better'[3]. Initially only two battalions were recalled, and when subsequently it was suggested that others might be replaced by militia battalions that had volunteered for overseas service, Wellington rejected the idea completely, being delighted to receive militiamen into existing regular bat-

[1] *Dispatches of Field-Marshal the Duke of Wellington*, ed. J. Gurwood, London 1834-38, Vol. XI pp. 52-3.

[2] *Ibid.*, Vol. X, p. 77.

[3] *Ibid.*, Vol. X, p. 629.

talions, but not in their own, for 'the officers have all the faults of those of the line to an aggravated degree, and some peculiarly their own'![4]. Ultimately three provisional battalions of militia were sent to the Peninsula, but they only arrived after the cessation of hostilities.

Some regiments bore designations other than just a county affiliation. Three were Fusilier regiments (of which the 7th and 23rd served in the Peninsula, plus the grenadiers of the third fusilier regiment, the 21st, as noted above), but apart from distinctions in uniform were ordinary line regiments. Eleven were originally Highland regiments, six of which abandoned Highland dress in 1809 (it was believed to inhibit the recruiting of non-Highlanders); three of those which continued to wear Highland dress served in the Peninsula (42nd, 79th, 92nd). By 1809 six regiments were designated as light infantry (43rd, 51st, 52nd, 68th, 71st, 85th), all of which served in the Peninsula, most notably the 43rd and 52nd in the Light Division. The 60th (Royal American) Regiment had the largest establishment of any, six battalions at the beginning of the Peninsular War and eight at the end, a mixture of line and rifle-men; the 5th Battalion 60th, the first rifle-armed regular battalion in the army, was that which served throughout the Peninsular War. The 95th Rifle Corps, which increased to a strength of three battalions, was also a corps armed exclusively with rifles, and regarded (with much justification) as among the highest élite in the army.

In addition to the Provisional Battalions mentioned above, extra battalions could be formed for particular purposes by assembling companies detached from their parent formations. These were usually styled 'flank battalions', formed from detached grenadier and light companies, such as those in Graham's army at Barossa: Browne's battalion (comprising two flank companies from each of the 1/9th, 1/28th and 2/82nd), and Barnard's battalion (four companies of 3/95th Rifles and the two flank companies of the 47th). The composite Grenadier Battalion employed in eastern Spain in late 1812, for example, was an even greater mixture, being composed of the grenadier companies from the 2/10th, 1/21st, 1/31st, 1/62nd and 1/75th Foot, and from the 3rd, 7th and 8th Line Battalions of the King's German Legion (for which see below). Other noted *ad hoc* units were the 'Battalions of Detachments' which served in the Talavera campaign, composed of recovered invalids from a number of corps.

Veteran Battalions, composed of soldiers considered unfit for full field service, performed garrison duty (the 4th Veteran Battalion was at Gibraltar 1808-14, the 7th there 1810-14), and one was formed in the Peninsula, at Lisbon in March 1813, from men in the depot there who were fit only for garrison duty; numbered originally as the 13th Veteran Battalion, it was awarded the battle-honour 'Peninsula' for its service.

Cavalry

The cavalry of the British Army was divided into heavy and light regiments, although in practice the 'heavies' of the line cavalry came to be as tactically adaptable as the light regiments, and almost as versatile in 'outpost' duty. The heavy cavalry consisted of the two regiments of Life Guards and the Royal Horse Guards (classed as 'Household Cavalry' although the status of the latter was not at the time officially so designated); seven numbered regiments of Dragoon Guards (of which the 3rd-5th served in the Peninsula); and five regiments of Dragoons,

---

[4] *Dispatches of Field-Marshal the Duke of Wellington*, ed. J. Gurwood, London 1834-38, Vol. XI, p. 140.

numbered 1-6 (the number 5 was vacant), of which the 1st, 3rd and 4th served in the Peninsula. (The appellation 'Dragoon Guard' did not imply 'guard' status in the continental sense, but was merely a distinction for those regiments which prior to 1746 had been titled 'Horse'). The nineteen light cavalry regiments were numbered in sequence after the 6th Dragoons, 7-25, and styled Light Dragoons; twelve served in the Peninsula. Four bore the additional title of Hussars (7th, 10th, 15th, 18th), wore hussar uniform, and served in the Peninsula: in the Corunna campaign and from March 1813, when three regiments were sent out as what was sometimes referred to as the Hussar Brigade, being joined by the 7th Hussars in October 1813.

From 1800 cavalry regiments comprised five squadrons of two troops each, of which two troops formed the depot at home; in 1811 the establishment was reduced to six 'service' and two depot troops. In September 1813 the light regiments, which had retained the ten-troop establishment, were increased to twelve, two continuing to serve as a home depot. In 1812 elements of the Household Cavalry were sent to the Peninsula, two squadrons each from the 1st and 2nd Life Guards and Royal Horse Guards, sufficient of each regiment being left at home to perform ceremonial duties.

The numerical strength of cavalry regiments was usually considerably below establishment; for example, at the beginning of the Corunna campaign average regimental strength (all light regiments) was 615; at Albuera 388 (two heavy regiments, average 380, one light); at Salamanca 354; at the start of the Vittoria campaign 412. As with the infantry, by 1813 some regiments had so declined in strength that Wellington intended to reduce four regiments to two troops each, sending home the surplus cadres to recruit; but again the Duke of York

objected and in March four regiments were sent home, with less-efficient new regiments sent in their place.

British cavalry often formed a smaller proportion of the whole army than did the larger mounted formations employed by some continental armies. At Talavera, for example, Wellesley's cavalry represented 14.4 per cent of his troops (their French opponents 17.4 per cent); at Busaco only two squadrons of the 4th Dragoons were present, but in the entire field army, including Portuguese, the mounted element represented only 8 per cent of the whole; at Salamanca the cavalry represented 11.6 per cent of the British forces, 8.3 per cent of the whole Anglo-Portuguese army. The British cavalry in the Peninsula was generally gathered in brigades, rising in number from two in June 1809 to eight in 1814 as the number of regiments increased over that period from eight to 19. In June 1811 the brigades were split into two divisions of cavalry, the 1st Division of three brigades and the 2nd of two, but they were amalgamated into a single division again in April 1813, the brigade remaining the principal tactical formation.

Artillery

Administered not by the Commander-in-Chief and Horse Guards, but by the Board of Ordnance under its Master-General, the Royal Regiment of Artillery comprised both foot and horse branches. The standard tactical unit was the 'brigade' or company of six cannon, usually five guns and a howitzer, named after its commanding officer (the modern term for such a unit, 'battery', at the time usually referred to an artillery position). Each of the Royal Artillery's ten battalions comprised ten companies, each forming an autonomous 'brigade' with an attached detachment from the separately-constituted Corps of Drivers; from 1808 each 'brigade' had an establishment of five officers and 136 other ranks. The principal field ordnance was originally 6- and 3-pdr. guns, but more effective 9-pdrs. (and 5½-in. howitzers) were introduced progressively during the period. There were twelve 'brigades' or troops of Royal Horse Artillery, with a similar establishment and attached complement of drivers; despite the introduction of 9-pdrs., some retained 6-pdrs. as late as Waterloo. One of the specialist Rocket Troops, formed 1813, served in the Peninsula, but rockets had been deployed (without much effect) earlier in the war; Wellington disliked them, believing them only of use for setting fire to a town, which he said he had no desire to do, but they were very damaging to enemy morale, if only by the unpredictability of their flight, and they were used to this effect late in the war.

Compared with the artillery of some continental armies, the British artillery field strength was often low, though it was increased during the war. In August 1808, for example, artillery was in such short supply that it had to be deployed in batteries of only three guns each; at Talavera there were only five companies, three with light 6-pdrs., one with heavy 6-pdrs., and one with 3-pdrs. Even at Vittoria there were only seven companies of 9-pdrs., two of heavy 6-pdrs., and four of light 6-pdrs.

In January 1813 Wellington commented on the dearth of artillery in his army compared with that of the French (whose Armies of the Centre, Portugal and South he believed would have 120 fieldpieces for the coming campaign, not including the siege-train). The previous October he had stated that the minimum necessary for his army would be ten 'brigades' of 9- or long 6-pdrs., four horse artillery troops and a 'brigade' of heavy guns, which would give a total of 90 guns. By

January he reported that the ordnance establishment 'is infinitely lower than that of any army now acting in Europe . . . and below the scale which I have ever read of for an army of such numbers'. The principal shortage was in horses to drag the guns: he noted that except for 18-pdrs., he had the ordnance, and the Portuguese had the gunners, but had no means of transporting them; so that while he was grateful for the despatch to the army of another horse artillery troop, 'adverting to the calibre and size of the guns used by the horse artillery, I [am] not desirous of increasing that description of force with the army beyond the four troops now with it; and I should wish to be permitted to apply the horses of the troop now coming to draw guns of larger calibre'[5].

The horse artillery was usually attached to the cavalry or Light Divisions, and each infantry division had its own 'brigade' of foot artillery. The artillery reserve generally consisted of the siege-train of heavier ordnance, 18- and 24-pdrs.; the quantity of guns available never permitted a large mobile reserve to be assembled for use as an offensive rather than support weapon, in the style of some continental armies. For siege work, even heavier guns were used, iron 32- and 42-pdrs., and early in the war ancient Spanish and Portuguese ordnance had to be employed. Latterly British naval guns were landed for use with the siege-train.

Engineers

The least successful part of the army, at least in the early stages of the war, the engineer service consisted of two sections. The Corps of Royal Engineers was composed exclusively of officers; under-strength and over-worked, 102 served in the Peninsula, of whom 24 were killed and one died of exertion. The

[5] *Dispatches of Field-Marshal the Duke of Wellington*, ed. J. Gurwood, London 1834-38, Vol. X, pp. 48-49.

rank-and-file was provided by the Royal Military Artificers, twelve companies stationed in garrisons, which sent small detachments to the field army; in November 1809, for example, their effective strength in the Peninsula was only 19 men. All manual work had to be done by infantrymen, often unskilled, and 'assistant engineer' officers were seconded from the line regiments to help out. William Napier was not unbiased but there was much truth in his assertion that 'To the discredit of the English government, no army was ever so ill provided with the means of prosecuting such enterprises [as sieges]. The engineer officers were exceedingly zealous . . . but the ablest trembled when reflecting upon the utter destitution of all that belonged to real service . . . the best officers and the finest soldiers were obliged to sacrifice themselves in a lamentable manner . . . The sieges carried on in Spain were a succession of butcheries, because the commonest resources of their art were denied to the engineers'[6]. Only after the second siege of Badajoz were attempts made to improve the situation, when at Wellington's behest the Royal Military Artificers or Sappers and Miners was formed (titled Royal Sappers and Miners from 1813), a corps of 'other ranks' trained in engineering and commanded by officers of the Royal Engineers. For the 1813 campaign some 300 were present with the army, and the conduct of siege operations improved markedly.

Because the engineer services were commanded by the Master-General of the Ordnance, in 1798 the Horse Guards created their own engineer unit, the Royal Staff Corps, officers of which served as individuals in staff and engineer duties, with the 'other ranks' of the battalion serving as overseers or foremen to the gangs of infantrymen-labourers.

Foreign Corps

A considerable proportion of the British Army in the Peninsula was of foreign composition, notably the King's German Legion. Raised from the king's Hanoverian citizens (Hanover being over-run by the French in 1803), and subsequently recruiting other nationalities, it became one of the army's finest elements. Its establishment expanded to encompass five regiments of cavalry (light and heavy dragoons, reorganised as light dragoons and hussars), all of which served in the Peninsula; two light infantry battalions (both Peninsula) and eight line battalions (all of which served in the Peninsula, albeit just the flank companies of the 3rd and 8th), four foot batteries (three Peninsula) and two horse batteries. Although organised generally as other units of the British Army, the line battalions had rifle-armed sharpshooter companies, and the two light battalions were armed partially with rifles, although as late as 1814 only about 60 per cent carried rifles. Other notable units included the Brunswick Oels Corps, which entered British service after its epic march across Germany in 1809; it included six troops of hussars which served in eastern Spain in 1813, and twelve companies of *Jägers*. Arriving in September 1810, three companies were detached to the 4th and 5th Divisions to supplement their skirmishing capability; the remainder served briefly in the 4th Division, transferred to the Light Division in November, and from about April 1811 served with the 7th Division. Other foreigners were drafted in and the corps got a bad reputation for desertion; as did the Chasseurs Britanniques, founded in 1801 from French *émigrés* but later including other foreign recruits. Arriving at Lisbon from Cadiz in January 1811, it served in the 7th Division until the end of the war, with especial distinc-

[6] Napier, W.F.P., *History of the War in the Peninsula*, London 1832-40, Vol. III pp. 525-26.

tion at Fuentes de Oñoro. Corps serving in eastern Spain included Dillon's Regiment (originally French, German and Italian in composition), De Roll's Regiment and Watteville's Regiment (originally Swiss); the Anglo-Italian Levy (formed partially from prisoners-of-war) and the Calabrian Free Corps, a light infantry unit raised in Sicily from Calabrian rebels in 1809 and organised in five 'divisions' of three companies each. A unit formed in the Peninsula, originally in 1808, was the small Corps of Guides, largely Spaniards or Portuguese who knew the country and who could act as interpreters (Wellington described their 'requisite qualities' as 'intelligence, some honesty, and a knowledge of Spanish or Portuguese languages, and English or French'[7]); with officers from the Royal Staff Corps.

Command and higher formations

The British Army operated with a smaller staff than that employed by some continental armies, with most duties being divided between the departments of the Adjutant-General and Quartermaster-General, the former officially responsible for equipment and discipline, the latter for quarters, conveyance of troops and marches, though their tasks overlapped and in the Peninsula it was the Quartermaster-General's Department that came to predominate, due to the efficiency of its head, Sir George Murray. The Commissariat was one of the 'civil' departments of the army, administered by the Treasury, and as the official transport corps, the Royal Waggon Train, was almost negligible in size, the transportation of supplies depended more upon hired waggoners and

vehicles, less efficient but usually providing the army with sufficient supplies, despite exasperated comments such as Wellington's: 'What do you think of empty carts taking two days to go ten miles on a good road? After all, I am obliged to appear satisfied, or they would all desert!'[8].

Conversely, there was no shortage of general officers, though Wellington had little say about who was sent to him, or who should be employed. Among his comments was this from January 1813, concerning 'the removal of officers found or supposed to be incapable of performing service in the field. I request that General Officers should not be sent out; and when those are sent out whom I conceive not to be fit for their situations, I request that they be removed. I am then to bear the responsibility or odium of their removal. What a situation then is mine! It is impossible to prevent incapable men from being sent to the army; and, when I complain that they are sent, I am to be responsible'[9].

At the commencement of the war, the only higher formation was the brigade; for the Vimeiro campaign, for example, Wellesley ordered his army in eight brigades, of between two and four battalions each. Moore began his campaign with similar organisation, in six principal brigades; Baird's contingent contained four. When they united at Mayorga, Moore reorganised his army, creating four divisions of two or three brigades each, plus two 'flank brigades' of light infantry. When Wellesley returned to the Peninsula in April 1809, the army was formed in nine brigades; from 18 June he instituted the divisional system which existed for the remainder of the war, and which became increasingly necessary as the army increased in strength. Initially

[7] *Dispatches of Field-Marshal the Duke of Wellington*, ed. J. Gurwood, London 1834-38, Vol. V, p. 571.

[8] *Ibid.*, Vol. VIII p. 514.

[9] *Ibid.*, Vol. X pp. 33-4

there were four infantry divisions, of two brigades each (four brigades for the 1st Division); the un-numbered Light Division was formed in February 1810. In August 1810 the 5th Division was created, and the 6th in October; the 7th was formed in March 1811. To most divisions, a Portuguese brigade was attached (only in rare cases were the Portuguese integrated at brigade level, notably in the Light Division), and there was also a complete Portuguese division, un-numbered but in effect forming the army's ninth division.

Skirmishing formed an important part of Wellington's system of tactics, so that each brigade was usually allocated a specialist company of riflemen or light infantry to augment the brigade's regimental light companies (battalion companies could also be utilised as skirmishers, though usually not so expert as those specially trained for the task). For combat, the light companies of a brigade or division could be assembled together to form an *ad hoc* light unit, but in other circumstances remaining part of their parent battalions. The specialist skirmisher companies were usually provided by the 5th Battalion 60th, the rifle-armed companies of which were distributed individually throughout the divisions, augmented from late 1810 by the Brunswick Oels light infantry. The specialist nature of deployment of the light regiments is exemplified by Wellington's comment of December 1812, regarding the decline in numbers of the 51st and 68th Light Infantry: that as for other weak units, he wished to send home the cadres of four companies of each, but as they were light infantry, he wished to keep the remainder as separate units, rather than combine them into a stronger provisional battalion which would be of less use.

No higher organisation than the division was ever established officially; references may be found to groupings of divisions which had a degree of autonomy, for example 'Hill's corps', but no official corps structure existed.

Royal Navy

The Royal Navy's significance on the Peninsular War was considerable, most notably in maintaining the security of the sea-routes from Britain to the Peninsula, and thus the line of communication for supplies and reinforcements. In this they remained unchallenged by the French navy's larger vessels, so that the transportation of troops, usually in hired vessels with naval escorts, from Britain and the Mediterranean, went unhindered. Naval squadrons and single ships – frequently frigates and smaller vessels – were used to launch raids upon the occupied northern and southern coasts of Spain, sometimes in conjunction with Spanish forces; and to interrupt the enemy's coastal traffic. The occupation of Santander, which enabled the army's maritime base to be transferred from Lisbon, thus radically reducing the length of the line of communication, was effected largely through the presence of the Royal Navy. Naval personnel served on land in numerous campaigns during the period, but only in a limited manner during the Peninsular War: apart from the many amphibious raids, naval gunners and artillery were employed later in the war, notably in the siege of San Sebastian.

Each warship carried a detachment of Royal Marines, the Admiralty's military force, which was organised in four 'Divisions' (Chatham, Portsmouth, Plymouth and Woolwich, numbered 1-4 respectively), each Division having an artillery company. By July 1808 the corps comprised 183 companies, though marines were allocated to ships (roughly on a scale of one per gun) irrespective of their original company. They provided the nucleus for all landing-parties, but there were in addition marine battalions formed for service in the Peninsula. The 1st Marine Battalion was created in September 1810, formed of two companies and the divisional artillery company from Plymouth, and a single companies from both Chatham and Portsmouth Divisions; each company had 80 privates and the battalion a total strength of 503 all ranks. It served in garrison in Lisbon, and was sent home to recruit to 500 rank and file in January 1812, serving subsequently on the north coast of Spain, notably at Santander. In August 1812 a 2nd Battalion was sent to Santander, that having companies of 69 of all ranks. In January 1813 both battalions were detailed for service in North America.

HOLLAND

The Kingdom of Holland was formed in 1806 from the previous Batavian Republic, with Napoleon's brother Louis as king. It maintained its own army until 1810 when Louis abdicated (never having been the compliant client Napoleon required), when both army and state were integrated into France. A Dutch brigade was sent to the Peninsula in 1808 under General David-Henri Chassé, which formed part of Leval's Division of IV Corps: 1st Battalion 2nd Line and 2nd Battalion 4th Line, with an artillery battery and the 3rd Dutch Hussars as part of the corps cavalry. The division served at Talavera (the 3rd Hussars as part of the Reserve Cavalry) and Ocaña, for example, and in 1810 the Dutch infantry was incorporated into the French line (123rd-126th Regiments). As a result of distinguished service in the Peninsula, the 3rd Hussars were elevated into the Dutch Royal Guard, but in 1810 the cadres of two squadrons were sent home, and later in the year the regiment largely passed into the new 2nd (Dutch) Chevau-Léger-Lanciers of Napoleon's Imperial Guard.

ITALY

The French satellite Kingdom of Italy was created in the north of that region, eventually extending to the boundary of the Kingdom of Naples; Napoleon was crowned king on 26 May 1805. Organised on French lines, the Italian army proved to be a most reliable asset for Napoleon. The seven numbered line and three (four from 1811) light infantry regiments each had, in French style, a depot and four field battalions, each battalion of one grenadier, one voltigeur and four fusilier companies. The cavalry consisted of two dragoon regiments (each of four squadrons of two companies each) and ultimately four chasseur à cheval regiments; artillery and supporting services were also organised on French lines.

The Corps of Observation of the Eastern Pyrenees included in its 2nd Division (commanded by the Italian general Joseph Lechi (or Lecchi)) battalions of the 2nd, 4th and 5th Line and one of the Velites of the Royal Guard, with the Chasseur regiment 'Principe Real' as part of corps cavalry. This became part of VII Corps where it was joined by another Italian division under General Pino, of 13 battalions drawn from the 1st and 2nd Light and 4th-7th Line Regiments, with the cavalry joined by the Chasseur regiment 'Real' and the Dragoon regiment 'Napoleone'. When Pino's division served at the siege of Rosas it was organised in three numbered brigades, the 1st and 3rd of infantry and the 2nd cavalry, and accompanied by a company each of horse and foot artillery, two train companies and the 4th company of sapeurs, totalling 9,422 all ranks. The Velites and 5th Line were represented by detachments, the other infantry regiments numbering nine battalions, with an average strength of 814.

The brigading was not constant; by the time of the siege of Gerona, for example, Pino's Division of 13 battalions was still in three brigades, but with the cavalry numbered as the 3rd, while Lechi's Division had its 1st brigade of three Italian battalions, its second of two Neapolitan battalions, and two squadrons of the Chasseur regiment 'Principe Real'. By the beginning of 1810 the Italians were concentrated into the 2nd Division of VII Corps. At the siege of Tarragona the Italian Division was commanded by General Peiri (or Peyri) and comprised two brigades of two battalions each of the 2nd Light and 4th, 5th and 6th Line, with the Dragoon regiment 'Napoleone' in Boussard's French cavalry brigade, with one company each of foot and horse artillery, train and sapeurs. A second division, under General Severoli, was ordered to join Suchet in 1811, three battalions each of the 1st and 7th Line and an extra battalion of each of both light regiments and the 4th and 6th Line, with drafts to reinforce the cavalry, artillery and engineers. At Saguntum the Italian Division was commanded by General Palombini, two brigades totalling eight battalions (3,897 men) plus 157 of the Dragoon regiment 'Napoleone' in two squadrons. By the siege of Valencia this had risen to ten battalions, with the dragoons increased to three squadrons and incorporated in Delort's French cavalry brigade; plus Severoli's Division of two brigades (three battalions each of 1st Light and 1st Line, two battalions 7th Line), with three squadrons of chasseurs and with the divisional cavalry augmented by the 9th French Hussars. Late in 1812 Palombini's Division transferred to the Army of the Centre (three battalions 3rd Light, two each 4th and 6th Line, Dragoon regiment 'Napoleone' and two batteries), while Severoli's Division remained with Suchet (two battalions each 1st Light and 1st Line, artillery, chasseurs, plus French 5th *Léger*); a battalion of 7th Line formed part of the garrison of Tarragona. (Morale cannot have been universally high: while passing through Navarre in 1812, for example, half the 3rd Battalion 6th Line deserted to join Mina!).

At Castro-Urdiales in 1813 Palombini's Division comprised only one brigade (2nd Light, 4th and 6th Line, total 5 battalions) plus the Dragoon regiment 'Napoleone' and one company each of horse and foot artillery, train and sapeurs. Units were reduced early in 1813 so that when Soult reorganised his army in July he had just one Italian brigade, under St. Paul, of the 2nd Light and 4th and 6th Line.

NAPLES

Following the expulsion from mainland Italy of the Neapolitan royal family, Napoleon made his brother Joseph King of Naples (February 1806); but when Joseph was removed to the throne of Spain, Napoleon's brother-in-law Joachim Murat was appointed king in his stead. Joseph had to create an army from almost nothing, so its recruits were largely impressed, the indigent or criminals, which accounts for their terrible record for desertion. With units organised in French style, the first Neapolitans were sent to the Peninsula early in the war, joining Lechi's Italian Division in the Corps of Observation of the Eastern Pyrenees: the 1st and 2nd Battalions of the 1st Neapolitan Line Regiment and three squadrons of the 2nd Chasseurs à Cheval (*Cacciatori a Cavallo*). In August 1808 two battalions of the 2nd Line went to Spain, joining Chabot's 6th Division of VII Corps (Lechi's Division being the 2nd). In May the Neapolitan infantry was concentrated in Zenardi's Brigade of Lechi's Division, but it had to be withdrawn from the siege of Gerona due to losses from desertion, illness and combat. Early in 1810 they were reinforced by two battalions of the 1st Neapolitan Light Infantry and three squadrons of the 1st Chasseurs à Cheval, with a draft of 1,000 men for the 1st Line, all ex-convicts, of whom half ran off before they even reached Spain. The Neapolitans were concentrated into a division under General Pignatelli, whose abilities were criticised by Macdonald, and the reinforcements which continued to be sent were of declining calibre. In July 1810 Napoleon wrote to Clarke: 'Let the King of Naples know that all his troops in Spain desert, and are in a wretched state, and that I will have no more of them. Order Marshal Perignon not to send any more, and General

Miollis to let none pass. They are a gang of thieves, and poison the country through which they pass'; and ten days later, 'I have no wish to crowd Catalonia with bad soldiers, or to increase the troops of banditti . . . I do not want any more Neapolitan troops in Spain, and . . . I will have no more'[1].

Consequently the strength of the Neapolitan contingent declined; at the beginning of 1811 the infantry numbered some 2,804 men, the cavalry 593. Pignatelli was succeeded in command by General Claude-Antoine Compère, though his divisional command declined to brigade strength. It served at Saguntum, and by early October 1811 comprised some 1,391 infantry and 169 cavalry; at the siege of Valencia some 1,153 infantry and 120 cavalry. At the end of the year it was ordered that the infantry in Spain be consolidated into a new 8th Line, of three battalions, with the surplus cadres returning to Naples. Guglielmo Pepe was appointed colonel of the new regiment, who in the post-Napoleonic age was to become one of the heroes of the struggle for Italian independence. The cavalry was reduced at the same time to two squadrons. Numbers continued to decline; in early 1813 the regiment was reduced to a single battalion, the cavalry to a weak company, and upon the news that Murat had changed sides, they were disarmed and interned.

PORTUGAL

The Army in 1807

Despite attempts to reorganise and strengthen after the Spanish War of 1801, upon Junot's entry into Portugal in December 1807 the Portuguese Army had regressed to its previous state of weakness, perhaps less than half the official establishment.

In May 1806 a radical reorganisation had divided the country into three districts, forming divisions to one or other of which all units were attached: the Northern, of the provinces of Minho and Tras os Montes; the Central, including Beira and Estremadura; and the Southern, Alemtajo and Algarve. There were

24 numbered infantry regiments, allocated at eight per division; most were named after the region in which they were formed, though three of the four Lisbon regiments bore the names of former distinguished commanders (1st Lippe, 4th Freire, 16th Viera Telles), and the 3rd and 15th retained the title 'Olivenza' even though that frontier fortress had been ceded to Spain by the Treaty of Badajoz on 6 June 1801, these two regiments being formed in northern Beira. Regiments previously had seven companies of 116 men each, but following the 1801 war were reorganised into two battalions of one elite and four 'centre' companies each, one battalion's élite com-

---

[1] *The Confidential Correspondence of Napoleon Bonaparte with his Brother Joseph*, London 1855, Vol. II pp. 131, 134.

pany being grenadiers and one light infantry; each company was supposed to be 150 strong, but generally they were very much below establishment.

The twelve cavalry regiments were 'medium': there were no specifically light or heavy regiments. Each had eight companies with a notional strength of 58 other ranks each, but they were greatly under-strength and had insufficient horses to mount even those who were under arms.

The 1806 reorganisation numbered the four existing artillery regiments and gave them new names: for the Northern Division the 4th Artillery (Oporto), for the Central the 1st (Lisbon), and for the Southern the 2nd (Lagos) and 3rd (Estremoz). Each regiment comprised seven companies of gunners, and one each of bombardiers, pontoneers and miners. Their duties were largely as garrisons for the frontier forts, but it was ordered that regimental field batteries should consist of two 3-pdrs., two 6-pdrs., a 9-pdr. and a 5-in. howitzer.

One of the few concessions to 'modern' tactics had been the creation of the Legion of Light Troops (or Experimental Legion, or Alorna's Legion, after the general who instigated and commanded it): it comprised eight companies of light infantry and six of cavalry, but its horse artillery battery had been transferred to the regular artillery in 1803.

Each of the three territorial divisions of the country supported 16 regiments of militia, each named from its area. There was in addition the *ordenanza*, a levy-en-masse organisation of companies nominally 250 strong, which could be combined into 24 numbered brigades, six in Estremadura, four each in Minho and the district of Oporto, five in Beira, two each in Alemtajo and Tras os Montes, and one in the Algarve.

The Portuguese Legion

Upon the French occupation, beginning with a decree of 22 December 1807 and finishing in February 1808, Junot disbanded the existing Portuguese army and militia, and formed instead six regiments of infantry, three of cavalry, and from the Legion of Light Troops a battalion of light infantry, for French service. On 21 March 1808 these were ordered to leave Portugal for Valladolid; many deserted but those who marched into Spain were formed, by a decree of 18 May 1808, into the *Légion Portugaise*, a 'foreign corps' of the French Army. Five infantry and two cavalry regiments were created; they were sent to France, but two units did participate in the Peninsular War. The 5th Portuguese Regiment and the *Bataillon de Chasseurs Portugais* formed the 2nd Brigade of General Gomes Freye d'Andrade's 2nd Division at the first siege of Saragossa, numbering 265 and 288 men respectively; they finally crossed into France in September 1808.

The re-formed Portuguese Army

Upon the first revolts against the French, some of the previous units attempted to re-muster, and it was these who participated in the early campaigning with Wellesley's expedition. The Council of Regency, established to govern Portugal in the name of the Regent, suggested that Wellesley be appointed head of the re-forming Portuguese Army; but when he declined, the British government appointed William Beresford. An inspired choice, he retained the previous regimental structure but instituted a complete overhaul of every aspect of the army, introducing experienced British officers at all levels from company upwards, and retaining only the best Portuguese officers. In consequence the Portuguese troops became an integral part of Wellington's army, some believing them equal to the British in their steadiness and reliability, probably from the inherent character of what one of their officers, John Blakiston, described as 'a patient good-tempered people'[1]. (Beresford's reorganisation applied initially only to units in Lisbon and the south: those beyond the Douro were already in the field and served in the 1809 campaign without the benefit of the reforms). Wellington attributed the improvement to the overhaul of the army's adminstration: 'notwithstanding that the Portuguese are now the *fighting cocks* of the army, I believe we owe their merits to the care we have taken of their pockets and bellies than to the instruction we have given them'[2].

Infantry

The 24 previous infantry regiments were re-constituted with two battalions of seven companies each, with flank companies as before, and a regimental establishment, including staff, of 1,550 all ranks. (Some sources indicate a British-style ten-company establishment from this time). Recruitment was by conscription, from May 1810 recruits receiving basic training at a central depot (until 1811 at Peniche, then moved to Mafra), and thus on campaign regimental strengths were kept to a reasonable level. For example, at Busaco regimental strength averaged 1,154, at Fuentes de Oñoro 892; in the Salamanca campaign brigade strength varied between 51 and 71 per cent of the establishment; in the Vittoria campaign between 62 and 82.5 per cent, with an average of 67 per cent. The importance of the Portuguese forces may be gauged by the fact that at

Salamanca they represented 40 per cent of the army's infantry, 41 per cent at Toulouse, and 49.7 per cent at Busaco.

One of the most proficient of the early corps was in British pay, the Loyal Lusitanian Legion, raised partly from Portuguese residents in Britain, but more in Oporto and Coimbra in August 1808. It was intended to comprise three infantry battalions of ten companies each, an artillery battery and three squadrons of cavalry, but the cavalry was never formed. It was commanded originally by the mercurial Sir Robert Wilson. They provided early evidence of the mettle of the Portuguese troops, when the Legion officer William Mayne attempted to hold the bridge at Alcantara with some 500 of his own men and the Idanha Militia. The latter, 'not being accustomed to any thing of this kind, and witnessing their officers and men falling and wounded on every side, made a precipitate retreat in a body'[3], which compelled the Legion to retire. Wellington commented that 'You are in error in supposing that the Portuguese troops will not fight. One battalion had behaved remarkably well with me; and I know of no troops that could have behaved better that the Lusitanian Legion did at Alcantara the other day; and I must add that if the Idanha à Nova militia had not given way, they would have held their post'[4].

To provide light infantry, in October 1808 the formation of six battalions of Caçadores (chasseurs) was authorised, and created in the following two months; each comprised five companies (including one of *atiradores* or *tiradores*, sharpshooters) each of 123 all ranks, and a battalion establishment of 628. Six more

[1] Blakiston,J., *Adventures in Three-Quarters of the Globe*, London 1829, Vol. II, p. 336.

[2] *Dispatches of Field-Marshal the Duke of Wellington*, ed. J. Gurwood, London 1834-38, Vol. X p. 569.

[3] Mayne, W., & Lillie, Capt., *Narrative of the Campaigns of the Loyal Lusitanian Legion during the Years 1809, 1810 & 1811*, London 1812, p. 242.

[4] *Dispatches of Field-Marshal the Duke of Wellington*, ed. J. Gurwood, London 1834-38, Vol. IV p. 350.

battalions were created in April 1811, the 7th-9th converted from the Loyal Lusitanian Legion and the 10th-12th newly-formed. It had been intended that all should have been armed with rifles, but these were not available initially, and subsequently were carried by about one-third to one-quarter of the men, the rest using the standard infantry musket.

Cavalry

Due in part to a shortage of suitable horses, the cavalry remained the least effective part of the army. Beresford reorganised the twelve regiments to have four squadrons of two companies each, each company of 72 all ranks and a regimental total of 595, but rarely was this strength attained. For example, the 1st and 11th Regiments in D'Urban's Brigade at Salamanca mustered only 482 all ranks combined (the 12th Regiment, also part of the brigade, was on baggage-guard duty); at Vittoria the three regiments of this brigade, plus the 6th Regiment, together mustered less than 900. Indeed, only six regiments were fully mounted and at least three were never mounted at all, but used for garrison duty. Performance in the field was patchy: for example, D'Urban's Brigade behaved well at Salamanca but infamously at Majalahonda only twenty days later, which led Wellington to comment that 'they must not be employed again alone, or with our cavalry, who gallop too fast for them, but only as they were on the 22nd July, viz., in support of our infantry, and with English dragoons with them'[5].

Artillery

Beresford retained the previous organisation of four regiments, each of ten companies (including one each of bombardiers, miners and pontoneers, the two latter transferred to the Artificers in October 1812 and replaced by gunners); each company had an establishment of four officers and 108 other ranks. While still serving in a garrison role, detachments were formed to create field batteries (or 'brigades'), armed with 3- and 6pdrs., with the more effective 9-pdr. being introduced subsequently. For example, at Busaco the 1st Regiment provided two batteries with 6-pdrs., the 2nd Regiment two with 3-pdrs., and the 4th Regiment one 6-pdr. battery. Five batteries were present in the Fuentes de Oñoro campaign (two from the 1st, three from the 2nd Regiment), while in 1812 some thirteen batteries were mobilised at some stage of the year. Only three were with the main field forces: one of 6-pdrs. and one of 9-pdrs. from the 1st and 2nd Regiments respectively, attached to the Portuguese Division; and one from the 1st regiment, with 24-pdrs., with Wellington's artillery reserve. Batteries of 3-pdr. mountain guns were a speciality, but there was no horse artillery. In October 1812 Wellington stated that their greatest problem was a shortage of horses to pull the guns: in 1810, he noted, there were nine brigades of six guns each with the army, 'But the financial difficulties of the Portuguese Government, and the irregularity of their system, have caused the destruction of nearly all the animals attached to draw these guns; and the equipment failed first in the quantity of ammunition necessary to be brought into the field to be useful, and afterwards in the draft for the guns themselves; and the service of one brigade after another has been discontinued, till at last there has been no Portuguese ordnance with this part of the army in this campaign, and only one brigade with Lieut. General Sir Rowland Hill'[6].

[5] *Dispatches of Field-Marshal the Duke of Wellington*, ed. J. Gurwood, London 1834-38, Vol. IX, p. 402.
[6] *Ibid.*, Vol. IX, pp. 500-01.

Engineers

Reorganised in November 1808, the engineer corps consisted of officers only, of whom there were 92 by 1812; their original duties concerned the border and coastal fortifications, but subsequently some served with the field army. The 'other ranks" engineer corps, the Artificer Battalion, was formed in 1812 and absorbed the artillery miners and pontoneers; three companies strong, it was reorganised in October 1813 with two augmented artificer companies, plus the pontoneer company as before.

Militia

The militia was re-formed in December 1808, 48 regiments divided into three groups of 16 as before, each of two battalions, one of which might be called for a period of between two and six months (it was unusual for both of a regiment's battalions to be mobilised simultaneously). Their primary function was defensive, as the British engineer John Jones wrote of the lines of Torres Vedras, that the 'militia, ill-organized peasantry and gunners, who, though totally unfit to act in the field, still being possessed of innate courage, were equal to defend a redoubt and work its artillery'[7]. Mobilised militia released regular troops for other duties; for example, in February 1811 Wellington commented that the presence of the Tavira Militia in Algarve would 'quiet the apprehensions of the inhabitants', and that 'The greater number of this description of men we have, the greater number of the better description we should have to dispose of'[8]. During the French invasion of 1810 the whole force was mobilised, some for garrison duty and others gathered in five

'divisions', partly defensive and partly for operations against the invaders' flanks and rear, the whole force about 50,000 strong. Commanders were instructed not to engage in the open field without support, but to defend passes and fords; where they did risk a field action they were usually defeated (an example was Trant's attempt to hold a position near Sardao on 30 September 1810: he had four militia battalions – Coimbra, Porto, Penafiel and a composite light battalion – and had to withdraw when the latter bolted at the very beginning of the action). As the threat of invasion receded, the militia's principal use was as a training-ground for conscripts for the regular army.

The *Ordenanza* (or *Ordenança*) was re-formed in 1808 with the same organisation as before, each of the 24 brigades comprising eight 'captaincies' of eight companies each; plus 16 legions for Lisbon, each of three battalions of ten companies each. Often their armaments consisted of no more than agricultural implements or pikes, though some did have muskets or civilian fowling-pieces. Wellington's mobilisation of these forces was probably largely to enhance patriotic feeling, to harass enemy stragglers and help defend suitable strongpoints, and to assist the 'scorched earth' policy to deny the French the ability to live off the land. Possibly as many as 70,000 were mobilised in 1810-11, but as the danger of invasion subsided, they acted more as a source of recruits for the militia. The fact that they usually had no uniform was a cause of concern: on 9 September 1810 Wellington wrote to Massena deploring the French practice of shooting the *ordenanza* they captured. He stated that when in the

[7] Jones, J.T., 'Memoranda relative to the Lines thrown up to cover Lisbon in 1810', in *Papers on Subjects connected with the Duties of the Corps of Royal Engineers*, Vol. III, London 1839, pp. 27-8.
[8] *Dispatches of Field-Marshal the Duke of Wellington*, ed. J. Gurwood, London 1834-38, Vol. VII pp. 238-39.

field they were subject to military law and demanded that they be treated accordingly.

In addition, there were a few urban volunteer corps, and in 1810 some 49 artillery companies were formed, associated with the *ordenanza*, to man the coastal defences and lines of Torres Vedras.

Higher formations

From early 1809 the infantry was formed into brigades for campaigning, each of two regiments and known by the name of its commander. From 29 September 1809 a more permanent organisation was established, and beginning in August 1810 a Caçadore battalion was added to almost every brigade. The composition of eight brigades remained unchanged throughout; others were of more ephemeral existence, and when the brigades were numbered in August 1813 (officially: numbers were used before) there were ten, each of two line regiments and a Caçadore battalion (save the 2nd or Algarve brigade, which comprised only the 2nd and 14th Line). Six of these brigades formed part of one of the numbered British divisions (only the 1st Division never had a Portuguese brigade attached); the 1st and 10th Brigades were independent, and the 2nd and 4th constituted the separate Portuguese Division. The 20th Line formed part of the Light Division October-December 1812, when it was replaced by the 17th Line, and the 1st and 3rd Caçadores also served with the Light Division (these were the only Portuguese units integrated into British formations at brigade level, rather than forming Portuguese brigades attached at divisional level)[9].

In October it was proposed (with the support of war minister Miguel Forjaz, whom Wellington described as 'the ablest statesman and man of business I have seen in the Peninsula'[10]) that the ten Portuguese brigades be concentrated into an independent army, perhaps to give greater prominence to General Francisco Silveira, conde de Amarante, one of the principal Portuguese commanders. Wellington was appalled at the prospect of any 'alteration of a system which, up to the present day, has answered admirably, has contributed in a principal degree to our great and astonishing success, and has enabled the Portuguese Government and nation to render such services to the cause, and has raised their reputation to the point at which it now stands . . . if the Portuguese troops were separated from the British divisions . . . and they were not considered . . . part of ourselves, they could not keep the field in a respectable state, even though the Portuguese Government were to incur ten times the expense they now incur'[11], so reliant were the Portuguese troops upon the British system of administration. The brigading remained unchanged to the end of the war.

Navy

The Portuguese navy's principal service during the period was to transport the royal family to Brazil, leaving Portugal in November 1807; the fleet consisted of the flagship *Principe Real* (90 guns), four 74- and three 64-gun ships of the line, and smaller vessels. Three 74-gunners, one 64 and some smaller ships were left in Portugal

[9] For the complicated lineage of the Portuguese brigades, including their commanders, see Ward, S.G.P., 'The Portuguese Infantry Brigades 1809-1814', in *Journal of the Society for Army Historical Research,* Vol. LIII (1975) pp. 103-12.

[10] *Dispatches of Field-Marshal the Duke of Wellington,* ed. J. Gurwood, London 1834-38, Vol. XI p. 184.

[11] *Ibid.,* Vol. XI, pp. 184-85.

in unserviceable condition; the ships of the line were repaired by the French (and most re-named) but they reverted to Portuguese control under the terms of the Convention of Cintra. In January 1813 Wellington authorised the deployment of Portuguese seamen to man the pontoon train, to be commanded by an officer of the navy.

THE RHEINBUND

The *Rheinbund* or Confederation of the Rhine was an organisation of principally German satellite states established by Napoleon. It originated on 12 July 1806 when sixteen German princes pledged their allegiance to France, and other states joined subsequently. Until the Confederation collapsed after Leipzig, these states provided troops in support of the French, including a number which contributed units to the Peninsular war. These corps were usually organised in French style, with six companies per battalion.

The first *Rheinbund* contingent entered Spain in October 1808, in Leval's Division, initially in IV Corps. Its brigading altered subsequently, but initially its 1st Brigade included a composite regiment from Baden, formed from that state's 2nd Battn. 3rd Line Regiment and 1st Battn. 4th, which in February 1809 was re-designated as the 4th Line, with the remaining battalions at home being united as the 3rd Line. The 1st Brigade was completed by two battalions of the 2nd Nassau Regiment and a Baden artillery battery. The 2nd Brigade was composed of Chassé's Dutch contingent; the 3rd Brigade comprised two battalions of Hesse-Darmstadt Gross-und-Erbprinz Regiment, the Frankfurt infantry battalion, and a half-battery of Hessian artillery. Also with the contingent were the Westphalian Chevauxlegers (numbered as the 1st Regt. after the formation of a 2nd in 1812), and the 2nd squadron of Nassau Chasseurs à Cheval. Detached to I Corps, the brigade was distinguished at Meza de Ibor and Medellin; the division was in excess of 4,500 strong at Talavera. Escort and garrison duty occupied much time thereafter, until the Hessians were detached to become part of the garrison of Badajoz, some 910 strong; they were lost upon the fall of the city.

The remainder — sometimes styled 'the German Division' but including the French 123rd Line (late Dutch), with the Westphalian and Nassau cavalry, served in the Army of the Centre (in July 1811 numbering about 4,870 men), but numbers declined and they became a brigade of Darmagnac's Division. At Vittoria the infantry brigade mustered 2,678; in July 1813 the Nassau cavalry was reinforced by its 1st squadron. When Soult reorganised the French armies, the brigade was allocated to Villatte's reserve, numbering little more than 2,000; the Nassau Chasseurs were allocated to Pierre Soult's Division, and the Westphalian Chevauxlegers, reduced to a single squadron, were transferred to Suchet, where they were joined by the Nassau Chasseurs from October 1813.

The changing situation in Europe led to the commander of the 2nd Nassau, August von Kruse, receiving a message from his sovereign that he should defect to the Anglo-Spanish side at first opportunity; so on 10 December 1813 he led his two Nassau battalions, and the Frankfurt battalion, over to the British. There they were welcomed; Wellington gave them a month's pay and arranged their passage home, via Britain. The Badeners, reduced to a single battalion, did not defect, evidently by mistake or from not having received instructions from their grand duke to that effect (the facts seem unclear); while the Barden artillery battery was serving with Darmagnac's division. The Badeners were disarmed by the French on the following day.

Another *Rheinbund* formation arrived in Catalonia in April 1809, the brigade of General François-Pierre-Joseph Amey. This comprised the 1st and 2nd Berg Infantry and the Würzburg Regiment (two battalions each), and a composite unit known (by its French title) as the *Bataillon des Princes* composed of a single company from each of six small states: Lippe-Detmold, Reuss, Schaumberg-Lippe, Schwarzburg-Rudolstadt, Schwarzburg-Sonderhausen, and Waldeck. (At the siege of Gerona the Würzburg Regiment numbered 1,519 all ranks, the 1st and 2nd Berg 1,310 and 1,313 respectively; there was also a detachment of Berg artillery, one officer and 38 other ranks). In May 1809 General Joseph Morio's Westphalian Division entered Catalonia: its 1st Brigade under General Hadeln comprised the 2nd and 4th Line (two battalions each), its 2nd under General Ochs including the 1st Light Infantry (one battalion) and 3rd Line (two battalions). At Gerona the 1st Light was 300 strong and the other six had a combined strength of 3,277; there were also two companies of Westphalian Foot Artillery, 3 officers and 77 other ranks combined.

The assault on Gerona caused a large number of casualties on these troops, and numbers declined in the subsequent minor operations. In June 1810 the *Bataillon des Princes* had ceased to be a viable formation and was broken up among the 5th and 6th *Rheinbund* Regiments (see below). The Berg contingent was reduced to battalion strength (its new designation was 1st Battalion, 1st Infantry) in 1810, and returned home in late 1811. The Westphalian Division shrank to a single battalion about 300 strong before it was withdrawn in early 1813.

In March 1810 the *Rheinbund* Division of General Marie-François Rouyer entered Spain; it also served in Catalonia. It comprised two brigades of regiments assembled from a number of states, and accorded *Rheinbund* numbers. The brigade under General François-Xavier de Schwarz (a French officer, though born in Baden) comprised the 1st Nassau Regiment (two battalions) and the 4th *Rheinbund* Regiment, which comprised a light battalion drawn from Saxe-Weimar-Eisenach and Saxe-Hildburghausen, and a line battalion from Saxe-Coburg-Saalfeld, Saxe-Gotha-Altenburg, and Saxe-Meiningen. The other brigade, commanded by Colonel Friedrich von Chambaud, comprised the 5th *Rheinbund* Regiment (1st Battalion from Anhalt-Bernburg, Anhalt-Dessau and Anhalt-Köthen, the 2nd from Lippe-Detmold and Schaumberg-Lippe); and the 6th *Rheinbund* Regiment (1st Battalion from Schwarzburg-Rudolstadt and Schwarzburg-Sonderhausen, the 2nd from Reuss-Greiz, Reuss-Schleiz-Gera, and Waldeck). They too suffered from desertions and casualties, notably in Schwarz's expedition to Manresa, and La Bisbal; what remained left Spain in January 1811, leaving the 1st Nassau behind. Another *Rheinbund* unit, the 2nd Battalion 3rd Berg Infantry, also served briefly in Catalonia. Following Kruse's defection, the *Rheinbund* units remaining in Catalonia were disarmed, even though there was no sign of their desertion: the survivors of the 1st Nassau Regiment, the Würzburg Battalion, Westphalian Chevauxlegers and Nassau Chasseurs à Cheval.

Another unit was the *Chevau-Légers de Berg*, formed in May 1807 by Murat who was Grand Duke of Berg. Two squadrons were raised by the time of his service in the Peninsula, but their service in Spain was little more extensive than that of Murat himself. After he left Spain the unit was broken up, most of the officers following Murat to Naples, while some of the other ranks went home to form a new regiment and others transferred into the Chasseurs à Cheval of the Imperial Guard, the corps having been attached to the Guard. Napoleon succeeded Murat as Grand Duke, and from March 1809 the title was transferred to Louis Bonaparte's son Louis, Napoleon's nephew, with Napoleon as regent during his minority. Napoleon ordered the formation of a replacement unit, known initially as the Berg Chasseurs à Cheval, but in December 1809 he ordered them armed with lances, and re-titled as the Lanciers de Berg (or Chevau-Légers-Lanciers). They went to Spain in June 1810 and served with the Guard cavalry in the Army of the North, including Fuentes de Oñoro, but their strength was reduced over the next two years and the survivors left the Peninsula in March 1813.

Writing largely of the *Rheinbund* troops in 1810, Lejeune made a comment applicable to many of the foreign contingents allied to France: he praised their bravery, humanity and discipline, 'but unfortunately they all hate being sent away from their own land to fight in the service of France in a cause about which they care nothing, and the authorities, instead of sending regular conscripts, make up the numbers of the regiments by buying men from the very dregs of the people. These substitutes bring their vices and their habits of insubordination with them, and many desert to the enemy'[1].

SICILY

King Ferdinand IV of Naples (III of Sicily) was driven from the mainland portion of his 'Kingdom of the Two Sicilies' by French invasion, and while Joseph Bonaparte, later Murat, reigned as Kings of Naples, Ferdinand and the legitimate royal family ruled in Sicily, supported by a British garrison and maintaining a Sicilian army. When the British expedition to the east coast of Spain was mounted, Sicilian troops were included, though Bentinck ordered that they were to remain in Spain only so long as they were not required for the security of Sicily, and that their employment on the Spanish coast was to be regarded as temporary, which rather conflicted with Wellington's instruction from the British government that the expedition was at his disposal. The first expeditionary force under Maitland was composed of British and British 'foreign corps', but the subsequent reinforcement included the Sicilian Estero Regiment (two battalions), a battalion of grenadiers, an artillery detachment and some 200 cavalry from the 1st Sicilian Regiment, together numbering about 2,250 men (about 1,260 of them in the Estero Regiment). The Estero Regiment and the Sicilian Grenadiers were brigaded together in Pastori's Brigade of William Clinton's 1st Division.

SPAIN

The Army in 1807-08

Following the war against France in 1793-95, attempts had been made to modernise and reorganise the Spanish military establishment; but a worsening financial situation and the most intractable problem, that of chronic shortages of manpower, served to undermine the efficiency of the army to a very considerable degree. The following provides a brief survey of the establishment of the army at the commencement of the war.

Separate from the remainder of the army was the Royal Guard, the senior of which was the Life Guard (*Guardias de Corps*), three

---

[1] Lejeune, L.F., *Memoirs of Baron Lejeune*, trans. Mrs. A. Bell, London 1897, Vol. II p. 47.

cavalry companies of 180 men each. The infantry comprised the *Guardias de Infanteria Española* (Spanish Guards) and the *Guardias de Infanteria Walona* (Walloon Guards), each of three battalions, each of six fusilier companies of 50 men and a grenadier company of 100. The *Guardias Albarderos* (Halbardier Guard) was a ceremonial palace guard company. The second cavalry corps was the *Carabineros Reales* (Royal Carabiniers), composed of four squadrons of four companies of 69 men each, plus a squadron of chasseurs and one of hussars that formed Godoy's guard, known from his title of Grand Admiral as the *Husares de la Guardia del Almirante*.

The 24 line cavalry regiments each comprised five squadrons of two companies each, each company with an establishment of three officers and 53 mounted and 13 dismounted other ranks. The twelve 'heavy' regiments were styled *Caballeria de Linea* ('Line Cavalry'), the remaining twelve light regiments consisting of eight regiments of Dragoons, two of *Cazadores a Caballo* (chasseurs: Regiments Olivenza and the Voluntarios de España), and two of Hussars (Maria Luisa and Españoles: regiments were identified by name, not a number). Between 1803 and 1805 the dragoons had been converted to chasseurs and hussars, but though re-converted back to dragoons, they are sometimes listed incorrectly as *cazadores* or *husares* as late as 1808.

The 45 line infantry regiments included 35 Spanish and 10 foreign. The Spanish regiments each comprised three battalions of four companies each, the companies being fusiliers for all but 1st Battalions, which had two grenadier and two fusilier companies; each company had an establishment of 3 officers, 21 NCOs, 3 drummers and 60 privates, espanded to 164 privates in wartime. Three of the ten foreign regiments were offi-

cially Irish (Irlanda, Hibernia, Ultonia) and one Italian (Napoles), all organised like the Spanish regiments. The remaining six foreign regiments were Swiss (Wimpffen, Reding senior and junior, Betschart, Traxler and Preux), each of only two battalions. A regiment's battalions might not always be stationed together; in mid-1808, for example, the senior line regiment, Rey, had one battalion at San Sebastian, one in Portugal and one in Galicia; while Regiment Jaen had battalions in different continents, two in Andalusia and one in the north African colony of Ceuta. Exemplifying the fact that units were usually under-strength, at this time only two regiments appear to have in excess of 2,000 rank-and-file, while eleven had less than 1,000, with the weakest barely 700. The Irish and Italian regiments averaged only 500 men.

There were twelve battalions of light infantry, each of six companies of 4 officers, 22 NCOs, 3 drummers and 105 privates, expanded to 175 privates in wartime. They were less under-strength than the line, averaging about 1,130 men each in mid-1808, and were sometimes deployed as half-battalions.

The four artillery regiments each had two battalions of five 6-gun batteries each (some had but 4 guns each, and six of the forty companies were horse artillery). There were some fifteen garrison companies (*Companies Fijas*), five artisan companies (*Obreros de Maestranza*), and 74 militia companies (*Milicias Disciplinadas*) among what might be termed an artillery reserve. The ordnance was a mixture of the French Gribeauval pattern (mostly the field-pieces of 4-, 8- and 12-pdr. types) and the older Vallière pattern, the heavier guns being used for garrison and siege duties (16- and 24-pdrs.). The engineers consisted of the Royal Engineers (*Real Cuerpo de*

Ingenerios), comprising about 173 officers, and the Royal Sappers and Miners (*Regimiento Real de Zapadores-Minadores*), of two battalions, each of one miner and four sapper companies, each of 5 officers and 120 other ranks.

There were 21 independent companies (*Companias Fijas*), a form of garrison troops, including eleven on the 'Costa de Granada' (protecting that coast, initially from north African pirate raids), others at Ceuta (cavalry) and Melilla in North Africa, and companies of *Escopateros* (mountain light infantry) in the Gibraltar region, two in Andalusia and one in Valencia.

The Provincial Militia (*Regimientos Provinciales de Milicias*) consisted of 42 regiments bearing the name of their region, each a single battalion 550-600 strong; with a two-battalion regiment in Mallorca (Majorca), and four two-battalion grenadier regiments, officially 1,600 strong (Old and New Castile, Andalusia and Galicia). The Urban Militia (*Milicias Urbanas*) comprised 114 companies in thirteen cities or towns: for example, there were 20 companies in Cadiz, 14 in Badajoz, 13 in the Gibraltar region, 12 in Corunna, 9 in Cartagena and 5 in Ceuta. There were 41 companies of Invalids fit for garrison duties (*Invalidos Habiles*): eleven in Andalusia, seven in Old Castile, six in Estremadura, five in New Castile and four each in Galicia, Navarre and Valencia; and 26 companies of incapacitated Invalids (*Invalidos Inhabiles*), eight each at Seville and Valencia and five each at Lugo and Toro.

At the outbreak of war some of the best elements of the army were serving under La Romana in support of the French in Denmark and north Germany: the cavalry regiments Rey, Infante and Algarbe, the Almansa and Villaviciosa Dragoons, the infantry regiments Asturias, Guadalajara, Princesa and Zamora, detachments of horse and foot artillery and a company of *Zapadores*. Most of the force escaped with British naval assistance, and returned to Spain.

The Army during the Peninsular War

At the beginning of the war, the problems of years of under-funding were compounded by the political situation. While many of the existing regiments survived, many new units were raised by provincial juntas, both they and the old regiments being filled with conscripts or volunteers deficient in training, equipment and experience. The political concept of a patriotic 'national army' could lead in some cases to the exclusion of some elements of the previous military heirarchy, though many retired officers were recalled to service. Furthermore, the new 'patriot' forces were usually extremely deficient in artillery and cavalry, arms necessary to bolster the inexperienced levies that comprised a large proportion of the forces deployed against the French. The consequence of half-trained, poorly-equipped troops with poor leadership was a number of severe defeats, which led to the Spanish troops in general gaining a poor reputation: 'nothing better than mere rabble – no organization, no subordination, but every one evidently pursued that plan which seemed right in his own eyes'[1]. Others recognised the real deficiencies: for example, Robert Blakeney declared that although 'Courage was never wanting in Spanish soldiers', they were 'left barefoot, ragged and half-starved. In this deplorable state they were brought into the field under leaders many of whom were scarcely competent to command a sergeant's outlying pic-

---

[1] Surtees, W., *Twenty-Five Years in the Rifle Brigade*, London 1833, p. 77.

quet'[2]. John Colborne stated that the Spanish people were brave, hardy, active, and abstemious, yet, the Central Junta and the presumption and obstinacy of most of the men placed at the head of the armies rendered their perseverance and courage useless'[3], and as Wellington noted, 'It cannot be expected that troops will march without provisions, or will fight without ammunition'[4]. When adequately provisioned and associated with reliable allies, however, the regular forces formed an important contribution to the Allied military effort, and could emulate the courage and determination displayed by the defenders of fortifications like Saragossa and Gerona.

The Royal Guard

Parts of the Guard disappeared early in the war and were not resurrected until the return of Ferdinand VII, for example the *Albarderos*. The *Guardia de Corps* was reconstituted at Cadiz in May 1813, with two squadrons of three troops each, of 60 all ranks, one to serve as a guard for the Cortes while the other could take the field. The infantry remained in existence, adding 4th battalions in 1810; it is noteworthy that Zayas's Division of Blake's army, which held 'the heights' so valiantly at Albuera, included the 2nd and 4th Spanish Guards, the 4th Walloon Guards, and two old regular regiments, Irlanda and Toledo.

Cavalry

Early in the war the official establishment of cavalry regiments was reduced to four, then three, squadrons of three companies each, and latterly to four squadrons of two companies each; but such establishments were more notional than actual, shortages of horses causing regiments to be very weak, sometimes fielding only one mounted squadron, with the dismounted men used as infantry, for example the 800-odd men who formed part of the garrison of Badajoz in 1811. From the beginning of the war many new units were created, some ostensibly with as many as five squadrons, others with only one, some of which existed for only a couple of years. These included all types of existing cavalry, plus several units of lancers, some styled 'Grenadiers' and a unit of cuirassiers (the *Coraceros Españoles*, 'Spanish Cuirassiers', two squadrons formed in May 1810 with one equipped with captured French cuirasses and helmets). Some corps changed their classification; for example, the *Granaderos de Fernando VII*, raised under the Conde de Fernan-Nuñez in September 1808, became the *Husares de Fernando VII* in May 1811, while others changed title: for example, the San Narciso Hussars, raised under Don Luis Decreff at Gerona in December 1809, subsequently became the Cataluña Hussars. In April 1811 a reorganisation established the regular cavalry as twelve heavy regiments and ten of dragoons (all but two of the latter retaining their titles as at the beginning of the war), and four each of hussars and *cazadores a caballo*; there were also regular squadrons of provincial cavalry, and others including some which had evolved from guerrilla bands. The notional strength of about 700 of all ranks was rarely, if ever, achieved in the field; for example, average regimental strength at Medellin was probably about 375, at Ocaña about 275, in Blake's army at Albuera probably about 350, at Saguntum barely 170.

---

[2] Blakeney, R., *A Boy in the Peninsular War*, ed. J. Sturgis, London 1899, pp. 311, 313.

[3] Moore Smith, G.C., *The Life of John Colborne, Field-Marshal Lord Seaton*, London 1903, p. 135.

[4] *Dispatches of Field-Marshal the Duke of Wellington*, ed. J. Gurwood, London 1834-38, Vol. X p. 415.

Infantry

While almost all of the regiments existing in 1807-08 survived, they were supplemented by a huge number of newly-raised units, many formed by the provincial juntas, of which some were of fairly ephemeral existence, and weak in numbers. The majority were only of one battalion, but some had more (for example, the 'Loyal Saragossans' (*Fieles Zaragozanos*) or Saragossa Volunteers (*Voluntarios de Zaragoza*), formed under Don Manuel de Enna on 30 December 1808, had an establishment of five battalions). Line regiments were usually named after their location, occasionally after an individual (for example the *Voluntarios Leales de Fernando VII*, three battalions raised at Talavera in September 1808), and many styled themselves 'Volunteers'; light battalions were often named *Cazadores* or *Tiradores*.

On 1 July 1810 an attempt was made to reorganise the regular infantry into 121 regiments, eight grenadier and 32 light battalions, plus the surviving Swiss regiments. Each line regiment was ordered to comprise three battalions, each of one grenadier company (113 all ranks), a *cazadore* company (105) and four fusilier companies (165); these were to include the old provincial militia regiments. The grenadier battalions were formed from the old militia grenadiers, each to comprise one *cazadore* and four grenadier companies, each of 134 all ranks. Light battalions were to consist of six companies of 206 all ranks. As before, the establishment strength (of about 880, over 1,200 for light battalions) can rarely have been attained: for example, average strengths at Gerona seem to have been about 500; at Ocaña about 800; at Albuera about 540; at Saguntum about 520.

The difficulty of maintaining multi-battalion regiments was recognised – for example, at Albuera all were single-battalion corps save Regiment Murcia, with two – and a new establishment was ordered on 8 March 1812, by which regiments were to consist of a single battalion, eight companies strong (including one of grenadiers, one of *cazadores*), each company of 125 all ranks. However, according to Wellington's correspondence of February-March 1813, a full-strength regiment could have eight companies of 150 each, a total of around 1,200, confirmed by some regimental returns. Wellington complained that 1,200 men were too many to be manageable in one unit, and by keeping up the numbers there was a tendency to include men physically capable only of garrison duty. His solution was to constitute regiments in two battalions of six companies each, each of a captain, two subalterns and 100 other ranks; or if the regiment were under-strength, the 2nd battalion should have only four companies. The regiment would thus be more manoeuverable, and while the two battalions could serve together in the same brigade if strong enough, otherwise the weaker 2nd battalion could be used as a source of replenishment for the 1st, with the less-effective men employed in garrison duty.

His suggestion, however, was not heeded, though in practice the strength of 1,200 was probably only rarely achieved: of the units with Wellington in mid-1813, for example, average battalion-strength seems to have been under 1,000, 685 at the Nivelle. About 168 infantry regiments served in the post-1812 period, which by 1814 had been reduced to 70 line, 53 light and 30 provincial militia regiments; 33 of the 35 regular regiments that had existed in 1807-08 were still extant, together with three Irish and two Swiss regiments. Included at the end of the war was the uniquely-named 'Imperial Alejandro' Regiment, created on 2 May 1813 under Alejandro O'Donnell, raised at St. Petersburg, named after the Tsar and intended to comprise five battalions of 1,000 men each, though actually it was composed of only three battalions of about 2,000 men in all. New regiments were formed until relatively late in the war: for example, line regiment Talavera was formed under Don Rafael Maroto as late as 30 October 1813.

In addition to the provincial militia, a huge number of local formations existed, from small companies to levy-en-masse style formations like the *Alarma Gallega* ('Galician Alarm'), which by 1811 numbered over 200,000 men. Some corps were of short duration, as exemplified by the 28 'tercios' of Migueletes formed in Catalonia from 15 May 1808; some were disbanded, in November 1809 thirteen were absorbed into the 1st and 2nd *Legion Catalana*, while the 1st and 2nd Gerona, 1st and 2nd Vich, 1st and 2nd Talarn and 2nd Cervera tercios ceased to exist upon the fall of Gerona on 10 December 1809, exemplifying the fact that the continued existence of such corps might depend upon the progress of the war.

Artillery

To the original four regiments, a fifth was added in December 1810, organised at Mallorca. From March 1811 these regiments were restricted to foot companies, with the horse batteries – officially four, later six squadrons – separated. Numbers of new, regional artillery units were formed, not part of this central formation. One of the greatest failings, the reliance upon hired civilians to move the guns, was not fully addressed until April 1813, when five (subsequently six) battalions of Artillery Train were formed, and some British ordnance was supplied. The engineer services remained in existence, with some new formations, the rank-and-file element expanded in 1811 to a regiment of six battalions.

Overseas corps

One of the 'overseas' corps relevant to the Peninsular war was the force styled *Tercios Espanoles de Tejas*, raised from 1804 for service in Texas. Of four infantry and two cavalry tercios planned, only two light infantry units (three companies each) were actually formed, and were stationed at Cadiz, never having been sent to Texas. They served at Bailen and in 1808 were converted to *Cazadore* battalions.

While the colonies in the Americas had provided an important source of revenue, many of the colonies were beset by internal unrest or even virtual cessession (in Mexico, for example, though still mostly under the colonial administration, there was a serious insurrection led by a priest, Father Michael Hidalgo, which began on 16 September 1810 but was crushed in two principal engagements by smaller but disciplined royalist forces, Hidalgo being executed on 30 July 1811). With such unrest, the financial support for patriot Spain fell dramatically, causing serious difficulties for the government, as well as causing some straining of relations with Britain. Detracting from the war effort against the French, this colonial 'second front' absorbed some 20,000 troops during the Peninsular War; in the spring of 1812, for example, the Army of Galicia was all but paralysed by the despatch of a large proportion of its trained artillerymen.

Territories not part of mainland Spain provided a limited amount of resources. A Buenos Aires battalion was formed in 1808 from Spanish prisoners of war taken at Montevideo by the British during their disastrous South American expedition (from the colonial corps *Blandenegues de la Frontera* and the *Regimiento Fijo de Buenos Aires* and Dragoons of the same). The regular battalion resident in the Canary Islands was sent to Spain in 1809 (Regiment Canarias fought in

Lardizabel's Vanguard Division at Albuera, for example), and the Ceuta Regiment served in the Peninsular War as well as serving as a garrison for the north African colonies.

Command and organisation

Although the Spanish Army maintained a traditional divisional system (in which at the outset the old regular, provincial militia and newly-formed units were combined without discrimination), the larger formations were originally in regional armies, based upon the administrative divisions within the kingdom. In addition to the 32 provinces (each headed by an Intendant, a treasury official), the country was divided into fourteen military regions: Aragon, Asturias, Old Castile, New Castile, Catalonia, Estremadura, Galicia, the Campo de Gibraltar, Granada, Navarre, Seville, Valencia and Murcia, and including the two offshore regions, the Balearic Islands and the Canary Islands. Each was headed by a Captain-General, Viceroy or Commandant-General. In October 1808, for example, there were five principal or front-line armies: Blake's Army of Galicia (almost 44,000 strong); Palafox's Army of Aragon (about 34,000), Galluzzo's Army of Estremadura (about 12,800), Castaños's Army of the Centre (about 51,000, and including the so-called 'Army of Castile' of General Pignatelli), and Vives's Army of Catalonia (about 20,000). The reserve forces comprised Reding's Army of Granada, San Juan's Reserve Army of Madrid, and reserves from Galicia, Asturias, Estremadura, Andalusia, and Murcia and Valencia, totalling perhaps 65,000. This exemplifies the fact that the term 'army' did not imply a particular level of strength or composition: for example, the Army of Galicia comprised six divisions and two independent brigades, while the Army of Catalonia, less than half the numerical strength of Galicia, comprised five divisions and a reserve. Other forces remained outside such organisations throughout.

Despite changes, regional identification of armies remained the principal method of distinction until 1811, when numbers were allocated to various forces, though territorial denominations continued to be used. The First Army was that of Catalonia, Second Valencia, Third Murcia, Fourth Andalusia (originally the troops at Cadiz), Fifth Estremadura, Sixth Galicia; the Seventh, Eighth and Ninth Armies covered the guerrilla forces of north-eastern Spain. Wellington indicated the disadvantages of maintaining so many armies in a letter to war minister José Maria de Carvajal in December 1812: that they perpetuated too many staffs and Captains-General for the number of troops involved, 'not only useless, but destructive of the resources by which troops could be maintained'. Castile and Estremadura, he noted, were the territory of Fifth Army, but in addition to its commander, both provinces maintained a Captain-General and staffs, with hardly any troops to command. Second and Third Armies together hardly amounted to two divisions, but had enough staff for two armies, while Seventh Army 'is composed almost entirely of bands of guerrillas; and the only corps that I know of in Spain that at all approaches in numbers the size of armies are the 4th and 6th'[5]. In the event, the Catalonians remained as First Army; Murcia and Valencia were consolidated as Second Army; the Andalusians became Third Army, and Fifth to Seventh Armies (Estremadura, Galicia, Castile) became the Fourth.

Writing as generalissimo of the Spanish forces, Wellington identified failings in lead-

---

[5] *Dispatches of Field-Marshal the Duke of Wellington*, ed. J. Gurwood, London 1834-38, Vol. IX, p. 598.

ership and logistical support: 'the discipline of the Spanish armies is in the very lowest state; and their efficiency is, consequently, much deteriorated. Neither officers nor troops having been paid for months, nay, some for years, it cannot be expected that the troops should be in very good order . . . not only are your armies undisciplined and inefficient, and both officers and soldiers insubordinate for want of pay, provisions, clothing, and necessaries, and the consequent endurance of misery for a long period of time, but the habits of indiscipline are such, that even those corps that have been clothed and regularly paid by my directions . . . are in as bad a state'[6].

Logistical problems remained, even taking into account the very considerable supplies provided by Britain; Wellington admitted 'the inconvenience and evils of the existing system' of 'allocating the revenues of certain provinces to the support of certain armies'; but 'bad as it is, it is the only one under which the army could get any thing'[7]. In March 1813 he reported that 'We have large bodies of men well clothed, armed and accoutred [but] it is doubtful whether I can realize any resources from the country, so as to be able to make any use of these troops as an army in the field'[8]. Three months later he reported that the Army of Reserve of Andalusia could not move because their Intendants had not collected the provision as ordered, and that the Army of Galicia 'is unprovided with mules to carry ammunition, or any thing else, on account of the neglect of the civil authorities in Galicia . . . The consequence is that this army, which is clothed, armed, and disciplined, cannot be brought into action with the enemy . . . Thus this campaign will be fought without the aid of a single Spanish corps, notwithstanding that it is supposed there are 160,000 troops in arms . . .'[9].

From mid-1813 the troops directly under Wellington's command comprised Fourth army (six divisions, rising to eight) and the Army of Reserve of Andalusia (two divisions), a total of about 46,000 in mid-1813. Much to Wellington's disapproval, Castaños was replaced by Freire in command of Fourth Army, with Giron transferred to command the Army of Reserve of Andalusia; Wellington remarked that 'in addition to the inconvenience and injury to the public of all the changes of this description in the midst of a military operation . . . directly in breach of the engagements made to me'[10]. To Bathurst he commented, 'We and the powers of Europe are interested in the success of the war in the Peninsula; but the creatures who govern at Cadiz appear to feel no such interest. All that they care about really is to hear praise of their foolish Constitution. There is not one of them who does not feel that it cannot be put into practice; but their vanity is interested to force it down people's throats'[11]. The number of Spanish troops with Wellington's army had declined to about 40,000 by the end of the war, the cavalry and two divisions of Fourth Army having been left in, or sent back to Spain, after the invasion of France, as was the whole of the Army of Reserve, though its two infantry divisions were called up again in February 1814.

---

[6] *Dispatches of Field-Marshal the Duke of Wellington*, ed. J. Gurwood, London 1834-38, Vol. IX, pp. 596-97.

[7] *Ibid.*, Vol. X, p. 622.

[8] *Ibid.*, Vol. X, p. 164.

[9] *Ibid.*, Vol. X, p. 415.

[10] *Ibid.*, Vol. X, p. 494.

[11] *Ibid.*, Vol. X, p. 474.

The Prince of Anglona's Third Army, 17,000 strong at the end of 1813, only crossed the Pyrenees in April 1814.

As with the Anglo-Portuguese forces, most of the commissariat depended upon hired civilians, though from August 1813 an attempt was made to militarise the muleteers, but supplies were not often forthcoming. Although the troops could distinguish themselves in action – for example at San Marcial when Anglo-Portuguese-style tactics were employed to good effect – from sheer necessity they had to plunder, the reason why Wellington used so few in the invasion of France. He wrote in November 1813, 'If I could now bring forward 20,000 good Spaniards, paid and fed, I should have Bayonne. If I could bring forward 40,000, I do not know where I should stop. Now I have both the 20,000 and the 40,000 at my command, but I cannot venture to bring forward any for want of means of paying and supporting them. Without pay and food, they must plunder; and if they plunder, they will ruin us all'[12]. It was this that led him to issue his harsh letter to Morillo in the following month, 'I did not lose thousands of men to bring the army under my command into the French territory, in order that the soldiers might plunder and ill treat the French peasantry, in positive disobedience of my orders'[13]. Nevertheless, his comments on what could be achieved with Spanish troops properly supplied is a reflection upon his opinion of their inherent qualities.

The quality of leadership remained low throughout the war. Some generals proved to be capable subordinate commanders, many were brave, but few approached the upper reaches of military capability. In later life Wellington commented that 'The Spaniards make excellent soldiers. What spoils them is that they have no confidence in their officers – this would ruin any soldiers – and how should the Spaniards have confidence in such officers as theirs?'[14]. This accords with his comment to Bentinck in 1813 that neither the British government nor army would like to see the British forces in eastern Spain 'under the command of any Spanish General that has appeared in the last one hundred and fifty years'[15]. That may be an exaggeration, but it was the combination of poor leadership, troops starved of resources and training and insufficiently equipped with artillery and cavalry, that led to the reverses suffered by the Spanish military during the period.

Guerrillas

The popular concept of the guerrilla may be misleading, in that many thus categorised were virtually the equivalent of regular soldiers. While many guerrilla forces originated with bands of civilians united in a patriotic cause, many of the earlier formations were composed of dispersed regular troops from the defeated armies, commanded by regular officers like Juan Diaz Porlier, 'El Marquesito'. By the time that most of these had been re-integrated into the army, some originally civilian bands had become established with semi-regular organisation; Espoz y Mina, for example, in 1810 named his command the Division of Navarre and divided it into three battalions. By the end of the war, despite defeats and dispersals, it comprised four Navarrese, three Aragonese and two Alavese

[12] *Dispatches of Field-Marshal the Duke of Wellington*, ed. J. Gurwood, London 1834-38, Vol. XI, pp. 306-07.

[13] *Ibid.*, Vol. XI, p. 391.

[14] Stanhope, Earl, *Notes on Conversations with the Duke of Wellington*, London 1888, p. 10.

[15] *Dispatches of Field-Marshal the Duke of Wellington*, ed. J. Gurwood, London 1834-38, Vol. X, p. 620.

infantry battalions, two Navarrese cavalry regiments and two companies of light horse, numbering about 11,000 and supported financially by a customs service that levied tolls considerably more efficiently than had the previous 'official' revenue service.

Many civilian bands were formed spontaneously, though the Central Junta issued orders on 28 December 1808 to regularise the size of bands or *partidas*, while others were authorised by local juntas. Their services varied from isolated operations to large-scale campaigns, often supporting or in concert with regular forces. Their operations may not have been entirely beneficial to the patriot cause: in some cases the guerrilla war was just an excuse for banditry, and there were complaints that the existence of guerrilla bands with their very loose discipline encouraged desertion from the regular forces. Wellington noted their limitations in June 1812: 'The guerrillas, although active and willing, and although their operations in general occasion the utmost annoyance to the enemy, are so little disciplined that they can do nothing against the French troops, unless the latter are very inferior in numbers . . .'[16]; but nevertheless they posed a serious problem to the French. Countless thousands of French troops were occupied in keeping open lines of communication and in sweeps against guerrilla bands, convoys and messengers were intercepted, garrisons besieged, and when the guerrillas were defeated they usually melted away and re-formed. The effect upon the morale of the French troops must have been profound, for as Marshal Macdonald noted of his period commanding the Army of Catalonia, 'The

enemy were ubiquitous, and yet I could find them nowhere, though I travelled through the length and breadth of the province'[17]. At their most effective they were of strategic significance; for example, the exertions of leaders like Longa and Porlier in 1810-11 paralysed the French commanders in northern Spain and probably prevented them from conquering Galicia or falling upon north-east Portugal.

A noted element of the guerrilla war was, all too often, cruelty of a most obscene description, on both sides. Some of the atrocity and counter-atrocity was not even spontaneous: an example was the announcement in December 1811 by General Louis Abbé, in Navarre, that not only would no quarter be given, but that relatives of insurgents would also suffer, and numbers were killed and their bodies hung along the road near Pamplona. Espoz y Mina – who hitherto had been taking and holding French prisoners in the conventional way – countered by killing some in retaliation. This savagery ended when Abbé withdrew his proclamation of extermination and Mina resumed offering quarter to his enemies. (A comment on the practices of some guerrillas was made by Sir George Collier of HMS *Surveillante*, regarding a joint operation between that ship and the band of 'El Pastor' against Bermeo in October 1811: 'only one prisoner was brought in, who owes his life to his having fallen into the hands of a guerilla (sic) recruit'[18], implying that a more experienced guerrilla would not have taken a prisoner!).

Many guerrilla commanders became more famous than the leaders of regular forces, and often were more competent, even if

[16] *Dispatches of Field-Marshal the Duke of Wellington*, ed. J. Gurwood, London 1834-38, Vol. IX, p. 242.

[17] Macdonald, J.E.J.A., *Recollections of Marshal Macdonald*, ed. C. Rousset, trans. S.L. Simeon, London 1892, Vol. II p. 16.

[18] *London Gazette*, 9 November 1811.

many had come from non-military or humble backgrounds; an example was General Baron Eroles, a civilian in 1808,who learned warfare and command in the field, and graduated to become a general of real skill, indefatigable, brave, active and competent. Javier Mina, 'El Estudiante', was one of the early heroes, succeeded upon his capture by his uncle, Francisco Espoz y Mina, whose forces are mentioned above. Juan Martin Diez; 'El Empecinado' ('the Obstinate') was another legendary leader whose forces became regularly organised and became part of the army proper. Don Julian Sanchez came from a humble beginning to become a dominant figure in Old Castile, with regularly-formed troops (his lancers dressed in captured French clothing) of especial use to Wellington, given their area of operations. A feature of the guerrilla commanders was the use of nicknames, as well-known as 'El Empecinado' to lesser characters styled, for example, El Capuchina, El Cura (also a priest, Geronimo Moreno), Manco (the turncoat Saturnino Albiun, 'one hand'), Chaleco (lit. 'waistcoat', Francisco Abad Moreno) and El Pastor ('the shepherd', Gaspar de Jauregi). Such names became so familiar as to be quoted in official documents, not just the better-known like 'the Empecinado' who appears under that name in British despatches: for example, in 1812 Wellington reported that Madrid had been occupied by 'Colonel Don Juan Palarea the Medico'[19] (El Medico: 'the doctor').

With the liberation of territory, the guerrilla bands had to be integrated into the regular forces, so that many took on the establishment of ordinary regiments, a process largely achieved by 1813 (for example, Espoz y Mina's Division of Navarre ranked as the 8th Division of Freire's Fourth Army). Such forces also became properly uniformed and equipped; Longa, for example, organised his command into four light infantry battalions and collaborated so well with Graham in 1813 that Wellington especially recalled Longa as one of the most able Spanish commanders.

While the guerrilla bands could not ultimately have propered without support from the regular forces (notably the Anglo-Portuguese war effort), they constituted a vital part of the resistance to the French, and were of considerable assistance to the regular armies. The number of French casualties they inflicted is impossible to determine, but it is likely that the minimum was 50,000, and perhaps very considerably more (Espoz y Mina claimed 40,000 for Navarre alone)[20]; but in keeping occupied countless thousands of French troops who could otherwise have been employed to much greater effect elsewhere, their contribution was of great significance.

Navy

The navy was in a very weak state at the beginning of the Peninsular War, never having recovered from the losses of Trafalgar. Its three principal bases were Ferrol, Cartagena and Cadiz, of which the latter was the most significant. The last martime loss before the end of Anglo-Spanish hostilities was the capture of a mistico and destruction of four gunboats by the 18-gun brig-sloop HMS *Redwing* in May 1808. Although communication was maintained with the overseas colonies, thereafter the navy's role in the Peninsular War was very limited, though

---

[19] *London Gazette*, 3 December 1812.

[20] see, for example, Tone, J.L., *The Fatal Knot: The Guerrilla War in Navarre and the Defeat of Napoleon in Spain*, Chapel Hill, N.C., 1994, p. 177.

involved operations like the frigate *Flora's* co-operation with HMS *Cambrian* in the raid on Bagur in September 1810. Naval personnel served on land during the war, however; there was, for example, a detachment of some 130 seamen attached to the artillery at the siege of Gerona. At the beginning of the war there were four battalions of marines, expanded in January 1809 to five regiments of two battalions each, with a sixth (of three battalions) added in September 1809; and a corps of Marine Artillery. These troops served on land during the war.

SPAIN: THE BONAPARTIST KINGDOM

From the outset, Joseph Bonaparte received the support of a part of Spanish society, largely from the upper echelons. Their motives ranged from a desire to retain the social order imperilled by popular uprisings, or in the belief that the Bonapartist regime would maintain law and order, to opportunities for personal advancement or enrichment. Those who took Joseph's side included such significant figures as the war minister, General Gonzalo O'Farrill (who held the same portfolio in Joseph's administration), François Cabarrus, the French-born finance minister, and Miguel José de Azanza, a viceroy of Mexico under the Bourbons and who, ennobled by Joseph as the Duque de Santa Fé, served as his ambassador in Paris and temporarily led the government during Joseph's absence. Others took some time to oppose Joseph, like the Duque de Infantado; he was the senior grandee present with the junta summoned to Bayonne to welcome the new king, though he did say that they must await the views of the Spanish people; Napoleon gave him a tongue-lashing and Infantado subsequently became a leader of the 'patriot' forces. Nor was the decision to support Joseph always taken early in the war; for example, when he surrendered Pensicola, without resistance, in February 1812, General Garcia Navarro remarked in his letter to Suchet that 'I followed with zeal, I might say with fury, the party which I considered the just one; but today I recognise the necessity for all of us to unite under our King, to render our country less unhappy, and I make my offer to you to serve him with the same enthusiasm'[1]. (Even if this were done for reasons of personal advancement, Navarro persuaded his officers to consent to his decision).

Support among the lower echelons of society was much less common, which greatly affected Joseph's ability to maintain an army. This was composed of the Royal Guard and the line formations.

---

[1] Belmas, J., *Journaux des Sièges faits ou soutenus par les Français dans la Péninsula de 1807 à 1814*, Paris 1836-37, Vol. IV, p. 248.

The Royal Guard

The most reliable part of Joseph's army, the Guard was formed in accordance with Napoleon's suggestions of late December 1808: 'Let each regiment be composed of four battalions, and each battalion of four companies containing 200 men . . . Admit no-one to it except the French conscripts whom I have ordered from Paris and Bayonne, and French soldiers who, either as prisoners with Dupont or otherwise, have been for less than a year in the Spanish service. Of these you may be sure'[2]. Joseph actually formed two battalions of grenadiers, expanded in 1809 to two regiments, Grenadiers and Tirailleurs (or Voltigeurs), of French personnel, with two battalions of Fusiliers, of Spaniards; there was a regiment of (French) Chevau-Légers and a Spanish Hussar regiment, of four and two squadrons respectively; a small Spanish mounted gendarmerie unit serving as a kind of *Maison du Roi*, formed in February 1811, the senior element in the Guard; a ceremonial palace-guard company of Halbardiers which had accompanied Joseph from Naples; and foot and horse artillery batteries and attendant train companies.

Line Regiments

The line formations were much less efficient, and some never progressed beyond the planning or cadre stage. The most reliable were probably the foreign regiments, the senior, *Royal Etranger*, being formed in December 1808 on Napoleon's instructions: 'There should be included in this regiment all the Austrians, Prussians and Italians who have passed the last ten years in Spain . . . appoint as colonel one of the chief officers of your guard, and . . . a chef de bataillon and six cap-

tains out of your guard, and the requisite number of sergeants . . . [it will] be composed of four battalions, each consisting of six companies, each company containing 200 men . . . one of the advantages of this will be to clear off the crowd of strangers who swarm in Madrid, and who may be put to some use'[3]. A second foreign regiment, *Royal Irlandais* (though containing few of Irish descent) comprised two battalions and apparently merged with *Royal Etranger* about 1812; the latter had but two battalions when disbanded in January 1814. In addition to these, many French officers were seconded to Joseph's army, including in staff and administrative positions, often with a rank higher than that held in French service.

The indigenous part of Joseph's army included six heavy cavalry regiments which never appear to have progressed much beyond cadre stage; a lancer regiment that barely attained company strength; a squadron of Guadaljara Hussars; and four weak *Cazadore a Caballo* regiments, formed 1809-10, of which the first three lasted until December 1813 (it was members of one of these that appear to have been involved in the action at Blascho Sancho in July 1812). Seven line infantry regiments were authorised, each of two battalions and a depot, numbered 1-7 and named after cities (respectively Madrid, Toledo, Seville, Soria, Granada, Malaga and Cordova), formed from January 1809, and two light infantry regiments (Castile and Murcia). Evidently Napoleon did not expect much from these, writing in January 1809 that 'They should not be allowed to approach within 10 leagues of Madrid. If you have officers enough to form the cadres, I think that

---

[2] *The Confidential Correspondence of Napoleon Bonaparte with his Brother Joseph*, London 1855, Vol. I, p. 380.

[3] *Ibid.*, Vol. I, pp. 379-80.

you will be able to obtain privates. These regiments are indispensible as a refuge for numbers of people who would otherwise become bandits; at the same time they will be useful as police'[4]. Probably not much more that the first two line regiments and the light infantry were ever operational, and the 1st and 2nd Line were incorporated into the 1st Castile Light Infantry in 1813, which was itself disbanded in January 1814. There were also two artillery battalions and some garrison companies, small engineer and gendarmerie units, and a small corps of Catalonian Guides, mounted and foot, for convoy escort duty.

The provincial militia, intended to continue the organisation existing under the previous monarchy, probably never amounted to much, but there were civic or urban militia units, sometimes styled *escopateros*, of more significance. Their prime function was to protect their own communities from the depredations of patriot regulars or guerrillas, albeit under the threat of French vengeance if they collaborated; in fact their real sentiments might lie with the 'patriots'. Some anti- or *contra-guerrilla* bands existed on similar lines, for example that led by one of El Empecinado's subordinates, Saturnino Albuin, 'El Manco', who changed sides after having been taken prisoner, and who also raised the Guadalajara Hussars.

The number of military *Juramentados* was never great, with many of the rank and file being deserters or ex-prisoners of war who would desert again at the first opportunity; consequently the army was never large. At Vittoria, for example, the Guard infantry numbered about 2,300, the Guard cavalry about 400, the three line regiments (Castile, Toledo, Royal-Etranger) together about 2,000, and the line cavalry (1st and 2nd *Cazadores a Caballo*, Guadalajara Hussars) about 600, plus a small artillery detachment, which was then virtually the whole of Joseph's disposable army.

While the Spanish rank and file could desert to join the patriot forces, a worse fate awaited the officers, who could expect no mercy: 'Cuesta shot 13 Spaniards in front of our lines, viz. 12 for Cowardice & one (an Officer tho' badly wounded & who sat in a chair) for being taken in the service of the valiant King Joe'[5].

A company of Spaniards participated in the defence of Badajoz in 1812; five officers (including *chef de bataillon* Nieto) and 'several' other ranks fell into Spanish hands at the surrender and were instantly shot. Another officer, Captain Farinas of the artillery, escaped that fate by standing in front of a mortar and firing it. The fear of reprisals explains why, when the French abandoned a territory, their retreating forces would be followed by a convoy of civilian *Afrancesados* and their dependents, such as the thousands who followed Soult when he evacuated Andalusia in September 1812.

When Soult reorganised his army in July 1813, he had Casapalacio's Spanish brigade of 1,160 men (regiments Castile, Toledo and Royal Etranger) and Joseph's Guard, three regiments under General Nicolas-Philippe Guy, Marques de Rio Milanos (an ex-ADC of King Joseph who had followed him from Naples and who became a general in French service in January 1814), three regiments numbering about 2,000. Subsequently the surviving Spanish regiments were disbanded, and the French personnel of the Guard absorbed into Napoleon's Young Guard, notably the 14th Voltigeurs.

[4] *The Confidential Correspondence of Napoleon Bonaparte with his Brother Joseph*, London 1855, Vol. II, p. 26.

[5] Account of Talavera by an unidentified British participant; MS, author's possession.

TUSCANY

The Treaty of Lunéville converted Tuscany into the Kingdom of Etruria, under Spanish control, but by the Treaty of Fontainebleau Charles IV ceded Etruria to France. It was divided into three *départements* as the 29th military district and ruled by a French administrator until in March 1809 Napoleon's sister, Elisa Bacciocchi, was made grand-duchess of Tuscany. In 1807 the Etrurian troops passed into French service, the infantry regiment becoming the 113th French Line Regiment, which continued to be recruited in the Tuscan *départements*. The Etrurian Dragoons, reconstituted as the Tuscan Dragoons in January 1808, served in the Peninsula, as part of Reille's 'Perpignan Division', two squadrons strong (250 men), along with two battalions of the newly-formed 113th. On 29 May 1808 the dragoons were converted officially into the French 28th Chasseurs à Cheval.

GLOSSARY

The following list of military and other terms includes many of especial relevance to the Peninsular War, and which may be encountered in the literature of the war.

AAG: British Assistant-Adjutant-General.

abanderado: Spanish colour-bearer.

abatis (or abbatis): breastwork or barricade constructed of trees or interwoven branches; from French *abbatre*, to cut down.

adjutant: junior administrative officer, or French warrant officer.

adjutant-commandant: French staff officer, usually serving as a divisional or corps chief of staff.

adjutant-general: staff officer; in British service, the adjutant-general's department was officially responsible for equipment and discipline.

adjutant-sous-officier: French senior warrant officer.

afrancesados: Spanish supporters of the French; afrancesamiento, 'Frenchification' or the attempt to introduce French systems or customs.

AG: British Adjutant-General.

aide-de-camp: junior staff officer, serving a general.

Alarma Gallega: local-defence militia raised in Galicia; lit. 'Galician Alarm'.

alarm post: in field or garrison, the place at which a unit assembled in case of alarm.

Albarderos: the Guardias Albarderos (lit. 'halbardier guard') was a unit of the Spanish royal bodyguard, a ceremonial part of the Casa Real.

alcalde: Spanish mayor.

alferes: Portuguese second-lieutenant.

alferez: Spanish second-lieutenant.

alpartagas: Spanish sandals, of the type worn by mountaineers.

ammunition: British colloquial description of any piece of issue equipment, e.g. 'ammunition boot'.

ammuzette: large-calibre musket or 'wall piece' fired from a defensive position.

approaches: siege-trenches approaching the enemy defences.

AQMG: British Assistant-Quartermaster-General.

armada: Spanish 'navy'.

artillerie à cheval: French horse artillery.

artillerie à pied: French foot artillery.

atirador: Portuguese Caçadore sharpshooter (also 'tirador').

avant-train: French artillery limber.

ayudante: Spanish adjutant.

ball: musket ammunition, referring either to the projectile, or to a complete cartridge, as in 'ball ammunition'.

bandera: Spanish 'flag'; applied to infantry regimental Colours.

Bank dollar: coining in silver being suspended in Britain in 1798 due to increase in the commercial value of the metal, overstruck Spanish and Spanish-American coins were issued as a substitute, equating with a five-shilling piece. They were either entirely overstruck, or punched with a 'countermark' of the king's head; they were current in both Britain and Spain, although in Britain they were officially-sanctioned tokens rather than true regal coinage.

banquette: in fortification, a firing-step behind a parapet.

barbette: a cannon fired *en barbette* over a parapet, without using an embrasure.

Barbuda, El: lit. 'The Beard', nickname of the guerrilla leader Jaime Alfonso.

barretina: the 1806-pattern false-fronted Portuguese shako.

bastion: (i) a four-sided fortification; (ii) a similar-shaped lace loop on a uniform, which in British service might be subdivided into shapes styled 'flowerpot' or 'Jew's harp'.

bât: pack or pack-saddle; orig. French but used in English to describe anything concerning baggage or provisions, hence 'batman'. Sometimes pronounced 'bau', e.g. 'bau-men'.

batalhão: Portuguese 'battalion'.

batallón: Spanish 'battalion'.

batardeau: a coffer-dam to retain water in a fortress-ditch.

battalion company: British infantry 'centre' company.

battering-train: siege-train of heavy ordnance.

battery: orig. a gun-emplacement, later used to describe a 6- or 8-gun artillery unit.

battery fascine: in fortification, a fascine 8 to 12 feet long, 10 to 12 inches thick (244-366 cm. x 25-30 cm.)

Belemite: British colloquialism for a malingerer (from the hospital at Belem, near Lisbon).

Bengal lights: a carcass or illumination-shell or firework composed of saltpetre, sulphur and red orpiment, which apparently burned with a bright blue light.

biscaïen: French term for a large bullet or slug, or for the component part of grapeshot.

bivouac: term often used in the modern sense of a camp in the field, though in the strictest sense it described a nocturnal camp in which the troops remained under arms, about one-third resting at any one time.

black strap: British colloquialism for wine, said to originate from a punishment used at Gibraltar (where wine instead of beer was issued).

blind: a construction used to conceal a besieger from the enemy, a barricade of brushwood, sandbags or gabions.

block-battery: a wooden floor for artillery, providing a solid base for firing guns.

blockhouse: fortified strongpoint.

bomb: mortar-shell; term applied loosely to all explosive projectiles.

bombardier: junior NCO of artillery, or one trained to prepare explosive shells.

bonnet: in fortification, a triangular position in front of a ravelin.

breaking ground: the commencement of a siege, when the first excavation was begun.

breastplate: small metal badge worn upon a shoulder-belt.

breastwork: protective parapet.

bricole: a rope or strap for dragging a field-piece by hand; a cannon fired *en bricole* when a shot struck a sloping revetment.

brigade: (i) a tactical formation of two or more infantry battalions or cavalry regiments; (ii) a British artillery company.

brigade-major: brigade staff officer.

brigadier: brigade-commander (an appointment rather than a rank). In French service, a cavalry corporal; in Spanish, a brigadier-general, ranking below *mariscale de campo.*

briquet: French term for a short infantry sabre.

Brown Bess: nickname of the British infantry musket, prob. orig. from the colour and 'buss', anglicization of German *buchse*, a gun; or a term of endearment.

Brown George: British colloquialism for an issue loaf.

budge-barrel: a powder-barrel, usually with rope hoops (so as not to strike sparks from metal bands), with leather lining and draw-string top; orig. French *bouget.*

busby: fur hussar cap (a term not in common use at this period).

caballeria de linea: Spanish 'line cavalry'.

cabecilla: guerrilla or bandit chieftain.

cabo: Portuguese corporal.

cabotage: coastal shipping of the sort used by the French to supply their coastal garrisons; caboteur or cabotier, a coasting vessel.

caçadore: Portuguese light infantry (lit. 'hunter'; also cazador).

caisson: ammunition wagon (orig. French).

camisade: nocturnal surprise attack, from Spanish *camisa*, a shirt, from the early practice of wearing a shirt over armour to distinguish friend from foe in the dark.

canister: artillery projectile of lead balls in a tin container.

cantinière: French sutleress.

capitão: Portuguese captain.

capitão mor: 'chief captain', either a feudal lord or senior magistrate responsible for calling out and leading Portuguese ordenanza.

caponnière: (i) covered communication-trench from an enceinte to a detached work; (ii) casemated fortification project-ing across a ditch for delivering flanking-fire.

caporal: French corporal.

capsquare: metal plate which secured the trunnion of a cannon-barrel to the carriage.

captain-general: Spanish commanding general (of a province, etc.)

carabineros: lit. 'carabiniers':the Carabineros Reales were a cavalry unit of the Spanish Royal Guard.

carabinier: (i) grenadier of French light infantry regiment; (ii) a variety of French heavy cavalry.

Caracol: nickname of Spanish guerrilla leader Toribio Bustamente.

carbine: short cavalry musket.

carcass (or carcase): incendiary or illumina-tion-shell, applied loosely to any illumina-tion device, e.g. a tar barrel.

carriage: the wheeled framework which sup-ported a cannon barrel.

cartel: arrangement between opposing armies to exchange prisoners.

cartouche: cartridge or cartridge-pouch (French).

Casa Real: Spanish 'royal household': applied to the royal bodyguard troops equivalent to the French *Maison du Roi.*

cascabel: knob at the 'sealed' end of a cannon barrel.

casemate: chamber in a fortress wall.

caserio: a stout house, especially in the Basque region, which could be used as a strongpoint.

case-shot: see 'canister'.

cavalier: raised battery, usually inside a bastion.

cazador: Spanish 'chasseur'.

cazador a caballo: Spanish 'chasseur à cheval'.

centre company: infantry 'battalion company', so called from their position in the centre of the line.

cerro: hill.

chacones: Spanish guerrilla nickname for those who sided with the French, after José Chacon, one of the most prominent Afrancesados in Navarre (a derivation like 'quisling').

Chaleco: lit. 'waistcoat', nickname of the guerrilla Francisco Abad Moreno.

chamade: signal by drumbeat or trumpet-call that a commander wished to confer with the enemy.

chandelier: wooden frame upon which fascines could be laid to cover men working in a trench.

Charleville: generic name for the French military musket, from one of its places of manufacture.

chase: segment of cannon barrel between chase-girdle and muzzle.

chasse-marée: light, swift coastal vessel, used by privateers; could also be used as a pontoon to form a bridge, such as that constructed over the Adour in 1814.

chasseurs: French light troops in general; more specifically, the 'centre' companies of light infantry regiment (lit. 'hunters').

chasseurs à cheval: French light cavalry.

chasseurs à pied: French light infantry, though the title was only used specifically for the light infantry of the Imperial Guard.

chef de bataillon: French battalion-commander (a rank rather than an appointment).

chef d'escadron: French cavalry squadron-commander.

chemin des rondes: sentry-walk around the top of a revetment.

cheval-de-frises: a barricade made of beams or planks studded with blades or spikes.

chevau-léger: French light cavalry.

Chinese light: illumination-shell composed of nitre, sulphur, antimony and orpiment.

Cholin: nickname of the Aragonese guerrilla leader Miguel Sarasa.

clinometer: instrument for measuring the gradient upon which a cannon stood.

clique: French colloquialism for *tête de colonne*.

Coehorn (or Coehoorn): a mortar, named after its designer.

coffret: French ammunition-chest.

cohorte: unit of French National Guard.

comisario de guerra: Spanish commissary.

command: the British term 'on command', encountered in muster-rolls, indicated personnel on detached duty.

commissaire ordonnateur: French chief commissary.

compagnie d'élite: French 'élite company', equivalent of British 'flank company', i.e. grenadiers and light infantry of an infantry battalion; the 1st troop of the 1st squadron of a cavalry regiment.

company: basic tactical unit within an infantry battalion or cavalry regiment, or a battery of artillery.

conductor: commissariat assistant who supervised the transport of stores; an artillery- or wagon-driver.

Conselho da Guerra: the traditional 'War Council' that ran military affairs in Portugal.

contador: Spanish administrative staff officer (lit. 'accountant').

coraceros: Spanish 'cuirassiers': the single regiment of 'Coraceros Espanoles' was formed in 1810 with equipment captured from the French.

cordon: (i) rounded coping-stone atop a revetment; (ii) chain of sentry-posts.

cornet: British cavalry second-lieutenant.

corneta: Spanish bugler.

Coronilla: term applied to the three provinces of Aragon, Catalonia and Valencia, which had formed the ancient kingdom of Aragon.

corps: generic term for any military unit; a *corps d'armée* was a formation of one or two divisions with all supporting services, virtually a miniature army.

corregidor: Spanish city governor or chief magistrate, royally appointed.

corso terraste: lit. 'land pirates': the concept of guerrilla formations authorised by the Centra Junta on 17 April 1809.

Cortes: Spanish parliament.

countermark: the over-stamping of a king's head device upon a Spanish silver coin to produce a variety of 'bank dollar', silver currency issued by the Bank of England and used both in Britain and the Peninsula.

counterscarp: a slope or retaining-wall on the outer side of a ditch.

countersign: password given in answer to a challenge.

covered-way (or covert-way): an infantry fire-step along a ditch.

crapaud: British nickname for French soldiers ('Johnny Crapaud'), lit. 'toad'.

croaker: British colloquialism for a complainer or pessimist, from the croaking of a raven, supposedly an omen of ill-luck.

crownwork: fortification of two small bastions with two long bastions at either side.

cruzada: lit. 'crusade', a Spanish guerrilla band composed of clerics, monks, etc., but more generally a levy en masse.

cruzados novos: Portuguese silver coins worth approximately 2s.6d. sterling.

cuartel: Spanish 'barracks'; 'uniforme de cuartel' was 'barrack dress' or what in English might be termed 'undress'.

cuerpo: Spanish 'corps', as in the title of a unit.

Cuerpo de Estado Mayor: Spanish general staff.

cuirassier: French armoured heavy cavalry.

Cura, El: nickname of the guerrilla leader Geronimo Merino, lit. 'the priest'.

DAAG: British deputy Assistant Adjutant General.

Daddy: nickname in the British Army for Rowland Hill, from his paternalistic attitude.

Damnation, Duke of: British nickname for Soult, from his title 'Duke of Dalmatia'.

DAQMG: British Deputy Assistant Quartermaster General.

dead ground: a hollow or fold in the terrain which would conceal troops from enemy fire.

Death or Glory Men: British nickname for the Brunswick Oels Corps, from the skull and crossed bones device upon their shakos.

defile: to reduce the frontage of a unit to permit it to pass through a narrow space or opening.

dehors: outworks some distance from a main fortification.

demi-brigade: prior to 1803, a French regiment; after that date the term was applied to any ad hoc, temporary formation.

demi-lune: a ravelin (lit. 'half-moon').

Deseado, El: nickname of Ferdinand VII, lit. 'the desired one'.

detachment: as in British 'battalion of detachments': a composite unit formed from a number of small contingents.

devil carriage: four-wheeled wagon for the transportation of heavy ordnance.

diario: 'uniforme de diario' was the Spanish term for 'everyday' uniform, or what might be termed 'service dress' in English, as different from full dress.

dispart: half the distance between the diameter of a gun-barrel at the base-ring and the swell at the muzzle; usually 1/56th of the length.

disputacion: Spanish provincial assembly or council.

division: (i) a formation of two or more brigades; (ii) in British service especially, two companies of a battalion acting in concert; (iii) also in British usage, two field-pieces with attendant vehicles.

dollar: name given to a Spanish silver coin, worth 4s.6d. sterling, or 20 reales.

dolphins: lifting handles of a cannon-barrel.

Douro: the name by which Wellington was generally known by his Portuguese troops, from his Portuguese title; its use also spread to the British army.

dragones: Spanish 'dragoons'.

dragoons: 'medium' cavalry, orig. mounted infantry.

ejercito: Spanish 'army'.

embrasure: opening in a parapet to enable guns to fire through.

Empecinado, El: 'the Obstinate': nickname of the guerrilla leader Juan Martin Diaz.

enceinte: fortress-wall or perimeter.

enfants-perdus: lit. 'lost children': French colloquialism for 'forlorn hope'.

enfilade: to fire upon the flank of a formation, raking its length.

ensign: British infantry 2nd lieutenant.

Enthusiastics: nickname of the British 4th Division, adopted after Wellington had referred to their enthusiastic conduct in the Pyrenees, prior to which they had been called 'the Supporting Division'.

envelope: a continuous enceinte.

escopeta: short, sturdy Spanish musket, the term evidently first recorded in 1517 and derived from the 15th-century Italian *schioppetto*.

escopeteros: light infantry, named from the escopeta musket; also the name given to home-defence units formed by Soult in Andalusia.

esplanade: open space between a citadel and the nearest buildings.

Estado Mayor de Artilleria: Spanish 'Artillery General Staff'.

Estudiante, El: 'the Student', nickname of the guerrilla leader Xavier Mina.

evolutions: drill-movements.

expense magazine: small magazine placed near a battery.

Extincta Primero Plano: originally an exclusive body of officers of the Portuguese Army, known as the Primero Plano, originally forming a royal bodyguard; the organisation was disbanded but former members were permitted to wear its distinctive scarlet uniform when at court.

facings: (i) coloured distinctions on a uniform, collar, cuffs, lapels, etc.; (ii) drill-movements.

family: colloquialism for a general's personal staff.

fanega: Spanish measure (of wheat, etc.) equivalent to 55 litres.

fascine: bundle of brushwood used in fortification.

fernandino: supporter of Ferdinand VII.

fidalgo: Portuguese noble.

Fighting Division: nickname for British 3rd Division.

file: line of men ranged behind one another (hence 'rank and file').

fire-ball: illumination-shell composed of rosin, sulphur, alum powder, starch, saltpetre, mealed powder and linseed oil.

firelock: flintlock musket.

fixed ammunition: artillery projectile with wooden 'sabot' attached.

flank company: grenadiers and light infantry of an infantry battalion, from their position on the flanks of the line.

flèche: arrow-shaped earthwork.

foreland: space between a rampart and its ditch, onto which lumps of destroyed rampart might fall without filling the ditch.

forlorn hope: advance storming-party, especially in the attack on a breach; from Dutch *verloren hoop*, 'lost party'.

fougasse: small mine (also fougade, foucade).

fourgon: French heavy transport wagon.

fourrier: French quartermaster sergeant or corporal.

Fraile, El: nickname of the guerrilla leader Agostin Nebot, lit. 'the Friar'.

fraises: stakes placed horizontally on the outward slope of a rampart to hinder an escalade; also known as 'storm pokes'.

frizzen: the part of a musket-lock from which the flint struck sparks.

furriel: Portuguese quartermaster-corporal.

fusil: in English, a light musket; in French, any musket.

fusilero: Spanish fusilier.

fusilier: generally a 'centre company' infantryman; in British service (often spelled 'fuzileer'), a member of a fusilier regiment (7th, 21st and 23rd Foot).

gabion: earth-filled wicker basket used in fortification; for 'gabion farci', see 'sap roller'.

gala: 'uniforme de gala' was Spanish 'full dress'.

gallery: large mine-tunnel in siegeworks.

galloper: ADC or message-bearer.

gambeto: voluminous Spanish overcoat.

garland: wooden framework used to keep roundshot in a neat pile.

garrochistas: Spanish irregular lancers, orig. Andalusian cattle-herders.

Garter guinea: alternative designation for the 1813 'military guinea', q.v.

gastador: Spanish infantry pioneer.

gendarme: orig. a French term to describe any armed man; later used to describe troops used in security or provost duties, notably the French *Gendarmerie d'Espagne*.

général de brigade, général de division: successive ranks of French general officer; a rank, not an appointment, so that a général de brigade did not necessarily command a brigade, nor was a brigade invariably commanded by one.

generalissimo: Spanish supreme commander (of all aspects of military organisation).

Gentleman's Sons: nickname of British 1st Division.

giberne: French cartridge-box,

glacis: slope descending from a fortification.

Goddam: French nickname for British troops, dating from the Hundred Years War, from the British use of this expression.

granadero: Spanish infantry grenadier; granaderos a caballo, Spanish 'horse grenadiers'.

grand division: in British service, a tactical unit of two infantry companies.

grand rounds: main inspection of sentries, usually conducted once a night.

grasshoppers: French nickname for British riflemen, from their green uniform.

graze: point at which a cannon-ball pitched; 'first graze' was initial point of impact, from where it ricocheted.

grenadier: élite infantryman, so called from being armed with hand grenades in earlier times, but not generally used in the Napoleonic era.

grog: loosely applied to any alcohol, but in British slang a mixture of rum and water; named from Admiral Vernon, who introduced it, alias 'Old Grog' from his wearing of grogram fabric.

Guardias de Corps: Spanish royal bodyguard cavalry.

Guardias Españoles: Spanish royal body-guard infantry.

Guardias Walones: Spanish 'Walloon Guards', royal bodyguard infantry.

guérite: sentry-box upon a fortress rampart; applied loosely to any sentry-box.

guerrilla: Spanish irregular or partisan soldier; lit. 'little war'. In Spanish the individual soldier was a *guerrillero*.

guias: Portuguese Army 'guides', those utilised in reconnaissance duty.

guinea: the standard British gold coin, worth 21 shillings sterling (one pound one shilling), last coined in Britain in 1799 until the issue of 1813 (see 'Military Guinea'); when sent to the Peninsula its official exchange-rate was 4 2/3 dollars, or 93 reales, 12 maravedis.

gun: an unchambered artillery piece (i.e. not a howitzer or mortar).

halberd: common name for the spontoon carried by British infantry sergeants, although a true halberd had an axe head.

half-brigade: in British service, a half 'battery' of artillery.

Halkett's Green Germans: British 7th Division nickname for the light battalions of the King's German Legion.

handspike: lever used to traverse a cannon.

hérisson: beam stuck with spikes, used as a *cheval de frises* for blocking a breach in a wall.

hidalgo: Spanish lower-ranking nobleman (from *hijo de algo*, 'son of something').

hornwork: fortification consisting of a bastion front and two branches at the sides.

housings: cavalry horse-furniture (shabraque and holster-caps).

howitzer: short-barrelled, chambered-bore cannon designed for high-angle fire.

Jaggers: British nickname for the 5th Battn. 60th Royal American Regt., an anglicization of *Jäger*, rifleman, from the predominantly German composition of that battalion.

jefe politico: Spanish political prefect of an area, or provincial governor.

Johnny: British nickname for the French; also 'Johnny Crapaud'.

Josefino: a follower of King Joseph.

juiz de fora: Portuguese chief magistrate of a town.

junta: Spanish administrative or governmental committee; provisional, often regional, body of government.

juramentado: support of King Joseph; lit., one who has sworn an oath.

KGL: King's German Legion.

knapsack: infantry pack.

Legiao de Tropas Ligeras: 'Legion of Light Troops', the official name of the experimental corps of the Portuguese Army formed by the Marquis de Alorna, and disbanded in December 1807.

legion: originally a military unit formed of more than one 'arm', containing infantry, cavalry, and/or artillery; the best-known in the Peninsular War were the King's German Legion, the Loyal Lusitanian Legion, and probably the Spanish *Leal Legion Extremena* commanded by the eccentric British officer John Downie. Other corps used the title but were not 'legions' in the original sense, e.g. the French *Légions de Réserve*.

Light Bobs: British colloquialism for light infantry; 'light bobbing', light infantry service.

limber: two-wheeled carriage connecting a fieldpiece to its team of horses; limber-box, an ammunition-chest carried on a limber.

linstock: pike holding a length of slow-match; orig. 'link-stock'.

lodgement: foothold made in a fortification by an attacker; strictly, such a position fortified to guard against counter-attack.

London Gazette: the British government's official newspaper, in which dispatches and details of commissions were published, hence 'gazetted' meant commissioned.

loophole: small aperture broken through a wall or palisade, to permit defenders to fire through.

lunette: (i) triangular fortification on or beyond a glacis; (ii) small fortification sited to one side of a ravelin.

madrier: long, robust plank used in fieldworks or temporary fortification.

magazine: (i) storage-dump for munitions; (ii) container for cartridges in addition to his ordinary cartridge-box.

Manco, El: nickname of the turncoat guerrilla Saturnino Albuin; lit. 'one-hand'.

Maneta: nickname of French general Louis-Henri Loison, from his having only one arm.

mantlet: wooden screen, often wheeled, protecting the diggers at the head of a sap.

maravedi: small-denomination Spanish coin, similar to a British farthing.

Marching Division: nickname for British 6th Division.

marechal de campo: Portuguese major-general.

maréchal des logis: French cavalry quarter-master.

mariscal de campo: Spanish major-general.

Marquesito, El: nickname of the guerrilla leader Juan Diaz Porlier, because he was a nephew of La Romana, *the* marquis.

marshal-general: highest-ranking officer in the Portuguese Army.

match: impregnated burning-cord for igniting cannon, etc.; 'slow-match', 'quick-match'.

mayor de plaza: Spanish town-major.

Medico, El: nickname of the guerrilla leader Don Juan de Palarea.

merlon: solid parapet between two embrasures.

milicias honradas: Spanish town militia recruited from the upper (propertied) classes.

milicias provinciales: Spanish 'provincial militia', battalions of infantry based upon geographical areas.

milicias urbanas: Spanish 'urban militia', companies based in towns.

Military Guinea: gold coin struck by the Bank of England in 1813 to remedy the shortage of coin with the army in the Peninsula; struck primarily from mohurs and pagodas brought from India, the only source of sufficient metal, production in Britain having stopped in 1799. Also styled a 'Garter Guinea' from the design on the reverse, it was the last guinea coined in Britain, being succeeded in 1816 by the sovereign of 20 shillings.

Minadores: Spanish miners (as in the *Regimiento Real de Zapadores-Minadores*).

Miqueletes (or 'migueletes'): Catalonian irregular light infantry, named after Miguel or Miquelot de Prats, a Catalan condottiere who served under Cesar Borgia (1476-1507); see also 'Somatenes'.

Miquelet lock: a design of flintlock mechanism, the name derived from the above, also known as the 'Spanish lock' from the preponderence of its usage in that country.

mistico: small Mediterranean coasting-vessel, between a xebec and a felucca.

moidore: Anglicization of the Portuguese *moeda d'ouro*, a gold coin.

Moniteur: French government's official newspaper.

Montero Mor: Portuguese 'Master of Horse' to the royal court; name by which the Conde de Castro Marin was often known.

Mozo, El: nickname of the guerrilla leader Xavier Mina, lit. 'the Youth'.

muff cap: British colloquialism for the fur hussar busby.

music: British term for regimental band.

musketoon: light musket.

muzzle droop: distortion of a cannon-barrel caused by overheating.

Napoleon: French coin, a twenty-franc gold piece which from 1803 replaced the Louis d'or (worth 24 *livres* before the Revolution). The five-franc piece replaced the silver *écu*, worth six *livres* before the Revolution. As a rough guide to comparative value, when Wellington entered France he issued a proclamation which equated the British guinea with 25 francs 20 centimes, the dollar with 5 francs 40 centimes, and a franc with 3 reales 24 maravedis.

nature: the weight or classification of an artillery piece.

necessaries: British term for items of personal kit provided at the soldier's expense.

Nosey: British Army nickname for Wellington (from his large nose).

obreros de maestranza: Spanish artillery artisans (lit. 'skilled workmen').

Observing Division: nickname for British 2nd Division.

obusier: French 'howitzer'.

Old Trousers: British nickname for the french drum-call *Pas de charge* which heralded every attack; hence 'here comes Old Trousers', 'the French are attacking'. Probably derived from the British nickname for grenadiers (who were supposed to lead the advance), 'Tow Rows', itself taken from the song *The British Grenadiers* and imitating a drum-beat, hence its use in this context.

ordenanca (or ordenanza): Portuguese second-line militia, a virtual feudal levy.

Ordens do Dia: Portguese military 'Orders of the Day'.

outpost: an outlying picquet; sentry-duty or scouting in general.

Owls: British nickname for members of the Brunswick Oels Corps (from 'Oels').

pagoda: gold coin from southern India, reckoned in 1818 to be worth $3\frac{1}{2}$ rupees; quantities were sent from Britain to the Peninsula to be converted into Portuguese coinage.

pamplonia: colloquialism for a loaf of bread of two to three pounds in weight, presumably named from the city.

pancada: Portuguese military punishment, of striking the miscreant's back with the flat of a sword-blade.

parados: a rearward parapet.

parallel: a siege-trench running roughly parallel to enemy fortification.

parapet: wall or earthern bank on the forward edge of a fortification.

park: artillery reserve.

parlementaire: an envoy sent under a flag of truce to negotiate with an enemy, for example in the case of the capitulation of a fortress (orig. French).

parole: (i) prisoner-of-war's promise not to escape or misbehave; (ii) a password.

partida: guerrilla band (regulated from December 1808 at about 50 men, but this rule was generally ignored).

paseo: 'uniforme de paseo' was Spanish 'walking-out dress'.

Pastor, El: nickname of the guerrilla leader Gaspar de Jauregui; lit. 'the Shepherd'.

patee: small horseshoe-shaped earthwork used to cover an exposed position or gate.

paterero: Spanish term for a large mortar, usually projecting stones.

Peer: 'The Peer' was a common British nickname for Wellington.

peloton: French platoon.

picker: wire needle used for cleaning a musket touch-hole.

picquet (or 'picket'): (i) an outpost or the men forming it; (ii) sharpened length of wood or stake used for tying horses to, fixing gabions in place, etc.

piece: a cannon (orig. 'fieldpiece').

Pillar dollar: Spanish silver coin, first struck in 1732, using silver from Spanish South American colonies, the name deriving from the device of the pillars of Hercules featured in the design.

Pioneers: nickname for the British 5th Division.

place of arms: enlargement of a covered way of a fortress where troops could be assembled for sorties.

plaster: greased patch used as wadding for loading a rifle.

pong: British colloquialism for bread, Anglicized pronunciation of Portuguese *paõ*, bread; 'yellow pong' was bread made from Indian corn.

porte-aigle: French 'Eagle'-bearer; porte-dra-

peau, flag-bearer; porte-étendard, cavalry standard-bearer.

portfire: holder for slow-match.

post: outpost, sentinel.

prepared ammunition: ball and propellant in a cartridge.

present: to 'present fire', to take aim.

prog: British colloquialism for food.

prolonge: rope used to drag a cannon, to obviate repeated unlimbering during movement over the battlefield.

provisional regiments: composite units assembled from detachments.

puente: Spanish 'bridge'.

puerto: Spanish 'pass'.

QMG: British Quartermaster-General.

Quarteis Generaes: Portuguese Quartermaster-General's Department.

quick-match: quick-burning match.

quinte: Spanish levy of conscription.

qui vive?: challenge issued by French sentries: 'who goes there?'

rampart: earthern or masonry wall forming the main part of a fortress defence.

random shot: strictly, an artillery term for a shot fired with the gun-barrel at 45° elevation upon a level plane.

ravelin: triangular detached fortification in front of a fortress wall.

real: small Spanish silver coin (lit. 'royal'); one-twentieth of a dollar, worth about $2^{1}/_{2}$d. sterling or 30 French centimes.

redan: V-shaped fortification.

redoubt: detached fortification, or a redan placed in a bastion.

refractaires: French civilians who refused to be conscripted.

régiment de marche: French provisional formation composed of drafts of a number of units.

reinforces: strengthening-bands upon a cannon-barrel.

Resurrection Men: British nickname for the 3rd Foot after Albuera, when so many returned to duty after recovering from wounds. In civilian argot, 'resurrection men' were those who stole newly-buried bodies and sold them for medical research.

retirade: in field fortification, a trench with a parapet, but used most commonly to describe retrenchment within a defence-line.

retrenchment: interior defences of a fortress, especially to cover a breach.

returns: in fortification, the turnings and angles of a trench.

revetment: retaining-wall of a fortress.

Rey Intruso: 'the intrusive king': a term for Joseph Bonaparte.

Rheinbund: the French-satellite organisation of the Confederation of the Rhine, or the troops pertaining to it.

rounds: inspection of sentries.

running ball: musket-charge without wadding.

sabot: wooden 'shoe' upon 'fixed ammunition'.

sap: narrow siege-trench.

sap roller: also 'gabion farci': a gabion rolled in front of a sapper to shield him from enemy fire. 'Sap faggot', an 8-inch (20 cm.) thick fascine, three feet (92 cm.) long.

Sargento Mayor de Plaza: Spanish Town Major.

saucissons: long, thin fascines (lit. 'sausages').

scarp: outer edge of a rampart.

scour: to enfilade a line at an exact right angle.

serrano: Spanish guerrilla band (lit. mountain-dwellers or mountaineers).

Servil: nickname given to the pro-monarchist faction in Spain by the Liberals; an opponent of the 1812 constitution (lit. a subservient one).

shell: explosive projectile.

sierra: Spanish 'mountain'.

silex: French musket-flint.

skilly: British colloquialism for thin, watery soup.

Slashers: nickname for the British 28th Foot, supposedly invented by Col. John Browne of Barossa fame to compensate for the regiment's lack of a 'royal' title.

sling-cart: two-wheeled vehicle for the transportation of heavy ordnance or mortars.

slow-match: slow-burning match.

slug: misshapen bullet or lump of lead fired from a blunderbuss or musket.

smallclothes: waistcoat, breeches and shirt.

Somatenes: Catalonian levy en masse, paid and armed by their parishes, who could assemble to fight whenever the alarm-bell (somaten) was sounded.

sous-lieutenant: French 2nd lieutenant.

spherical case-shot: shrapnel shell, an explosive shell filled with balls.

spiking: method of rendering a cannon inoperable by hammering a metal spike into the touch-hole.

sponge: the reverse end of an artillery rammer, used to swab out the bore of a cannon to extinguish burning fragments prior to re-loading.

spontoon: short or half-pike carried by sergeants of British line infantry.

spring-spike: artillery spike which expanded when inserted into the touch-hole of a cannon, requiring drilling to remove it.

squadron: cavalry regimental sub-unit, usually comprising two troops.

steel: alternative designation for a frizzen.

storm-poles: palisade planted on a scarp, projecting horizontally or slightly downwards.

subdivision: British artillery unit of one gun, crew and ammunition-wagon.

suelta: a Spanish 'Compañia Suelta' (lit. 'loose' or 'detached') was an independent company of infantry.

Supporting Division: nickname of the British 4th Division before they were re-named 'Enthusiastics'.

Surprisers: nickname of the British 2nd Division, after Arroyo dos Molinos.

Sweeps: nickname for the British 95th Rifles, from their dark green uniforms and black facings.

tambour: (i) French 'drum' or 'drummer'; (ii) small palisaded fortification.

tenaille: small fortification in a ditch in front of a wall.

tenaillon: small fortification one one side of a ravelin.

teniente: Spanish 'lieutenant'.

teniente general: Spanish 'lieutenant-general'.

Teniente de Rey: Spanish lieutenant-governor (of a town).

tercio: the 16th-century Spanish term for a large body of troops continued to be used to describe special formations, including some of the units raised in 1808.

terreplein: wide upper part of a rampart.

testoon (or 'tester'): archaic British term for a small silver coin, a sixpence in sterling but at the time still applied to equivalent Iberian coins; orig. from French *teston*, *teste* (*tête*), the head, from such coins bearing the depiction of a sovereign's head.

tête de colonne: French unit's colour-party, musicians, pioneers, etc.; lit. 'head of col-umn', where these would march.

Tio Pepe: nickname of Joseph Bonaparte, lit. 'Uncle Joe'.

tirador: Portuguese caçadore sharpshooter (also 'atirador'); Spanish light infantry.

tiraillade: skirmish-fire, from French *tirer*, to shoot.

tirailleur: French term for a sharpshooter, although not used as a unit-title except for some regiments of Young Guard and foreign corps.

toise: old French unit of measurement used for measuring fortifications; equivalent to 6.395 English feet.

Tommy: British colloquialism for bread; 'brown Tommy' was that issued to the army, while 'white Tommy' or 'soft Tommy' was a naval term to distinguish bread from biscuit.

town-major: assistant to the governor of a fortress or garrison.

trabajo: 'uniforme de trabajo' (lit. 'working uniform') was Spanish fatigue dress.

train d'artillerie: French artillery drivers and transport.

train des equipages: French 'equipment train': transport-corps for others than artillery.

tren: Spanish 'train' (transport); tren de artilleria, artillery train.

trench fascine: fascine four to nine inches thick (10-23 cm.), four to six feet long (122-183 cm.).

troop: cavalry sub-unit equating with an infantry company.

trou de loup: wolf-pit, q.v.

trunnions: lugs projecting from a cannon-barrel, securing it to the carriage.

vales: lit. 'vouchers' (Spanish); bills for payment issued by the commissariat in lieu of cash.

vedette: cavalry scout.

vent: touch-hole in a cannon-barrel; the 'ventsman' was the gunner who placed his thumb over the vent during the loading procedure.

vivandière: French sutleress.

Vivares de Exercito: Portuguese Army's commissariat department responsible for the acquisition of victuals.

voltigeur: French light company member in an infantry regiment; lit. 'vaulter'

volunteer: in the British Army, an aspirant officer serving in the ranks in the hope of gaining a commission.

wad hook: screw-ended shaft to extract unfired cartridges from a cannon.

wall-piece: large-calibre musket mounted on a fortress wall.

water fascine: fascine six feet long (183 cm.), one or two feet thick (30-61 cm.) weighted with stones to make it sink into wet or marshy ground.

windage: the difference between the bore of a gun and the size of shot.

wing: half an infantry battalion, or more loosely any element of a battalion greater in size than a company.

wolf-pit: cone-shaped pit, usually 6 feet deep (183 cm.) and 4 to 5 feet wide at the top (122-152 cm.), used as an anti-personnel trap; often styled by its French name, *trou de loup*.

worm: corkscrew device for extracting an unfired charge from the barrel of a gun.

zapadores: Spanish 'sappers'.

zigzags: approach-trenches in siege-works, from their configuration.

REFERENCES

The literature on all aspects of the Peninsular War is vast. The titles listed below include many of the most significant, while concentrating upon English-language editions, which are the most accessible for an English-speaking audience. Bibliographies of much greater length, and including more Spanish, French and Portuguese publications, may be found, for example, in *Napoleonic Military History: A Bibliography*, ed. D.D. Horward, London 1986; *The Peninsular War: A New History*, C.J. Esdaile, London 2002; Vol. IX of the Greenhill reprint of Oman's history, *A History of the Peninsular War: Modern Studies of the War in Spain and Portugal, 1808-1814*, ed. P. Griffith, London 1999; *Britain and the Defeat of Napoleon 1807-1815*, R. Muir, New Haven & London, 1996; and in the 'Bibliographic Essay' in *The Wars of Napoleon*, C.J. Esdaile, London 1995.

The following bibliography includes divisions into categories by subject, and the war chronologically; though it is perhaps more appropriate to mention here the Osprey 'Campaign' series of titles, including *Vimeiro 1808*, *Bussaco 1810* and *Fuentes de Oñoro 1811* by René Chartrand, *Badajos 1812*, *Salamanca 1812* and *Vittoria 1813* by Ian Fletcher, and *Corunna 1809* by the present author.

'General' works

Arteche y Moro, J.G. de *Guerra de la Independencia: Historia Militar de España de 1808-14*, Madrid 1868-1903.

Chandler, D.G., *Dictionary of the Napoleonic Wars*, London 1979.

Chandler, D.G., *The Campaigns of Napoleon*, London 1967.

Esdaile, C.J., *The Peninsular War: A New History*, London 2002 (very important modern study).

Fletcher, I. (ed.), *The Peninsular War: Aspects of the Struggle for the Iberian Peninsula*, Staplehurst 1998.

Fletcher, I., & Cook, A., *Fields of Fire: Battlefields of the Peninsular War*, Staplehurst 1994.

Foy, M.S., *History of the War in the Peninsula, under Napoleon*, London 1829

(published originally as *Histoire de la Guerre de la Péninsule, sous Napoléon*, Paris 1827).

Gates, D., *The Spanish Ulcer: A History of the Peninsular War*, London 1986.

Geoffrey de Grandmaison, C.A., *L'Espagne et Napoléon*, Paris 1908-31.

Glover, M., *The Peninsular. War 1807-1814: A Concise Military History*, Newton Abbot 1974.

Glover, M., *Wellington's Peninsular Victories*, London 1963.

Grasset, A.L., *La Guerre d'Espagne*, Paris 1914-32.

Lachouque, H., *Napoleon's War in Spain*, London 1982 (trans. of *Napoléon et la Campagne d'Espagne*, ed. J. Tranié & J.-C. Carmigniani, Paris 1978).

Lovett, G.H., *Napoleon and the Birth of*

Modern Spain, New York 1965.

Nafziger, G.F., *Imperial Bayonets: Tactics of the Napoleonic Battery, Battalion and Brigade as found in Contemporary Regulations*, London 1996.

Napier, W.F.P., *History of the War in the Peninsula and in the South of France from the Year 1807 to the Year 1814*, London 1828-40 (the great, classic early history).

Oman, C.W.C., *A History of the Peninsular War*, Oxford 1902-30 (still the greatest and most detailed work in English. Two important additional volumes were added to the Greenhill reprint: Vol. VIII, Hall, J.A., *The Biographical Dictionary of British Officers Killed and Wounded, 1808-1814*, London 1998; Vol. IX, Griffith, P. [ed.], *Modern Studies in the War in Spain and Portugal, 1808-1814*, London 1999).

Paget, J., *Wellington's Peninsular War: Battles and Battlefields*, London 1990 (includes useful guide to the battlefields).

Parkinson, R., *The Peninsular War*, London 1973.

Priego Lopez, J, *Guerra de la Independencia 1808-14*, Madrid 1972-2000.

Sarrazin, J., *History of the War in Spain and Portugal from 1807 to 1814*, London 1815.

Severn, J.K., *A Wellesley Affair: Richard, Marquess Wellesley and the Conduct of Anglo-Spanish Diplomacy, 1809-1812*, Tallahassee 1981.

Smith, D.G., *The Greenhill Napoleonic Wars Data Book*, London 1998 (includes orders-of-battle for most actions).

Weller, J., *Wellington in the Peninsula*, London 1962.

Windrow, M., & Embleton, G.A., *Military Dress of the Peninsular War*, London 1974.

Wyld, J., *Maps and Plans, showing the Principal Movements, Battles & Sieges in which the British Army was Engaged during the War from 1808 to 1814, in the Spanish Peninsula and South of France*, London 1840 (valuable collection of maps).

The Campaigns: 1808-09

Anderson, J., *The Spanish Campaign of Sir John Moore*, London 1906.

Balagny, D.E.P., *Campagne de l'Empereur Napoléon en Espagne 1808-09*, Paris 1902-06.

Bradford, W., *Sketches of the Country, Character and Costumes in Portugal and Spain, made during the Campaign and on the Route of the British Army in 1808 and 1809*, London 1812.

Davies, D.W., *Sir John Moore's Peninsular Campaign*, The Hague 1974.

Glover, M., *Britannia Sickens: Sir Arthur Wellesley and the Convention of Cintra*, London 1970.

Gordon, A., *A Cavalry Officer in the Corunna Campaign*, ed. H.C. Wylly, London 1913.

Hibbert, C., *Corunna*, London 1961.

Moore, J.C., *A Narrative of the Campaign of the British Army in Spain commanded by His Excellency Lieutenant General Sir John Moore K.B.*, London 1809.

Porter, R. Ker, *Letters from Portugal and Spain written during the March of the British Troops under Sir John Moore*, London 1809.

The Campaigns: 1810-11

Chambers, G.L., *Bussaco*, London 1910.

Fletcher, I., *Bloody Albuera: The 1811 Campaign in the Peninsula*, Marlborough 2000.

Grehan, J., *The Forlorn Hope: The Battle for the Spanish Frontier 1811-1812*, London 1990.

Horward, D.D., *The Battle of Bussaco: Massena vs. Wellington*, Tallahassee 1965.

Pelet, J.J., *The French Campaign in Portugal 1810-11*, trans. & ed. D.D. Horward, Minneapolis 1973.

The Lines of Torres Vedras

Grehan, J., *The Lines of Torres Vedras*, Staplehurst 2000.

Norris, A.H., & Bremner, R.W., *The Lines of Torres Vedras*, Lisbon 1980.

Sieges

Belmas, J., *Journaux des Sièges faits ou Soutenus par les Français dans la Péninsule, de 1807 à 1814*, Paris 1836-7 (very important early history).

Fletcher, I., *In Hell Before Daylight: the Siege and Storming of the Fortress of Badajoz*, Tunbridge Wells 1984.

Horward, D.D., *Napoleon and Iberia: the Twin Sieges of Ciudad Rodrigo and Almeida, 1810*, Tallahassee 1984.

Jones, J.T., *Journals of the Sieges undertaken by the Allies in Spain*, London 1814.

Myatt, F., *British Sieges of the Peninsular War*, Tunbridge Wells 1987.

Napier, W.F.P., *English Battles and Sieges in the Peninsula*, London 1855 (taken largely from his *History* but with some additions).

Rudorff, R., *War to the Death: the Sieges of Saragossa 1808-1809*, London 1974.

The Campaigns: 1812

Lawford, J.R., & Young, P., *Wellington's Masterpiece: the Battle and Campaign of Salamanca*, London 1972.

Marindin, A.H., *The Salamanca Campaign*, London 1906.

Muir, R., *Salamanca 1812*, Newhaven & London 2001.

Sarramon, J., *La Bataille des Arapiles*, Toulouse 1978.

The Campaigns: 1813-14

Batty, R., *Campaign of the Left Wing of the Allied Army, in the Western Pyrenees and South of France in the Years 1813-1814*, London 1823.

Beatson, F.C., *Wellington: The Bidassoa and Nivelle*, London 1931.

Beatson, F.C., *Wellington: The Crossing of the Gaves and the Battle of Orthez*, London 1925.

Beatson, F.C., *With Wellington in the Pyrenees*, London 1914.

Clerc, J.C.A., *Campagne de Maréchal Soult dans les Pyrénées occidentales en 1813-14*, Paris 1894.

Robertson, I.C., *Wellington invades France: the Final Phase of the Peninsular War 1813-1814*, London 2003.

Vidal-Abarca, J., *La Batalla de Vitoria 175 Años Despues*, Vitoria 1988.

The Guerrilla War

Alexander, D.W., *Rod of Iron: French Counterinsurgency Policy in Aragón during the Peninsular War*, Wilmington, Delaware, 1985.

Brandt, H. von., *The Two Minas and the Spanish Guerrillas*, London 1825.

Tone, J.L., *The Fatal Knot: the Guerrilla War in Navarre and the Defeat of Napoleon in Spain*, Chapel Hill, N. Carolina, 1994.

Naval Operations

James, W., *The Naval History of Great Britain from the Declaration of War by*

France in 1793 to the Accession of George IV, London 1878 (new edn.)

Woodman, R., *The Victory of Seapower: Winning the Napoleonic War 1806-1814*, London 2001.

The Nations: France

Bucquoy, E.L., *Les Uniformes du Premier Empire* (ed. Lt.Col. Bucquoy & G. Devautour: series of books which reprint the Bucquoy uniform cards, with historical text); volumes include (all published in Paris): *Dragons et Guides* (1980); *Etat-Major et Service de Santé* (1982); *Gardes d'Honneur et Troupes Etrangèrs* (1983); *La Cavalerie Légère* (1980); *La Garde Impériale: Troupes à Cheval* (1977) and *Troupes à Pied* (1977); *L'Infanterie* (1979); *Les Cuirassiers* (1978).

Bueno, J.M., *Los Franceses y sus Aliados en España 1808-1814*, Madrid 1996.

Dempsey, G.C., *Napoleon's Mercenaries: Foreign Units in the French Army under the Consulate and Empire, 1799-1814*, London 2002.

Elting, J.R., *Swords Around a Throne: Napoleon's Grande Armée*, London 1989 (very important modern study).

Malibran, H., *Guide . . . des Uniformes de l'Armée français*, Paris 1904, r/p Krefeld 1972 (primarily concerned with uniform-regulations but including details of organisation and lineage).

Martinien, A., *Tableaux par Corps et par Batailles des Officiers Tués et Blessés pendant les guerres de l'Empire*, Paris 1899.

Rogers, H.C.B., *Napoleon's Army*, London 1974.

Smith, D.G., *Napoleon's Regiments: Battle Histories of the Regiments of the French Army, 1792-1815*, London 2000.

The Nations: Great Britain

Brett-James, A., *Life in Wellington's Army*, London 1972.

Chappell, M., *The King's German Legion*, Parts 1-2, Oxford 2000.

Fletcher, I., *Galloping at Everything: The British Cavalry in the Peninsular War and Waterloo 1808-15, A Reappraisal*, Staplehurst 1999.

Fletcher, I., *Wellington's Army*, London 1996.

Fletcher, I., *Wellington's Foot Guards*, London 1994.

Fletcher, I., *Wellington's Regiments*, Tunbridge Wells 1994.

Fortescue, Hon. Sir John, *History of the British Army*, London 1899-1930 (still a most valuable work on the subject).

Fosten, B., *Wellington's Heavy Cavalry*, London 1982.

Fosten, B., *Wellington's Infantry* (Parts I & II), London 1981-2.

Fosten, B., *Wellington's Light Cavalry*, London 1982.

Gates, D., *The British Light Infantry Arm 1790-1815*, London 1987.

Glover, M., *Wellington's Army in the Peninsula 1808-1814*, Newton Abbot 1977.

Glover, R., *Peninsular Preparation: The Reform of the British Army 1795-1809*, Cambridge 1963.

Guy, J., (ed.), *The Road to Waterloo: The British Army and the Struggle against Revolutionary and Napoleonic France*, London 1990.

Haythornthwaite, P.J., *The Armies of Wellington*, London 1994.

Haythornthwaite, P.J., *Wellington's Specialist Troops*, London 1988.

Muir, R., *Britain and the Defeat of Napoleon 1807-1815*, New Haven & London 1996.

Oman, C.W.C., *Wellington's Army*, London 1912.

Reid, S., *Wellington's Highlanders*, London 1992.

Rogers, H.C.B., *Wellington's Army*, London 1979.

Smith, C. Hamilton, & Haythornthwaite, P.J., *Wellington's Army: The Uniforms of the British Soldier 1812-1815*, London 2002.

Verner, W., *History and Campaigns of the Rifle Brigade*, London 1919 (mostly concerns the Peninsular War).

Ward, S.G.P., *Wellington's Headquarters*, Oxford 1957.

The Nations: Portugal

Chartrand, R., *The Portuguese Army of the Napoleonic Wars* Parts I-III, Oxford 2000-01.

Newitt, M., & Robson, M., *Lord Beresford and British Intervention in Portugal, 1807-1820*, Lisbon, 2004.

Pivka, O. von, *The Portuguese Army of the Napoleonic Wars*, London 1977.

The Nations: Spain

Bueno, J.M., *El Ejercito y la Armada en 1808*, Malaga 1982.

Buena, J.M., *Uniformes Espanoles de la Guerra de Independencia*, 1989.

Chartrand, R., *The Spanish Army of the Napoleonic Wars* Parts I-III, Oxford 1998-99.

Esdaile, C., *The Duke of Wellington and the Command of the Spanish Army 1812-1814*, London 1990.

Esdaile, C., *The Spanish Army in the Peninsular War*, Manchester 1988.

Glover, M., *Legacy of Glory: The Bonaparte Kingdom of Spain 1808-13*, London 1971.

Pivka, O. von, *Spanish Armies of the Napoleonic Wars*, London 1975.

Biographies

A small number of biographical works of some of the most important personalities are listed below:

Anglesey, 7th Marquess of, *One-Leg: the Life and Letters of Henry William Paget*, London 1961.

Barault-Rouillon, C.H., *Le Maréchal Suchet, duc d'Albufera*, Paris 1854.

Brett-James, A., *General Graham, Lord Lynedoch*, London 1959.

Brownrigg, B., *The Life and Letters of Sir John Moore*, London 1921.

Chandler, D.G. (ed.), *Napoleon's Marshals*, London 1987.

Chastenet, J., *Godoy, Master of Spain*, trans. J.F. Huntington, London 1953.

Combermere, Viscount, *Memoirs and Correspondence of Field-Marshal Viscount Combermere, from his Family Papers*, ed. Mary, Viscountess Combermere & W.W. Knollys, London 1866.

Conegliano, duc de., *Le Maréchal Moncey*, Paris 1902.

Connelly, O., *The Gentle Bonaparte: Biography of Joseph, Napoleon's Elder Brother*, London 1968.

Craufurd, Revd. A.H., *General Craufurd and his Light Division*, London, n.d.

Delavoye, A.N., *Life of Thomas Graham, Lord Lynedoch*, London 1880.

Du Casse, Baron A., *Mémoires et Correspondance Politiques et Militaires du Roi Joseph*, Paris 1854-57; a section in translation is *The Confidential Correspondence of Napoleon Bonaparte with his Brother Joseph*, London 1855.

Dupont, P.A., *Mémoires de Général Dupont: Relation de la Campagne d'Andalousie* Paris 1824.

Ellesmere, Earl of, *Personal Recollections of*

the Duke of Wellington, London 1904.

Fanshawe, Sir E.G., *Hew Dalrymple at Gibraltar and Portugal in 1808*, London n.d.

Girod de l'Ain, M., *Vie Militaire du Général Foy*, Paris 1900.

Glover, M., *Wellington as Military Commander*, London 1968.

Griffith, P. (ed.), *Wellington Commander: the Iron Duke's Generalship*, Chichester 1985.

Hayman, Sir Peter, *Soult: Napoleon's Maligned Marshal* London 1990.

Haythornthwaite, P.J., *Who Was Who in the Napoleonic Wars*, London 1998.

Hibbert, C., *Wellington: A Personal History*, London 1997.

Horricks, R., *Marshal Ney: The Romance and the Real*, Tunbridge Wells 1982 (r/p as *Military Politics from Bonaparte to the Bourbons: Life and Death of Marshal Ney*).

James, L., *The Iron Duke: A Military Biography of Wellington*, London 1992.

Jourdan, J.B., *Mémoires militaires du Maréchal Jourdan*, ed. Vicomte de Grouchy, Paris 1889.

Lannes, C.L.M., *Le Maréchal Lannes, duc de Montebello*, Tours 1900.

Le Marchant, Sir Denis, *The Memoirs of the Late Major-General Le Marchant*, London 1841.

Longford, Countess of: *Wellington: Years of the Sword*, London 1969.

Marmont, A.F.L., *Mémoires du Maréchal Marmont, duc de Raguse, de 1792 à 1841*, Paris 1857.

Marshal-Cornwall, Sir James, *Massena*, Oxford 1965.

Maxwell, Sir Herbert, *The Life of Wellington*, London 1900.

Mina, F.E., *A Short Extract from the Life of General Mina, published by Himself*, London 1825.

Miot de Melito, A.F., *Memoirs of Count Miot de Melito, Minister, Ambassador, Councillor of State . . .*, ed. T. Fleischmann, 1881.

Moore, Sir John, *The Diary of Sir John Moore*, ed. Sir J.F. Maurice, London 1904.

Myatt, F., *Peninsular General* [Picton], Newton Abbot 1980.

Oman, C., *Sir John Moore*, London 1953.

Parkinson, R., *Moore of Corunna*, London 1976.

Pigeard, A., *Les Etoiles de Napoléon*, Entremont-le-Vieux, 1996 (biographies of French Marshals, Generals and Admirals).

Polt, J., *Garspard Melchor de Jovellanos*, New York 1971.

Priego y Llovera, P., *El Grande de España: Capitan-General Castaños*, Madrid 1958.

Robinson, H.B., *Memoirs and Correspondence of Lieutenant-General Sir Thomas Picton*, London 1836.

Ross, M., *The Reluctant King: Joseph Bonaparte, King of the Two Sicilies and Spain*, London 1976.

Rousseau, F., *La Carrière du Maréchal Suchet, duc d'Albufera*, Paris 1898.

Sidney, Revd. E., *The Life of Lord Hill*, London 1845.

Six, G., *Dictionnaire Biographique des Généraux & Amiraux Français de la Révolution de de l'Empire 1792-1814*, Paris 1934.

Stanhope, Earl, *Notes on Conversations with the Duke of Wellington*, London 1888.

Suchet, L.G., *Memoirs of the War in Spain from 1808 to 1814*, London 1829.

Teffeteller, G.L., *The Surpriser: The Life of Rowland, Lord Hill*, Newark, N.J., 1983.

Thoumine, R.H., *Scientific Soldier: A Life of*

General Le Marchant 1766-1812, London 1968.

Wellington, Duke of, *Dispatches of Field-Marshal the Duke of Wellington*, ed. J. Gurwood, London 1834-38.

Wellington, Duke of, *Supplementary Despatches & Memoranda of Field Marshal the Duke of Wellington*, ed. 2nd Duke of Wellington, London 1858-72.

Wilette, L., *Le Maréchal Lannes, un D'Artagnan sous l'Empire*, Paris 1979.

Memoirs

The Peninsular War produced a huge volume of memoirs and personal reminiscences; extensive bibliographies of works available in English may be found in Sir Charles Oman's *Wellington's Army* (London 1912) and in the new Vol. IX of the Greenhill reprint of his *History of the Peninsular War: Modern Studies of the War in Spain and Portugal 1808-1814*, ed. P. Griffith, London 1999. Some of the most memorable are listed below:

Anon., *A Soldier of the Seventy-First*, ed. C. Hibbert, London 1975 (orig. 1819).

Anton, J., *Retrospect of a Military Life*, Edinburgh 1841.

Blakeney, R., *A Boy in the Peninsular War*, ed. J. Sturgis, London 1899.

Blakiston, J., *Twelve Years' Military Adventure, in Three Quarters of the Globe*, London 1829.

Cooper, J.S., *Rough Notes of Seven Campaigns in Portugal, Spain, France and America*, Carlisle 1869 (r/p 1914).

Costello, *Memoirs of Edward Costello*, London 1857; r/p as *The Peninsular and Waterloo Campaigns: Edward Costello*, ed. A. Brett-James, London 1967.

Fletcher, I. (ed.), *Voices from the Peninsula:*

Eyewitness Accounts of Soldiers of Wellington's Army 1808-1814, London 2001.

Gleig, Revd. G.R., *The Subaltern*, Edinburgh 1872.

Grattan, W., *Adventures with the Connaught Rangers 1809-14*, London 1847, r/p ed. Sir Charles Oman, London 1902.

Harris, B.R., *The Recollections of Rifleman Harris*, ed. H. Curling, London 1848, r/p ed. C. Hibbert, London 1970 (in which Harris's name is given incorrectly as John).

Kincaid, Sir John, *Adventures in the Rifle Brigade, in the Peninsula, France and the Netherlands 1810-15*, London 1830.

Kincaid, Sir John, *Random Shots from a Rifleman*, London 1835.

Larpent, F.S., *The Private Journal of Judge-Advocate F.S. Larpent*, London 1853.

Lawrence, W., *The Autobiography of Sergeant William Lawrence*, ed. G.N. Bankes, London 1886.

Leach, J., *Rough Sketches in the Life of an Old Soldier*, London 1831.

Marbot, J.B.A.M., *The Memoirs of Baron de Marbot*, trans. A.J. Butler, London 1913.

Maxwell, W.H. (ed.), *Peninsular Sketches; by Actors on the Scene*, London 1844.

Rocca, A.J.M., *In the Peninsula with a French Hussar*, London 1990 (orig. published as *Memoirs of the War of the French in Spain*, trans. M. Graham, London 1815).

Schaumann, A.L.F., *On the Road with Wellington: the Diary of a War Commissary*, trans. A.M. Ludovici, London 1924.

Sherer, M., *Recollections of the Peninsula*, London 1823 (published as 'by the Author of "Sketches of India"').

Simmons, G., *A British Rifle Man*, ed. W. Verner, London 1899.

Smith, Sir Harry, *The Autobiography of Sir*

Harry Smith 1787-1819, ed. G.C. Moore Smith, London 1910.

Tomkinson, W., *The Diary of a Cavalry Officer in the Peninsula and Waterloo Campaign*, ed. J. Tomkinson, London 1895.

Warre, W., *Letters from the Peninsula*, ed. Revd. E. Warre, London 1909.

Wheeler, W., *The Letters of Private Wheeler, 1809-28*, ed. B.H. Liddell Hart, London 1951.

Wood, G., *The Subaltern Officer*, London 1825.

Fiction

Unlike some aspects of the Napoleonic Wars - notably actions at sea - the Peninsular War has not produced a very large quantity of fiction in English, at least until the advent of Bernard Cornwell's very popular *Sharpe* series (from 1981). Some of the best known works of Peninsular fiction were among the earliest, notably Charles Lever's *Charles O'Malley, the Irish Dragoon* (1841); this includes characters that can be recognised from historical personalities, the story being influenced by Lever's contact with half-pay officers during his residence in Brussels. The same decade saw the publication of James Grant's *The Romance of War; or, The Highlanders in Spain* (which supposedly sold 100,000 copies within a month of publication); it also bears the stamp of authenticity, being based on the experiences of the author's father, Lieut. John Grant of the 92nd, who was wounded at Maya. It was the start of a series of military novels by Grant, who had himself served as an infantry officer, and who became a noted authority on military affairs (though he maintained his literary licence: his *King's Own Borderers* (1865) includes the Corunna campaign, in which the regiment of the title, the 25th, did not serve).

Subsequent publications include works by authors not known especially for military subjects, although some were based upon fact or closely resembled the truth, for example Sir Arthur Conan Doyle's *Brigadier Gerard* stories - the hero consciously based upon Marbot - and Georgette Heyer's *The Spanish Bride* (1952), the story of Harry and Juana Smith. Works aimed at a more juvenile audience include the prolific G.A. Henty's *With Moore in Corunna* (1898) and *Under Wellington's Command* (1899) (in which the hero serves in the Portuguese Army), to the more modern, Ronald Welch's *Captain of Foot* (1959). Other noted authors to have produced Peninsular fiction include R.F. Delderfield (*Too Few for Drums*, 1964; *Seven Men of Gascony*, 1973, part of which is set in Spain); and C.S. Forester, most notably *The Gun* (1959), one of the few Peninsular War stories to have been filmed, until the *Sharpe* series. At their best, such works of fiction not only entertain but can be informative in reflecting the spirit of the period - and more akin to the most entertaining of the contemporary memoirs - as well as presenting the facts in a form rather more digestible than some of the histories.

Few of the most famous poets were inspired by Peninsular themes, with exceptions like Byron's *Childe Harold* and Wordsworth on the Convention of Cintra. It did inspire poets of second rank, however, and amateurs, sometimes at considerable length (William Hersee's *The Fall of Badajoz*, for example, ran to 52 octavo pages when printed). Most of these followed a 'patriotic' tone in celebrating a victory, for example Mrs. John Philippart's *Victoria* (sic):

'High beat each British and Castilian heart
And every soldier siez'd the ready brand;

Proud they advanc'd with life itself to part,
And grasped their weapons with a giant's
hand'

(*Gentleman's Magazine*, August 1813, p.
150), although Mary Russell Mitford, whose
reputation as a literary figure of some
prominence was just beginning, depicted
the horrors of war graphically in her *Portugal: an Ode:*

'Thy teeming earth still reeks with blood;
The full gorg'd ravens loathe their food;
And corses of the unburied slain
Taint thy pure breeze, and load thy plain'

(*Gentleman's Magazine* June 1811, p. 567).
The power of the Peninsular War to continue to provide poetic inspiration is
demonstrated by a recent publication, Harry
Turner's *Against all Hazards: Poems of the
Peninsular War*, Staplehurst 2001.

Periodicals

Although relatively few periodicals have
been devoted exclusively to the Napoleonic
Wars, the Peninsular War features quite
strongly in a number of those concerned
with military history in general. These
range from the long-established, scholarly
and prestigious 'society' publications like
the *Journal of the Society for Army Historical Research* (established 1921) and the
Carnet de la Sabretache (established
1893), to modern commercial productions
like *Military Illustrated* and *The Age of
Napoleon* (UK) and *Military History*
(USA). Donald Horward's *Napoleonic Military History: A Bibliography* (London
1986) contains an extensive listing of relevant publications, including (in the section
on the Peninsular War) a listing of Spanish
and Portuguese publications. One of the
most important sources of memoirs, reminiscences and comments on the war is the

publication founded in 1827 and usually
styled the *United Service Journal* (originally *The Naval and Military Magazine*, it
became *The United Service Journal and
Naval and Military Magazine* in 1829, *The
United Service Magazine* in 1842 and *Colburn's United Service Magazine & Naval
and Military Journal* in 1843). Among
countless accounts, comments and correspondence by participants in the Peninsular War it included the first publication of
the memoirs of Costello and Grattan, for
example.

Web resources

The intention in this section is to provide
details of some of the more useful websites. The list is by no means exhaustive,
and a quick browse through the links section of any of the below will throw up a
host of additional sites.

www.wtj.com

Among a plethora of military documents
and articles the *War Times Journal* contains an archive of rare and unusual on-line
editions of military memoirs, headquarters
dispatches, official correspondence and
eyewitness accounts. Texts includes dispatches, orders and correspondence from
the headquarters of Arthur Wellesley, the
Duke of Wellington during the Peninsular
and Waterloo campaigns, *The Recollections
of Marshal Macdonald* and Marshal
Suchet's memoirs of the war in Spain.

www.napoleonguide.com

The Napoleonic Guide is a general website encompassing the whole of the
Napoleonic Wars. It has more than 2000
pages of information including articles,
biographies and treatises on warfare.

www.napoleonseries.org

Another general Napoleonic website containing articles written by professionals and amateurs, including biographies, interviews with authors, histories of specific conflicts, analyses of diplomacy in the period, etc. Other useful aspects include a lively discussion forum, a list of frequently asked questions, reviews and online documents. Of specific note, the latter includes: The Convention of Fontainebleau, Documents Pertaining to the Convention of Cintra and the Inquiry into the Convention of Cintra.

www.1808-1814.org

A very useful Spanish language website which provides a different perspective from the English language sites; includes timelines, biographies, articles, reviews, details of battles and much more.

www.napoleonicsociety.com

A nonprofit educational body, which promotes the study of the Napoleonic Era in accordance with proper academic standards.

www.fsu.edu/~napoleon
www.revolutionaryeurope.org

Both of these sites are academic bodies and provide useful publications.

www.napoleonic-literature.com

Provides out-of-copyright Napoleonic texts in electronic format. Particularly relevant to the Peninsular are: *The Memoirs of Baron de Marbot*; *The Services of the Royal Regiment of Artillery in the Peninsular War 1808 to 1814* by Major John H. Leslie, Royal Artillery; *Adventures in the Rifle Brigade* by Captain John Kincaid; *The Mem-*

oirs of Baron Lejeune, translated and edited from the original French by Mrs Arthur Bell; and *Lord Blayney's Narrative* by Major-General Lord Blayney.

www.peninsularwar.org

Battle reports with maps, a useful starting point.

www.britishbattles.com

Contains battle reports and maps of the major engagements in the Peninsula involving the British Army.

www.peninsular-resource.com

Dedicated to the expansion of historical knowledge and understanding of the Peninsular War.

ORDERS OF BATTLE

Army organisation may be demonstrated by sample orders-of-battle, like the two shown below. Strength, where this can be ascertained, is shown by the numbers in parentheses (all ranks).

WELLINGTON'S ARMY AT SALAMANCA

The statistics of unit-strengths are those for 15 July 1812, deducting the casualties and missing incurred in the action at Castrejon/Castillo on 18 July, which in some cases were considerable: for example, the 14th Light Dragoons lost 75 all ranks, the 3/27th 72, the 1st K.G.L. Hussars 70. Actual strength at the Battle of Salamanca was probably slightly lower than the figures given below, to take into account a few who may have fallen in during the previous week; though some of those returned as wounded and missing from 18 July may have remained with, or rejoined their regiments.

Staff

Commander: Arthur Wellesley, Earl of Wellington.
Marshal Sir William Beresford.
Acting head of Quartermaster-General's Department: Lt.Col. William H. De Lancey.
Acting head of Adjutant-General's Depart-

ment: Lt.Col. John Waters.
Commander of Royal Artillery: Lt.Col. Haylet Framingham.

Cavalry (Lt.Gen. Sir Stapleton Cotton Bt.)

Maj.Gen. John G. Le Marchant's Brigade: 5th Dragoon Guards (325), 3rd (329) and 4th Dragoons (358).
Maj.Gen. George Anson's Brigade: 11th (375), 12th (321) and 16th Light Dragoons (258).
Maj.Gen. Victor Alten's Brigade: 14th Light Dragoons (272), 1st K.G.L. Hussars (329)
Maj.Gen. Eberhardt O.G. von Bock: 1st (363) and 2nd K.G.L. Dragoons (407).
Brig.Gen. Benjamin D'Urban's Portuguese Brigade: 1st and 11th Dragoons (total 482, not including 12th Dragoons, detached at rear as baggage-guards).
Artillery: 'I' Troop, Royal Horse Artillery (Brevet-Major Robert Bull).

1st Division (Maj.Gen. Henry Campbell)

Maj.Gen. Hon. Thomas W. Fermor's

Brigade: 1/Coldstream Guards (954), 1/3rd Guards (961), 1 coy. 5/60th (57). (Light companies of this brigade were united to form a battalion under Lt.Col. Alexander Woodford).

Maj.Gen. William Wheatley's Brigade: 2/24th (421), 1/42nd (1,079), 2/58th (400), 1/79th (674), 1 coy. 5/60th (54). (2/58th had been ordered to join 5th Div. on 1 June but remained with 1st Div. until after the battle of Salamanca).

Maj.Gen. Siegesmund von Löw's Brigade: 1st (641), 2nd (627) and 5th (555) Line Battns. K.G.L.

Artillery: Brevet-Major Robert W. Gardiner's Coy., 8th Battn. Royal Artillery.

3rd Division (Maj.Gen. Hon. Edward Pakenham)

Lt. Col. John A. Wallace (of the 88th)'s Brigade: 1/45th (442), 74th (443), 1/88th (663), 3 coys. 5/60th (254).

Lt.Col. James Campbell (of the 94th)'s Brigade: 1/5th (902), 2/5th (308), 2/83rd (319), 94th (347).

Brig. Gen. Manley Power's Portuguese Brigade: 12th Caçadores, 9th and 21st Line (total 2,197).

Artillery: Capt. Robert Douglas's Coy., 9th Battn., Royal Artillery.

4th Division (Lt.Gen. Hon. Galbraith Lowry Cole)

Maj.Gen. Sir William Anson's Brigade: 3/27th (561), 1/40th (513), 1 coy. 5/60th (43).

Lt.Col. Henry Ellis (of the 23rd)'s Brigade: 1/7th (476), 1/23rd (442), 1/48th (420), 1

coy. Brunswick Oels Corps (54).

Col. William Stubbs's Portuguese Brigade: 7th Caçadores, 7th and 23rd Line (total 2,554).

Artillery: Capt. Friedrich Sympher's No. 4 Coy., K.G.L. Artillery.

5th Division (Lt.Gen. James Leith)

Lt. Col. Hon. Charles Greville (of the 38th)'s Brigade: 3/1st (759), 1/9th (666), 1/38th (800), 2/38th (301), 1 coy. Brunswick Oels Corps (78).

Maj.Gen. William Pringle's Brigade: 1/4th (457), 2/4th (654), 2/30th (349), 2/44th (251), 1 coy. Brunswick Oels Corps (69).

Brig.Gen. William Spry's Portuguese Brigade: 8th Caçadores, 3rd and 15th Line (total 2,305).

Artillery: Capt. Robert Lawson's Coy., 8th Battn. Royal Artillery.

6th Division (Maj.Gen. Henry Clinton)

Maj.Gen. Richard Hulse's Brigade: 1/11th (516), 2/53rd (341), 1/61st (546), 1 coy. 5/60th (61).

Lt.Col. Samuel V. Hinde (of the 32nd)'s Brigade: 2nd (408), 1/32nd (609), 1/36th (429).

Brig.Gen. D. Luiz Rezende's Portuguese Brigade: 9th Caçadores, 8th and 12th Line (total 2,631).

Artillery: Capt. John P. Elige's Coy., 8th Battn. Royal Artillery (commanded by Capt. William Greene, Eligé having been killed at the Salamanca Forts).

7th Division (Maj.Gen. John Hope)

Col. Colin Halkett (of the 2nd K.G.L. Light Battn.)'s Brigade: 1st (569) and 2nd (494) Light Battns. K.G.L., 9 coys. Brunswick Oels Corps (596).

Maj.Gen. J.H.C. de Bernewitz's Brigade: 51st (307), 68th (338), Chasseurs Britanniques (713).

Col. Richard Collins's Portuguese Brigade: 2nd Caçadores, 7th and 19th Line (total 2,168).

Artillery: 'E' Troop, Royal Horse Artillery (Capt. Robert Macdonald).

Light Division (Maj.Gen. Charles Alten)

Col. Andrew F. Barnard (of the 95th)'s Brigade: 1/43rd (748); 4 coys. 2/95th Rifles and 5 coys. 3/95th (392).

Maj.Gen. John O. Vandeleur's Brigade: 1/52nd (799), 8 coys. 1/95th Rifles (542).

Portuguese: 1st Caçadores attached to Barnard's Brigade, 3rd Caçadores to Vandeleur's (total 1,067).

Artillery: 'A' Troop, Royal Horse Artillery (Brevet-Major Hew D. Ross).

Other formations

Brig.Gen. Denis Pack's Independent Portuguese Brigade: 4th Caçadores, 1st and 16th Line (total 2,605).

Brig. Gen. Thomas Bradford's Independent Portuguese Brigade: 5th Caçadores, 13th and 14th Line (total 1,894).

Reserve Artillery of Wellington's army included Capt. Frederick Glubb's Coy.,

5th Battn. Royal Artillery (actually commanded by 2nd Capt. William Power), with heavy artillery; Capt. John May's Coy., 1st Battn. Royal Artillery (actually commanded by 2nd Capt. Henry Baynes), with the ammunition train (and without guns); and Major Sebastian J. de Arriaga's Coy., 1st Regt. of Portuguese Artillery (armed with heavy [24-pdr.] howitzers).

Strengths of Royal Horse Artillery (416); Foot Artillery (Coys. present: Gardiner's, Douglas's, Lawson's, Eligé's, May's) (685); K.G.L. Artillery (78); Arriaga's Coy., Portuguese Artillery (114); Royal Engineers/Artificers (21); Royal Staff Corps (86); Royal Waggon Train (139).

Spanish Division (Gen. Carlos de España): Lanceros de Castilla; 2/Princesa, 2/Jaen, 3/1st Sevilla Regts.; Tiradores de Castilla, Cazadores de Castilla (total 3,360).

LANNES'S ARMY AT THE SECOND SIEGE OF SARAGOSSA

The following demonstrates a typical organisation of two *corps d'armée* and supporting troops; strength (all ranks) are in parentheses. The ranks of *Général de Division* and *Général de Brigade* are given as 'Gén. de Div.' and 'Gén. de Bde.' respectively. Unit-titles are generally rendered in English, e.g. '20th Coy., 1st Regt.' rather than '20me Cie., 1er Régt.'

General Staff

Commander: Marshal Jean Lannes, duc de Montebello.
Chief of General Staff: Gén. de Div. Bernard G.F. Frère.
Deputy chief of General Staff: Adjutant-Commandant Dumolard.
Commander of artillery during the siege: Gén. de Div. François-Louis Dedon-Duc-los.
Commander of Engineers during the siege: Gén. de Bde. André-Bruno de Frévol, comte de Lacoste (succeeded after his death by Col. Joseph Rogniat).

III CORPS

Commander: Gen. de Div. Jean-Andoche Junot, duc d'Abrantes.
Chief of Staff: Gén. de Bde. Jean-Isidore Harispe.
Commander of Artillery: Gén. de Bde. Joseph-Christophe Couin.

1st Division (Gén. de Div. Charles L.D. Grandjean)

Headquarters detachment: 2nd Léger (100); 1 battn. 70th Line (407).
1st Brigade (Gén. de Bde. Pierre-Joseph Habert): 4 battns. 14th Line (2,122), 2 battns. 2nd Vistula Legion (1,225).
2nd Brigade (Gén. de Bde. Anne-Gilbert de Laval): 3 battns. 44th Line (1,784), 2 battns. 3rd Vistula Legion (1,138).

2nd Division (Gén. de Div. Louis F.F. Musnier)

1st Brigade (Gén. de Bde. Jean-Antoine Brun): 4 battns. 114th Line (2,235), 2 battns. 1st Vistula Legion (1,163).
2nd Brigade (Gén. de Bde. Jean-Nicolas Razout): 4 battns. 115th Line (2,206).

3rd Division (Gén. de Div Antoine Morlot)

1st Brigade (Gén. de Bde. Claude Rostolland [or Rostollant]: 2 battns. 5th Léger (1,244), 2 battns. 116th Line (878).
2nd Brigade (Gén. de Bde. Jean-Pierre Augereau): 4 battns. 117th Line (1,532).
3rd Brigade (Gén. de Bde. Claude-Joseph Bujet [or Buget]: 4 battns. 121st Line (2,187), 4 battns. 2nd Légion de Réserve (2,507).

Cavalry (Gén. de Bde. Pierre Watier)

4 sqdns. 4th Hussars, 4 sqdns. 13th Cuirassiers (336), detachment of 2nd and 10th Hussars (113), detachment of 1st Provisional Hussars (309), detachment of cavalry *régiment de marche* (dragoons and chasseurs) (396), detachment of Gendarmerie (27), detachment of 'Lanciers polonais' (21).

Artillery (Gen. de Bde. Joseph-Christophe Couin)

Staff: 13 officers
Foot Artillery: 20th Coy., 1st Regt. (81); 7th, 18th, 21st and 22nd Coys., 3rd Regt. (179); 7th Coy., 5th Regt. (50).

Horse Artillery: 7th Coy., 5th Regt. (71).
Ouvriers: 2nd Coy. (5).
Train: 4th, 5th and 6th Coys., Imperial Guard (199); 5th Coy., 6th *bis* Battn. (101); 2nd and 4th Coys., 12th *bis* Battn. (102).

V CORPS

Commander: Marshal Adolphe-Edouard-Casimir-Joseph Mortier, duc de Trévise.
Chief of Staff: Gén. de Div. Joseph-Augustine Daultanne.
Deputy Chief of Staff: Adjutant-Commandant Dambouski.
Commander of Artillery: Gén. de Div. Louis-François Foucher.
Commander of Engineers: Col. Guillaume Dode.

1st Division (Gén. de Div. Louis-Gabriel Suchet)

1st Brigade (Gén. de Bde. Pierre Dumoustier): 3 battns. 17th Léger (2,302), 4 battns. 34th Line (2,590), 3 battns. 40th Line (2,246).
2nd Brigade (Gén. de Bde. Jean-Baptiste Girard): 3 battns. 64th Line (2,222), 3 battns. 88th Line (2,471).

2nd Division (Gén. de Div. Honoré T.M. Gazan, comte de La Peyrière)

1st Brigade (Gén. de Bde. Jacques-Julien Guérin): 3 battns. 21st Léger (1,827), 3 battns. 100th Line (2,632).
2nd Brigade (Gén. de Bde. Eloi-Charle-

magne Taupin): 3 battns. 28th Léger (2,230), 3 battns. 103rd Line (2,553).

Cavalry (Adjutant-Commandant Henri-Pierre Delaage)

3 sqdns. 10th Hussars (777), 3 sqdns. 21st Chasseurs (731), detachment Gendarmerie (26).

Artillery (Gén. de Div. Louis-François Foucher)

Staff: (13 officers).
Foot Artillery: 5th Coy., 1st Regt. (97); 1st, 2nd, 15th and 20th Coys., 5th Regt. (285); 11th Coy., 6th Regt. (86).
Horse Artillery: 3rd Coy., 6th Regt. (65).
Ouvriers: 4th Coy. (32).
Pontonniers: 4th Coy., 1st Battn. (73).
Train: 4th, 5th, 6th and 9th Coys., 3rd Battn. (320); 1st-6th Coys., 5th *bis* Battn. (566); 3rd and 5th Coys., 8th *bis* Battn. (136).

Engineers (Col. Guillaume Dode)

Staff: (7 officers).
Sapeurs: 5th Coy., 2nd Battn. (65).

SIEGE ARTILLERY

(Gén. de Div. François-Louis Dedon-Duclos)

Staff: (15 officers).
Foot Artillery: 4th, 14th and 19th Coys., 3rd

Regt. (232); 10th, 13th and 15th Coys.,
6th Regt. (185).
Pontonniers: 2nd Coy. (71).
Ouvriers: 2nd Coy. (31).
Train: 2nd Coy., 6th *bis* Battn. (23).

SIEGE ENGINEERS

(Gén. de Bde. André-Bruno de Frévol, comte de Lacoste)

Staff: (40 officers).
Mineurs: 7th Coy. (73), 8th Coy. (88), 9th
Coy. (77).
Sapeurs: 6th and 7th Coys., 1st Battn. (183);
1st, 3rd and 4th Coys., 2nd Battn. (275);
2nd, 4th and 6th Coys., 3rd Battn. (321).

BATTLES, NUMBERS AND LOSSES

Some of the important Peninsular War actions are listed below, with estimates of the numbers of troops involved, and losses incurred, although different statistics may be encountered in various sources.

In some cases it is arguable which formations should be reckoned as engaged in any particular action; for example, only about one-third of Wellesley's army was really involved at Roliça, a total of less than six battalions, and only eleven of his sixteen units suffered any fatalities, with the aforementioned five-and-a-half battalions sustaining some 92 per cent of the overall losses. (Even the infantry regiments that sustained no casualties at all received the battle-honour 'Roleia' (sic), albeit comparatively later than some; although the 20th Light Dragoons, which had three men wounded, did not receive the honour).

Statistics concerning casualties are even more problematic. British and Portuguese casualties were reported with as much accuracy as possible under the circumstances, but losses admitted by the French in particular often seem to have been too low. The details of British and Portuguese losses quoted here are derived from the returns reported initially, as published in the *London Gazette* (the issue is quoted in each case, by 'LG' and date of publication); these are sometimes slightly at variance with statistics published at a later date, which might, for example, take into account men returned originally as 'missing' but who subsequently rejoined their units. The stated percentages of losses compared to an army's overall strength, including both casualties and 'missing'/prisoners, are only approximate. Orders-of-battle and more comprehensive statistics may be found, for example, in *A History of the Peninsular War*, Sir Charles Oman, Oxford 1902-30, and in *The Greenhill Napoleonic Wars Data Book*, D.G. Smith, London 1998.

MEDINA DE RIO SECO 14 July 1808
Blake and Cuesta 21,700
Losses over 3,000, about 14%.

Bessières 13,700
Losses over 400, about 3%.

BAILEN 19-22 July 1808
Castaños about 33,000
Losses less than 1,000, about 3%.

Dupont about 18,000, **Vedel**
about 10,000.
Losses: about 17,635 prisoners,
about 2,000 casualties, many
deserters.

ROLIÇA 17 August 1808
Wellesley about 13,500, **Trant** (Portuguese)
2,375; of which about 4,635 (British)
actually engaged.
Losses: 479 (LG 3 Sept. 1808), 3% of
whole force, 3.5% of British, 10.3% of
those actually engaged.

Delaborde 4,350
Losses: about 600, about 13.8%.

VIMEIRO 21 August 1808
Wellesley 16,778, **Trant** (Portuguese)
2,000.
Losses 720 (LG 3 Sept. 1808), 4.3%.

Junot 13,050
Losses about 1,800-2,000,
about 13.8-15.3%.

TUDELA 23 November 1808
Castaños about 30,000, of which about
23,000 principally engaged.
Losses about 4,200, of which about
4,000 from main force engaged; 14%, or
about 17.4% from main force.

Lannes 34,000
Losses about 470, 1.4%.

CORUNNA 16 January 1809
Moore about 15,000
Losses 'seven to eight hundred'
(LG 24 Jan. 1809), about 4.7-5.3%.

Soult about 20,000
Losses about 1,500, 7.5%.

MEDELLIN 29 March 1809
Cuesta 24,000
Losses about 10,000, 41.6%.

Victor 17,500
Losses about 1,000, 5.7%.

OPORTO 12 May 1809
Wellesley about 23,000 (not all engaged)
Losses 121 (LG 25 May 1809), 0.5%.

Soult 13,000 (not all
engaged)
Losses about 600, plus 1,500
captured in hospital; 4.6%,
16.2% including those in hospital.

TALAVERA 27-28 July 1809
Wellesley 20,641; **Cuesta** more than 34,000
Losses: 27 July 846, 28 July 4,521 (LG
15 Aug. 1809); Cuesta reported loss of
1,201 but his army was engaged so lightly
that this must include deserters. British
loss 26%, Spanish 3.5%.

Joseph and Jourdan about
46,100
Losses 7,268, 15.8%

OCAÑA 18-19 November 1809
Areizaga 51,500
Losses 18,000, 35%.

Joseph and Jourdan 33,500
Losses less than 2,000, 6%.

BUSACO 27 September 1810
Wellington about 52,000, but 2nd and 4th
Divisions not engaged, so total about
34,000.
Losses 1,253 (LG 15 Oct. 1810), 3.7% of
those engaged.

Massena about 64,000, but VIII
Corps not engaged, so about
47,000.
Losses about 4,000, 9.8% of
those engaged.

BARROSA 5 March 1811
Graham 5,217; **La Peña** about 10,000 (most
not engaged).
Losses: Graham 1,243 (LG 25 March 1811),
23.8%; La Pena 300-400, 3-4%.

Victor about 10,160.
Losses about 2,380, 23.4%;
of those engaged against
Graham, 28.8%.

FUENTES DE OÑORO 3-5 May 1811
Wellington 37,500.
Losses: 3 May 263, 5 May 1,526 (LG 26 May
1811), 4.8%

Massena about 48,450.
Losses: 3 May 652, 5 May
2,192, 5.8%.

ALBUERA 16 May 1811
Beresford 20,358 (of which 10,201
Portuguese), **Blake** 12,073,
Castaños 2,561.

Soult about 24,000.
Losses about 7,000, 29%.

Losses: British 4,158, 40.9%; Portuguese 389, 3.8% (LG 3 June 1811), Beresford's total loss 22.3%; Blake 1,307, 10.8%; Castaños 258, 10%; total Spanish loss 10.6%.

ARROYO DOS MOLINOS, 28 October 1811

Hill about 10,000.
Losses: 72 British and about 30 Spanish (LG 2 Dec. 1811), 1%.

Girard about 4,000 (Hill thought about 3,100).
Losses: perhaps 2,500 or more (about 1,300 prisoners taken); 62.5%, or if Hill's estimate were correct, 80%.

CIUDAD RODRIGO, storm 19 January 1812

Wellington: exact number of troops involved in storm not clear.
Losses in storm: British 104 killed, 350 wounded, 5 missing; Portuguese losses in general total (LG 22 Feb. 1812).
Losses in siege (9-19 January): British 154 killed, 680 wounded, 5 missing; Portuguese 24 killed, 136 wounded, 2 missing. (LG 1 & 22 Feb. 1812).

Barrié: at commencement of siege, 1,818, of whom 163 sick in hospital.

BADAJOZ, storm 6 April 1812

Wellington: exact number of troops involved in storm not clear.
Losses in storm: British 651 killed, 1,349 wounded, 22 missing; Portuguese 155 killed, 545 wounded, 30 missing.
Losses in entire siege: British 820 killed, 3,007 wounded, 33 missing; Portuguese 215 killed, 780 wounded, 30 missing (LG 24 April 1812).

Philippon: original strength stated 4,453, plus 300 in hospital and 250 non-combatants (cantinières, etc.) (Belmas V pp. 364-6). Actual strength may have been rather more.

SALAMANCA 22 July 1812

Wellington: about 30,200 British, 17,800 Portuguese, 3,360 Spanish.
Losses: 3,176 British, 10.5%; 2,038 Portuguese, 11.4%; 6 Spanish. Overall loss 9.9% (LG 16 Aug. 1812).

Marmont 49,600
Losses about 14,000, 28.2%.

BIAR AND CASTALLA 12-13 April 1813

Murray about 18,700 (British and British-foreign corps, but including more than 8,000 Spanish and about 1,200 Sicilians).
Losses: British 397, Spanish 262, Sicilian 9, total 3.6% (LG 18 May 1813).

Suchet about 13,500
Losses perhaps 1,200, 8.9%.

VITTORIA 21 June 1813

Wellington about 81,000, of whom probably more than 52,000 were British; about 8,000 Spanish.
Losses (LG 3 July 1813): British 3,308, 6.4%; Portuguese 1,049, 3.6%; Spanish 553, 6.9%. Overall loss about 6%.

Joseph and Jourdan probably more than 57,000.
Losses probably more than 8,000, 14%.

PYRENEES (Maya, Roncesvalles, Sorauren, etc.) 25-30 July 1813

Wellington: forces actually engaged about 40,000.
Losses (LG 16 Aug. 1813): British 3,841, Portuguese 2,258, Spanish 204, total loss about 15.8%. Corrected returns of Portuguese casualties are considerably lighter (see Oman VI p. 773), which if correct would reduce the casualty-rate to about 14.4%.

Soult: forces actually engaged about 53,000.
Losses: Soult reported 12,563, which was probably too small a figure. If 13,000, casualty rate would would be 24.5%.

SAN SEBASTIAN, storm 31 August 1813

Graham: exact number of troops employed in storm not clear, but probably about 6,200.
Losses 2,376, 38.3%.

Rey: original garrison 3,185 including 52 civilian employees; on 15 Aug. 2,996 including 53 civilians.

SAN MARCIAL and associated actions,
31 August-1 September 1813

Wellington: forces engaged probably about 22,500.
Losses: British 417, Portuguese 525, Spanish 1,679; total 11.6% (LG 14 Sept. 1813).

Soult: forces engaged probably about 34,000.
Losses: 3,808 reported, 11.2%.

227

PASSAGE OF THE BIDASSOA 7 October 1813

Wellington: forces engaged about 24,000.
Losses (LG 18 Oct. 1813): British 579,
Portuguese 235, Spanish 'about 750';
about 6.5%.

Soult: forces available about
36,000.
Losses: 1,676 reported but
probably more; if 2,000,
5.5%.

NIVELLE 10 November 1813

Wellington: about 39,000 British,
24,240 Portuguese, 25,373 Spanish.
Losses (LG 25 Nov. 1813): British
2,116 (5.4%), Portuguese 582 (2.4%),
Spanish about 800 (3.2%); overall loss 3.95%.

Soult about 61,400.
Losses: 4,321 reported; if
actually about 4,500, loss was
about 7.3%.

NIVE (including ST. PIERRE) 9-13 December 1813

Wellington: forces engaged about 44,000.
Losses: British 2,675, Portuguese
2,344, Spanish 26 (LG 30 Dec. 1813);
overall 11.5%.

Soult about 65,900.
Losses about 5,900-6,000;
overall 9%.

ORTHEZ 27 February 1814

Wellington: forces engaged 26,798 British,
17,604 Portuguese.
Losses (LG 20 March 1814): British
1,665 (6.2%), Portuguese 609 (3.4%);
overall 5.1%.

Soult: forces engaged about
36,000 plus elements of the
Division of Reserve of
Toulouse which came up late
(3,750).
Losses 3,985 reported; about 11%.

TOULOUSE 10 April 1814

Wellington: forces engaged about
24,000 British, 13,000 Portuguese,
10,000 Spanish.
Losses (LG 26 April 1814): British 2,124
(8.8%), Portuguese 607 (4.7%), Spanish 1,928
(19.2%); overall 9.9%.

Soult about 42,000.
Losses: 3,236 reported,
7.7%.

BAYONNE 14 April 1814

Hope about 8,000 engaged.
Losses (LG 27 April 1814): British
811, Portuguese 32; overall 10.5%.

Thouvenot about 6,000 engaged
Losses 905, 15%.

PENINSULAR WAR CASUALTIES

Given the qualifications noted for the statistics in pp. 223-228, it is possible to determine average rates of killed and wounded, as proportions of total casualties, for actions where reliable statistics exist. Some of these are listed below, but the statistics are *approximate*; it is likely that a considerable proportion of those originally returned as 'missing' were actually not prisoners, but killed or wounded, while in the longer term the proportion of fatalities would increase as some of those listed originally as wounded would not survive. An average taken over a selection of actions would seem to suggest that about 14 per cent of the total casualties would be killed (excluding any wounded who died subsequent to the preparation of the original returns); the ferocity of the fire recounted for some actions would seem to be reflected by those cases where the initial fatality-rate was significantly higher, notably the storming of Badajoz and San Sebastian, and Albuera. The percentage of the whole represented by officer casualties also reflects their exposure to fire on such occasions.

Percentages of killed, wounded and missing
as a proportion of the whole toll of casualties; the officer casualty-rate is also expressed as a percentage of the total casualties:

	killed	wounded	missing	officer casualties
British, Vimeiro	18.7	74.2	7.1	6.0
British, Talavera	14.9	72.9	12.2	4.4
French, Talavera	10.4	86.7	2.9	3.7
British, Busaco	17.0	78.1	4.9	6.5
Portuguese, Busaco	14.5	82.3	3.2	5.0
British, Barrosa	16.3	83.7	-	5.0
French, Barrosa	11.7	81.5	6.8	4.3
British, Fuentes de Oñoro	11.5	70.6	17.9	5.6
Portuguese, Fuentes de Oñoro	20.8	62	17.2	4.5
French, Fuentes de Oñoro	12.1	80.4	7.5	6.3

	killed	wounded	missing	officer casualties
British, Albuera	21.2	65.7	13.1	5.0
Portuguese, Albuera	26.2	67.1	6.7	4.6
British, Ciudad Rodrigo (storm)	19.9	79.1	1.0	7.2
British, Badajoz (storm)	32.2	66.7	1.1	13.0
Portuguese, Badajoz (storm)	21.2	74.7	4.1	7.3
British, Salamanca	12.2	85.5	2.3	6.6
Portuguese, Salamanca	14.9	77.2	8.9	4.3
British, Vittoria	15.2	84.8	-	5.7
Portuguese, Vittoria	14.3	85.7	-	5.6
Spanish, Vittoria	16.1	83.9	-	2.7
British, San Sebastian (storm)	33.1	64.5	2.4	6.3
Portuguese, San Sebastian (storm)	49.9	49.6	5.0	6.6
Spanish, San Marcial	15.6	80.2	4.2	6.3
French, Bidassoa	9.6	54.7	35.7	4.9
British, Nivelle	13.1	84.1	2.8	6.8
Portuguese, Nivelle	11.3	86.1	2.6	6.9
French, Nivelle	10.4	61.0	28.6	4.3
British, Orthez	12.7	85.5	1.8	4.4
Portuguese, Orthez	10.8	82.8	6.4	4.8
French, Orthez	13.6	52.1	34.3	4.2
(excluding prisoners, killed 20.7, wounded 79.3)				
British, Toulouse	14.7	85.4	0.8	7.1
Portuguese, Toulouse	12.8	87.2	-	4.3
Spanish, Toulouse	10.6	89.3	0.1	5.3
French, Toulouse	10.0	73.3	16.7	7.1

Officer casualties as a proportion of officers present could vary dramatically. Approximate percentages include: British, Busaco, 4.8; British, Fuentes de Oñoro, 6.4; British, Nivelle, 6.5; British, Vittoria, 8.4; French, Fuentes de Oñoro, 9.4; British, Salamanca, 13.7; British, Barrosa, 26.3; French, Barossa, 29.6; British, Albuera, 39.0.

MEASUREMENTS OF DISTANCE

With no universal system of measurement existing in Europe, errors in the calculations of distance could be made at the time, and subsequently; for example, the nine-day ride of Sir Charles Vaughan from the Tudela to Corunna, via Madrid, which he estimated as 188 leagues or 790 English miles, was actually 595 miles. The mis-calculation of the forced march of the Light Brigade to Talavera, traditionally 62 miles in 26 hours, when probably actually 42 miles in that time, is another example of an error probably arising from confusion over what constituted a league.

English measurements were as follows, with approximate metric equivalents:
12 inches = 1 foot (30.479 cm.)
3 feet = 1 yard (91.4 cm.)
5½yards = 1 rod, pole or perch (502.7 cm.)
4 rods, poles or perches = 1 chain (22 yards, 20.11 m.)
10 chains = 1 furlong (220 yards, 201.1 m.)
8 furlongs = 1 mile (1,760 yards, 1.609 km.)

Prior to the adoption of the metric system (by which 1 metre, a ten-millionth part of a line drawn from the Pole to the Equator, was equivalent to 39.3708 English inches), France used the *toise*, a measurement retained (by many nations) for military purposes, such as the measurement of fortifications:
12 inches = 1 foot
6 feet = 1 toise (182.87 cm.)
although the measurement of a 'foot' was not constant; those relevant to the Peninsula included the following, as percentages of an English foot:
English 1.000
Madrid 1.001
Paris 1.068
Toledo 0.899
(which are approximations: the Paris foot, for example, was actually 1.067977 of an English foot).

Measurements of distance might also be expressed in paces, normally calculated to be 2½ English feet (76.19 cm.), but the 'geometric pace' was taken to be equivalent to 5 French feet or 6.1012 English feet. A British military handbook of the period (*The Bombardier and Pocket Gunner*, R.W. Adye, London 1802), stated that the following definitions were current, to which approximate modern equivalents have been added:

	Geometric paces	English yards	Metres
English mile	868	1,760	1,609
	(by calculation, 865.4)		
French league	2,400	4,881	4,462.25
Spanish league	2,286	4,649	4,250.3
Scottish league	1,500	3,050.6	2,788.25

An English league was stated to be 3 miles (4.83 km.), although in maritime usage, it represented one-twentieth of a degree, 3 geographical miles or 3.456 statute miles (5.56 km.), a nautical mile being reckoned as 6.080 feet (1.15 statute miles, 1.85 km.).

In the first half of the nineteenth century, however, there were four 'leagues' in use in Spain, expressed as a number of *varas*, a unit of measurement approximating to 33 English inches (83.82 cm.). With approximate equivalents, these were:

Legales castellanas (Castilian leagues): 5,000 *varas*, 2.63 English miles (4.23 km.)

Maritime leagues or *legales, una hora de camino* ('one hour's journey'): 6,626 *varas*, 3.49 English miles (5.61 km.)

Legales géograficas or *de camino real* ('on the king's highway'): 7,572 *varas*, reckoned as four English miles (6.43 km.) though not exact.

Legales de España ('Spanish leagues'): 8,000 *varas*, 4.2. English miles (6.77 km.)

For further details, and an explanation of how mistakes in calculation could occur, see the Talavera appendix (pp. 481-92) of *History and Campaigns of the Rifle Brigade*, Col. W. Verner, London 1919, Vol. II.

SIEGES

Sieges featured in the Peninsula perhaps more prominently than in any other campaign of the Napoleonic Wars, and under normal circumstances the attacker required immense resources. The necessary forces were calculated by the British engineer Lt.Col. John T. Jones, presuming that the extent of the place to be attacked was some 180 *toises* in length (about 350 metres), including a ravelin. He stated that for a successful undertaking, the first night's trench-digging would require 3,000 men, but 2,000 for each successive day, with four shifts per day making 8,000. To protect them, a trench-guard was required of three-quarters of the strength of the garrison, which varied markedly in the Peninsula: at the second siege of Saragossa there were probably in excess of 29,000 troops, not including civilian irregulars[1], whereas the French defended Badajoz with about 5,000 (including 300 in hospital), San Sebastian with just less than 3,000, Burgos with 2,000, Ciudad Rodrigo with 1,800 and Monzon with just 100. The trench-guard could operate with three shifts per day, so that the total number required would amount to two and one-quarter times the strength of the garrison. For camp-duties, escorts and fatigues, a force of one-tenth of the combined workers and trench-guards was required, in four shifts.

To besiege a garrison of 5,000 men, therefore, Jones stated that a trench-guard of 3,750, in three shifts, would add 11,250 men to the 8,000 workers, making 19,250. For camp duties, one-tenth of these, multiplied by four shifts, added a further 7,700, producing a total of 26,950, exclusive of men required to fill the gaps caused by casualties and sickness. Paradoxically, because the number of trench-diggers was constant, the proportion of besiegers to besieged fell with the increase in strength of the garrison; which was the reason, Jones stated, why the accepted practice was that the proportion of attackers to defenders should be 5 to 1 with a garrison of 15,000, 6 to 1 with 10,000, 7 to 1 with 5,000 and 8 to 1 with 3,000 defenders[2].

Two celebrated examples demonstate that such theories could not always be applied in reality. For the 29,000 troops forming the garrison of Saragossa during the second

[1] Belmas, J., *Journaux des Sièges faits ou soutenus par les Français dans la Péninsule, de 1807 à 1814*, Paris 1833-7, Vol. II pp. 343-47 apparently over-estimates the total force by some 3,100, by including units detached from the garrison; see Oman, Vol. II p. 624.

[2] Jones, J.T., *Journals of the Sieges undertaken by the Allies in Spain*, London 1814, pp. 334-7.

siege (excluding the civilian defenders), by these calculations the French should have deployed more than 102,000 troops, whereas they actually had just over 49,000; and at Gerona in 1809, the original garrison of 5,700 (some 3,600 reinforcements were received subsequently) should have required a besieging-force of about 30,000, whereas the French actually had about 17,000 in the siege plus a covering force of some 15,700.

The expenditure of ammunition was immense, as exemplified by the quantities used by the British in the sieges of Badajoz in 1812 and San Sebastian:

	Badajoz	San Sebastian
24-pdr. roundshot (rounds)	18,832	43,367
18-pdr. roundshot	13,029	9,303
24-pdr. grapeshot	1,051	2,094
	(including 158 rounds fabricated from 1,268 rounds of 3-pdr. roundshot)	
18-pdr. grapeshot	328	–
24-pdr. case-shot	112	–
18-pdr. case-shot	168	–
5½-inch common shell	507	–
8-inch common shell	–	7,766
10-inch common shell	–	3,755
5½-inch spherical shell	1,319	–
8-inch spherical shell	–	2,198
24-pdr. spherical shell	–	1,930
18-pdr. spherical shell	–	150
Total rounds	35,346	70,563

Presuming powder to be one-third the weight of solid shot, one-quarter the weight of case-shot, and presuming a 12-oz. (340 g.) charge for howitzer shells, the weight of munitions expended at Badajoz amounted to more than 437 tons (about 440,000 kg.) and more than 900 tons (915,000 kg.) of shot at San Sebastian, for which 5,579 barrels of powder of 90 lbs. (40.86 kg.) each were used, adding a further 224 tons (about 228,000 kg.) When infantry ammunition and engineering supplies are added (at Badajoz, for example, some 2,726 gabions, 1,476 18-foot (5.49 m.) fascines and 20,000 sandbags were used), the scale of the logistical requirement for a successful siege becomes apparent[3].

[3] Jones, J.T., *Journals of the Sieges undertaken by the Allies in Spain*, London 1814, pp. 144, 244.

THE PROVINCES OF IBERIA

Spain

Until 1833, when Spain was divided into 47 mainland and two island provinces, there were thirteen mainland provinces, originating with the ancient kingdoms and principalities from which the modern country was constructed.

***Andalucia* (or Andalusia):** Spain's southernmost province, bounded on the west by Portugal (Alemtejo and Algarve), on the north-west by Spanish Estremadura, north-east by New Castile, east by Murcia and by the Mediterranean in the south. In 1833 it was divided into eight provinces named after the following cities: Almeiria (the eastern part of the old kingdom of Granada), Cadiz (the principal seaport, of great commercial and military significance, which became the capital of 'patriot' Spain when the Central Junta moved there, and withstood a long French blockade), Córdova (or Córdoba, on the right bank of the River Guadalquivir, once the capital of Moorish Spain), Granada (once among the wealthiest of Spanish cities, and the last of the Moorish states, falling to Spain in 1492), Jáen (a city with Moorish fortifications), Huelva (which only developed real prosperity in the later nineteenth century, with the exploitation of the nearby Rio Tinto copper mines), Malaga (one of the most important ports, once the capital of a Moorish kingdom), and Seville (chief city of Andalucia, on the left bank of the Guadalquivir, traditionally known for its loyalty to the monarchy, and the residence of the Central Junta until it moved to Cadiz). Other significant locations included Andujar, Ayamonte, Bailén (or Baylén, site of the greatest Spanish victory of the Peninsular War and near the battlefield of Las Novas de Tolosa, where Alfonso VIII defeated the Moors in 1212), Barossa, Baza, Bornos, Ronda, and Tarifa. South of Cadiz is Cape Trafalgar, site of the great naval battle of 1805.

***Aragon*:** province of north-eastern Spain, bounded on the west by Old Castile, on the north-west by Navarre, on the north by the Pyrenees and France, on the east by Catalonia, south-east by Valencia, and south-west by New Castile. In 1833 this ancient kingdom was divided into three provinces named after the cities of Huesca (near the right bank of the River Isuela), Saragossa (Spanish Zaragoza, capital of the kingdom of Aragon, site of the defeat in 1710 of the forces of Philip V by an Allied force including British troops and General James Stanhope, and in the Peninsular War the location of the most epic of all sieges); and Teruel (on the left bank of the Guadalquivir). Other significant locations included Alagón, Alcañiz, Belchite, Epila and Jaca (on the frontier road from Saragossa to Pau, known as 'most noble and most loyal' for its support of Philip V during the War of the Spanish Succession).

Asturias: the northern province bounded in the west by Galicia, on the north by the Bay of Biscay, on the east by Old Castile and to the south by León. The heir to the Spanish throne took the title of 'Prince of (the) Asturias', the plural version from the province's old division into Asturias d'Oviedo, and Asturias de Santillana, the latter becoming the western portion of Santander. In 1833 the province was re-named after its principal city, Oviedo, the early capital of the kings of Asturias, and on the *camino real* from Gijon, via León, to Madrid. Gijon, the home-town of Jovellanos, was of considerable commercial significance by virtue of being the most important harbour between Ferrol and Santander.

Basque Provinces: the three provinces of Alava, Vizcaya (or Biscay) and Guipuzcoa were bounded by Old Castile on the west and south, the Bay of Biscay in the north, France on the north-east and Navarre on the east. Although under the authority of the Spanish crown, the Basque provinces enjoyed considerable autonomy, and preserved their own laws and customs; they were, for example, mentioned separately from Spain in the Treaty of Utrecht (1713). Alava's capital was Vittoria (or Vitoria), an important commercial centre on the route from Madrid to France and the port of San Sebastian. Guipuzcoa, bounded on the north-east by the River Bidassoa, had San Sebastian as its capital; other places of some significance included Irun, on the left bank of the Bidassoa, opposite the French town of Hendaye; Fuenterrabia (or Fontarabia), also on the left bank of the Bidassoa, originally fortified but with defences dismantled when captured by the French in 1794; and the harbours of Bermeo, Lequeitio and Pasajes. Vizcaya was a province rich in minerals, hence the importance of Bilbao, one of the principal seaports of Spain: the English colloquialism for a sword, 'bilbo' or 'bilboa' (sic), was testimony to its reputation for the manufacture of steel.

Catalonia (**Cataluña**): province of north-eastern Spain, known for its patriotic and independent spirit, bounded on the west by Aragon (to whose monarchy it had been a principality), on the north by the Pyrenees and France, to the east by the

Mediterranean and to the south by Valencia. In 1833 it was divided into provinces named after the following four locations: Barcelona, the capital of Catalonia, one of the great cities of Spain and the industrial and commercial centre of the east of the kingdom; Gerona (besieged 25 times in its history, mostly unsuccessfully); Lérida (also the site of several sieges and taken by the French in 1707); and Tarragona (like Barcelona a seaport of considerable importance). Other locations of some note included Balaguay, Figueras (an important frontier fortification), Hostalrich, Igualada (some twelve miles [19.3 km.] from the remarkable mountain and monastery of Montserrat, 30 miles [48.3 km.] north-west of Barcelona), Manresa, Mataró (an important port), Palamos, Reus (where British traders had been established in the mid-eighteenth century), Rosas, Tortosa (an important location on the River Ebro), Valls and Vich.

Estremadura (or **Extremadura**): province of western Spain, bounded on the west by Portugal (Beira and Alemtejo), on the north by León, north-east by Old Castile, east by New Castile, and Andalusia on the south; as with Portuguese Extremadura, its name was derived from the Latin for 'far shore'. In 1833 it was divided into two provinces named after the cities of Badajoz (the great frontier fortress on the River Guadiana), and Cáceres. Other locations of note included Albuquerque, Almàraz, Alcántara (seven miles [11.3 km.] from the Portuguese frontier, its name in Arabic - 'the Bridge' - taken from the great Roman bridge that crossed the Tagus), Llerena, Olivenza (ceded to Spain by Portugal after the war of 1801), Plasencia, Trujillo, Valencia de Alcántara (the old border fortress captured by Portugal in 1664 and 1698), and the battlefields of Albuera, Arroyo dos Molinos and Medellin.

Galicia: the mountainous north-westerly province, bordered on the west by the Atlantic, north by the Bay of Biscay, north-east by Asturias, south-east by León, and on the south by Portugal (Entre Minho e Douro and Tras os Montes). In 1833 it was divided into four provinces named after Corunna (La Coruña, a very important port by virtue of its sheltered harbour on a difficult coast), Lugo (the old capital of Galicia, notable for its Roman walls), Orense (with an ancient bridge over the River Miño [Minho]), and Pontevedra (named from its Roman bridge). Other significant locations included Ferrol (El Ferrol, from the mid-eighteenth century an important naval base, the object of the British landing in 1800); Mondoñedo, Santiago de Compostella (the ancient capital, one of the most famous pilgrimage centres in

Christendom), Tuy (an ancient frontier fortress on the right bank of the River Miño [Minho]), and Vigo (an important port by virtue of its sheltered harbour, the object of a number of British maritime operations, notably in 1702 and 1719).

León: the westerly province named from the city that was its capital, it was bordered on the west by Portugal (Tras os Montes and Beira), the north by Asturias, the east by Old Castile and the south by Estremadura. From 1833 it was divided into the three provinces named after the cities of León (the old capital of the kingdom of León), Salamanca (whose Roman bridge crossed the River Tormes, and the prosperity of which was founded originally upon the presence there of its great university), and Zamora (on the right bank of the River Duero [Douro], which was crossed there by a notable bridge). Other locations of some significance included Alba de Tormes, Astorga, the great border-fortress of Ciudad Rodrigo on the River Agueda, Mansilla, Tamames, Toro (the ancient fortified town with a crossing of the Duero), Villafranca, and the battle-sites of Benevente, Fuentes de Oñoro and Sahagun.

Murcia: the south-easterly province bounded on the west by Andalucia, on the north by New Castile, on the east by Valencia and on the south by the Mediterranean. From 1833 it was divided into the two provinces named after the city of Murcia (on the left bank of the River Segura) and the town of Albacete (famous for the manufacture of cutlery, notably daggers). Also in the province was the great port and naval base of Cartagena, and Almanza, site of the victory of the Duke of Berwick's Franco-Spanish army over an allied force in 1707.

Navarre: the northern province (formerly a kingdom which incorporated part of France), bounded on the west by Alava, north-west by Guipuzcoa, north-east by the Pyrenees and France, south-east by Aragon, and south-west by Old Castile. In 1833 it was not divided into smaller regions. Its capital and principal fortress was Pamplona (or Pampeluna); other locations of note included Tudela (on the right bank of the River Ebro, noted for its ancient bridge), Maya and Roncesvalles (two of the only three roads from Navarre into France, the latter [French Roncevaux] being probably best known for the death there in battle in 778 of Charlemagne's warrior Roland), and Sorauren. The routes through the Pyrenees and into France led to the severe fighting there in 1813.

New Castile (**Castilla la Nueva**): the southern part of the old kingdom of Castile was that recovered second from Moorish control, hence the appellation 'new'. Occupying the centre of Spain, with the Guaderrama mountains roughly separating New from Old Castile, its western border was with Estremadura, north with Old Castile, north-east with Aragon, east with Valencia, south-east with Murcia and south with Andalucia. In 1833 it was divided into five provinces named after the cities of Madrid (the national capital from the time of Philip II), Ciudad Real, Cuenca (with its bridge over the River Jucar), Guadalajara (with an ancient bridge over the River Henares), and Toledo (once the capital, the centre of Christianity in Spain as witnessed by its magnificent cathedral, with bridges over the Tagus, and renowned for arms-manufacturing). Other locations of significance included Alcalá de Henares (with a university second only to Salamanca), Almonacid, Aranjuez (on the left bank of the Tagus, site of a notable royal palace and of the 1808 insurrection), Arzobispo, Ocaña, Siguenza, Uclés, Talavera (correctly Talavera de la Reina, known thus from once being the property of the queens of Castile, with its bridge over the Tagus), and the great royal palace of the Escorial, north-west of Madrid. In what became the provinces of Cuenca, Ciudad Real, Toledo and Albacete (Murcia) lies the area of La Mancha (named from the Arabic Al Mansha, 'wilderness' or 'dry land'), much of the action of *Don Quixote* taking place there, in the neighbourhood of Alcázar de San Juan.

Old Castile (**Castilla la Vieja**): occupying north-central Spain, Old Castile was bordered on the west by Léon, on the north by the Bay of Biscay, the north-east by Vizcaya, Alava and Navarre, on the east by Aragon, and the south by New Castile. In 1833 it was divided into eight provinces named after the following cities: Avila (on the right bank of the River Adaja, seat of a university until 1807), Burgos (capital of Old Castile, on one of the principal roads of the kingdom, hence its strategic importance), Logroño (an ancient walled town with bridge across the Ebro), Palencia (on the left bank of the River Carrion), Santander (a port with an excellent harbour, hence its significance as Wellington's advanced base), Segovia (a seat of the old Castilian court), Soria (on the right bank of the River Duero), and Valladolid (once the capital, and possessing a noted university). Other locations of significance included the Biscayan sea-port of Castro Urdiales, La Granja or San Ildefonso (a royal estate and palace, hence the treaties of that name), Espinosa de los Monteros, Gamonal, Medina de Rio Seco, and Somosierra, like the foregoing a battle-site of the Peninsular War.

Valencia: an eastern province bounded in the west by New Castile, north-west by Aragon, north-east by Catalonia, east by the Mediterranean, and south-west by Murcia. In 1833 it was divided into three provinces named after Valencia (the capital), Castellón de la Plana and Alicante, all with harbours. Other locations of significance included the port of Burriana, Castalla, Sagunto (also known as Saguntum or Murviedro), Villarreal, and the lagoon of Albufera de Valencia, about seven miles south of Valencia (from which Suchet took his title as duc d'Albufera as a reward for the capture of Valencia; subsequently its revenues were given to Wellington in recognition of his services to Spain).

Balearic Islands (**Islas Baleáres**): Spain's province in the Mediterranean was of considerable importance due to its excellent harbours, and comprised two principal groups of islands. In the west was Ibiza (Iviza, capital Ibiza or La Ciudad), Formentera and four islets; more significant was the western group of Majorca (Mallorca, capital Palma), Minorca (Menorca), and seven islets, including Cabrera, where French prisoners-of-war were sent during the war. Minorca had been held by the British from time to time during the eighteenth century, and was finally ceded to Spain by the Peace of Amiens; its capital, Port Mahon (Puerto Mahón) had one of the finest harbours in the Mediterranean, hence its strategic importance. The Balearic Islands were staunchly loyal to the 'patriot' cause, and sent troops to the mainland (Whittingham's Division was organised in Majorca).

Canary Islands (**Islas Canarias**): Spain's Atlantic province was included in the captain-generalcy of Andalusia for administrative purposes, until it was made a separate province in 1833. It consisted principally of the islands of Grand Canary (Gran Canaria), Tenerife (or Teneriffe), Fuerteventura, Lanzarote, Palma, Gomera and Hierro; its principal towns were Santa Cruz de Tenerife (the administrative capital) and Las Palmas. The archipelego had its own regular battalion and territorial militia, and sent troops to serve on the mainland.

Portugal

Portugal was divided into six provinces, corresponding largely to the natural divisions of the geography of the country. In 1833 the provinces were subdivided into districts, each named after its principal town.

Alemtejo: its name meaning 'beyond the Tagus', this southerly province was bounded on the south-west by the Atlantic, the north-west by Portuguese Estremadura, the north by Beira, the north-east by Spanish Estremadura, the south-east by Andalucia, and the south by Algarve. In 1833 its districts were named after the towns of Beja, Evora, and Portalegre; other locations of note included Campo Mayor (Campo Maior), Elvas (the chief frontier fortress south of the Tagus, facing Badajoz), and Estremoz (once an important frontier defence).

Algarve: the smallest of the six provinces, its name (from Arabic) indicating a western-lying land, it occupied the southernmost part of Portugal, bounded on the north by Alemtejo, on the east by Andalucia (the estuary of the Guadiana forming the boundary), and by the Atlantic on south and west. In 1833 it was named as the district of Faro, from its chief town, a seaport; another significant location was Lagos, possessed of a deep harbour. Nearby is Cape St. Vincent, off which Admiral Sir John Jervis won his great victory in 1797.

Beira: the mountainous central province (the Sierra de Estrella runs north-east to south-west through its centre), on the west it was bounded by the Atlantic, by Entre Minho e Douro on the north-west, Tras os Montes on the north-east, by León and Spanish Estremadura on the east, by Alemtejo in the south, and by Portuguese Estremadura on the south-west; the northern and south-eastern frontiers were marked by the Douro and Tagus respectively. In 1833 it was divided into five districts, named after the towns of Aviero (a port, with a canal to the Atlantic constructed from 1801), Castello Branco, Coimbra (the ancient capital on the north bank of the River Mondego, with a noted university), Guarda, and Vizeu. Other locations of note included the great frontier fortress of Almeida, facing Ciudad Rodrigo; Busaco (or Bussaco; the mountain-range was the Sierra de Bussaco); Figuera da Foz (a port on the north bank of the Mondego; Lavos, on the south bank, was used as a landing-point by the British in 1808), and Sabugal.

Entre Minho e Douro (**or Minho**): the north-western and second smallest province, it was bounded on the west by the Atlantic, north by Galicia, east by Tras os Montes and to the south by Beira; as the name implies, it was also bounded by the Rivers Minho (Miño) and Douro (Duero) in north and south respectively. In 1833 it was divided into the districts named after the town of Braga (the seat of the archbishop who was primate of Portugal), the city of Oporto (Portuguese Porto, the capital, a major commercial centre and the second city of the kingdom after Lisbon), and the port of Vianna do Castello. Other locations of note included the port of Povoa de Varzim, and Guimarães with its ancient fortifications.

Estremadura (or Extremadura): the south-western province, divided almost equally into two by the Tagus, was bounded on the west by the Atlantic, on the north and north-east by Beira, and on the south and east by Alemtejo. In 1833 it was divided into three districts named after the cities of Lisbon (Lisboa, the capital, on the Tagus, the city which had suffered from the devastating earthquake of 1755), Leiria, and Santarem. Other locations of note included Abrantes (on the right bank of the Tagus, from which Junot took his title), Cintra (Sintra), Mafra (noted for its monastery and royal palace), the battle-sites of Roliça and Vimeiro, the important seaport of Setubal, Thomar, Torres Novas and Torres Vedras.

Tras os Montes: the north-eastern province, literally 'across the mountains', was bordered by Entre Minho e Douro on the west, Galicia to the north-west, León to the north-east and east, and Beira to the south. In 1833 it was divided into the districts named after the towns of Braganza (Bragança), which gave its name to the royal dynasty that ruled Portugal 1640-1853, and Villa Real. Also in the province was Chaves, long an important fortress on the northern frontier, which was regarded as the *chaves* ('keys') of northern Portugal. The district adjacent to the Douro was known as 'Paiz de vinho' or 'wine country'.

Offshore territories: the Madeira islands, in the north Atlantic, consist primarily of Madeira itself (capital Funchal) and Porto Santo (capital also Porto Santo); other towns of significance on Madeira (in that they possessed their own militia battalions) were Calheto and São Vicente. Madeira had a British garrison at the time of the Peninsular War. The Azores (Açores), some 830 miles (1,335 km.) from the Portuguese mainland, in the Atlantic, is an archipelego, of which the largest islands are São Miguel, Terceira and Pico; Terceira was the centre for the military establishment on the islands.

INDEXES

GENERAL INDEX

INDEX OF BATTLE AND SIEGE SITES

INDEX OF PLACE NAMES

INDEX OF NAMES